The Global Luther

The Global Luther

— A Theologian for Modern Times —

Edited by Christine Helmer

Fortress Press
Minneapolis

THE GLOBAL LUTHER
A Theologian for Modern Times

Cover image: "Yoga Man," Nicholas Wilton. Used by permission.
Cover design: Laurie Ingram
Book design: PerfecType, Nashville, TN

Library of Congress Cataloging-in-Publication Data

The global Luther : a theologian for modern times / edited by Christine Helmer.
    p. cm.
  Proceedings of a conference held Feb. 21-23, 2008 at Northwestern University.
  Includes bibliographical references (p.   ) and indexes.
  ISBN 978-0-8006-6239-4 (alk. paper)
  1. Luther, Martin, 1483-1546. I. Helmer, Christine.
  BR332.5.G66 2009
  230'.41092--dc22
                            2009001252

The paper used in this publication meets the minimum requirements of American
National Standard for Information Sciences — Permanence of Paper for Printed Library
Materials, ANSI Z329.48-1984.

Printed in Canada

13 12 11 10 09 1 2 3 4 5 6 7 8 9 10

Contents

Contributors

Peter J. Burgard is Professor of German at Harvard University and works on literature, art, architecture, philosophy, and psychoanalysis. His publications include essays on Caravaggio, Opitz, Gryphius, Hoffmannswaldau, Grimmelshausen, Goethe, Herder, Lessing, Nietzsche, Mann, Kafka, Adorno, Ibsen, Miller, and Warhol. His books include *Idioms of Uncertainty: Goethe and the Essay* (1992), *Nietzsche and the Feminine* (1994), *Barock: Neue Sichtweisen einer Epoche* (2001, ed.), and, in progress, *Figures of Excess: Toward an Aesthetic of the Baroque*.

Jacqueline A. Bussie is Associate Professor of Religion at Capital University. She is the author of *The Laughter of the Oppressed* (2007), which won the 2006 Trinity Prize, and numerous articles in the areas of theology, religion and culture, and Christian ethics. She serves on the executive board of the Lutheran Academy of Scholars and is currently Vice-President of the Midwest American Academy of Religion.

Theodor Dieter is Research Professor and Director of the Institute for Ecumenical Research in Strasbourg, France. An ordained pastor of the Evangelical Lutheran Church in Württemberg, Germany, Dieter is known particularly for his involvement in the complex negotiations that led to the *Joint Declaration on the Doctrine of Justification* between Lutheran and Roman Catholic Churches. He has taught and lectured at many institutions around the world, including the University of Tübingen, Luther College in Decorah, Iowa, and the Lutheran Theological Seminary in Hong Kong. His publications include *Der junge Luther und Aristoteles* (2001) and numerous articles in Luther studies, ecumenical theology, and social ethics.

Krista Duttenhaver is an instructor in the Program of Liberal Studies and a doctoral candidate in systematic theology at the University of Notre Dame. She specializes in nineteenth- and twentieth-century systematic theology in the European context, with particular interests in soteriology and suffering, and political and feminist theology. She is completing a dissertation entitled *Christian Platonism as a Radical Politics: Simone Weil and the Mystical-Political*.

Hans-Peter Grosshans is Professor of Systematic Theology and Director of the Institute for Ecumenical Theology at the University of Münster, Germany. He has held the position of Study Secretary for Theology and the Church of the Lutheran World Federation (LWF) and has taught at various universities, including Tübingen, Hamburg, Munich, and Zürich. He is the author of *Luther* (1997) in the Fount Christian Thinkers series, *Theologischer Realismus* (1996), and *Die Kirche—irdischer Raum der Wahrheit des Evangeliums* (2003). He was coeditor of both the Festschrift for Eberhard Jüngel (2004) and a collection of essays entitled *Kritik der Religion* (2005).

Christine Helmer is Professor of Religion and Adjunct Professor of German at Northwestern University. She has taught theology at the Claremont School of Theology and Harvard Divinity School. She is the author of *The Trinity and Martin Luther* (1999) and is contributing editor or coeditor of numerous volumes in the areas of Schleiermacher studies, philosophy of religion, and biblical theology, most recently *The Multivalence of Biblical Texts and Theological Meanings* (2006).

Paul Helmer has taught until recently as Associate Professor of Music at McGill University in Montreal, Quebec. He has published in the areas of Western Christian liturgy. His books include an edition and recording of the *missa sancti iacobi* (1992) and *Le premier et le secont livre de fauvel* (1997). His most recent work is *Growing with Canada* (2009), a book on the musical émigrés from Europe who came to Canada between 1933 and 1948. He is a concert pianist with extensive performing and recording credits as both soloist and chamber musician.

Peter C. Hodgson is Charles G. Finney Professor of Theology Emeritus in the Divinity School of Vanderbilt University, where he taught from 1965 to 2003. He is the author, editor, and translator of over twenty books on various topics of systematic and historical theology. His most recent works are *The Mystery Beneath the Real* (a study of George Eliot) (2001), *Hegel and Christian Theology* (2005), *Liberal Theology: A Radical Vision* (2007), and a translation of Hegel's *Lectures on the Proofs of the Existence of God* (2007).

James W. Jones is Professor of Religion at Rutgers University. He holds doctorates in both Clinical Psychology and Religious Studies as well as an honorary doctorate from the University of Uppsala in Sweden. He is the author of eleven books, the most recent being *Waking from Newton's Sleep: Dialogues on Spirituality in an Age of Science* (2006) and *Blood That Cries Out from the Earth: The Psychology of Religious Terrorism* (2008). He is a Fellow of the American Psychological Association and currently serves as the vice-president of the International Association for the Psychology of Religion.

Allen G. Jorgenson is Associate Professor of Systematic Theology and Assistant Dean at Waterloo Lutheran Seminary at Wilfrid Laurier University in Waterloo, Ontario. He is the author of essays on the topics of Luther, public theology, and worship, as well as *The Appeal to Experience in the Christologies of Friedrich Schleiermacher and Karl Rahner* (2007).

Volker Leppin is Professor of Church History at the University of Jena, Germany. He taught at the universities of Zürich and Frankfurt and is an ordained pastor in the Evangelical Lutheran Church in Thuringia. He has published extensively in the areas of theology, philosophy, and mysticism in the late middle ages, particularly on William of Ockham and the Reformation. Among his many books are *Luther privat: Sohn, Vater, Ehemann* (2006), *Martin Luther* (2006), and most recently *Die christliche Mystik* (2007) and *Die Wittenberger Reformation und der Prozess der Transformation kultureller zu institutionellen Polaritäten* (2008).

Antti Raunio is Professor of Systematic Theology at the University of Helsinki. He has published numerous essays on Luther's theology, ecumenical theology, ethics, the theology of love, and the Golden Rule. He is coeditor of *Luther und Theosis* (1990) and author of *Summe des christlichen Lebens: Die Goldene Regel als Gesetz der Liebe in der Theologie Martin Luthers* (2001).

Risto Saarinen is Professor of Ecumenical Theology at the University of Helsinki. He served as Research Professor at the Institute for Ecumenical Research in Strasbourg from 1994 to 1999. He is author of numerous books, articles, and encyclopedia entries in both English and German. His most recent book is entitled *God and the Gift: An Ecumenical Theology of Giving* (2005).

Birgit Stolt was Professor of German Philology and Literature at the University of Stockholm, Sweden, from 1980 to 1992. She has been a member of many prestigious academic institutions, including Fellow at the Institute of Advanced Studies in Berlin, member of the Royal Academy of Letters, History, and Antiquities in Stockholm, the Royal Society of the Humanities in Uppsala, and vice-president of the International Group for German Language and

Literature (IVG). She was awarded an honorary doctorate in theology from the
University of Uppsala. Her publications include numerous articles in the areas
of Luther scholarship, rhetoric, style, theories and practices of translation, and
bilingualism, and books on Luther, most recently *Martin Luthers Rhetorik des
Herzens* (2000), and in Swedish, *Luther själv* (2004).

Ronald F. Thiemann is Benjamin Bussey Professor of Theology at Harvard
University. An ordained Lutheran pastor and a specialist on the role of religion
in public life, Professor Thiemann is the author of *Revelation and Theology:
The Gospel as Narrated Promise* (2005), *Constructing a Public Theology: The
Church in a Pluralistic Culture* (1991), and *Religion in Public Life: A Dilemma
for Democracy* (1996). His current book project is entitled *Prisoners of Conscience: Public Intellectuals in a Time of Crisis*.

Vítor Westhelle is Professor of Systematic Theology at the Lutheran School
of Theology at Chicago. He is the author of *The Scandalous God: The Use and
Abuse of the Cross* (2006), and two other books, on ecclesiology and postcolonialism, are awaiting release. His areas of expertise include nineteenth-
century theology and philosophy, Luther and Lutheranism, postcolonialism,
sociology of religion, and theology and literature. He has taught in several faculties of theology, among them Luther Northwestern Theological Seminary in
Saint Paul, Minnesota, and Escola Superior de Teologia, Brazil, the University
of Natal, South Africa, and the University of Aarhus, Denmark.

Munib A. Younan is Bishop of the Evangelical Lutheran Church in Jordan
and the Holy Land. He has been an outspoken advocate of peace with justice
and non-violence in the Holy Land for decades. He has also been a leader in
interfaith dialogue with Christians, Muslims, and Jews and is an initiator of the
new Council for Religious Institutions in the Holy Land. He is Vice-President
of the Lutheran World Federation and President of the Fellowship of Middle
East Evangelical Churches. He is the author of *Witnessing for Peace* (2003)
and has written many articles, speeches, and lectures on religion, politics, and
peace-building in the Middle East. Recently he received an Honorary Doctorate of Divinity (D.D.) from Wartburg University, Iowa, and the Finnish Peace
Prize 2001 from the Finnish Christian Peace Movement.

Abbreviations

BoC *The Book of Concord: The Confessions of the Evangelical Lutheran Church.* Trans. Charles Arand et al. Ed. Robert Kolb and Timothy J. Wengert. Minneapolis: Fortress Press, 2000.

LW Luther's Works—American Edition. 55 Vols. Ed. Jaroslav Pelikan and Helmut T. Lehmann. St. Louis, Mo. and Minneapolis: Concordia Publishing House and Fortress Press, 2002.

NEB *The New English Bible with the Apocrypha.* Ed. C. H. Dodd et al. Oxford and Cambridge: Oxford University Press and Cambridge University Press, 1970.

NRSV *New Revised Standard Version: The New Oxford Annotated Bible with the Apocrypha.* Ed. Bruce M. Metzger and Roland E. Murphy. New York: Oxford University Press, 1991.

RGG *Religion in Geschichte und Gegenwart.* 4th Edn. 9 Vols. Ed. Hans Dieter Betz et al. Tübingen: Mohr Siebeck, 1998–2007.

WA D. Martin Luthers Werke: Kritische Gesamtausgabe. 67 Vols. Ed. J. K. F. Knaake et al. Weimar: H. Böhlau, 1883–1997.

WABr D. Martin Luthers Werke: Kritische Gesamtausgabe: Briefwechsel. 18 Vols. Ed. G. Bebermeyer et al. Weimar: H. Böhlau, 1930–1985.

WADB D. Martin Luthers Werke: Kritische Gesamtausgabe: Deutsche Bibel. 12 Vols. Ed. P. Pietsch et al. Weimar: H. Böhlau, 1906–1961.

WATr D. Martin Luthers Werke: Kritische Gesamtausgabe: Tischreden. 6 Vols. Ed. K. Drescher et al. Weimar: H. Böhlau, 1912–1921.

Foreword

The adjective *global* associated with the proper noun *Luther*, in the geographical sense, is oxymoronic. Globes existed in Martin Luther's Europe, as did maps of the known world. But the world in which Luther traveled was a tiny diamond-shaped chunk of what was to become Germany—474 kilometers long from Wittenberg to Augsburg, and 334 kilometers from Marburg to Leipzig. He was certainly aware of the alien "Turk," his name for the threatening Muslim presence, but his writings provide no road-map for what centuries later came to be called "foreign missions." A provincial of the provincials, he wanted to help reform the church so that the pure gospel would be preached until the imminent end of the world in the territories not far from his front yard. The concept of the "global" would have been as foreign to him as putative news from the star Arcturus would be to us.

Yet Christine Helmer and her colleagues audaciously and creatively project a "Global Luther." At first glance, the biographies of the authors still suggest provincialism. Most of the historians are from Northern Europe and North America. (One hopes that a second volume in a sequence convened and edited by Professor Helmer will also feature scholars from "everywhere else.)" The chapter by Bishop Munib A. Younan provides a sample of what is to come in the decades ahead, when interreligious activity will test Luther-an witness and scholarship. The presence of Africans, Asians, and Latin Americans would help break the mold of Luther scholarship shaped and often frozen in the old "Luther homeland(s)." Yet most of the chapters in this book already do that, in an exciting fashion.

Speaking of a mold being broken might suggest that the authors here are iconoclasts, seekers of novelty, trash-talkers about the work of their intellectual antecedents. Not at all. They show respect for such work and then engage in revisionism that will advance a new global receptivity to Luther scholarship. If readers will not here find a demolition of the Luther image, they will also

not find the treatment of Luther as icon and idol. Most of the historians represent and interpret conventional findings of Luther scholarship and move
on from there to challenge readers to probe further. For example, chapters
reflecting contemporary Finnish Luther scholarship revisit the key texts familiar to all who have read Luther or who are informed Lutherans. Then they
provide turnings and openings for understandings in cultures that were alien
to the sixteenth-century Reformers, just as they have become alienated from
the world that the Reformers, led by Luther, took for granted. "Psychoanalysis,"
"Liberation," and such words in chapter headings do not demand rejection of
sixteenth-century affirmations, but they will elicit revisionist thinking for the
academy, church, and larger culture alike.

Editor Helmer teases readers in her line one: "The study of Luther is an
intellectual enterprise fraught with risk." She invites readers to take up the risk
with the authors herein. We associate "risk" with "rewards." They will be manifest to any who take this intellectual tour of a sometimes figurative, sometimes
literal Luther "globe." It is time and this is the place from which to take off with
guides who demonstrate their trustworthiness as they deal with the familiar
and then their risk-taking as they venture to the horizon of the unfamiliar in
appropriating the figure and significance of Martin Luther.

Martin E. Marty

CHAPTER 1

Introduction
– Luther beyond Luther –
Christine Helmer

T he study of Luther is an intellectual enterprise fraught with risk, not least the risk that any approach may present an embarrassment to religious movements stamped with Luther's name. Someone investigating the "historical Luther" runs the risk of stepping on contemporary Lutheran denominational toes. Likewise, someone examining the "Catholic Luther" will bump up against strong commitments to a distinct Protestant identity, while yet another examining the "reformation Luther" may irritate Catholic sensibilities with stories of a rebel monk and his uncompromising idea of justification by Christ's work alone. The study of Luther may also raise the specter of Luther's anti-Judaism. Luther is associated, as perhaps no other Christian theologian, with the evil of the Holocaust. This association poses a challenge to Luther studies for addressing the stubborn anti-Semitism in Christianity's history and theology. The risk of religious dialogue today requires scholarly clarification of the historical issues at stake in Luther's own works and creativity in advocating for religious peace in today's global context.

Yet Luther remains, in spite of the risks, a theologian who provokes and challenges on topics from religion to spirituality, from Christian theology to economics. Luther himself was a theologian who wagered his life and vocation, even European Christendom, to test out ideas that changed the world. Those who study Luther should be asked to do the same, to take intellectual risks—sometimes even with personal and vocational consequences—and to dare to promote energetic and dangerous ways to understand loving and just ways of construing self, world, and God today.

"The Reformer"

In his Psalm commentary of 1532, Martin Luther invokes the tradition of biblical interpretation that determines a proper name according to the genus that it represents.[1] Paul is acknowledged as "the Apostle," for example, although the New Testament recognizes at least twelve other apostles. Aristotle is known throughout the entire middle ages as "the Philosopher," a term that is attributed to many other thinkers in Western history. The identification of name with genus situates those so designated in the rarified company of figures who have transcended their contexts and become associated with intellectual, social, pedagogical, and political movements of global proportions.

So history has attributed to Martin Luther (1483–1546) the genus that he is reputed to have initiated, "the Reformer," the title by which Luther is known around the world. Many other reformers were associated with the sixteenth-century Protestant reformation—John Calvin (1509–1564), Geneva's reformer, for example, or Katharina Zell (1497/98–1562), Strasbourg's reformer—and with other reformations vital to the Christian church's historical development. "The Reformer" himself often recalled his spiritual predecessor John Hus (c. 1372–1415), the theologian who attempted to reform the church's practice of distributing the sacraments in only one kind (the bread), for which he was burnt at the stake at the Council of Constance. Yet the name representing the genus "Reformation" is attributed to Luther alone. Any religious or political movement that aspires to the status and outcome of reform will appeal inevitably to Luther to authorize its ideas and to inscribe its story into the tradition of meanings and associations his name connotes. Most recently, "Luther" has been used to designate religious and political reformers in Islam.[2] And in the fall of 2008, the Chilean government instituted October 31 as a national holiday, provocatively celebrating Protestant churches in a country that is dominantly Roman Catholic.[3] The worldwide call of Luther's name still today highlights the global significance of his reforms in religious,

---

1. This strategy, technically known as "antonomasia . . . makes a proper noun out of a common noun, [so that] it is transferred to other things": LW 12:82 (*Exposition of Psalm 2*; to verse 12; 1532).
2. Recently, Tariq Ramadan: see Paul Donnelly, "Tariq Ramadan: The Muslim Martin Luther?" (Feb. 15, 2002), http://dir.salon.com/story/people/feature/2002/02/15/ramadan.
3. See "Hola, Luther," from *The Economist* (Nov. 6, 2008).

cultural, historical, and political perspective. What "the Reformer" means globally transcends his distinct person and particular work.

   This book aims to highlight Luther's global impact, in particular those
ideas and actions associated with "the Reformer" that circulate in contemporary discussions. Such a goal requires looking at a number of factors in order
to underline the powerful potential of Luther for today. A methodological
awareness is in order concerning the way Luther's ideas have transcended their
original context and taken on a life of their own. When questions are asked
of Luther that pertain to contemporary issues—the matter of peace among
global religions today is at the forefront of this book's interest—a two-step
methodology is required. First, such questions must be posed in ways that are
conscious of the contentious and ambivalent history of Luther's reception.
Only after this may we turn to the creative appropriation of Luther's theological repertoire for more productive conversations in the contemporary world.
Sober historical study is the necessary complement to exploring the imaginative potential of Luther's ideas for transforming thought and action.

Reading Luther in Context

Luther's biography has functioned in the history of Western Christianity as
more than the story of an individual life. It is taken as a paradigm of Christian experience. Luther's dramatic experiential movement from a life lived
under the accusing law to a life set free in its psychological, spiritual, and
social dimensions by the gospel is the paradigm of conversion at the heart of
the Christian religion. Christianity since its origins in the New Testament has
been captivated by the experience of paradigm shift. The Christian religion
has come to signify the shift from false gods to the true God, from unbelief
to faith, from law to gospel. There are severe problems associated with the
conversion model. It is linked directly to Christianity's supersessionism and
Christian anti-Semitism. It struggles to admit the tenacity of abusive behavior that persists after conversion. Luther persecuted the "heretics" even after
personally experiencing the grace of Christ, as Augustine had done centuries before following his conversion. Any responsible retrieval of Luther must
acknowledge these problems.

   Yet the attraction of the conversion model persists, and it is Luther's
particular shaping of this model that rivets the imagination. The emotions
of an epoch were concentrated in Luther's fears of hell, of Christ the judge,
and of the devil—or God hidden in nature—and in Luther's abhorrence of a
God who exacted love but set up creation in such a way that loving God was

an impossibility. The age's inner life is evident too in Luther's terrible anxiety about the human requirement to cooperate with divine grace. That era's hopes, in turn, were quickened by Luther's sudden, intimate glimpse into the Father's heavenly heart that calmed his soul. Luther's conversion from the old became the synecdoche for an era poised on the cusp of the new. Conversion's power fueled the hagiography, while historical and theological scholarship has worked hard to demythologize it. Luther's conversion was not instantaneous but the result of many years of intellectual and spiritual struggle in the monastery and of exercising critical thinking in the genre of the disputation. The Ninety-Five Theses did not catapult the German states to reformation but merely provided the occasion for an academic debate. Yet the legend of the solitary monk who spoke up for freedom against overwhelming odds still excites its audience. Even the academic theologian must acknowledge that Luther's globally imaginative impact is more interesting than dusty study of historical facts.

This book admits that Luther's person and work have great appeal. His ideas about justification, his theology of the cross, and his challenging, even dangerous, remarks about the hidden God have been the subject of fascination and speculation for five hundred years. These classic ideas from Luther cannot, however, be entirely chalked up to a reformation paradigm shift. Responsible historical scholarship looks at the complicated links of these ideas to the middle ages. The Luther known by his global impact must be contextualized as "Catholic," at least in some respects. The impact of Luther's liturgical "re-alignment" (to use Paul Helmer's phrase in this volume) and hymn compositions, for example, cannot be imagined without seriously considering his indebtedness to medieval musicological traditions. Luther's notion of universal priesthood must be taken, to use another example discussed by Allen Jorgenson, in continuity with medieval traditions of conciliarism. The "global Luther" invites interest in the "Catholic Luther," and this interest follows Heiko Oberman's famous lead in sketching continuities between late medieval philosophy and theology and Luther.[4] Furthermore, a "global Catholic Luther" might help explain why Luther's thoughts about suffering and love (in the essays by Krista Duttenhaver and Antti Raunio) can appear strange but pose unique ways of addressing the cross of daily human life today. There is just one caveat: if the global Luther is also Catholic, then he might pose an embarrassment as well as a creative challenge to both Lutheran and Roman Catholic identities.

---

4. Heiko A. Oberman, *The Harvest of Medieval Theology: Gabriel Biel and Late Medieval Nominalism* (Cambridge: Harvard University Press, 1963).

If Luther's relation to his catholicity is controversial, his dismissive relation to non-Christian religions must be rejected today. Luther is well known
for his invective against Jews and Judaism. Although this attitude has been
historically contextualized in medieval Christianity by scholars, its political
appropriation by twentieth-century National Socialism in Luther's native Germany cannot present anything short of a horrific abomination. *Kristallnacht*
was carried out on the eve of the anniversary of Luther's birthday, on Nov. 9,
1938, and motivated by the hate-filled polemic that Luther had articulated
in 1543. Christian scholarship today, responsible to an age that counteracts
religious violence with strong advocacy for interreligious dialogue, tolerance,
and peace, has met Luther with critical evaluation. Munib Younan's paper,
"Beyond Luther: Prophetic Interfaith Dialogue for Life," speaks precisely to
the contemporary challenges to build bridges of peace and justice between
Christians, Jews, and Muslims. The move beyond Luther requires describing all
aspects of being human, the psychological, political, rational, and emotional,
as they are intertwined in complex and distorted ways. The task also includes
prescribing ways to orient these aspects toward the good of individual and
community. Luther's own biography witnesses to the interplay between all
factors—his idea of justification has a psychological component that drives his
complex religious outbursts. If this study is to contextualize the deep insights
of Luther's ideas positively in the contemporary global situation, then it must
take into consideration the human subject who engages—with varying degrees
of distortion and wholeness—this task.

Reading Luther beyond Context

It is an academic impossibility to distinguish neatly between Luther as
reformer in his historical context and the meaning of reformation as understood by different generations appealing to Luther as authority and inspiration. Luther is so decisively a figure that has transcended his past—in terms of
meaning, authority, and inspiration for subsequent generations—that the task
of representing and understanding Luther as he sought reformation in his own
particular time is a perennial historical problem. Appeals to Luther to justify
positions held long after the sixteenth century have overlaid his reformation
with a surplus of meaning. It is not possible to strip this entirely away.

The historical dilemma presents a unique opportunity, however. Rather
than studying the Reformer with the goal of finding the "historical Luther,"
Luther studies could begin instead with an appreciation for Luther as a legend with global status. Did his treatise on Christian freedom not contribute

significantly to the history of the modern West's quest for freedom and liberation, from Hegel to Martin Luther King Jr.? Did Luther's translation of the
Bible not mark a linguistic turn for the German language that is analogous to
the creative revolution that Shakespeare achieved for the English language?
Did Luther's religious and theological focus on the individual *coram deo*
("before God") not lead to the modern preoccupation with subjectivity, exemplified by philosophers in the Lutheran tradition, preeminently Immanuel
Kant and Søren Kierkegaard? And did not Luther's lonely stand against pope
and emperor offer a powerful inspiration to those speaking truth to power?

When Luther's ideas are viewed in different times and places, they can be
plumbed at a depth-dimension that he did not himself explore and for implications of which he was probably not aware. Luther was audacious in thinking
through theological distinctions—for example, the justifying God and the sinful human—as well as theological identities—the unity of God and humanity
in Christ. His reconceptualizations had a transformative impact in revising
notions of priesthood and freedom, faith and truth, God's frightening hiddenness and God's eternal burning love. Luther's glimpses of the reality of self,
world, and God have inspired centuries of interpretation in various religious,
cultural, and political forums. But to solicit Luther as viable conversation partner for today's stormy discussions is also to acknowledge that his ideas have
been fraught with danger, and that even in their all-too-human ambivalence,
they have a visionary dimension of a truth that must be heard today.

The task of engaging Luther in contemporary dialogue also requires a flex-
ibility of mind: if the history of the Protestant religious reformation is to have
anything to say to social-cultural and political histories, or if Luther's own
provocative contributions to discussions of sin and grace are to be understood
by those who are not born into the Lutheran succession, these topics must be
communicated in such a way that they are interesting and accessible to others.
Conversely, psychological, musicological, literary-linguistic, and philosophical
contributions to the study of Luther can open up new avenues in interpreting
Luther's theology. Justification is not solely about the individual *coram deo*, for
example; it refers to the transformation of the human person that engages all
faculties of being human: emotion, reason, language, and community.

Contemporary interdisciplinary interest is testimony to Luther's own
efforts in the sixteenth century. His education in the liberal arts served as
the foundation for his own facility in extending theology into areas of music,
language, philosophy, and psychology. Luther's prolific hymn composition presupposes his musical and musicological training that was later transmitted into
the Protestant tradition of choral singing and organ preludes. Luther's striving

to make the Bible available to the literate population led to his commitment to words and their meanings that then became the subject for discussion in German departments and the history of hermeneutics. Luther's deep religious interests compelled him to explore history and philosophy, metaphysics and logic, as theologically appropriate tools to describe the religious realities he had experienced.

By orienting its focus to the global and sometimes Catholic Luther, this book goes beyond the Luther who has, for many centuries, been associated with Germany, and with its history and theology. The "German Luther" is undoubtedly the legacy given to the contemporary world to study and appropriate.[5] The "Reformer" as he appears today bears the contours of interpretation in distinctly German Protestant categories—his neo-Kantianism, the insidious dualism that is highlighted as characteristic of his thinking, and the "word event" character of his theology are interpretations that are closely bound up with German intellectual history. Yet the last half-century has witnessed a rapidly growing global dimension to the study of Luther. The Finnish reception of Luther, to use one example, has paved a significant interpretative way to both Luther's philosophical-anthropological ideas of the human person as justified in the very depths of the soul and to the important ecumenical implications of this new insight. This volume addresses new forays beyond the "German Luther" as they are represented by scholars of Luther and scholars interested in Luther. It is intended to set a new trend in global scholarship that does justice to "the Reformer," as one who has truly succeeded in transcending his own person, his religion, and his nationality.

The Global Luther Project

The assumption behind Luther as "a theologian for modern times" is that theologians should and can speak to and intimately engage with their world. Luther found a language that fired up his contemporaries. He is admired as one of the most successful models of theological communication in the history of Christianity. This book highlights Luther's facility in engaging the pressing questions of his times in the context of themes that are driving the contemporary imagination. Life's opacity to rationality, reality's coldness, and God's mysterious silence are described alongside glimpses of God's undying love for human persons. *The Global Luther* is divided into particular themes

---

5. See the section entitled, "The American Luther's German Pedigree," in Christine Helmer, "The American Luther," *Dialog* 47/2 (Summer 2008): 118–20.

structuring five sections. Individual introductions are provided at the beginning of each distinct section.

The first section, "Luther's Global Impact," outlines the broad parameters of Luther's extraordinary impact. Luther's contributions to West and world are sketched in the areas of culture, intellectual history, and global religions. The history of modern language cannot be written without acknowledging his Bible translation and literary compositions, the history of freedom that encompasses Luther, Hegel, and Martin Luther King Jr., in its embrace, and the history of relations between global religions that have Luther to criticize and to overcome.

The title of section two, "Living in the Midst of Horrors," alludes to Luther's hymn, "In the Midst of Life We Are,"[6] to give expression to the task, challenge, and despair of living in the world today. The primary interpretational matrix for focusing Luther's insights is the interplay between psychological, spiritual, religious, and theological factors. This interplay is becoming more and more a consensus in discussions of Luther that seek to develop a robust anthropology on the basis of Luther's understanding of the human person living simultaneously in the states of sin and grace. The continued interest in Luther's own complicated psychological history is fleshed out in a number of ways, including descriptions of his religious dispositions, spiritual distresses, and images of God inherited from his parental home that help explain his psychological fears, religious polemic, and theological tensions.

The third section, "Language, Emotion, and Reason," looks at an even more specific determination of the human person. The human person is not only one theologically determined by law and gospel before God, but lives an embodied life in relation to others. Hence this section focuses on human subjectivity as the interplay between faculties and capacities that express and structure human life. Language and emotions are constitutive of human subjectivity. If justification justifies the human truly, then language and emotions will express this transformation. Reason is also a significant part of Luther's anthropology, particularly as it shapes and relates the different spheres of thinking—music, metaphysics, mathematics, logic—with which Luther was intimately familiar.

The fourth section, "Luther's Theology for Today," highlights Luther's specific, distinctive ideas that have had a lasting impact in Lutheran traditions and beyond. Justification is without doubt the most famous. The doctrine of justification did, after all, lead to the Western schism that has only recently been addressed with the signing of the *Joint Declaration on Justification* in 1999. This

---

6. The first line continues: ". . . Aye in Death's embraces" (LW 53:275).

section treats the extension of justification into areas of justice, particularly the Lutheran ethics that are represented in the Nordic welfare states. A study of Luther's theological achievement would not be complete without mentioning his theology of the cross, and, in the context of building interreligious bridges, its constructive implications for a theology of religions.

The fifth section, "Politics and Power," addresses the ecclesial and political dimensions of human life in the world. Luther's insights in this regard have also had a powerful impact, particularly the idea of the priesthood of all believers and the liberative potential that this idea conveys. Yet this insight together with ideas concerning reformation of ecclesial and political structures is tempered by a disturbing ambivalence that is inscribed into Luther's rhetoric as well as into the reality of history. The realism of Luther's theology is its test of truth: as people and powers, religious believers and political folk are thrown together into the teeming struggles of history, they can only momentarily grasp the actuality of justification without ever really embodying it definitively and permanently. Perhaps in this realism lies Luther's potential for today. Human life is shot through with ambivalence and ambiguity; ideas and actions, even those of the Christian, are modeled after God's hiddenness on the cross.

I note the particular translations used in this book. The *New Revised Standard Version* of the Christian Bible is cited, except where otherwise indicated. All references to Luther in English are taken from Luther's Works—American Edition (LW), except where otherwise indicated. In the many cases where Luther's text has not yet been translated into English, references are made to the critical edition of Luther's works in the Weimarer Ausgabe (WA). Translations of the Weimarer Ausgabe are provided by the respective author, and significant discrepancies between LW translation and WA original are noted. Equivalent passages in the WA are given for the LW when possible. References to the English version of Luther's Small and Large Catechisms (1529) are taken from the recent edition published by Fortress Press of the *Book of Concord*.

The Global Luther also includes the medium of sound to highlight one of Luther's most important contributions to Western culture. The recording included in this volume demonstrates the musical development throughout the middle ages of the famous Latin Sequence *Victimae paschali laudes*. Luther's Easter hymn, *Christ lag in Todesbanden* ("Christ Jesus Lay in Death's Strong Bands"),[7] stands in the tradition of this musical trajectory, which culminates

---

7. The title in LW is "Death Held Our Lord in Prison" (53:255).

in the organ chorale prelude by J. S. Bach. The performance was recorded in the Charles Palmerston Anderson Chapel of Saint John the Divine at Seabury-Western Theological Seminary in Evanston, Illinois, on November 19, 2008. The program was created by Paul Helmer. Andrew Lewis conducted the Bella Voce choir of Chicago, the chapel organ, and an early music ensemble composed of two cornetts and two sackbuts. Edward Hoke of Audiospark in Evanston, Illinois, was the sound engineer.

Part One
Luther's Global Impact

This book is about Martin Luther's history-shaping ideas. The purpose is celebration but also critical engagement with Luther in a new time for the world. The most important of Luther's ideas, such as freedom and justification, have ambivalence and ambiguity written right into their original formulations. Indeed, the five-hundred-year history of interpreting Luther has been, to a great extent, inspired and provoked by this ambivalence, which is the ground of Luther's theological creativity. In this first section, the bold vision and insidious danger of Luther's most crucial ideas are described, measured by appreciative and critical distance.

The question is one of contextualization: What happens when Luther's ideas are contextualized in his own time and then beyond? If Luther is to be understood as a theologian for today, he must be able to address today's most pressing questions, which in turn presupposes that Luther had something important to say in the past.

One word captures what Luther's name, life, and work were all about: *freedom* was inscribed—by his own decision—into his name. Martin Luder created the name "Luther" for himself, as Peter Hodgson notes, deriving it from the Greek word for freedom (*eleutheria*). The name came to connote a new experience, Christ's creation of freedom and life for the sinner in the place of death and hell. Luther's Christian freedom precipitates—as the "urban legend" of Luther's life goes—the history of freedom as constitutive of the modern

West. For philosophers in Luther's footsteps—for example, Georg Wilhelm Friedrich Hegel and Søren Kierkegaard—freedom is a key characteristic of the human individual, as it is of world history. Persons together with their world are destined for freedom. When Michael King Jr.'s birth certificate was altered to Martin Luther King Jr., his life too was inscribed into the history of freedom.

Freedom is actualized in the reality of history as struggle. Freedom's articulation in language is visionary, but its concretization is in the ambivalence of power and suffering. This fundamental ambivalence marks Luther's struggles even after his alleged tower-experience (*Turmerlebnis*) with depression and devil, driving his persevering denigration of the religious other. Europeans after Luther took this ambivalence into intra-Christian struggles and into Christianity's relation to other global religions, particularly to Judaism and Islam. Creative and critical inquiry is required to reorient Luther's idea of freedom for today. Luther's life and work are oriented to freedom, and so he himself must be liberated from aspects of his own ideas in order to set personal, political, and religious expressions of freedom into motion in ways that he might not even have imagined.

Risto Saarinen, Peter C. Hodgson, and Munib A. Younan each consider Luther in this section from the perspective of his global impact, moving between historical interpretation and contemporary concerns. Saarinen describes the significance of Luther's life as "urban legend" in theology, modern literature, and philosophy. Hodgson contextualizes Luther's view of freedom in the West's history of freedom, particularly in the American civil rights movement. Younan describes and then offers ways to recontextualize today one of the most problematic issues in Luther's thought, the relation of Christianity to global religions. These three essays set the parameters for the entire volume, showing how Luther's original texts are mined for their novel insights and proposing how Luther can be read today for our times, even if Luther himself must be transcended.

CHAPTER 2

Luther the Urban Legend

Risto Saarinen

mportant historical figures are notoriously immortalized in hagiography. Hagiography assigns an aura of powerful transhistorical transcendence to the deeds, personalities, and teachings of its subjects, while comparisons are continuously drawn between great men and women of the past. Martin Luther is no exception in this regard. Hagiography swirled around Luther right from the alleged beginnings of the Reformation with the hammering of the Ninety-Five Theses to the door of the Wittenberg castle church. Luther was sensationally portrayed as a new Apostle Paul or a new Augustine, a charismatic and revolutionary figure who pointed to a new dawn in the church's and the world's history. Luther was famously portrayed as a forerunner of modernity. He brought values modernity holds dear out from under medieval darkness: the importance of individual freedom and the fundamental equality of all human persons. Modern Lutheran social and ethical commitments, such as universal education and healthcare as well as social welfare, can be traced back to Luther's original ideas.

The scholarly task for historians and theologians is to sort through the various layers of Luther's hagiography, the "urban legend" that is Luther. The category of urban legend is usually taken as a story assumed to be true, while in reality it is not. In this sense, historians concerned with historical accuracy must separate story from history. A different meaning of urban legend is perhaps more pertinent to this chapter. This meaning takes an urban legend as a story that is transmitted as a true story, yet the participants in transmission do not know its actual truth value.[1] Urban legends are characterized by their embellishments. They are told and understood without critical concern for the story's true origins and faithful development. They can describe a modest event in fantastic terms and can represent a side remark as a profound innovation that has powerfully shaped subsequent generations. They may contain seeds of truth, but more often than not these seeds take on many and different distortions as they grow.

Irrespective of their truth value, urban legends can serve as important factors in shaping history and group identity. Once a large group firmly believes a particular story to be true, the story plays an important role in influencing the group's dispositions, thoughts, and actions. Urban legends and stories fascinate and delight, yet their functions in building past and present identity are complicated and multilayered. Often, the heroes and heroines are not entirely empty canvasses onto which the legends are projected. In some cases, hero and heroine are very concerned with the ways in which they will be remembered in subsequent generations and actively take part in shaping this memory.

This chapter discusses some urban stories circulating around the person and thought of Martin Luther. Obviously, the task of giving a comprehensive account of all the legends associated with Luther and his Reformation is beyond the scope of this chapter. Luther is an urban legend par excellence because his person and thoughts have been packaged countless times and in infinite variation. Thus we restrict ourselves to a few exploratory probes into different soils in order to sample the rich variety. The evaluations and judgments here are intended to stimulate discussion of Luther: the man, the work, and the history of interpreting him.

The historical Luther is hidden behind five hundred years of text and tradition. It is a most difficult task to find him and then to understand him as he would have understood himself. Luther had a complex and multifaceted personality. His prodigious literary output documents four event-filled decades, makes use of many literary genres from sermon to aphorism, and covers an extraordinary range of topics from children to church. Any discrete literary element in this vast corpus can be interpreted, and in many cases has been interpreted, for very different purposes. We first examine a famous story that relates Luther to the Christian past in order to illustrate the various ways in which Luther has been read, interpreted, and appropriated. We then discuss

---

1. The concept is from modern folklore. See for example Jan Harold Brunvand, *Too Good to Be True: The Colossal Book of Urban Legends* (New York: Norton, 2001).

a few other stories that connect Luther to more recent historical events and contemporary trends.

Paul, Augustine, and Luther: The Conversion

The biographies of great religious leaders typically report a decisive moment, a *kairos*, that marks a radical and innovative shift in life and thought. The New Testament figure Saul of Tarsus, for example, was stunned by a vision of light on his way to Damascus. Saul also heard a voice that reproached him for persecuting Jesus (Acts 9:3-5). This decisive moment precipitated Saul's conversion to be a follower of Jesus. Saul became the Apostle Paul. A similar story is part of Augustine's biography. In his search for Christianity, the church father Augustine also saw a vision and heard a voice.[2] Lady Continence appeared to him and urged him not to rely on his own strength but to entrust himself to God. Augustine then heard a voice from under the fig tree saying, "tolle et lege," which means, "pick up and read." Augustine turned to a passage from Paul's letter to the Romans and was converted. He remembers that "a light of relief from all anxiety flooded into" his heart.[3] A religious conversion is, in the stories of both Paul and Augustine, preceded by a miraculous event. Seeing things and hearing things highlight the dramatic character of conversion. The paradigm of conversion, exemplified by two of the most important figures in Christianity, shapes our understanding of key religious experiences.

Martin Luther's conversion story recapitulates this paradigm. The conversion is said to have taken place upon his decision to enter the monastery of Erfurt. On July 2, 1505, Luther experienced a severe thunderstorm in Stotternheim.[4] Terrified by the lightning and thunder, he cried out to Saint Anne for help. He sincerely promised to become a monk if he were saved. We have here a vision and a voice, as with Paul and Augustine, although with Luther the miraculous aspect is connected to the storm's lightning and thunder. Luther's father is skeptical and entertains the possibility that his son has been deluded. But as we all know, Luther enters the monastery.

Like Paul, Luther walks on the road and encounters his moment of *kairos*. Like Augustine, he is a young man thirsty for life and does not regard monastic

---

2. Saint Augustine, *Conf.*, 8:11, 27–12, 30. Cited in *Confessions*, trans. Henry Chadwick, The World's Classics (Oxford: Oxford University Press, 1992), 151–54.
3. Saint Augustine, *Conf.*, 8:12, 29. Cited in *Confessions*, trans. Chadwick, 153.
4. This account is taken from Andreas Lindner, "Was geschah in Stotternheim? Eine problematische Geschichte und ihre problematische Rezeption," in *Martin Luther und das monastische Erbe*, ed. Christoph Bultmann, Volker Leppin, and Andreas Lindner, Spätmittelalter, Humanismus, Reformation 39 (Tübingen: Mohr Siebeck, 2007), 93–110.

celibacy or "continence" in laudatory terms. The stories of Paul, Augustine, and
Luther are so successfully united in the urban legend that three different religious horizons are fused. We sometimes do not remember which of the three
read the letter to the Romans, which one was struck down by lightning, and
which one personally met Jesus. The legend brings Paul, Augustine, and Luther
into close contact with God as well as into contact with each other.

A theologian reflecting at length on these matters may detect some contradictions concerning the role the story plays in Luther's overall biography.
Luther promised to become a monk and immediately entered the monastery.
At a later moment in his life, Luther decided to leave the monastery, very
critical of the "holy" lives of monks and nuns. Does this contradiction prove
that Luther's father was right? Was the thunderstorm not a real vision and
voice but a delusion? These questions open up conflicting interpretative possibilities; a theologian must smooth out the inconsistencies. One example of
ironing out the wrinkles might be: Luther became religious as a result of a
thunderstorm, but his conversion did not yet signal the true faith of his later
Reformation breakthrough. Yet this interpretation presents an interpretative
difficulty. If Luther's conversion is regarded as incomplete, then the analogy
to Paul and Augustine breaks down. Both Paul and Augustine were enthusiastically religious before their respective conversions. The main point of their
conversion stories was to show how their conversion precipitated a right and
true Christian faith.

A modern Protestant theologian may also have some difficulties with the
miraculous element of "seeing things and hearing things." Generally speaking,
miraculous sights and sounds are not taken seriously by mainline Protestants.
Proper Christians should rely on word and sacrament, not on supernatural
revelation. Yet coincidentally, the supernatural element in Luther's conversion
has powerful pedagogical appeal. Children and young people recall the dramatic event more easily than the articles of the Augsburg Confession (1530).
Drama also situates Luther in good company—with the two greatest heroes
of early Christianity.

The story of Luther's conversion in a thunderstorm is a complex event
that has both exemplary and problematic aspects. What really happened on
July 2, 1505? A historian would first answer the question by stating the obvious: no one was close enough to the event to witness and record it. Posterity only knows of this event from Luther's later recollections and from
some remarks made by his friends. The Table Talk mentions the event several
times, but in these entries Luther is already creating the legend of his own
beginnings.

Two earlier records stem from 1519 and 1521. They are generally considered to be the most reliable sources.[5] The first of these records is a letter written by Crotus Rubeanus to Luther in 1519. Rubeanus, a student friend, remarks that "the heavenly lightning struck Luther down as a second Paul and moved him to the corner of the Augustinians [the monastery of the Augustinian eremites]."[6] Already, three heroes are mentioned in this earliest report of the happening: Luther, Paul, and Augustine. Luther scholars have also noticed that Luther was called "the second Paul" before 1519.[7] The religious horizons of Luther and Paul had already been fused in the very first historical records of Luther's own conversion.

Luther also reports the event in his 1521 text *The Judgment of Luther on Monastic Vows* by comparing himself to Augustine. As was the case of the early church father, the passions of youth were burning in the young student when lightning struck him down. He feared a sudden death. He decided to enter a monastery, although his father questioned the sanity of his son's conversion experience. Luther's father would have liked him to marry rather than to base his life on a vision and a vow of celibacy.[8]

The two early records conflate Luther's experiences with those of Paul and Augustine. One important figure, however, is missing from these early stories: the stories do not mention Saint Anne. She comes into the picture only much later, in a Table Talk stemming from 1539. Luther's late Table Talk tells the same story of the thunderstorm but with a different nuance. The later Luther is generally critical of his earlier decision to enter the monastery, and he recalls his invocation of Saint Anne with a touch of sarcasm: "In my fear I cried: help me, Saint Anne, I want to become a monk. But God understood this promise in a Hebrew manner. Anne is a name that means 'under grace,' not according to the law. Afterward I repented of this promise."[9] In this first mention of Saint Anne in the Table Talk, Luther interprets the event to suit his theological purpose.[10] He describes the monastery as a place under the law. The invocation of Saint Anne is a cry that God understands paradoxically, contrary to the intentions of the young student. Saint Anne ultimately serves the purpose in this interpretation of evangelical freedom rather than representing the monastery's captivity.

---

5. All this evidence is listed and discussed in Lindner, "Was geschah in Stotternheim?"
6. WABr 1:543, 107–108 (no. 213; Oct. 16, 1519). (Translation R. S.)
7. Lindner, "Was geschah in Stotternheim?" 99.
8. LW 44:253–54, WA 8:573–74.
9. WATr 4:440, 9–11 (no. 4707; 1539).
10. Lindner, "Was geschah in Stotternheim?" 98. Referring to Cornelis Augustijn, *Luthers Intrede in Het Klooster* (Kampen: Kok, 1968).

The very first memories of Luther's conversion link him to Paul and Augustine. The mantle of greatness from Paul and Augustine is passed on to Luther. The later recollections are, however, self-critical and diminish the importance of the decision. Luther does not even mention the conversion event in his 1545 autobiography. He only notes sarcastically that he remained Saul in the monastery rather than Paul.[11] The self-critical reflection offers some evidence for both sensationalizing the conversion as well as for minimizing its significance.

The story of Luther's conversion introduces us to the complex world of narrative reports. Contemporary narrative theory has rejected the assumption that a narrative first invokes a naked event that historians can access by uncovering and exposing the legends wrapped around it. Historical analysis is not a process of disclosure; history shows the enormous complexity of and multiple perspectives on the past. History is interwoven with narrative that both constitutes the event and interprets it.

The event of Luther's conversion is not exhausted by analyzing the historical facts pertaining to July 2, 1505. This event is first created by later recollections and interpretations. A conversion may be momentary, but the meaning of conversion only gradually emerges over a long period of time. The entire meaning of the event can include contradictory elements. In Luther's case, the thunderstorm oriented Luther to the right path, but it also brought him down the wrong one. Luther's father mistakenly interpreted the event as delusion, but he was also right in criticizing it. Luther followed the example of Paul and Augustine, but he also distanced himself from their conversion narratives.

Luther and Shakespeare: Two Different Mentalities

One genre of urban legend connects the larger-than-life person to his predecessors. Luther is, for example, connected to Paul and Augustine. Another genre connects the heroine to her followers and perhaps other, later figures. This second genre is particularly important in our discussion of Luther's global impact. Later currents of thought may flow in close proximity to Luther's own thinking, or they might run in an entirely different direction.

Luther was German. Although the German state did not exist in the sixteenth century, Luther's writings established the German language as a

---

11. LW 34:327 (*Preface to the Complete Edition of Luther's Latin Writings*, 1545), WA 54:179, 27–28; Lindner, "Was geschah in Stotternheim?" 109.

unifying force and gave rise to many important aspects of German cultural identity.[12] If we want to appropriate the German Luther in a global context, we need to figure out the relationship between the German and the transcultural aspects of his thought. This is not an easy task. We initiate this discussion by relating Luther to other cultural mentalities, beginning with the easiest point of comparison: namely, the mentality of the English-speaking culture.

With which early modern figure would an average English-speaking college or university student today be most familiar? If we look at classic literary texts, William Shakespeare is the obvious answer. Shakespeare is regarded as the major creative force in the development of the English language and literary culture. He occupies a similar position to Luther in terms of cultural significance. Shakespeare has been formative to the English mind-set in ways that resemble Luther's significance to German-speaking people.

Let us imagine how a truly sympathetic reader of Shakespeare might evaluate the relationship between the English poet and the German reformer. The following picture might emerge.[13] Shakespeare is most interested in individual lives and their fates as they emerge in manifold variety. Life is both comic and tragic. Sympathy with suffering is commendable, but one-sided seriousness is not the best way to take advantage of all that life has to offer. Religious people, like Luther, have a tendency to disregard the great variety of life because they think they have found an absolute answer to all questions. In reality, however, they only ask a very limited set of questions. Religious people tend to be hypercritical and lack a sense of humor. Shakespeare upholds healthy emotions as a positive dimension of life. He allows for divine agency but does not claim to have a normative viewpoint on religious issues. Hence, Shakespeare is a much better guide for modern people than the narrow-minded professor from Wittenberg.

This story makes several assumptions by comparing Shakespeare to Luther and exposes crucial differences between British and German mentalities. Its assumptions reflect broad stereotypes that are not very helpful when considering important questions regarding the power of cultural influence. Instead, I

---

12. See Heinrich Bornkamm, *Luther im Spiegel der deutschen Geistesgeschichte: Mit ausgewählten Texten von Lessing bis zur Gegenwart*, 2nd rev. edn. (Göttingen: Vandenhoeck & Ruprecht, 1970).
13. Literature on Shakespeare and religion is vast. It is often claimed that Shakespeare was not only religious but that he was Roman Catholic. See, for example, Eric S. Mallin, *Godless Shakespeare (Shakespeare Now!)* (New York: Continuum, 2007); David N. Beauregard, *Catholic Theology in Shakespeare's Plays* (Newark: University of Delaware Press, 2007). In contrast to these studies, I focus on Shakespeare's Protestant characteristics.

turn to the more specific task of laying the historical groundwork for Luther's impact on Shakespeare.[14]

Scholars have noticed Shakespeare's comments on Luther and Lutheranism in *Hamlet*. Denmark is, after all, the Lutheran country closest to England. The prince of Denmark is said to have studied in Wittenberg. Furthermore, Hamlet's characteristic depression has been compared to Luther's heroic melancholy, particularly highlighted in sixteenth-century literature. Both Luther and Hamlet are often linked to Hercules, the classical symbol of heroic melancholy.[15] Shakespeare's best known allusion to Luther's Reformation in *Hamlet* is the wordplay about the emperor at the 1521 Diet of Worms. Hamlet responds to the question as to where he has put Polonius's body: "Not where he eats, but where he is eaten; a certain convocation of politic worms are e'en at him. Your worm is your only emperor for diet: we fat all creatures else to fat us, and we fat ourselves for maggots."[16]

Another important connection between Hamlet and Luther is their common criticism of philosophy. Hamlet's less than positive view of philosophy is immortalized in the famous line: "There are more things in heaven and earth, Horatio, than are dreamt of in your philosophy."[17] Luther and Hamlet hold a similar view of God as hidden. The hidden God (*deus absconditus*) is concealed under its opposite, the cross of Christ, and cannot be reached by means of philosophy. Another important similarity between Shakespeare's *Hamlet* and Luther is their common melancholy. Something rotten in the continental European spirit remains depressed as well as preoccupied with the dark side. Both figures were intimately acquainted with heroic melancholy. The urban story is not merely a product of later times, but its truth is based on real people and their writings.

The play most "Lutheran" in character that Shakespeare wrote is not *Hamlet* but *Measure for Measure*. The plot of Shakespeare's comedy is taken from Luther, namely from his *Temporal Authority: To What Extent It Should Be Obeyed* (1523). Luther tells the story as follows:

---

14. The following discussion is based on Tibor Fabiny, "The Strange Acts of God: The Hermeneutics of Concealment and Revelation in Luther and Shakespeare," *Dialog* 45/1 (Spring 2006): 44–54.
15. Fabiny, "The Strange Acts of God," 51.
16. *Hamlet* 4:3. Cited in William Shakespeare, "Hamlet," in *The New Folger Library Shakespeare*, ed. Barbara Mowat and Paul Werstine (Washington: Washington Square, 2003), 197.
17. *Hamlet* 1:5. Cited in *The New Folger Library Shakespeare*, 67.

A certain nobleman took an enemy prisoner. The prisoner's wife came to ransom her husband. The nobleman promised to give back the husband on condition that she would lie with him. The woman was virtuous yet wished to set her husband free; so she goes and asks her husband whether she should do this thing in order to set him free. The husband wished to be set free and to save his life, so he gives his wife permission. After the nobleman had lain with the wife, he had the husband beheaded the next day and gave him to her as a corpse. She laid the whole case before Duke Charles. He summoned the nobleman and commanded him to marry the woman. When the wedding day was over he had the nobleman beheaded, gave the woman possession of his property, and restored her to honor.[18]

Luther understands the story to refer to the worldly (temporal) authority's capacity to adapt the law to real situations. Temporal authority should not "make reason a captive of letters" but is mandated to keep "written laws subject to reason."[19]

Shakespeare's version of this story in *Measure for Measure* complicates the relationship between law and reason. The play's heroine is Isabella, a young nun who first pleads for her brother's freedom with the argument that mercy is better than punishment. The nobleman in charge of the prisoner wants to sleep with the nun. He turns Isabella's own argument on behalf of mercy against her. He claims that her belief in grace and mercy is so sincere that she should be able to forgive herself; she and her brother need not feel guilty for paying this price for his freedom. Isabella sticks more to her guns than the wife in Luther's story and staunchly refuses to sleep with the nobleman. As a result, the nobleman in Shakespeare's play accuses Isabella of failing to act according to her own principles. The nun initially claims that grace and mercy are greater than the law, but she cannot apply this principle to her own moral situation.

The dialogues between Isabella and the nobleman are profound theological treatises that tease out the relationship between law and gospel, justice and mercy. Shakespeare is well aware of Luther's distinction between law and gospel. The English poet agrees on the importance of this distinction but is also critical of it. He uses the circumstance of Isabella's confusion to show that people who proclaim the superiority of mercy do not necessarily understand its relationship to law and justice.[20]

---

18. LW 45:128–29, WA 11:279, 35–80, 11.
19. LW 45:129, WA 11:280, 118–119.
20. I have studied the theology inherent in this dialogue in more detail in a Finnish article: Risto Saarinen, "Luterilainen Seksuaalietiikka, Luther ja Shakespeare," in *Kirkko ja usko*

A careful reader of *Measure for Measure* will notice that the relationship between Luther and Shakespeare is more complex than any superficial story can tell about the differences between German and English mentalities. Shakespeare may be critical of Protestantism, but he understands very well the careful distinction between law and mercy. The heroine of *Measure for Measure* is very Lutheran in character. Her only fault is that her Lutheran theology is not as consistent as she first believes. The male hero of this play is Duke Charles. He appears only at the end of the play to rectify the situation and to punish the nobleman. The Duke metes out justice without appealing to explicit arguments. Although Isabella's reasoning has been exposed as contradictory, it is nevertheless the best reasoning offered in the play.

The dialectic between law and gospel, justice and mercy, transcends the boundaries of nationality and mentality. Shakespeare is clearly familiar with this dialectic and appeals to it in order to ask the important question concerning grace and mercy. The underlying issue is the perennial question: How can we find a merciful God? Or: How can we understand which actions count as merciful? In *Measure for Measure*, Shakespeare addresses these same questions that propelled Luther to his Reformation, but in discussing them Shakespeare also shows that the discovery of merciful actions may be even more difficult than Lutherans usually believe. The difficult and thought-provoking questions of mercy and law have been posed consistently since the sixteenth century. This fact is very likely due to Luther's enduring global impact.

Luther and Kierkegaard: Individualistic Faith

Søren Kierkegaard is another great thinker who has deeply probed the topic of mercy. Like Shakespeare, Kierkegaard prominently represents the interrelated issues of nationality, mentality, and Lutheranism. It is customary in Northern Europe to see Kierkegaard as a true representative of Lutheranism. Lutheran Pietists in particular have welcomed Kierkegaard as their patron saint. Kierkegaard represents the individual struggle of modern conscience and points out the exemplary way to be a Christian in the modern era. Kierkegaard's thought is a great place to start the discussion in this section of Martin Luther's relationship to the legends of modernity and individualism.

The so-called "Luther-Renaissance" (*Lutherrenaissance*) of the 1920s is largely responsible for connecting Luther to Kierkegaard. This German

---

tämän päivän Suomessa, ed. Aku Visala (Helsinki: STKS, 2007), 72–91. See also Fabiny, "The Strange Acts of God."

intellectual movement combined an admiration for Kierkegaard's individualism with a view of Luther through the lenses of modern philosophical schools. The professor from Wittenberg emerges in the writings of Karl Holl and some later scholars—for instance, Lennart Pinomaa and the young Jaroslav Pelikan—as a sixteenth-century Kierkegaard who struggles with his own conscience and executes a leap of faith, standing alone and strong against the entire world.[21] In this trajectory of Luther research, the German reformer is not primarily a harbinger of modernity but is cast in almost postmodern terms. Luther as postmodern figure does not believe in grand narratives but constructs his own existence through an inner struggle with anxiety, desperation, and temptations (*Anfechtungen*).

Luther scholars have appealed to Kierkegaard in order to promote a religious worldview that retreats from nationalism and moves toward subjective freedom. Kierkegaard's Lutheran religion is an individual and private conviction. This individualistic sense of Lutheranism has been appealing for both European and American Lutherans. A case in point is Karl Holl, known as a meticulous historian and as representative scholar of the "Luther-Renaissance." Even Holl succumbed to the individualistic interpretation of Luther and gushed: "Luther finally addresses the issues that Paul, the great groundbreaker, had foreseen and that Søren Kierkegaard, as well as Nietzsche, had grasped in the nineteenth century."[22]

Holl refers in the above quote to Luther's struggle with genuine repentance, or the act of contrition. The individualistic interpretation that Holl and his followers promoted was based primarily on Luther's earliest monastic texts. These texts exhibit Luther's inner struggles, sometimes to the extreme. Luther aims to renounce everything. In his own words, he attempts "to nail himself so high on the cross that his own feet no longer touch the ground."[23] Holl is perhaps right in assigning Kierkegaardian and Pietist features to Luther, particularly as Luther expresses himself in this uncompromising way. But Luther developed these ideas as he got older.

---

21. See Bornkamm, *Luther im Spiegel*, 114–17, 156; Lennart Pinomaa, *Der existentielle Charakter der Theologie Luther* (Helsinki: AASF, 1940); Jaroslav Pelikan, *From Luther to Kierkegaard: A Study in the History of Theology* (St. Louis: Concordia, 1950).
22. Karl Holl, *Gesammelte Aufsätze*, vol. 1, *Luther* (Tübingen: J. C. B. Mohr [Paul Siebeck],1927), 24–25. (Translation R. S.)
23. "Hoc autem est suspendi in cruce, ubi nusquam tangit terram in qua confidat; haec est via proficientium." (WA 1:102, 40–103, 2 ["Sermon on the Feast of Saint Andrew"; sermons from 1514–1517]); see also Bo Kristian Holm, *Gabe und Geben bei Luther: Das Verhältnis zwischen Reziprozität und reformatorischer Rechtfertigungslehre*, Theologische Bibliothek Töpelmann 134 (Berlin: de Gruyter, 2006), 57.

Luther recognized at a later point that this path of true repentance did not lead to real renunciation but to self-righteousness. As he nailed himself ever higher on the cross, he ascended by his own works and did not achieve self-denial. Contemporary Luther scholars point out that the so-called "theology of self-humiliation" (*Demutstheologie*) is only a transitory phase in Luther's development. Later, at least after 1518 or 1519, Luther insisted that the world was God's good gift to be affirmed, not renounced. More importantly, Luther admitted that the process of renunciation could not be turned into a universal rubric. If the process is understood as a disciplined prescription, self-righteousness is the inevitable result. A person engaged in achieving self-denial does not demonstrate trust in God but justifies himself or herself through ascetic practices.[24]

The Danish philosopher of the nineteenth century is much more careful in his reception of Luther than are the twentieth-century Kierkegaardians. As a young man, Kierkegaard appreciated Luther's honest struggle with conscience and temptations. As he grew older, he increasingly judged Luther's relationship to both world and society to be problematic. For Kierkegaard, ascetic discipline necessarily belongs to true Christianity. When Luther left his exaggerated asceticism behind and began to affirm worldly institutions, he compromised his own reformatory ideals. Luther's marriage in particular was, in Kierkegaard's interpretation, an inauthentic act that showed complicity with the world. Luther did not ultimately have what it took to follow the existential dialectic.[25] In this manner, Kierkegaard understood the key difference between himself and Luther much better than the Luther scholars who were and continue to be enchanted by the Danish radical.

Luther and Modernity: The Affirmation of Ordinary Life

The issue of individualism, or subjectivity, exposes one important connection between Luther and modernity. But many other topics are also relevant to this connection. One common nineteenth- and early twentieth-century association linked Luther to Kant. Immanuel Kant was seen as the philosopher of Protestantism par excellence, and his connection to Luther underlined this title.[26] It is Luther's concept of freedom that even today promotes Luther as a

---

24. For a detailed documentation of this development, see Holm, *Gabe und Geben*.
25. See Bornkamm, *Luther im Spiegel*, 95–100.
26. See for example, Risto Saarinen, *Gottes Wirken auf uns: Die transzendentale Deutung des Gegenwart-Christi-Motivs in der Lutherforschung*, Veröffentlichungen des Instituts für

forerunner of modernity. Prominent scholars like Gerhard Ebeling and Hans Reiner claim that Luther is the first thinker to have formulated the phrase "freedom of conscience."[27]

This claim is misleading. The phrase already appears in late antiquity. Boethius speaks of the "conscientiae libertas" in his *Consolation of Philosophy*, and Cassiodorus mentions the "libera conscientia" in his writings.[28] But the misleading claim contains a seed of truth. The term "freedom of conscience" was rarely mentioned in medieval Latin. It became prominent only after Luther and Calvin, conceptually framing later discussions of individual freedom and basic human rights. Luther did not invent the phrase; he contributed to its prominence. It should be noted in today's context of interreligious dialogue that the sixteenth-century use of the phrase did not imply the same type of respect or toleration that was developed in the Enlightenment. The radical Reformers did not in any way enjoy the same freedom of conscience that Luther or Calvin claimed for their adherents.[29] I summarize the result of this trajectory: Luther did not invent the term "freedom of conscience"—the term is older, the phenomenon younger than the Reformation. And yet, Luther contributed to the emergence of this phenomenon as well as to the understanding of the term according to its current meaning.

Other issues bring Luther to bear on modern individual rights. The connection between Luther and modernity in view of these issues is just as complicated as the issue of freedom. The rights and practices pertaining to sexual ethics are a good example of this complex relationship. Luther is well known for allowing pastors to marry. Many historians and theologians have evaluated his influential opinion of marriage as an affirmation of human sexuality and liberation from oppressive practices.[30] A careful reader of Luther's influential treatises on marriage may, however, see a different picture. Luther often denies in these treatises that humans have the capacity to control their sexuality. It is better to marry than to burn (1 Cor 7:9); celibacy only leads to graver sin

Europäische Geschichte/Abteilung Abendländische Religionsgeschichte 137 (Stuttgart: Franz Steiner, 1989).

27. Hans Reiner, "Gewissen," in *Historisches Wörterbuch der Philosophie* (Basel: Schwabe, 1974), 3:583; Gerhard Ebeling, *Lutherstudien III* (Tübingen: Mohr Siebeck, 1985), 385–86.

28. Boethius, *De Cons. Philo. 1*, prose 4; Cassiodorus, *Variarum Libri XII*, 1, 4, 5, 9, 12, 1.

29. On the complex history of toleration, see Benjamin J. Kaplan, *Divided by Faith: Religious Conflict and the Practice of Toleration in Early Modern Europe* (Cambridge: Harvard University Press, 2007).

30. For a summary of research on this topic, see John Witte, *Law and Protestantism: The Legal Teachings of the Lutheran Reformation* (Cambridge: Cambridge University Press, 2002), 199–256.

because genuine control cannot be attained. In Luther's view, living with a woman without having sex with her is more difficult than waking the dead.[31]

Luther radicalizes Augustine's view of sexuality as an uncontrollable power. His sexual ethics are based on this negative premise. Marriage is permitted to all because it is the lesser evil. Yet as a "lesser evil," it is not regulated by freedom of spousal agreement. Marriage must be regulated by society at large. Given this negative judgment on eros, Luther's view of sexual ethics cannot be easily harmonized with a position affirming eros as a positive power. It is the latter interpretation that has emerged in Luther scholarship as a dominant one: the Reformation's secularizing effect on marriage is justified by the Reformer's healthy affirmation of created powers. Luther's view does not support this happy end. Rather, Luther promotes marriage as a concession to the problematic power of sex.

The restraining force of marriage in Luther's sexual ethics is analogous to the power over this institution that Luther assigns to worldly and ecclesial authorities. Luther assumes that Christians are so morally weak that they must be governed by society's legal ordinances. Spousal consent alone does not warrant marriage. Both parental consent and a public notice of the intended marriage are also required. Christendom had for 1500 years and until Luther adhered to the Roman practice of regarding marriage as a contract between two partners. The Lutheran Reformation added the additional requirement of legal authorization. This political innovation might possibly be the only matter that the Council of Trent took over from the Reformation.[32]

Lutherans do not usually interpret Luther's view of sexuality and marriage in this manner, but it is entirely possible and historically appropriate to do so. Luther's relationship to modern views of marriage and sexuality is ambivalent. It is likely that the institution of marriage was socially upgraded as a result of the Reformation, but human sexuality continued to be regarded in Augustinian terms. Luther's global impact in this respect must be investigated further.

Luther's affirmation of ordinary life, not of human sexuality, remains his important contribution to the discussion. The term "ordinary life" refers to both family relations and professional relations. Among contemporary thinkers, Charles Taylor has highlighted the importance of this topic as a link between

---

31. LW 7:84, WA 44:362, 29–30 (*Lectures on Genesis*; to Gen 39:10; possibly 1544): "Habitare enim cum muliere, et eam non cognoscere, plus est quam mortuos excitare."
32. Albert Stein, "Luther über Eherecht und Juristen," in *Leben und Werk Martin Luthers von 1526 bis 1546: Festgabe zu seinem 500. Geburtstag*, ed. Helmar Junghans (Berlin: Evangelische Verlagsanstalt, 1985), 171–86.

the Reformation and modernity. In his *Sources of the Self*, Taylor claims that the Reformation was characterized as "the affirmation that the fullness of Christian existence was to be found within the activities of this life, in one's calling and in marriage and the family. The entire modern development of the affirmation of ordinary life was, I believe, foreshadowed and initiated, in all its facets, in the spirituality of the Reformers."[33] Charles Taylor, like Karl Holl, Gerhard Ebeling, and many other scholars before him, sees the Reformation as a forerunner of modernity. His interpretation, however, does not limit modernity to Kierkegaardian subjectivity, the freedom of individual conscience, or an emancipatory view of human sexuality. The main topic of Taylor's *Sources of the Self* is the concept of modern selfhood that Taylor derives from the Reformation's idea of a communitarian virtue of partnership and active participation in worldly vocation. Taylor does not rehearse the usual case for modernity's individualism and its indebtedness to the Reformation.

Rather, Taylor's argument focuses in detail on the concept of renunciation. While Socrates and the Stoics claimed that they do not, in fact, lose anything in renouncing the world, Christians have always experienced that, in renouncing the world, they really lose something of God's good creation. Thus, "Christian renunciation is an affirmation of the goodness of what is renounced." Renunciation and asceticism are ambivalent phenomena that may lead to a real loss of the good life. In Taylor's view, the Protestant reformers were very much aware of this ambivalence. They preached a sort of asceticism; they enthusiastically affirmed an inner-worldly asceticism that did not renounce ordinary life.[34]

Taylor's analysis can be used to interpret Luther's monastic experiences. Luther first renounced his worldly life upon entering the monastery. Yet, as he recalls later in life, Luther was driven to renounce this first renunciation. Only after he had renounced the monastery, hence a second renunciation, could he affirm the goodness of ordinary life available through evangelical freedom. The second renunciation did not eliminate the idea of renunciation. It added another contour to the idea, opening up the many possibilities associated with the affirmation of ordinary life.

Taylor's description of modernity is very different from interpretations of modernity that situate Luther in Kierkegaardian terms. In these interpretations, the Danish philosopher remains on the path of the first renunciation. Kierkegaard's hostility to ordinary life is shaped by the subject's individualistic

---

33. Charles Taylor, *Sources of the Self: The Making of the Modern Identity* (Cambridge: Cambridge University Press, 1989), 218.
34. Taylor, *Sources of the Self*, 219–21; see also Charles Taylor, *A Secular Age* (Cambridge: Harvard University Press, 2007), 16–18.

reductionism. Individuality is gained at the cost of the world, which is seen as a banal and dull reality. In contrast, Luther's theology views ordinary life in delightful, positive terms. Life's diverse vocations, roles, and tasks are positively affirmed in spite of sin's enduring power and the will's bondage to it. Luther's treatises on marriage can be viewed in light of this specific affirmation of ordinary life rather than as prescriptions for a sexual ethic. The treatises contextualize marriage by affirming everyday face-to-face encounters in the community. This innovative contextualization brings Luther in much closer proximity to Shakespeare than to Kierkegaard. Shakespeare's eye for the tiny details of ordinary life and his wonderfully profound intuitions of relationship in community are characteristics of Protestantism in Taylor's sense.

The Global Luther: Lessons to Be Learned

A few basic ideas have come from our exploratory drillings into the rich soil of Luther and his historical impact. My communitarian interpretation of Luther's theology shows how Luther's thought provides cultural insights that make a dialogue with poets like William Shakespeare and philosophers like Charles Taylor important. A communitarian perspective can be used also to criticize the linking of Luther to an individualistic understanding of human rights or a subjectivistic understanding of philosophy. Luther gradually learned to appreciate ordinary life with its communitarian ideals. This perspective was not his weakness, as Kierkegaard claimed, but his strength. In Luther's affirmation of the ordinary lies, in my view, the most important global impact of the Reformation. Ordinary life is a dominant theme in Luther's theology, together with its ideals of good education, social equality, and willingness to love and help one's neighbor.

I make these claims on behalf of Luther's theology of ordinary life without any intention of promoting a cultural Protestant viewpoint. I am not in favor of advocating a superficial accommodation of Luther's theology to various cultural institutions. I merely emphasize that a careful historian and a careful theologian will detect many significant points of contact between the Reformation and modern Western culture. Our cultural grasp of modernity is informed by the urban legends that tell the Reformation's story. These stories are often as old as the events they illuminate—and conceal. The stories and legends belong to history as its constitutive elements.

In addition to the communitarian emphasis, Charles Taylor's interpretation of Luther and the West also offers some transcultural possibilities in understanding the concept of reformation. The importance of this concept

arises when we ask whether other confessions or religions can have reformations. A very recent discussion concerning the "Islamic reformation," for example, suggests that the emergence of mass education and mass communication
constitute a new situation in which the larger group can become an agent of
religion in a stronger sense than before.[35] The comparison with the European
Reformation is plausible in terms of mass education and mass communication.
An affirmation of ordinary life constructs responsible subjects in a civil society in a new sense, since the notion of ordinary life promotes education and
both the exchange of goods and information. Any closer comparison between
these different reformations requires more precise historical and conceptual
analysis.

It is perhaps more difficult to address the issue of whether "Martin
Luthers" can arise in other confessions and religions. While some discussion
regarding the possibility of an "Islamic Luther" occurs, the evidence I have con-
sulted is not very illuminating.[36] One can speak of different reform attempts,
both conservative and liberal, in current Islam, but the spokespersons of these
initiatives do not discuss them in view of Martin Luther's personality traits or
his theological program. It is, nevertheless, of great interest that the name of
Luther can have a symbolic value for such a unique reform program.

Another difficult comparison follows from the affirmation of ordinary life
that I have introduced in this section. I am thinking of the role of Josemaria
Escriva de Balaguer and Opus Dei in twentieth-century Spain. Opus Dei has
promoted the affirmation of ordinary life and good education in civil society
and has thereby been instrumental in the rise in social and educational levels
in Spain. Opus Dei shares other ideals with the Reformation, for example, the
autonomy of professional life and the idea of secular vocation as a religious
calling.[37] Most contemporary Lutherans, as well as most Opus Dei members
would, however, be embarrassed by this comparison.

A final observation concerns the connection that Charles Taylor draws
between the Reformation and the emergence of Puritanism. Not all Lutherans
would be comfortable with this association. But could it be the case that modern Lutherans are allergic to the "re-formation of life" preached by Calvinists
and Puritans? If we take the affirmation of ordinary life as a central tenet of the

---

35. Dale Eickelman, "Inside the Islamic Reformation," *The Wilson Quarterly* 22 (1998): 82.
36. A review of this topic in recent literature is found in Roman Loimeier, "Is There Something like Protestant Islam?" *Die Welt des Islams* 45/2 (2005): 216–54.
37. For further reading on Opus Dei, see John L. Allen, *Opus Dei: An Objective Look behind
the Myths and Reality of the Most Controversial Force in the Catholic Church* (New York:
Doubleday, 2005).

Reformation, we might get at how Calvinists and Puritans can be said to follow Luther's cultural insights. This comparison could be helpful in attempting to understand the contemporary quasi-Puritan reformation movements in Catholicism and Islam. These reformations are not confined to doctrines; they could be understood primarily as renovations of life in all its dimensions.

Ordinary life must at the same time be balanced with ideals of true mercy and self-renunciation. It was Luther's insight that a one-sided asceticism and an overscrupulous moralism must be tempered in order to make room for acts of mercy and the affirmation of the created world. The search for a merciful God is, in light of this affirmation, an anti-individualistic, crosscultural and, finally, global challenge.

The Masks behind the Man

We read Luther today with an unprecedented degree of familiarity due to the media in which Luther's works are communicated. We can search digitally or in book indexes for any remark he uttered on any issue and upon any occasion. We ask his opinions on various matters as we randomly click our way through search engines. We engage him as a friend or familiar companion from the distant past. This familiarity characterizes modern biographical treatments of Luther's personality and lifestyle. We see him as a human being among equals.

This impression is, however, quite misleading. Luther writes texts for us in which he reveals to us the person he wishes us to see. He does not speak to us as a friend and companion. Rather, he wears his coat of arms and his war paint. He addresses his hearer as authoritative professor in a lecture room, or ordained pastor at the pulpit, and as famous polemecist and best-selling author, even as media celebrity. In order to understand his message correctly, we should not mistake him for a companion with a human face. We should engage him as he self-consciously asks to be seen by us: as a person in a certain role, wearing a mask.

A primary hermeneutical assumption of modernity is that a person is more genuine when he or she speaks without a mask, as himself or herself. This assumption is just another urban legend. We are not interested in the speeches of the American President as himself. We listen because he or she is an important officeholder. We should not listen to a sermon because the pastor is a nice person but because she occupies a specific role and performs a particular task. Instead of the mask, modernity stresses the face. The masks are hidden behind the person.

The sixteenth century differs from ours in this regard. The social rules of the community and the rhetorical rules of composing texts dictate the sixteenth-century assignment of specific roles and authority to the speaker. Lutheranism has been historically conscious of the different roles a speaker assumes, whether as pastor, as *paterfamilias*, as worldly authority, or simply as citizen. In this ethic, the idea that a genuine self could exist "behind" these roles is not entertained. Such a modern assumption should, therefore, not be projected back into sixteenth-century texts. The question regarding the "genuine self" as illusion is an intriguing one. I am not postmodern enough to make this claim. I am merely advocating the hermeneutical position that texts from the past should be read as descriptive of social and cultural roles and norms rather than as personal diaries.

The theme of "Luther the urban legend" already presupposes a neat distinction between fact and legend. But in the world of historical texts, there is no clear distinction between the two. The example of Luther's conversion shows that the earliest records are already interpreted in terms of Paul's and Augustine's conversion. The records do not prove the modern position that isolates an original individual experience from subsequent interpretation.

Yet even the important example of conversion can be understood in a different way. The different conversions are read simultaneously. The justification for this fusion of horizons is part and parcel of the Christian tradition. Christians are deeply familiar with the conversion experience from both the Bible and Augustine. They can identify their own experiences as "conversions" by interpreting their experiences through the lenses of ancient texts. The accounts they read, the *legenda*, serve as the hermeneutical matrix for identifying their own experiences. The legend is primary. It is then secondarily applied to personal experience so that, in a third step, definite events can be seen to take place and shape. In this sense, the matrix or the mask is primary. The face is then shaped to suit the mask.

CHAPTER 3

Luther and Freedom

Peter C. Hodgson

Luther as a Witness to Freedom

In April 1963, Martin Luther King Jr. wrote an open letter from the Birmingham city jail in which he responded to criticisms of the civil rights movement by white moderates. He concluded that it was not so bad to be called an "extremist." Was not Jesus an extremist for love? Or Amos an extremist for justice? Or Paul for the Christian gospel? Then King asked: "Was not Martin Luther an extremist: 'Here I stand; I cannot do otherwise, so help me God.'" This is the first of two references to Luther in King's public discourse.[1]

Was Luther a witness to freedom, indeed an extremist in its cause? Did he play a significant role in "the history of the progress of the consciousness of freedom"? The philosopher Hegel, who regarded himself as a Lutheran, certainly thought so. Hegel famously remarked that the history of freedom is a long and arduous one; it has consumed several millennia and the goal has

---

1. Martin Luther King Jr., *Why We Can't Wait* (New York: Harper, 1964), 92. My linking of Luther and King in this chapter is a way of addressing "the global Luther" (and global *eleutheria*). Hegel also contributes—if not to a global then to a philosophical perspective. I am not a specialist in Luther studies, nor am I a Lutheran. My interest in Luther comes principally through my engagement with Lutheran philosophers and theologians of the nineteenth and twentieth centuries, from Georg Wilhelm Friedrich Hegel and Ferdinand Christian Baur to Ernst Troeltsch and Paul Tillich. In the first two sections, I offer my own interpretation of two key Luther texts. Discussion of the extensive secondary literature on them and on Luther more generally is not possible within the bounds of this chapter.

not yet been attained. In the ancient Oriental world, only *one* was free, the despot. The consciousness of freedom first awoke among the Greeks, but they like the Romans knew that only *some* were free, male citizens of the state. The conviction that *all* human beings by nature are free, that freedom of the spirit is humanity's very essence, first dawned in Christianity through its faith that in Christ all are redeemed and accepted as God's children. This conviction did not, however, become immediately efficacious. The practice of slavery continued, modulating into feudalism. Freedom did not predominate in the Roman and later the Holy Roman Empires. And in time the church came to resemble an Oriental despotism.[2]

At this point, Luther plays a critical role in Hegel's scenario. Echoing a distinction Luther himself drew, he said that "we Lutherans have a better faith" than a "worthless, historical faith," which simply assents to an objective creed or refers to past events.[3] Ours is a living, spiritual faith that renders efficacious within us the liberating relationship to God that Christ proclaimed and enacted. We are at home with ourselves and with God, and all externality, all institutional and juridical mediation, is banished. God is spirit and is present for us only in the mode of subjectivity and spirituality: free spirit related to free spirit. Luther's "simple doctrine" was that the specific embodiment of divinity occurs not in external and sensuous forms but in faith and spiritual enjoyment (communion).[4] This faith is produced by the Holy Spirit and gives an assurance of eternal and absolute truth that is the common property of all humanity. In this truth Christian freedom is actualized; here the "banner of free spirit" is unfurled. The task of subsequent history was to bring the freedom and reconciliation implicit in this vision of Christianity into objective and explicit realization. Luther began the process by attacking the abuses and authority of the Roman church and setting up the Bible and the testimony of the Spirit in its stead. He did not go far, however, in reforming the state or changing the social and economic conditions under which people lived, and his efforts resulted initially in a schism of the church and religious wars. Neither he nor the other Reformers elaborated their "speculative content" philosophi-

---

2. Georg Wilhelm Friedrich Hegel, *Lectures on the Philosophy of World History. Introduction: Reason in History*, trans. H. B. Nisbet (Cambridge: Cambridge University Press, 1975), 54–55. Similar formulations are found in Hegel's lectures on the history of philosophy. See his *Vorlesungen über die Geschichte der Philosophie*, part 1, ed. Pierre Garniron and Walter Jaeschke (Hamburg: Felix Meiner, 1994), 35–37, 96, 193–97.
3. Hegel, *Geschichte der Philosophie*, 1:174.
4. Against the trend of neo-Kantian Luther scholarship, which continues to the present day, Hegel's reading of Luther affirmed a real ontological participation of the believer in Christ. See the essays in Carl E. Braaten and Robert W. Jenson, eds., *Union with Christ: The New Finnish Interpretation of Luther* (Grand Rapids: Eerdmans, 1998).

cally, and as a consequence, a Protestant orthodoxy ensued on one side, with its rigid scripture-principle, and an antireligious secularism on the other. Hegel regarded his own speculative philosophy as an attempt in part to recover the free theology of the Reformation.[5]

Admittedly, Hegel's portrayal of Luther is idealized and one-sided. But it captures an important dimension of this complex and contradictory figure. What Hegel gives us is the Luther of *The Freedom of a Christian*, not the Luther of *The Bondage of the Will* or of the later polemical controversies and apocalyptic worldview. The "Open Letter to Pope Leo X," which accompanied *The Freedom of a Christian* (1520), is an important document in its own right.[6] It was written by a still-obscure monk who clearly had been liberated from bondage to authority and felt free to speak the truth to power. He addressed the pope as an equal and offered advice liberally. He remarked that all Christians are servants of Christ (the pope being merely "the servant of servants"), and he implied that the only true authority is that of Scripture, reason, and conscience. He employed a good deal of satire and mockery (but they are nothing as compared with his later demonizing of opponents). Can you imagine such a letter being written even today, say by an assistant professor to a university president or an employee to a CEO? Apparently, when Luther changed the spelling of his name from Luder to Luther, he discovered within it the Greek word for freedom, *eleutheria*, and sometimes he signed his letters as Eleutherius, "the free one."[7]

"A Christian is a perfectly free lord of all, subject to none." The first of the two famous theses of *The Freedom of a Christian* means that the word of God alone gives freedom, liberating us from earthly lords, legal requirements, and human institutions. The gift is unlimited and universal, but it must be inwardly appropriated: all that is needed is the faith by which God's word is believed, accepted, trusted. This faith is more than forensic or verbal; it entails an ontological participation in Christ, like the iron that glows in fire. Faith unites the soul with Christ as a bride to her bridegroom; they become one flesh, a true marriage, the royal marriage of God and humanity in which God's freedom becomes humanity's freedom.[8]

---

5. Georg Wilhelm Friedrich Hegel, *Lectures on the History of Philosophy*, vol. 3, ed. and trans. Robert F. Brown et al. (Berkeley: University of California Press, 1990), 94–101; G. W. F. Hegel, *The Philosophy of History*, trans. John Sibree with an introduction by C. J. Friedrich (New York: Dover, 1956), 412–27.
6. LW 31:334–43.
7. Martin Marty, *Martin Luther* (New York: Viking, 2004), 32.
8. LW 31:344–54.

"A Christian is a perfectly dutiful servant of all, subject to all." The second thesis is more complex and seems to have four distinct aspects as Luther expounds it. First, we are bound in service because, given our earthly lusts, we must discipline our bodies and subject them to the Spirit—a monastic perspective on servanthood.[9] Second, a Christian consecrated by faith does good works. Luther is quite certain that good works do not make a good person; rather a good person does good works. By a "good person," he means Christian and only Christian persons. Good works could not make a Jew or a Turk or a humanist a good person.[10] Third, a Christian does not live for him- or herself alone but for all people on earth. We are called to live a life for others, not for ourselves. Free from works as a means of salvation, or as merits that deserve rewards, we should, like Christ, empty ourselves and become servants of all, making our works a gift to others.[11] Fourth, Christians are subject to the governing authorities and should stay in their own profession and station. For the sake of peace and order, they should not disrupt the social fabric or oppose unjust and violent tyrants unless the latter demand something contrary to God. (Are not injustice and violence contrary to God's will?) The freedom of a Christian applies principally to the inner, spiritual kingdom, not to the external, worldly kingdom.[12]

Both theses are problematic in the sense that they presuppose the distinction between lord and servant, the deep structure of which is the master-slave relationship. Freedom cannot be adequately defined in terms of relationships of inequality. Luther's intent in *The Freedom of the Christian* may have been to subvert the distinction in the realm of spirit, but it gets reestablished in *The Bondage of the Will*.

The Mystery of Freedom

Freedom poses a profound mystery to theology. How can divine and human freedom be copresent and efficacious without the one threatening or annihilating the other? The great consensus in theology from the early church fathers through the Reformers was that God is an absolute sovereign who controls and determines all finite, worldly activities. The royal metaphor and its accompanying logic of divine sovereignty meant that God alone is truly free and that human freedom, if it exists at all, is purely a divine gift. There

---

9. LW 31:358–59.
10. LW 31:360–63.
11. LW 31:364–68.
12. LW 31:369–74.

can be no independent basis of freedom in human nature, as the humanists claimed, for this would constitute a rivalry to and a limitation of the divine freedom. Only in the modern world did it become possible to grasp how two freedoms can be present to each other in such a way that both are affirmed and enriched. Hegel's great insight was that freedom *must* be present to and exist for the sake of its *other*. Freedom is not principally autonomy or self-will or free choice (*Willkür*) but a presence-to-self that is mediated through and dependent upon presence-to-another. Freedom requires a community of freedom in which otherness and difference are essential and reciprocal recognition occurs within a relationship of equality. Hegel applied this model to divine-human as well as interhuman relations. Thus, in order for God to be God, God must let the world go forth from God's self into freedom, and God relates to this world in the modality of empowerment and persuasion rather than command and control.[13]

Luther struggled mightily with the mystery of freedom, but he did not arrive at the modern insight. Despite his great originality and boldness, and despite his envisioning of the suffering and death of God on the cross, when it came to the question of the divine-human relationship, he was still operating principally with late-medieval categories. He certainly did affirm the presence and reality of reason in fallen humanity. In *The Disputation concerning Man* (1536), he says that "reason is the most important and the highest in rank" of all created powers; indeed it represents "something divine" in humanity. It is the means by which humans rule over nature; but human reason does not know itself a priori, does not know that its efficient cause is God, does not know that it can be freed from the power of the Devil only through Christ. Fallen reason is tainted but not destroyed; something remains in which faith can be formed; and reason is incomprehensible without freedom. "If there were no reason, the will would be like that of cattle, just as we see that we [by contrast] are drawn to righteousness and joy."[14] Something in us has the capacity to be drawn. In his *Theses concerning Faith and Law* (1535), Luther distinguishes between true faith, the gift of the Holy Spirit, and "acquired or historic faith" (a distinction that Hegel noticed). The latter is a mere intellectual acceptance of the creed, without attendant assent and trust, whereas the former involves an existential/ontological participation in and rebirth through the power that grasps and transforms us.[15] Assent, trust, participation, and

---

13. See my discussion of these matters in *Hegel and Christian Theology: A Reading of the Lectures on the Philosophy of Religion* (Oxford: Oxford University Press, 2005).
14. LW 34:137–39, 144.
15. LW 34:109–13.

rebirth entail an activity of reason and will that cannot be coerced and must in this sense be free.

It is unfortunate that the controversy between Erasmus and Luther focused on the category of "free will" or "free choice" (*liberum arbitrium*). Free will may be a condition of possibility of true freedom (the freedom of a Christian), but it does not get at the heart of freedom as conceived by either Luther or Hegel. In *The Bondage of the Will* (1525), Luther found it all too convenient to embrace Erasmus's rather careless definition of free choice as "a power of the human will by which a man can apply himself to the things which lead to eternal salvation, or turn away from them."[16] This made it seem as though Erasmus were positing a power of will by which humans merit or accomplish salvation on their own, leaving nothing to grace and the Holy Spirit. Never mind that this was not in fact Erasmus's position. It provided Luther the opportunity to insist that, in light of humanity's bondage to sin and evil and the absolute sovereignty of God, this kind of free choice is an illusion and contrary to every word of Scripture.[17]

Most of the controversy was consumed by the tedious citation of scriptural passages that were used as proof texts in defense of the freedom or the bondage of the will. Erasmus appealed to the rhetoric and language of Scripture, which presupposes that humans are responsible beings who make decisions and choices. What point is there in having a scripture without a human response, without minds and hearts that need to be persuaded and converted? Scripture is not a code of divine laws and dicta but a complex narrative discourse that employs diverse rhetorical strategies from many points of view. Luther attempted to refute this fairly obvious fact by selectively citing specific passages that teach divine predestination and foreknowledge, human depravity and incapacity, and so on.[18] He thus was led to a counterintuitive interpretation of Scripture as a whole; or at least he did not address the paradox that, while Scripture seems rhetorically to presuppose that humans are free and responsible beings, it teaches (in places) that in fact they are not.

Luther was intent on avoiding the trap of saying that God's use of the human will is coercive. God "does not work in us without us, because it is for this he has created and preserved us, that he might work in us and we might cooperate with him." What sort of "cooperation" is this? It is different from the power and the operation that belong to free choice in itself. We do nothing on our own but only through the will of the omnipotent God as manifested

---

16. LW 33:103.
17. LW 33:103–11.
18. LW 33:119–24, 132–38, 141, 209–11, 254–62.

in God's general governance of the world or in the special gift of grace. Our will is active and in this sense uncoerced, but what activates it is God's will. Thus Luther can say that we are like the tools of a carpenter, or a lame horse ridden by a horseman, or clay in the hands of a potter.[19] Can this be a genuine cooperation if our operation is simply and solely God's operation? It seems to be more like the "cooperation" expected of citizens in a totalitarian state, hence more like acquiescence and obedience than genuine co-working. There may not be actual coercion, but one knows what the limits are and internalizes them, subordinating personal freedom to the will of the state (or party). This analogy is not inappropriate because in the final analysis, Luther's God is a totalitarian, an absolute monarch—tragically so, since Luther's vision in *The Freedom of a Christian* and elsewhere was of the love, grace, and goodness of God, of God's liberation from human tyranny by subjecting God's self to that tyranny on the cross.

Swept along by his polemic against Erasmus, Luther arrived at a stark and consistent formulation of the logic of absolute divine sovereignty—more stark and consistent than many theologians who shared the same basic premises. God alone works both good and evil in us; all things come about by sheer necessity. The only way to account for the existence of sin and evil in the world is to conclude that God causes or wills them. The omnipotence of God entails foreknowledge and predestination, indeed, double predestination, given the fact of evil. A God who is not absolutely omnipotent would be a "ridiculous God."[20]

Luther elaborated on both the foreknowledge and the predestination. If God is not deceived in what God foreknows, then the thing foreseen must of necessity take place; otherwise "you take away faith and the fear of God, make havoc of all the divine promises and threatenings, and thus deny his very divinity." The necessity imposed by the divine foreknowledge is not of force with reference to work but of infallibility with reference to time. Thus, the human will must necessarily do what it does willingly if God foreknows it, and of course God foreknows everything.[21] As for double predestination, it alone explains why God wills to save some and harden the hearts of others. The difference between good and evil, the acceptance and rejection of grace, cannot be explained by reference to human freedom and worldly contingency. The sole explanation is concealed in the depths of divinity, in the "hidden

---

19. LW 33:154–56, 175–76, 182–85, 191–92, 242–43.
20. LW 33:112, 164–75, 189, 191.
21. LW 33:185–95.

and awful will of God" that is not to be inquired into but reverently adored. Human reason cannot bridge the gap between the hidden and the revealed will of God, *deus absconditus et revelatus*. Reason may wonder why God's majesty does not remove or change the defect in *all* persons rather than some, why God imputes the defect that all humans share in common to some but imputes righteousness to others. Reason may be offended by these paradoxes, but it has neither the right nor the power to inquire into them. If "we do not let God's will alone have the will and the power to harden and to show mercy and to do everything, we attribute to free choice itself the ability to do everything without grace."[22] This bleak conclusion shows how irreconcilably the two freedoms, divine and human, clash for Luther. In the clash, one prevails and the other seems to be reduced to an implement.[23]

The Limits of Luther's Vision

We have already been considering one of the limitations of Luther's vision of freedom, indeed the principal one from a theological point of view. His all-too-consistent elaboration of the doctrines of absolute divine sovereignty, foreknowledge, and double predestination excludes human freedom as any sort of meaningful reality in relationship to God. It is just these doctrines that led to a progressive discrediting of theology in later centuries. Even today, their espousal causes thoughtful people to turn away from Christian faith (while it attracts others to embrace it uncritically). At the same time, these doctrines seem starkly inconsistent with Luther's great insight into the freedom of a Christian as one who is inwardly transformed by the Holy Spirit, liberated from external authorities and the burden of works as a means to salvation and who is therefore free to serve others and love God without regard to personal interests. With Christian freedom, the whole question of merit and reward becomes irrelevant, but then it is reintroduced into the debate over free will

---

22. LW 33:138–40, 171–74, 177–81, 190.
23. Gerhard Ebeling offers an eloquent interpretation and defense of Luther's treatment of freedom and bondage, summarized in the paradoxical formulation that humanity's freedom must be defined more closely as its bondage, and its bondage as its freedom (*Luther: An Introduction to His Thought*, trans. R. A. Wilson [Philadelphia: Fortress Press, 1970], chap. 13, esp. 211). For me the formula founders on the doctrine of double predestination: the bondage of those whose hearts are hardened is in no sense freedom but the most abject and everlasting hell. Moreover, as I have said, I do not believe that freedom is properly defined in terms of bondage, even to God, for bondage presupposes a master-slave relationship as opposed to a relationship of mutuality and divinely-given equality.

where it skews the discussion by putting human freedom into rivalry with divine grace.[24]

There are other limitations. Christian freedom does not carry over very far into the realm of society, politics, and economics. It does not mean that Christians are placed above earthly powers, nor does it mean that they are all equally priests who have a right to minister publicly and teach. Rather, they must subject themselves to the governing authorities, recognizing that their lordship is spiritual rather than temporal.[25] David Whitford remarks that Luther never advocated social or political freedom in the modern sense. Rather, his understanding of freedom was religious and paradoxical, based on distinctions between law and gospel and the two kingdoms. In the spiritual kingdom, freedom and equality prevail, whereas the earthly realm is governed by the sword and hierarchical authority. "Luther advocated obedience because he feared the chaos of anarchy more than the tyranny of authority. However . . . he did not advocate a blind, totalizing, quietist approach to authority that has become the cliché."[26] So, for example, he insisted on freedom of conscience in religious matters and refused to recant at the Diet of Worms. He opposed the imposition of religious reforms by force of law. He allowed for certain forms of political resistance but opposed armed rebellion and the use of violence. Presumably the option of nonviolent civil disobedience as an effective political strategy did not exist in the late-medieval, pre-democratic world. But one wonders what would have happened had Luther stepped into the situation with the peasants, gained control from Thomas Müntzer, and advocated peaceful resistance instead of a holy war. Instead, he believed that the peasants were being driven by a satanic spirit.

The latter belief indicates a further limitation in Luther's vision. As Mark Edwards points out, he intensified an apocalyptic worldview that had been common to Western Christendom for over a thousand years. In this view, from the very beginning of the world the forces of good and evil, truth and falsity, God and the Devil have been locked in deadly combat, and persons and institutions are allied on either one side or the other. Luther became convinced

---

24. Christine Helmer has helped me to understand that Luther wrote in different genres and that these genre distinctions play an important role in interpreting his thought. The genre of the contentious disputation on free will is clearly different from that of the irenic treatise on Christian freedom. But are these genre differences sufficient to account for the deep theological tensions between these works?

25. LW 31:354–56, 369–74.

26. David M. Whitford, "Luther's Political Encounters," in *The Cambridge Companion to Martin Luther*, ed. Donald L. McKim (Cambridge: Cambridge University Press, 2003), 179–91; quotation from 181.

that he was engaged in a climactic phase of this conflict, that his real opponents were not men but devils, and that the stakes were eternal salvation and damnation. Tragically, he was unable to break this totalizing paradigm, and it drove him toward increasing self-righteousness, vulgarity, and the demonizing of opponents. His attitude toward the Jews was a consequence of the paradigm. Convinced that the entire Old Testament bears witness to the coming of Christ, Luther grew increasingly annoyed with the rabbinic exegesis that refused this interpretation. When the Jews failed to convert to Christianity after having the true meaning of Scripture revealed to them by the Reformation, he concluded that they and their religion were indeed ruled by the Devil and must be severely repressed. The same was true of the Turks.[27]

Luther in a global context needs to be rescued from his own worst instincts and reinforced in his truest insights.

What's in a Name? Martin Luther and Martin Luther King Jr.

On the evening of April 3, 1968, Martin Luther King Jr. delivered a remarkable speech in which he had a premonition of his impending death. He began by wondering how he would respond if the Almighty asked him, "Martin Luther King, which age would you live in?" He would take his mental flight to the Israelites as they escaped from bondage in Egypt and traveled through the wilderness toward the promised land. He would move on to Greece to see the great philosophers engaged in conversation around the Parthenon, then to the heyday of the Roman Empire and the new day of the Renaissance. "But I wouldn't stop there. I would even go by the way that the man for whom I'm named had his habitat. I would watch Martin Luther as he tacked his ninety-five theses on the door at the church in Wittenberg." But he wouldn't stop there. He would watch as a vacillating President Lincoln signed the Emancipation Proclamation; he would keep going on through the civil rights movement right up to the present moment in Memphis, Tennessee, and he would thank

---

27. Mark U. Edwards Jr., "Luther's Polemical Controversies," in *The Cambridge Companion to Luther*, 192–205. Bernhard Lohse's argument, in *Martin Luther's Theology: Its Historical and Systematic Development* (trans. Roy A. Harrisville; Minneapolis: Fortress Press, 1999), xi, that "Luther's attitude toward the Jews is a marginal theological issue, not at all part of the central claims," is not credible. It is implicit in even the few texts I have considered (e.g., LW 31:347–49; 34:112, 168).

the Almighty for allowing him to be in this place for yet another chapter in the long history of the struggle for freedom.[28]

That King should mention Luther in his last speech is noteworthy, and he captures well his relationship to his namesake by saying that he would watch for a while but then move on. The story of how he came by the name is fascinating. Just as Luther himself changed his name, so also did King's father, Martin Luther King Sr. In accord with the wish of his mother, King Sr. was baptized Michael, after the archangel; but his father had preferred the names of his own two brothers, Martin and Luther. As Michael became a young man, he began to change his name. First, he called himself Michael Luther King; then in 1934, after a visit to Germany, he changed it to Martin Luther King. By this time, he was the pastor of a prominent Atlanta church, and the name seemed suitable. His eldest son, born in 1929, was baptized Michael King Jr. But in elementary school, he was called Martin or M. L., and in 1957, his birth certificate was altered to Martin Luther King Jr.[29] Through a series of fortuitous circumstances, it seems that Providence was preparing a name for a great leader.

A linkage to the Reformers was present in the consciousness of the black church. Martin Luther could be seen as the Moses of Protestantism, leading his people out of Babylonian captivity to the Roman church. Martin Luther King Jr. became the Moses of the civil rights movement, leading his people out of bondage to segregation and racism. Martin Luther needed Martin Luther King to correct and concretize his own vision of freedom. Martin Luther King benefited from the name of Martin Luther: it conveyed his prophetic role, lent him authority as a religious and political leader, and in a hidden way linked him with the biblical word for freedom, *eleutheria*.

King may have reflected on the significance of his name in private, but he rarely mentioned it in public. When he was a doctoral student at Boston University (1951–1955), he became a disciple of the last generation of personalist theologians, notably Edgar Brightman but also Harold DeWolf, Walter Muelder, Peter Bertocci, and others. These thinkers created a fertile matrix of American liberal theology, and King imbibed of it deeply. One of his most interesting papers was a comparative evaluation of the theologies of Luther and Calvin. Luther's whole theology, he wrote, is complicated by his view of

---

28. Martin Luther King Jr., "I See the Promised Land," 3 Apr. 1968, in *A Testament of Hope: The Essential Writings of Martin Luther King Jr.*, ed. James Melvin Washington (San Francisco: Harper, 1986), 279–80.
29. Editorial introduction to *The Papers of Martin Luther King Jr.*, ed. Clayborne Carson et al., vol. 1 (Berkeley: University of California Press, 1992), 31, incl. n. 98.

God as an absolute sovereign power who predestines some to salvation and others to damnation. His view of human nature was deeply pessimistic, and he recognized human freedom only in matters unrelated to salvation. Both Reformers placed undue emphasis on the sovereignty of God, losing sight of the central reality of divine love (Luther a little less so than Calvin). Their notion of original perfection and catastrophic fall is refuted by the theory of evolution and by Jesus himself, who showed that humans can move toward God and who appealed to the hidden goodness in their nature. Any doctrine of humanity devoid of freedom leads into needless paradoxes; freedom is both a moral and a metaphysical necessity. But King concluded that his severe criticisms of Luther and Calvin should not minimize the importance of their message. "Their cry does call attention to the desperateness of the human situation. They do insist that religion begins with God and that man cannot have faith apart from him. They do proclaim that apart from God our human efforts turn to ashes and our sunrises into darkest night. Much of this is good, and may it not be that its re-emphasis by the neo-orthodox theologians of our day will serve as a necessary corrective for a liberalism that at times becomes all too shallow?"[30]

King studied Hegel's philosophy in a year-long seminar taught by Brightman and Bertocci. The seminar focused on the early theological writings, the phenomenology of spirit, the logic, and the philosophy of right. Perhaps the philosophy of world history was included as well. King did not write any papers on the latter, but evidences of the influence of Hegel's philosophy of history are scattered here and there in his essays and speeches of the civil rights period. King's way of thinking came to incorporate the Hegelian dialectic, moving toward synthesis and the reconciliation of opposing elements (by contrast with the dualistic or paradoxical thinking of Luther). In his doctoral dissertation, he criticized what he regarded as the one-sided monism of Paul Tillich and the one-sided pluralism of Henry Nelson Wieman, and he sought to work out a synthesis of their views.[31]

---

30. Martin Luther King Jr., "A Comparison and Evaluation of the Theology of Luther with That of Calvin," 15 May 1953, in *The Papers of Martin Luther King Jr.*, vol. 2 (Berkeley: University of California Press, 1994), 175–91 (quotation from 191). In this paper as in others he wrote during his studies, we see King functioning in the world of white academic liberal theology. The world of the black church and black preaching was quite different. Perhaps something of the latter comes through in the final remarks, which reflect also his familiarity with Reinhold Niebuhr. King was already an outstanding preacher who was much in demand.
31. *The Papers of Martin Luther King Jr.*, 2:196–201, 531–35.

The Boston personalists were strong champions of free will and of universal human freedom and dignity. They helped to make the University's School of Theology an attractive institution for African American students. Their views resonated well with King's emerging convictions about the role of the black church in the struggle against segregation and inequality. In papers and examinations, he made it clear that, for him, freedom is a central value and the essential foundation of ethics. He reflected Brightman's philosophy in arguing that if rational, purposive choice is not effective at the center of life, goodness is not possible. Freedom is also necessary for the act of reason, and without reason human personality is inconceivable. Thus freedom has epistemological and metaphysical as well as ethical implications. The founder of personalism, Borden Parke Bowne, was the most forthright champion of freedom, divine and human. Brightman modified Bowne's absolute theism in the direction of a finite God, a conscious person who struggles and has to work with the given in every moment. God's power is limited, but God's goodness is infinite. Divine power is limited by the fact of pluralism—the reality of difference and the presence of independent powers vis-à-vis each other and God. King calls this, following Brightman, a "quantitative pluralism," but it can be linked with a "qualitative monism," which affirms that all of reality has its ultimate ground in God, whose nature is love and whose work in history is freedom. Such a conviction gives persons the confidence to act and make decisions in the absence of theoretical certainty. Moral responsibility prevents the luxury of avoiding action and simply contemplating the wreckage of history.[32] Here the theoretical bases of King's life mission were being worked out in a way that, when combined with the rhetoric and substance of black preaching, became an explosive force. Resources were being assimilated that enabled King to transcend the limitations of Luther's theological worldview, while at the same time he began to incorporate the Reformer's driving and courageous spirit.[33]

Martin Luther King received his Ph.D. in June 1955. He had little time to relish his accomplishment. He had already begun his pastorate at the Dexter Avenue Baptist Church in Montgomery, Alabama, and by the following autumn he found himself engaged in the organization and leadership of the Montgomery Bus Boycott.

---

32. *The Papers of Martin Luther King Jr.*, 2:71–75, 110–13, 532–33.
33. In drawing contrasts between the two figures, I do not mean to imply that Luther's work was impaired by his polemics and prejudices while King's was pure and saintly. King was not a saint. He had his own flaws and weaknesses, which have been much discussed. Both men were enormously gifted but fallible and imperfect agents of a spiritual force that transcended them.

Nonviolent Resistance, the Dream of Freedom, and a Glimpse of the Promised Land

In speeches during and after the boycott, King began to elaborate on the strategy that had proved so effective, that of nonviolent resistance. Mohandas Gandhi had drawn the attention of black leaders for many years, and King had learned about him from Mordecai Johnson while at Crozer Theological Seminary. Perhaps he had had conversations with Howard Thurman, dean of the chapel at Boston University, who was familiar with Gandhi and a pacifist. In 1959, King himself traveled to India to study Gandhi's philosophy. But even before then, he was quite eloquent in describing a "new and powerful weapon" that would help to build a "new world order" to replace the old order of colonialism, exploitation, and segregation. It would do so in such a way that would avoid demonizing opponents and that might in fact transform them into better persons by appealing to their consciences and feelings of guilt.[34] The latter point was elaborated in an article published in *The Christian Century* early in 1957. Two possibilities present themselves in the struggle against oppression and injustice: violence and nonviolence. Violence leads to futility and solves no social problems but rather creates new and more complicated ones. Nonviolent resistance is not a method for cowards because it does resist and it accepts the consequences of disobeying unjust laws. It does not seek to defeat or humiliate opponents but to win their friendship and understanding. It is not an end in itself but seeks redemption and reconciliation, creation of the beloved community. Its attack is directed against forces of evil rather than against persons who are caught in those forces. It avoids not only external physical violence but also internal violence of spirit: at its center is the principle of love, by which it breaks the chain of hatred and retaliation. It has the conviction that the God of the universe is on the side of truth and justice, that God is involved in the struggle and will enable it to overcome, someday.[35] Such a sensibility is far removed from Luther's polemical and apocalyptic worldview.

King's theology of freedom was set forth in various speeches and writings. At a conference in Nashville in December 1962, he described the ethical demands

---

34. Martin Luther King Jr., "Address to the Montgomery Improvement Association," 14 Nov. 1956, and "Facing the Challenge of a New Age," 3 Dec. 1956, in *The Papers of Martin Luther King Jr.*, vol. 3 (Berkeley: University of California Press, 1997), 428–29, 452–63. In the second of these addresses, imagery is first employed that later appeared in the "I Have a Dream" speech of 1963.
35. Martin Luther King Jr., "Nonviolence and Racial Justice," 10–11 Jan. 1957, in *A Testament of Hope*, 5–9.

of integration.[36] Integration, he insisted, is the ultimate goal, not desegregation. We do not want a society where people are "physically desegregated
and spiritually segregated, where elbows are together and hearts are apart."
He knew that desegregation would be relatively easy to obtain and enforce,
but that integration was a long, distant, and unenforceable goal because it
involves an inward transformation: something must touch the hearts and
souls of human beings and bring them together spiritually. He described three
preconditions of integration. First, there must be a recognition of the sacred-
ness of human personality. This recognition is deeply rooted in both our religious and our political heritage. The Hebraic-Christian tradition expresses it
with the conviction that *every* human being is created in the image of God,
that this image is universally shared in equal portion by every person, that
there is no graded scale of essential worth. The same truth is affirmed by the
Declaration of Independence. Here King embraces the Hegelian idea that
all human beings are free as such; and he extends the Lutheran vision of the
freedom of the Christian from the purely spiritual realm to the social and
political world. Second, there must be a recognition that freedom entails the
capacity to deliberate, choose, and respond. Without such freedom, life itself
is shackled and destroyed. The system of slavery and segregation wreaked
havoc on black people for generations by constricting this freedom. (From a
black perspective, would not Luther's "bondage of the will" seem to involve
a similar constriction of the human spirit?) Finally, there must be recognition of the solidarity of the human family. Integration is the goal because we
basically are all one: God has made of one blood all nations. The category of
"race" is inappropriate because physical differences are insignificant as compared to the commonalities of human nature. Moreover, humans are social
creatures, engaged from the beginning of civilization in the great adventure
of community. The universe is so structured that things do not work out
rightly otherwise. The self cannot be a self without other selves; all human
beings are caught up in a network of mutuality. King mentioned John Donne
at this point, but he might have referred to Hegel's community of freedom
or Luther's servanthood on behalf of others. He might have gone further and
said that the category of "religion," like that of "race," is inappropriate as a
divider of humanity. Surely he would have rejected Luther's repudiation of
Jews and Muslims, seeing in them a reflection of his own people and their
subjugated condition.

---

36. Martin Luther King Jr., "The Ethical Demands for Integration," 27 Dec. 1962, in *A Testament of Hope*, 117–25.

King's most famous expression of these ideas is found in his keynote address for the march on Washington in August 1963.[37] Despite present shameful conditions and the many difficulties that lie ahead, King said that he still had a dream, "a dream deeply rooted in the American dream that one day this nation will rise up and live out the true meaning of its creed." He quoted the words of the great hymn, "My Country 'Tis of Thee." He ended with a call to let freedom ring from every mountain and mountainside. Then he said, "we will be able to speed up that day when all of God's children—black men and white men, Jews and Gentiles, Catholics and Protestants—will be able to join hands and to sing in the words of the old Negro spiritual, 'Free at last, free at last; thank God Almighty, we are free at last.'" It is notable, I think, that this dream avoids the imagery and fatalism of apocalyptic. It eschews a dualism that splits history into warring camps or that divides the spiritual realm from the secular. It expresses a faith that God is at work in the history of freedom, but it knows that God does not control or determine the outcome. While our individual destinies are in the hands of God, our social destiny is, with God's help, our responsibility.

On the night before he died, King told his audience that he had seen the promised land. He described what happened several years earlier in New York City when he was autographing his first book. A demented black woman stabbed him. The tip of the knife blade was on the edge of his aorta, and the next morning, the *New York Times* reported that if he had sneezed, he would have died. During his recuperation, he received many letters— from the President and Vice President, the Governor of New York, and other famous people, but he did not remember what they wrote. One letter, how- ever, he would never forget. "Dear Dr. King," it said, "I am a ninth-grade stu- dent at the White Plains High School. . . . While it should not matter, I would like to mention that I am a white girl. I read in the paper of your misfortune and of your suffering. And I read that if you had sneezed, you would have died. And I'm simply writing you to say that I'm so happy that you didn't sneeze." King continued by saying that *he* was happy that he hadn't sneezed. If he had, he would have missed most of the civil rights movement, and he would not be in Memphis tonight. There had been threats, and he knew that difficult days lay ahead. But it did not matter to him now because he had been to the mountaintop and seen the promised land. "I may not get there

---

37. Martin Luther King Jr., "I Have a Dream," 28 Aug. 1963, in *A Testament of Hope*, 217–20.

with you. But I want you to know tonight, that we, as a people, will get to the promised land."[38]

The sneeze is a sign of the fragility of life and the contingency of history. I think Luther would have appreciated the sneeze, although theoretically he did not allow for the contingency of history. Had he lived in the twentieth or twenty-first century, he might have said something like this: "Our lives hang by a thread, a sneeze. We are in the hands of God. On our own, we strive, suffer, and die. Our salvation, our true freedom, comes from God alone. To be sure, our earthly responsibility is to make this world into an image of God's promised land. And yes, the freedom of a Christian is a freedom that is shared by all of God's children. What happens in the world every day, while it happens independently and through its own processes, is not 'without God,' indeed it is God's work.[39] God's great work is the realization of freedom. But this work is not completed in history. It is completed only in God, who *is* the promised land."

38. Martin Luther King Jr., "I See the Promised Land," 3 Apr. 1968, in *A Testament of Hope*, 285–86. The next morning he walked out onto his motel room balcony, and that was the end.
39. Hegel is helping Luther a bit here. See Hegel, *The Philosophy of History*, 457.

CHAPTER 4
Beyond Luther
— Prophetic Interfaith Dialogue for Life —
Munib A. Younan

The essence of Martin Luther's theology was his experience of justification by grace through faith, of being set free from his bondage to sin by the love of God in Christ so that he could live to serve God and others in joyful freedom. The question that drove him and others of his day was: How do I find a merciful and gracious God? Though this question remains, today there are also other questions.

Where is God in a world torn apart by fear of the other, violence, war, and injustice, with much of it committed in the name of God? What does justification by faith look like to people who live under occupation and oppression? What does justification by faith look like to people whose entire lives are captive to fear in our present age where extremism, terrorism, xenophobia, anti-Semitism, Islamophobia, and Christianophobia are haunting our mindset? How do we live with other faiths? How can we together be stewards of our earth and resources?

The future of global Lutheranism depends on our ability to speak God's liberating gospel so that it is relevant for today's human condition. It lies in our ability to look theologically at our modern world, interpreting the human condition and the questions of the times, then listening to and giving fresh voice to God's saving activity in the midst of brokenness. Justification today must go beyond the preoccupation with the freed, forgiven individual. Justification must bring God's healing liberation to communities of different faiths that are trying to live in peace and yet are trapped in oppression, injustice, and fear. Justification today must speak to the millions with HIV-AIDS, the thousands dying daily from starvation, the millions living under ethnic, religious, and political violence. Justification must be less preoccupied with eternal salvation and more attuned to the gospel's message to set free and restore right relations in this world. Justification today means witnessing to the biblical message of *shalom* and *salaam* that the risen Christ brought to the disciples locked in their upper room behind doors of fear. The biblical message today must speak to us in our locked rooms of dehumanization, xenophobia, oppression, demonization, and perversions of truth, sending us out as ministers of reconciliation and salvation.

The Holy Scriptures have been abused by many to justify violence and oppression, especially in the Middle East conflict. Each religion is good at pointing the finger at the other and blaming the other for extremist behavior. But each religion has its own respective work to do. We Christians are no exception. Hans Küng said, "No peace among nations without peace among religions. And no peace among religions without dialogue."[1] This dialogue must be a prophetic dialogue for life among all faiths. It speaks the truth about reality yet dares to seek the common values for justice, peace, reconciliation, love, forgiveness, mutual respect, and human dignity for all. A study Commission on International Affairs in Norway said it well in 2002: "The great world religions have both similarities and fundamental differences. And one of the most important similarities is actually a conviction that it is part of the innermost essence of religion to be a source of peace and reconciliation."[2]

This is the great challenge: "Respect for plurality and diversity is put to the test in a special way in worldviews and beliefs that hold—each independently and in its own respective traditions—that they know the Truth itself. The credibility of religious convictions is put to the test in their desire for peace."[3] Justification by faith—the basis of Lutheran identity—helps us to work with other religions. It takes up the following important questions. How do we evaluate Luther's comments on Judaism and Islam in the modern world? Is it really possible to build a healthy theology that leads to peace and justice

---

1. Hans Küng, "No World Peace without Religious Peace," in *Christianity and the World Religions: Paths of Dialogue with Islam, Hinduism, and Buddhism,* trans. Peter Heinegg (Garden City: Doubleday, 1986), 443.
2. "Vulnerability and Security: Current challenges in security policy from an ethical and theological perspective," Prepared by the Commission on International Affairs in the Church of Norway Council on Ecumenical and International Relations (2002), 26; http://www.kirken.no/english/doc/Kisp_vulnerab_00.pdf.
3. Ibid.

among all God's children—regardless of religion, race, or ethnicity—on the foundation of Martin Luther's medieval theology that actually dehumanized others? If we decide that our present task is to work toward mutual under-standing and dialogue, then what does it mean to be "evangelical" in today's complicated world of religions? I begin with a discussion of Luther's under-standing of Judaism and Islam in his own writings and then provide my own evaluation of Luther's theology of religions for today, followed by a proposal for a dialogue for life among global religions.

Luther and Judaism

Martin Luther's attitude toward Jews changed throughout his life. Until 1536, he expressed concern for their situation and was enthusiastic at the prospect of converting them to Christianity. After 1537, he demonized them and urged their harsh treatment, even persecution.

When Martin Luther began lecturing at the University of Wittenberg in 1513, he had rarely encountered Jews, nor had he ever lived in close proxim-ity to them. He inherited a tradition of both theological and cultural hostility toward them. He was also strongly influenced by the Augustinian tradition, which held that Jews are sacred because they were given the Old Testament but missed the key revelation of the Messiah. The fact that they could not find the Messiah meant that "God has shown the grace of his mercy to His Church 'in the midst of her enemies,' for, as St. Paul says: 'By their offense salvation has come to the Gentiles.' "[4] Luther's own late-medieval culture viewed Jews "as a rejected people, guilty of the murder of Christ, and capable of murdering Christian children for their own evil purposes."[5]

Although hostility and suspicion characterized the way Christians saw Jews in the middle ages, Luther's first treatise on Jews advocated that they be treated in a friendly manner. Luther published an essay in 1523 entitled, *That Jesus Christ Was Born a Jew.*[6] Luther's outlook toward Judaism was positive but called for a missionary stance. Luther hoped that the clarity of Christ's gospel brought about by the Reformation would inspire Jews to convert to Christianity. He suggested that if Jews were dealt with in a friendly fashion

---

4. Saint Augustine, *City of God*, Bk. XVIII, ch. 46. Cited in Augustine's *City of God*, abridged version from trans. by Gerald G. Walsh et al., ed. Vernon J. Bourke, Image Books (New York: Doubleday, 1958), 417.
5. Mark U. Edwards Jr., *Luther's Last Battles: Politics and Polemics, 1531–1546* (Minneapolis: Fortress Press, 2005), 121.
6. LW 45:195–230.

and instructed carefully by the Holy Scriptures, many might become "genuine Christians and turn again to the faith of their fathers, the prophets and patriarchs."[7] In his commentary *The Magnificat* (1521), he wrote, "We ought, therefore, not to treat the Jews in so unkindly a spirit, for there are future Christians among them."[8] Luther's strategy was sensible and gradual: "Let them first . . . begin by recognizing this man Jesus as the true Messiah; after that they may . . . learn also that he is true God."[9]

In his later years, Luther's theological view of Jews remained consistent with his position in 1523, while his practical recommendations for their treatment became very severe. Wilhelm Maurer sees a clear development between 1513 and 1546 in Luther's pronouncements on Judaism. According to Maurer, (1) Luther regarded Jews as a people suffering under the wrath of God. (2) Without divine intervention they were incorrigible and impossible to convert by human efforts. (3) Their religion remained hostile to Christianity and they could not cease blaspheming God and Christ. (4) A "solidarity of guilt" existed between Christians and Jews, a common suffering under God's wrath, a common resistance to Christ, a common attempt to gain one's righteousness and salvation apart from Christ, and a common need for grace.[10]

Many theologians ask why Luther proposed to secular authorities such harsh treatment of Jews. Luther writes in *On the Jews and Their Lies* (1543): "First to set fire to their synagogues and schools and to bury and cover with dirt whatever will not burn. . . . Second, I advise that their houses be razed and destroyed. . . . Third, I advise that all their prayer books and Talmudic writing . . . be taken from them. . . . Sixth, I advise that usury be prohibited to them, and that all cash and treasure of silver and gold be taken from them. . . . And you, my dear gentlemen friends who are pastors and preachers, I wish to remind faithfully of your official duty, so that you too may warn your parishioners concerning their eternal harm."[11] This harsh polemic is characteristic of Luther, who often appealed to apocalyptic books, such as John's Revelation, when pronouncing judgment on those he disfavored.

---

7. LW 45:200.
8. LW 21:354 (to Lk 1:55).
9. LW 45:229.
10. Mauer published two major essays on Luther's understanding of Jews: Wilhelm Maurer, *Kirche und Synagoge: Motive und Formen der Auseinandersetzung der Kirche mit dem Judentum in Laufe der Geschichte* (Stuttgart: Kohlhammer, 1953) and "Die Zeit der Reformation in Kirche und Synagogue," in *Kirche und Synagoge: Handbuch zur Geschichte von Christen und Juden; Darstellung mit Quellen*, vol. 1, ed. Karl Heinrich Rengstorf and Siegfried von Kortzfleisch (Munich: Klett-Cotta, 1968), 375–428.
11. LW 47:268, 268, 269, 270, 273.

Luther tended in stressful situations to demonize his interlocutors, for example Roman Catholics or Jews. Church historian Roland Bainton referenced this polemic in his biography of Luther: "One could wish that Luther had died before ever this tract was written. Yet one must be clear as to what he was recommending and why. His position was entirely religious and in no respect racial."[12] Dietrich Bonhoeffer wrote in a letter to his parents, "As long as a hundred years ago Kierkegaard said that today Luther would say the opposite of what he said then."[13] Mark Edwards argues that Luther surveyed his own times in light of this archetype. Luther classified the papacy as the antichrist, the Turks as Gog (Rev 20:8), the little horn in the Book of Daniel (Dan 8:9) as contemporary Jewry and the remnant of a rejected people suffering under God's wrath, and his Protestant opponents as the false prophets and apostles who had plagued the true prophets and apostles of old.[14]

Luther contextualized his disagreements with his opponents in terms of a cosmic struggle between God and Satan. When he attacked Jews, Catholics, Turks, or "fanatics," he was not attacking mere humans. Rather, he was attacking Satan, the spirit of the false church motivating these opponents. All of humanity was divided between true and false church. The issues separating true from false church were not semantic: they distinguished the saved from the damned. Luther was convinced that he was living on the eve of the last judgment. Richard Marius states: "Although the Jews for him were only one among many enemies he castigated with equal fervor. Although he did not sink to the horrors of the Spanish Inquisition against Jews, and although he was certainly not to blame for Adolf Hitler, Luther's hatred of the Jews is a sad and dishonorable part of his legacy, and it is not a fringe issue. It lay at the center of his concept of religion. He saw in the Jews a continuing moral depravity he did not see in Catholics."[15]

12. Roland Bainton, *Here I Stand: A Life of Martin Luther* (Nashville: Abingdon, 1978), 297.

13. Dietrich Bonhoeffer, *Letters and Papers from Prison*, trans. Reginald Fuller et al., ed. Eberhard Bethge (New York: MacMillan, 1971), 123.

14. Mark U. Edwards Jr., "Toward an Understanding of Luther's Attacks on the Jews," in *Luther, Lutheranism, and the Jews: A Record of the Second Consultation between Representatives of the International Jewish Committee for Interreligious Consultations and the Lutheran World Foundation Held in Stockholm, Sweden, 11–13 July, 1983* (Geneva: Lutheran World Federation, 1984), 27–28.

15. Richard Marius, *Martin Luther: The Christian between God and Death* (Cambridge: Harvard University Press, 1999), 482.

Contemporary Lutheran Church Responses to Luther on Judaism

The Lutheran Church around the world has acknowledged its responsibility for the Holocaust in a spirit of repentance. A number of important documents have been issued by the Lutheran churches. In 1981, the first consultation of the Lutheran World Federation (LWF) and the International Jewish Committee on Interreligious Consultations (IJCIC—a joint agency of five major Jewish organizations) addressed joint questions such as the concept of the human being in Lutheran and Jewish traditions. From July 11–13, 1983, the LWF met with the Jewish community for a second dialogue and acknowledged the "openness of views" and "spirit of mutual respect for the integrity of our faith communities," affirmed "the integrity and dignity of our two faith communities and repudiate[d] any organized proselytizing of each other," and committed to "trust replacing suspicion and with reciprocal respect replacing prejudice. To this end, we commit ourselves to periodic consultations and joint activities that will strengthen our common bonds in service to humanity."[16]

In 1988, I attended a consultation in Sigtuna, Sweden, to discuss the document "Ecumenical Considerations on Jewish-Christian Dialogue." We concluded: "The teachings of contempt for Jews and Judaism in certain Christian traditions proved a spawning ground for the evil of the Nazis and the Holocaust. The church must learn to preach and teach the gospel so that it cannot be used toward contempt."[17]

The LWF document, "A Shift in Jewish-Lutheran Relations?" decisively claims that a theology of justification by faith does not support anti-Semitism.[18] The Evangelical Church in Germany (EKD) published a statement in 1950: "We confess that we have become guilty before the God of compassion by our omission and silence and then share the blame for the terrible crimes committed against Jews by members of our nation."[19] Studies in 1975, 1991, and 2000 examined the theological issues at stake in Jewish-Christian relations. Discussions focused on common uses of terms, for example "covenant," and explosive issues, such as the evangelization of Jews, the interpretation of

---

16. *Luther, Lutheranism, and the Jews*, 9–11.
17. "The Ways of God—Judaism and Christianity," a document for discussion within the Church of Sweden (endorsed by the Board of the Church of Sweden, Sept. 19, 2001); http://www.sidic.org/fr/docOnLineView.asp?class=Doc00418.
18. LWF Document no. 48, ed. Wolfgang Grieve and Peter N. Prove (Geneva: Lutheran World Federation, 2003).
19. Online from Nov. 9, 2000: http://www.ekd.de/ekd-texte/christen_juden_2000_vorwort.html. (Translation M. Y.)

Old Testament promises referring to the Holy Land and the Palestinian-Israeli conflict, and common moral responsibilities of synagogue and church in the modern world.

Numerous other churches, such as the Lutheran Church–Missouri Synod, the Lutheran Church of Bavaria, and the Evangelical Lutheran Church in America (ELCA), have formulated statements addressing anti-Semitism. In its 1994 "Declaration to the Jewish Community," the ELCA publicly repudiated the anti-Jewish views of Martin Luther, expressed repentance for Christian complicity in hatred and violence against Jews through the centuries, and committed itself to building a relationship with the Jewish people based on love and respect.[20] This document is the basis for any Lutheran understanding concerning its relation to the Jewish community.

In September 2004, our church, the Evangelical Lutheran Church in Jordan and the Holy Land (ELCJHL), initiated a statement that condemns anti-Semitism. I stated that, "as a Palestinian Christian living under Israeli occupation, our church is concerned about the reemergence of anti-Semitism around the world, particularly in Europe. There can be no justification for anti-Semitism. There is a clear distinction between the politics of the state of Israel and the attitudes of the Jewish people." I called on the LWF to reiterate its clear statements from the past by insisting, "We must fight anti-Semitism." The statement was unanimously accepted by the Council of the LWF: "The LWF Council voted to express its grave concern at the growth of anti-Semitism around the world and to restate its rejection and abhorrence of anti-Semitism."[21]

In 1987, Jewish and Christian laity and clergy formed an interfaith coalition, the Institute for Christian and Jewish Studies (the *Dabru Emet*). They were concerned that ignorance, fear, and hostility all too often define the Jewish-Christian encounter. They were committed to in-depth studies of sacred writings and traditions in order to "reexamine the meaning of [respective] religious assumptions," "question the theological distortions and misconceptions that have contributed to the historical conflict between Christians and Jews," and "develop resources within our respective communities that inspire both Christians and Jews to appreciate the legitimacy and distinctiveness of one another."[22]

---

20. "Guidelines for the Lutheran-Jewish Relations of the ELCA," 16 November 1998; http://www.elca.org/ecumenical/interreligious/jewish/guidelines.html; and "Declaration of the Evangelical Lutheran Church in America to the Jewish Community," 8 April 1994; http://www.elca.org/ecumenical/interreligious/jewish/declaration.html.
21. Minutes of the LWF Council (2004), summarized by M. Y. on Sept. 4, 2004; http://www.elcjhl.org/resources/newsletters/04/04sep.htm.
22. http://www.icjs.org/what/njsp/dabruemet.html.

Luther and Islam

Luther and Islam,[23] like Luther and Judaism, must be contextualized in the
middle ages and not appropriated as a guideline for the future. Luther lived
during a time when fear of Islam was dominant. The Turks had extended their
military power into Europe and were at Vienna's doorstep in 1529. Gregory
Miller explains it succinctly: "To a large degree, the Turkish threat was so terrifying because many Germans understood the conflict between the Habs-
burgs and Ottoman Empires to be a struggle not between political powers but
between the face of Christendom and that of its arch-enemy, Islam."[24] In this
respect, Martin Luther was a man of his times.

Luther, like others, read this event through apocalyptic lenses. As early as
1518, Luther identified the Islamic faith (inseparable from "the Turks") as the
"scourge of God." He believed that Muslims were God's punishment upon
a sinful Christendom, which had, among manifold other sins, tolerated the
papal abomination. The Turks would function as a German schoolmaster who
must correct and teach the German people to repent of their sins and to fear
God.

Sarah Heinrich and James L. Boyce explain that Luther's position was
framed throughout this period by his perspective of the two realities, civil and
spiritual, and the duties appropriate to each.[25] Luther repeatedly argued on
the basis of Romans 13 for the obligation of obedience to all secular authority.
According to Luther, God had instituted secular authorities, even the Turkish
captors, for the preservation of order. His position was often charged for representing the Reformation's reluctance to fight against the Turkish invaders and
thus hinder good morale on the part of Europe's defenders.

Luther was more concerned with Christians at home than with the Turks.
He used the occasion of Europe's war with the Turks to articulate a theodicy;

23. I list Luther's writings on Islam: *On War against the Turk* (1529), in LW 46:157–205;
"Heerpredigt wider den Türken (1529)" ("Sermon against the Turks"), in WA 30/2:160–197;
Vorwort zu dem Libellus de ritu et moribus Turcorum (1530), in WA 30/2:205–8 [*Preface to
the Tract on the Religion and Customs of the Turks*, trans. Sarah Heinrich and James Boyce,
"Martin Luther: Translations of Two Prefaces on Islam," *Word and World* 16/2 (Spring 1996):
258–62]; *Appeal for Prayer against the Turks* (1541), in LW 43:215–41; *Verlegung des Alcoran
Bruder Richardi, Prediger Ordens* (1542), in WA 53:272–396; *Vorrede zu Theodor Biblianders
Koranangabe* (1543), in WA 53:569–72 [*Preface to Theodor Bibliander's Edition of the Qur'an*,
trans. Sarah Heinrich and James Boyce, "Martin Luther: Translations of Two Prefaces on
Islam," *Word and World* 16/2 (Spring 1996): 262–66].
24. Gregory J. Miller, "Luther on the Turks and Islam," in *Harvesting Martin Luther's Reflections on Theology, Ethics, and the Church*, ed. Timothy L. Wengert (Grand Rapids: Eerdmanns,
2004), 185.
25. Heinrich and Boyce, "Martin Luther: Translations of Two Prefaces," 252.

the present catastrophe was God's punishment for Christians. Luther issued to Christians a call for contrition and mandate for inner preparation. It was clear in the *Explanations of the Ninety-Five Theses* (1518) that "to fight against the Turk is the same as resisting God, who visits our sin upon us with this rod."[26] In his *On War against the Turk* (1529), Luther uses the same language, describing the Turk as "the rod of God's wrath" by which "God is punishing the world." This conviction led him to call for leaders who would exhort the people "to repentance and prayer" because "we have earned God's wrath and disfavor, so that he justly gives us into the hands of the devil and the Turk."[27]

In his *Preface to the Tract on the Religion and Customs of the Turks* (1530), Luther writes: "We see that the religion of the Turks or Muhammad is far more splendid in ceremonies—and, I might almost say, in customs—than ours, even including that of the religious or all the clerics. The modesty and simplicity of their food, clothing, dwellings, and everything else, as well as the fasts, prayers, and common gatherings of the people that this book reveals are nowhere seen among us—or rather it is impossible for our people to be persuaded to them."[28] Luther expresses admiration for the Turks' way of life and then ridiculed the religious customs of his own day. He writes in the same text: "Our religious are mere shadows when compared to them [Muslims], and our people clearly profane when compared to theirs."[29]

Martin Luther thought the religion and customs of "Muhammadism" should be published and publicized. In 1542, he was delighted to own a translation of the Qur'an in Latin. He read it firsthand in order to understand Islam properly. Luther also—and to our amazement—convinced the Council of Basel in December 1542 to lift the ban on the Latin translation of the Qur'an undertaken by the printer Oporinus. The ban was lifted provided that the Qur'an be published and distributed outside of Basel. Both Martin Luther and Philipp Melanchthon wrote prefaces to the Bibliander translation, published in 1543.[30] As Heinrich and Boyce write, Luther's "actions in support of the publications of the Qur'an and his written remarks argued repeatedly for a clear and honest presentation of matters of religion so that the truth might be pursued and the false refuted through consideration of what is, not of some perversion or monstrosity."[31]

---

26. LW 31:91–92.
27. LW 46:170–71.
28. Trans. Heinrich and Boyce, "Martin Luther: Translations of Two Prefaces," 259.
29. Trans. Heinrich and Boyce, "Martin Luther: Translations of Two Prefaces," 259.
30. Miller, "Luther on the Turks and Islam."
31. Trans. Heinrich and Boyce, "Martin Luther: Translations of Two Prefaces," 256.

Nevertheless, Luther's views did not originate in the context of open dialogue. His intention was to equip Christians against the teachings of Islam that he thought contradicted the Christian doctrines of salvation and justification.[32] Luther believed that Islam was a faith patched together from the faith of Jews, Christians, and heathens. He saw the chief theological differences between Christianity and Islam manifested in the following two ways:

1. The Muslim faith is a faith of justification by works. Luther summarized it like this: "If you are pious and just, and if you perform good works, you are saved."[33] According to Luther, the prayer of the Muslim is, "May God spare my life, that I may atone for my sin."[34] Thus, for Luther, the Muslim possesses a false righteousness that strives to be holy, not through faith in the merits of Christ, but through his own self-chosen works.[35] The Muslim strives to "do good according to the light and understanding of reason and to be saved in this way."[36]

2. According to Luther, the Muslims believe like their ancestor Nestorius that "only Mary's Son, not God's Son, died for us."[37] The Muslims hold Christ to be "an excellent prophet and a great man"[38] who preached to his own line and completed his work before his death just like any other prophet. Christ, however, is not as great a prophet as Muhammad, who is to be "worshiped and adored in Christ's stead."[39] Thus, the Muslims storm against the teaching of Christ as true God[40] and refuse to accept the testimony of Jesus that he is true God and true man.[41] The doctrinal disagreement is about the two natures of Christ, which is the central doctrine for Christianity.

Luther's eschatology was crucial to his view of Islam. As Gregory Miller succinctly puts it, "In place of the crusade, Luther saw a spiritual eschatological battle."[42] Luther derived his understanding of Islam from Daniel's dream concerning the four beasts in Daniel 7. In Daniel's vision each beast represented,

---

32. See his *Preface to Theodor Bibliander's Edition of the Qur'an*, trans. Heinrich and Boyce, "Martin Luther: Translations of Two Prefaces," 262-66.
33. LW 22:500 (*Sermons on the Gospel of St. John*; to John 3:35; 1537–1540).
34. LW 24:349 (*Sermons on the Gospel of St. John*; to John 16:11).
35. LW 24:242 (to John 15:8).
36. LW 24:371 (to John 16:14).
37. LW 22:350 (to John 3:16).
38. LW 22:18 (to John 1:3).
39. LW 22:137 (to John 1:16).
40. LW 22:394 (to John 3:16).
41. LW 22:468 (to John 3:32).
42. Miller, "Luther on the Turks and Islam," 197.

according to Luther, the kingdoms of Egypt, Greece, and Assyria, with the last beast signifying the Roman Empire. Luther identified the small horn, which had displaced the above-mentioned kingdoms (Daniel 7:20), with the origin of Islam. Finally, Luther ends his eschatological predictions with these words: "But just as the pope is the antichrist, so the Turk is the very devil incarnate. The prayer of Christendom against both is that they shall go down to hell, even though it may take the Last Day to send them there; and I hope that day will not be far off."[43]

One may ask, "Doesn't Martin Luther identify non-Christian religions with specific eschatological events?" In his article "Luther, the Turks, and Islam," Robert O. Smith writes, "Luther was not a modern dispensationalist looking for a scientific system of biblical interpretation. When read into the Bible, such schemes are allegorical. . . . In his preface to the Book of Revelation . . . Luther states that [t]he second woe is 'the sixth [evil] angel, the shameful Muhammad with his companions, the Saracens, who inflicted great plagues on Christendom, with his doctrines and with the sword.' . . . Finally when 'these last woes combine [Islam and the papacy] and make a final concerted attack on Christendom . . . all hell is loose.' "[44] Martin Luther was not an extremist in his time, but when he read his own context through the lenses of biblical prophecy, he was driven to such a view.

Contemporary Lutheran Church Responses to Luther on Islam

Luther was remarkable for his time in that he advocated the importance of understanding Islam and the Qur'an. He taught that it is only by understanding Islamic faith on its own terms that Christians could effectively witness to their faith. He thereby set an historic example.

As Luther taught, we must try to understand the other, and the other's religion. Going beyond Luther, we must apologize and make it our responsibility to rehumanize where our religions have dehumanized. We should apologize to one another for the harm we have caused one another.

I ask a serious and principled question: Had Martin Luther known that there would be Palestinian Lutherans carrying the message of his teaching of justification by faith in an Arab and Muslim context, would he have written differently? Luther was a person of his time, and his language expresses the

---

43. LW 46:181 (*On War against the Turks*).
44. Robert O. Smith, "Luther, the Turks, and Islam," *Currents in Theology and Mission* 34/5 (Oct. 2007): 335.

roughness of his time. I am, however, surprised that this burdensome past has not been taken seriously enough. For this reason, as a Palestinian Christian, I urge the LWF and its member churches to make a shift in the Lutheran-Muslim dialogue. I call the followers of Luther to repent as well as to apologize to Muslims for any offense that Lutherans have issued against them and their religion. This recommendation follows the lead of an LWF Council in September 2004 that voted to "express its grave concern at the growth of anti-Muslim feeling around the world, particularly in the context of the 'war on terror.' "[45]

Especially in a time of growing Islamophobia, we must not read every doctrine of other religions from the correctness of our own doctrines. Although our church father Luther brought us the freshness of the gospel, today's Lutherans can learn from Palestinian Christianity on how to live in dialogue with Muslims. What would Dr. Luther say today to Palestinian Lutherans who are witnessing to the Muslims in the Arab world through education and *diakonia* (care for neighbor)? We might be surprised. Luther was far ahead of his time. He reminded us of the importance of the Muslim reality. We share his regret that scholars do not seek to understand Islam as it understands itself. Luther was right when he encouraged his followers to understand the Qur'an in order to understand the Muslim faith. The time has come to invest more in understanding Islam rather than fearing it.[46]

Luther, the Doctrine of Creation, and a Prophetic Interfaith Dialogue

The Lutheran World Federation has been engaged in developing what it calls "diapraxis." Danish Lutheran theologian Lissi Rasmussen proposed this term

---

45. Resolution on Israel-Palestine, LWF Council (2004) (see footnote 21).
46. There are signs of hope. A code of conduct aimed at finding common positive values between religions was signed in January 2008 at a conference in Amman, Jordan, as a response to the 2005 Muhammad cartoon controversy that began in Denmark. Roman Catholic, Orthodox, Eastern Orthodox, and Evangelical Christians in Palestine, Jordan, Syria, Lebanon, Egypt, and Iran pledged respect for all religions, their prophets, holy writings, and doctrines; the security of an access to all holy places; freedom of expression that does not harm the other's beliefs or sentiments; and the initiation of dialogue in order to achieve justice, peace, development, and human dignity for all: http://www.coexistence jordan.org/App/ Public/News/ArticleDetails.asp. The "Amman Message," developed by King Abdullah of Jordan in 2004, seeks to strengthen the moderate voices of Islam by holding up common values of justice, compassion, and nonviolence and standing against extremism and violence in the name of religion: http://www.coexistencejordan.org/amman_msg.shtm. A similar initiative was issued by 138 Muslims to Christians in the fall of 2007. The text, *A Common Word between You and Us*, quotes verses from both the Bible and the Qur'an, claiming that religion's essence is the love of God and the love of the neighbor as one's self: http://www.acommonword.com.

to signal the new kind of prophetic interfaith dialogue that we need to culti-vate: "I see dialogue as a living process, a way of living in co-existence and pro-existence. Therefore, I want to introduce the term 'diapraxis' . . . By diapraxis I do not mean the actual application of dialogue but rather dialogue as action. We need a more anthropological contextual approach to dialogue where we see diapraxis as a meeting between people who try to reveal and transform the reality they share."[47] By adopting this kind of prophetic dialogue for life, we stand for abundant life for every human being and for the love and freedom Christ brings to all of God's creation. We are set free from the slavery of a sys-tem of exclusive doctrinal truth claims as the basis for living with one another as well as the many historical corruptions of the Christian faith.

Being justified by faith returns us to the real meaning of biblical justice. Justification describes the ambiguous situation in which we human beings find ourselves. We are at the same time sinners and saints, always in need of the justice and liberation that God graciously gives us. Justification means being simultaneously judged and freed. Those of us experiencing injustice in the world are promised the wonderful hope of justice through Christ's cross and resurrection. Yes, we are victims of injustice, but as we are saved by God's grace, we never allow injustice to have the final word.

The central tenet of Lutheranism has shifted from an individualis-tic understanding of justification to the reconciliation of people with each other in community and a life of justice, peace, compassion, and healing. The important question now is: What will it take to bring healing and wholeness? Although the law must continue to be respected, the motives and initiatives shift toward mercy and healing for the future rather than remaining fixed on the punishment and pain for the past.

We who live in the world of religion must also restore what we have destroyed. We must commit ourselves to rehumanize together where our reli-gions have dehumanized. We must work together to forge a prophetic dia-logue for life that urgently confronts the very real human rights violations of our day and we must dare to work together to forge common values of peace with justice, compassion, and reconciliation. This call arises from Luther's the-ology of creation.

---

47. *Lutheran World Information Magazine* 4 (2005): 4; Ingo Wulfhorst, LWF Study Secretary for the Church and People of Other Faiths, explains further that: "Diapraxis involves dia-logue, thus theological discourse on what is commonly shared as well as the differences in the respective faith traditions can never be excluded, despite the inherent complexities, deep-rooted prejudices and conflicts. By sharing their common pain, people of different faiths are enriched by the 'otherness' of the other," *Lutheran World Information Magazine* 4 (2005): 5.

The doctrine of creation is expressed in the worth and human rights of every human being. Lutheran theology emphasizes both creation and redemption. For centuries, we emphasized the theology of redemption more than the theology of creation. This overemphasis on "justification by faith" got Luther into trouble with Jews and Muslims. We are to correct this imbalance and take the theology of creation very seriously in living with other faiths. The intention of Genesis 1:27 is that we are all—male and female, Jews, Muslims, Christians, and others—created in God's own image. This means that we share equal humanity. We are all children of God, equally worthy of love and dignity. Every human being should enjoy the freedom of religion and one's own convictions.

As Luther pointed out, God works in the world through law and gospel. The gospel is God's saving word, incarnate in Jesus. The law, according to Luther, is the word by which God preserves creation through demands that we care for the earth and its people. While other religions generally disagree with the Christian understanding of the gospel, there tends to be a lot of agreement about God's expectations for human life on this earth and about our responsibilities for meeting them. Lutherans must be concerned with human actions in the world. Lutheranism cannot adopt Luther's own criticism that non-Christian religions are much too concerned with human actions in the world.

We as Lutherans must never give up our theological conviction that human actions in this world cannot bring us salvation. Nevertheless, we could stress more that we have been placed on this earth together with all humans precisely to be stewards of the earth and of each other. When we emphasize this point, we fulfill God's basic expectations without deemphasizing the gospel. We can care for this earth although this stewardship does not draw us, as faith in Christ does, into the life of God. Yet we can stress stewardship all the more when we have been incorporated into God's saving word in Jesus, when we begin to have "the mind of Christ" (Phil 2:8), through whom we know that God has "loved the world" (John 3:16). While we may have different motivations to engage in a dialogue for life, Christians can participate actively with people of other religions to serve the world as part of the common human vocation.

Living and Serving with Other Religions

Martin Luther's concern was to convert Jews and Muslims to Christianity. As an Arab Palestinian Christian Evangelical Lutheran, I have had to learn what it means to live my faith in Christ among three strong monotheistic religions.

Muslims in Palestine call me their bishop. They come to me with problems; we share feasts together. We have similar relations with many Jewish friends. We have established a dialogue group for Jewish and Christian leaders called the Jonah group. Together, we are enriched by one another's faiths, and we challenge one another about how our respective faiths compel us to treat our neighbor. Together we engage the world, seeking common values of justice, love of neighbor, forgiveness, and reconciliation. In our world of extremism and violence, we work toward nonviolence and moderation by living out a prophetic dialogue for life.

This dialogue for life has six key points. First, this dialogue must engage urgently the immediate suffering of people. Dialogue can never succeed until the dialogue partner understands the pain of the other. Just as Palestinians—and all humans—must understand the deep trauma of the Holocaust, Israelis—and all humans—must understand the pain of the Nakba and the continuing occupation. Though we should not compare our sufferings, we must understand each other. Only when we understand the pain of the other will we truly accept our common humanity.

Second, this dialogue must challenge the structures and realities of injustice, just as Jesus did. Like the incarnation, dialogue must be embodied in the flesh and the truth. We cannot afford to gesture toward dialogue without ever breaking through to the realities on the ground. In the Palestinian-Israeli conflict, Jews, Christians, and Muslims discuss the root cause of the conflict: Israeli Jews attribute the conflict to violence and the denial of their existence. Palestinian Christians and Muslims say that it is occupation. We must come together to discuss the holy writings and traditions of the three religions: Do any of our religions promote violence, the denial of the other, or occupation?

Third, this dialogue should be a catalyst for reconciliation through rigorous self-examination. In my book *Witnessing for Peace*,[48] I challenge each of us to look at our own respective religions: Are we a source of conflict and disagreement or a catalyst for reconciliation? Have we built bridges or widened the gap between people? It is always easy to blame another's religion without examining one's own. It is very tempting to use religion for narrow, selfish purposes—especially for justifying political interests. The key to a robust Lutheran theology of justification is the call to be brokers of justice, instruments of peace, and ministers of reconciliation.

Fourth, the dialogue for life cannot be merely an intellectual exercise but must have a spiritual dimension in order to be deep and enduring. We must

48. Minneapolis: Fortress Press, 2003.

submit ourselves to God's will. In this way, God helps us to be self-critical, while at the same time transforming us so that we can walk on the path to justice and security. We are to learn about the other's spirituality in order to stand together before God.

Fifth, this dialogue for life also calls us to work toward democracy and to build modern civil societies. Dialogue for life invites us to explore how our religions view citizenship. As a Palestinian Christian, I am not a *dhimmi* or a minority but an integral part of Arab Palestinian society. Modern societies must wrestle with the tension between loyalty to religion and country and the task to uphold fully equal rights and responsibilities among all.

Sixth, a prophetic dialogue for life means that we all share in a common responsibility to seek social justice in the whole world and to promote abundant life for all. We must use our shared biblical traditions and sacred scriptures to seek common values of compassion, justice, peace, forgiveness, and nonviolence. We must stand against war and militarization and must work for freedom, equality, tolerance, and democracy. We must work together for the healing of the world by eradicating poverty, HIV-AIDS, and other illnesses by caring for our globe's ecological health. We must also work together to fight against any kind of extremism as well as to uphold religious freedom and minority rights. Dialogue for life calls us together as stewards.

If Luther was a man of his time, we are to be people of our times, envisioning anew "what conveys Christ" ("was Christum treibet") in this day and age. If justification by faith drives us to understand that the essence of religion is the love of God and thus the love of neighbor, then justification by faith helps us see that religion is no longer part of the problem. Religion becomes part of the solution in this theology of love. "For freedom Christ has set us free. Stand firm, therefore, and do not submit again to a yoke of slavery" (Gal 5:1).

We are to see God in the other and to accept the otherness of the other. We are set free from being right in doctrine and freed to love each other in relationship. We are set free from earning our way by theology to experiencing and sharing the grace of God we have been given in Christ. Because of this, we can stand firm against extremism, violence, and hate, becoming the people of faith that God meant us to be, striving in God's mysterious vineyard for the peace we are meant to share.

Part Two

Living in the Midst of Horrors

The "urban legend" of Luther's life has elicited fascination and provoked questions since the earliest rumors of this legend. Luther's own experience of Christian freedom has continued to compel religious interest, particularly as this experience dovetails with a key paradigm of Christian existence, that of conversion. Luther's conversion has been linked to the history of the Western church on the one hand as the Protestant innovation and on the other to European history as the herald of modernity. Preoccupation with Luther's biography channels interest in many details about life in early sixteenth-century Saxony.

Aspects of Luther's biography are of interest today particularly in light of current fascination with religious experience. Erik Erikson's well-known 1958 work turned Luther's experience into the subject of psychological investigation. Erikson's study is of significance today because it poses questions at the biographical intersection of psychological, spiritual, religious, intellectual, and theological factors. Luther's theology was produced by the man Luther, and so his theology can be probed for insights into the relationship between person and work. The essays in this section work out the interrelationship between psychological and theological aspects of Luther's more dramatic ideas, particularly his crass polemic against other religions and his bitter struggle with the opaque, even terrifying, side of God. The result is a complex personal makeup of psychological, emotional, spiritual, and religious factors.

Further questions precipitated by Luther's psychological and religious personality have to do with how life is lived "in the midst of death." Living constantly with the threat of imminent execution, Luther's psychological and religious life revolved around issues and questions with which he was also preoccupied theologically. The wondrous certainty of faith against psychological depression and the remarkable resistance of hope against imminent destruction by plague and war bear the marks of deepest ambivalence in Luther. His is a robust anthropology, articulated with a realism won by experience. It presents an alternative to an anthropological model of coherent personal development, and its inconsistencies and pathos may help us see in a new way the most difficult aspects of life today in the midst of the horrors of global economic meltdown and seemingly unending political and social violence. By probing the links between experience and doctrine, and between life and death, this section develops Luther's anthropological realism informed by the duality of sin and grace as key to his theological insights.

The essays here contextualize Luther's life and work by the question of what it means to be human in the face of experiences that defy any resolution of meaning. James W. Jones opens the discussion from the perspective of his academic discipline of psychology, exploring Luther's doctrine of justification through the complexity of Luther's own psychology and emotional makeup. Volker Leppin shows how Luther's theology, particularly the deepest tensions in his doctrine of God, are embedded in a personal biographical matrix. One important aspect of Luther's understanding of life "in the midst of horrors" is the experience of suffering. Krista Duttenhaver works out a theology of suffering in the dialogue between Luther and a twentieth-century thinker, Simone Weil. Jacqueline A. Bussie ends this section with a hope that soberly acknowledges the contemporary reality of degradation of humans by humans. Luther's robust and ambivalent understanding of both human reality and divine complexity presents an uncomfortable resource for current questions of life, religion, and humanity. This is the argument of the entire book.

CHAPTER 5

Luther and Contemporary Psychoanalysis
— Living in the Midst of Horrors —
James W. Jones

I must begin with two confessions, surely an appropriate way to begin a discussion of Luther. The first is that I am no fan of the "discipline" of psychohistory. For example, having read some of Luther's works rather carefully in the last few months, I think Erik Erikson's *Young Man Luther* tells us more about Erikson and his approach to religion—a very insightful approach, to be sure—than it does about Luther.[1] Second, when I read Luther's writings in preparation for writing this chapter, I was struck profoundly by how "other" they appeared to me. This is clearly a person, a mind, an outlook all formed by experiences that are significantly different from my own and from those of the patients I treat and the people who trained me as a psychologist. In addition, no psychological investigation can give a complete account of another human being, especially one as complicated and conflicted as he who called himself "the prophet of the Germans."

Psychoanalysis, Theology, and History

We begin by mentioning briefly—without time to develop them in any depth—several concerns at the interface of psychoanalysis, historical studies, and theology.

---

1. Erik H. Erikson, *Young Man Luther: A Study in Psychoanalysis and History* (New York: Norton, 1958).

First is the issue of source material. The clinician has the patient in front of her. She can check her interpretations against the patient's own self report. Plus, she has the patient's nonverbal reactions, which are so important in communication. Obviously, none of that applies to a personage from the middle ages. Can we really make a patient out of a historical personage?

Second, historians are trained to understand figures in their own historical context. Psychology, especially if it claims to be "scientific," appears to appeal to universal laws and transcultural generalizations. Can we really apply modern psychological categories to a radically pre-modern person?

Third, an issue always, always raised when psychology enters the theological world is "reductionism." Must psychology follow Freud and Jung and all of today's various psychological subspecialties in making psychological processes, however theorized, the independent variable and making religion and theology the dependent variables, making them simply manifestations of more fundamental, *psychological* realities?

Fourth, on the other hand, both historians and theologians are concerned about motivation. History is, among other things, a narrative of human behavior. It is poor history that simply reports events and offers no explanation of what motivated them. Likewise, just as every psychological theory is an implicit theory of human nature, so every theology is an implicit theory of human motivation. And motivation is, inevitably, a psychological concern.

It is a symptom of the conflicted relationship between Luther and psychology that I must begin by saying what I am *not* going to do. Despite his obvious depression and self-confessed inner torment, I am not going to treat Luther as an example of psychopathology. Like many larger-than-life figures, he was a man often at the mercy of overwhelming appetites. He was a person of extremes: he went from an extreme of scrupulosity and asceticism to moments of extreme indulgence in food, drink, and speech. He also had a powerful fixation on his bodily processes, which he could describe in excruciating detail. And like many polemicists, he could articulate his own position best by saying what he was against: he needed opposition in order to feel alive. All of this makes him a fascinating and complicated human being. None of it makes him necessarily sick. So I will not be putting Dr. Luther on Dr. Freud's or Dr. Jones's couch.

Quite the reverse: given his conflicted and psychologically ambiguous character, it is a tribute to Luther's psychological strength and resilience that he was able to use his conflicts, torments, and volcanic emotions in the service of a creative and constructive theological project. Luther acknowledged this when he wrote "living, yea dying, and being damned makes a theologian, not thinking, reading, or speculating."[2]

I will comment on some of the creative connections between his psychological situation and his theological formulas, but first a word about the psychological hermeneutic that I use here.

Contemporary Psychoanalytic Hermeneutics

Contemporary relational theory represents a fundamental revision of earlier psychoanalytic views of human nature. Phenomena that Freud attributed to biological instincts, the relational theorist sees as the consequence of interpersonal experience. Human relationships are not, as Freud thought, the product of antisocial impulses gradually modified into socially accepted forms out of a compromise between fear and desire. Rather, human experience is structured around the establishment and maintenance of connections with others. The nature of these connections—pleasurable, frustrating, or distant—and not their instinctual motivation is what influences the quality of our interpersonal experiences. The self develops from the *internalization* of infant-caregiver interactions. If these episodes carry sufficient parental attunement, they contribute to positive self-formation. Their psychological import comes from the meaning they acquire in the context of early interpersonal encounters. Such a view theorizes the unconscious as neither the container of biological drives and defenses against them, nor as the carrier of universal archetypal forms, but rather as the internalization of relational episodes laid down in the course of our development. These relational themes echo and re-echo through our devotional practices, spiritual disciplines, and cherished philosophical and theological convictions.[3]

Since the beginnings of psychoanalysis with Freud's writings, psychoanalytic clinicians have applied various clinical theories—developed in the psychic struggle of patient and therapist—to understanding the passions and motivations that drive religious belief and practice (and also the rejection of religious belief and practice) and that are expressed in and through rituals, theologies, stories, and songs from the various religions of the world. An important implication of all psychoanalytic psychologies is that theological beliefs and claims

---

2. WA 5:163, 28–29 (*Operationes in Psalmos*; 1519–1521). Cited in Erikson, *Young Man Luther*, 251. (Translation J. W. J.)
3. See James W. Jones, *Contemporary Psychoanalysis and Religion: Transference and Transcendence* (New Haven: Yale University Press, 1991), 62–67.

are never purely cognitive but rather express potent affects, strongly held sensibilities about self and world, and deeply felt wishes and fears, all of which are often unconscious. From a contemporary psychodynamic perspective, the ideas we find convincing, the experiences we undergo, as well as the behaviors we act out all express deeper, often unconscious, relational templates. Theological beliefs and convictions, like all beliefs and convictions, are carriers of profound early experiences and developmental processes. To understand them fully involves comprehending more than their cognitive content.

A religion is, among other things, a complex of relationships: with a divine figure, with a teacher or leader, with a sacred text or set of symbols, with a set of ideas, with a community of coreligionists. Such relationships embody certain patterns, and these patterns often reflect and repeat relational patterns in other areas of a devotee's life: a search for an authority figure or the rejection of all authority, a deep longing or attachment or a drive to keep aloof and distant from others, a need for absolute certainty or a fear of any commitments. These and many other patterns reverberate through the gods that are believed in or rejected, the dogmas of Christianity and the speculations of the theologians, and the philosophies of the skeptics. From the standpoint of relational psychoanalysis, the accepting or rejecting of the gods, the longing for a savior or the lure of a spiritual discipline, the attraction of a purely materialistic worldview or the call of martyrdom all carry certain interpersonal themes, thoughts, and affects. It is the task of a contemporary psychodynamic inquiry to unpack those patterns and the cognitions, affects, and behaviors that carry them.

Clinicians listen for repeating themes and patterns in a patient's life, not only in behavior but also in ways of thinking and feeling. In religious texts and religious practices, patterns repeat as well. It is that method of interpretation, which I have refined and used for several decades both in working with religious patients and studying and teaching religious texts and practices, that I am here applying to Martin Luther by listening for psychological-religious themes that echo in his writings.

Psychoanalysis is here more of a method, a way of listening and reading, than a theoretical paradigm. Also, the clinical encounter is experienced as more of a dialogue than an authoritative doctor interpreting and prescribing from on high for a passive patient. Such a stance approaches the issues raised previously from a rather different perspective than the more classical Freudian and Jungian paradigms, which assumed that the doctor knew the patient better than the patient knew himself. The therapist brings not an infallible theory but rather a way of listening and responding. Thus the patient is taken primarily on his own terms rather than having a master theory imposed on him. The possibility of reductionistic mischief being done, while not being eliminated, is significantly weakened. At most, a reductionistic approach is understood as a heuristic for generating a hypothesis and not as an absolute description of the reality of the other. Also, in a dialogue the patient addresses the therapist as much as the therapist addresses the patient.

In the following observations I listen for some psycho-religious themes in Luther's writings and in what little we know of his life history. Hopefully, I will allow myself to be addressed by Luther as well as addressing him from within the perspective of psychology.

Turning a Wrathful God into a Loving God

While he battled with princes in the political realm, with theologians in the intellectual realm, and with God and the devil in the spiritual realm, Luther appears convinced that the most fundamental site of battle is within the human soul. "Whether man believes it or not, it is most certain and true that no torture can compare with the worst of all evils, namely, the evil within man himself. The evils within him are more numerous and far greater than any which he feels. If a man were to feel his evil, he would feel hell, for he has hell within himself."[4] Locating the primary site of personal struggle within the self is certainly something the psychoanalyst can affirm.

Probably the most significant theological-psychological transformation Luther accomplished was turning a wrathful God experience into a loving God experience. It is a commonplace observation that Luther's early life was consumed by a guilty conscience and the concomitant dread of a wrathful and punitive God. When Luther cries out in the midst of the *Fourteen Consolations* (1520), "Can there be an evil more dreadful than the unrest of a gnawing conscience?"[5] one certainly can hear the voice of experience. This claim is substantiated further by Luther's frequent recalling of his spiritual director's insistence on reminding Luther of God's love in reaction to Luther's terror in the face of a wrathful God—for example, Johannes von Staupitz's response to Luther's seizure of panic in the monastic choir that "it could not have been Christ who terrified you for Christ consoles."[6]

---

4. LW 42:125 (*Fourteen Consolations*; 1520).
5. LW 42:136.
6. Erikson, *Young Man Luther*, 37.

A firsthand experience with a tormenting conscience and the punitive
God of wrath and judgment comes through clearly in Luther's *A Meditation
on Christ's Passion* (1519):

> They contemplate Christ's passion aright who view it with a terror-
> stricken heart and a despairing conscience. This terror must be felt as
> you witness the stern wrath and the unchanging earnestness with which
> God looks upon sin and sinners, so much so that he was unwilling to
> release sinners even for his only and dearest Son without his payment of
> the severest penalty for them. . . . If the dearest child is punished thus,
> what will be the fate of sinners? It must be an inexpressible and unbear-
> able earnestness that forces such a great and infinite person to suffer and
> die to appease it. And if you seriously consider that it is God's very own
> Son, the eternal wisdom of the Father, who suffers, you will be terrified
> indeed. The more you think about it, the more intensely will you be
> frightened.[7]

Christ's suffering is the necessary price for our sins—a traditional theme
heavy with psychological and theological meaning. Such a view rests upon
an image of God as just and punitive but also loving and forgiving. But his
justice and righteous anger are in the foreground here, his love and forgiveness in the background. God's love and mercy are obscured by his outrage at
transgression, his need for vengeance, and his vindictive anger. "How many vir-
gins, youths, and those whom we call innocents are there! How many monks,
priests, and married couples! All their lives they seemed to be serving God,
and now, perhaps because of a single lapse, they are being punished forever.
It must not be denied that God's justice is the same in the [case] of every sin,
hating and punishing it in whomever it is found."[8]

Such a God insists that sacrifices be made, that his justice be satisfied and
his wrath appeased before he can forgive. This theology also rests upon a view
of humanity as consisting of disobedient transgressors with eternal damnation
as their deserved and inescapable fate. To internalize such a theology, one must
be brought to the felt realization of the full extent of his or her sinfulness.
Luther does this masterfully by transforming his own experience of torment
into a homiletical tour-de-force:

> You must get this thought through your head and not doubt that you are
> the one who is torturing Christ thus, for your sins have surely wrought

---

7. LW 42:8.
8. LW 42:133 (*Fourteen Consolations*).

this. . . . Therefore, when you see the nails piercing Christ's hands, you can be certain that it is your work. When you behold his crown of thorns, you may rest assured that these are your evil thoughts, etc. For every nail that pierces Christ, more than one hundred thousand should in justice pierce you, yes, they should prick you forever and ever more painfully! When Christ is tortured by nails penetrating his hands and feet, you should eternally suffer the pain they inflict and the pain of even more cruel nails, which will in truth be the lot of those who do not avail them-selves of Christ's passion.[9]

In this theological world, the emphasis falls almost entirely on guilt and the weight of disobedience. The self is haunted by what W. R. D. Fairbairn calls "an internal saboteur," in this case a tormenting conscience. To its endless demands, sacrifices must be offered, penalties paid, purifications undertaken. Clinically, this way of experiencing the self, others, and God is almost always associated with depression and obsessive-compulsive symptoms. This certainly reminds one both of Luther's scrupulosity as a monk—scrupulosity so great that Luther reports that his confessor once demanded that Luther bring him "real sins to confess"—and of the "melancholy" that dogged him all his days. "Sometimes my confessor said to me when I repeatedly discussed silly sins with him, 'You are a fool. God is not incensed against you, but you are incensed against God. God is not angry with you, but you are angry with God.'"[10]

The patient in such a condition is almost always surprised that the thera-pist accepts him. Much of the struggle of therapy with such patients is the struggle to enable them to accept the therapist's acceptance. They often fight against accepting it. Some never do. And even those whose treatment has been most successful can fall back into bouts of depression and the sadistic conscience under stress. While it often brings relief for the patient to under-stand the origin of his vindictive conscience in his early life, the main agent of change is the therapeutic relationship itself and the experience with the therapist of both a new way of relating and the means to begin to internalize that experience.

Luther's writings lay bare the psychology behind this theology: a burden of guilt is the psychological soil out of which grows this way of understand-ing the work of Christ as a sacrifice and an expiation of God's justice and the requirement that transgressions be punished severely. And if the soul does not

---

9. LW 42:9 (*A Meditation on Christ's Passion*).
10. LW 54:15 (Table Talk no. 122: "Treatment of Melancholy, Despair, Etc."; Nov. 30, 1531).

naturally feel such a burden (as Luther apparently did), it must be brought
to feel it by rhetorical power. To be psychologically effective, this theology
requires that an internal conflict be experienced between the self and its conscience. Here again Luther could serve as a paradigm. If it can be appropriated
psychologically and experientially, the work of Christ will bring relief from
the burden of guilt by paying the price needed to satisfy God's wrath. But
psychologically, the crucial question is, can such a juridical transaction even
be appropriated experientially? Or more precisely, what are the psychological
preconditions for being able to appropriate it or that make it experientially
impossible?

Strikingly, for Luther this theology of the wrathful, vindictive God is
not the end of the story, either personally or theologically. The *Meditation on
Christ's Passion* follows the Holy Week trajectory, moving from the torture of
Good Friday to the glory of Easter. The *Fourteen Consolations* follows the same
deep structure. The first seven consolations are negative and involve meditating on seven "evils" found in human life. The second seven are positive and
involve meditating on seven "blessings." Again, this mirrors the Holy Week
trajectory of suffering leading to resurrection and glory. Luther writes in his
Meditation on Christ's Passion,

> If we allow sin to remain in our conscience and try to deal with it there,
> or if we look at sin in our heart, it will be much too strong for us and
> will live on forever. But if we behold it resting on Christ and [see it]
> overcome by his resurrection, and then boldly believe this, even it is dead
> and nullified. Sin cannot remain on Christ, since it is swallowed up by
> his resurrection. Now you see no wounds, no pain in him, and no sign of
> sin . . . In his suffering Christ makes our sin known and thus destroys it,
> but through his resurrection he justifies us and delivers us from all sin, if
> we believe this.[11]

Now we meditate on the glorified Christ and see there an example of God's
love:

> You must no longer contemplate the suffering of Christ (for this has
> already done its work and terrified you), but pass beyond that and see
> his friendly heart and how this heart beats with such love for you that it
> impels him to bear with pain your conscience and your sin. Then your
> heart will be filled with love for him, and the confidence of your faith
> will be strengthened. Now continue and rise beyond Christ's heart to

---

11. LW 42:12.

God's heart and you will see that Christ would not have shown this love for you if God in his eternal love had not wanted this, for Christ's love for you is due to his obedience to God. Thus you will find the divine and kind paternal heart, and, as Christ says, you will be drawn to the Father through him . . . We know God aright when we grasp him not in his might or wisdom (for then he proves terrifying), but in his kindness and love. Then faith and confidence are able to exist, and then man is truly born anew in God.[12]

Psychologically speaking, a figure-ground shift has taken place. At first, God's judgment was in the foreground and his mercy in the background. Now his mercy is in the foreground and his judgment in the background. Christ now radiates love rather than provoking us to fear. Christ is now a figure of beneficence whose love for us motivates us to identify with him and to serve him out of love, not terror. Psychologically, we have moved from fear into love, from terror into desire, from Christ as judge to Christ as ideal.

Here there has been a change not only in the image of God—a God of wrath replaced by a God of love—but also in the understanding of human nature. What we might call Luther's "Good Friday theology" assumed that, at most, humanity could be educated through punishment and its external behavior modified through fear. Now there is the suggestion that humanity might be motivated by gratitude and be able to internalize an example of love. The possibility of a more internal transformation is hinted at. The human problem has shifted from dealing with a punitive conscience to facilitating a transformation of the self.

These appear as very profound changes psychologically and theologically. Psychologically, we need to ask about what facilitated these changes. In my experience, profound changes in a person's image of God normally signal changes in their sense of self and, normally, such changes are facilitated by the relationship the patient has with the therapist. For example, the accepting and empathic relational experiences, along with increased self-understanding, catalyzes increased self acceptance and a less judgmental conscience. Did Luther's relationship with Staupitz serve that psychotherapeutic function?

Luther, of course, describes this change in theological, not psychological, terms—as an embrace of a doctrine of justification by faith. To that we now turn.

---

12. LW 42:12.

Justification by Faith

The psychologist prefers to begin from experience and move from there to reflection. So I would begin this discussion of the psychological themes in Luther's theory of justification by faith with the experience that led Luther to this theology.

> The words "righteous" and "righteousness of God" struck my conscience like lightning. When I heard them I was exceedingly terrified. If God is righteous [I thought], he must punish. But when by God's grace I pondered, in the tower and heated room of this building, over the words, "He who through faith is righteous shall live" [Rom. 1:17] and "the righteousness of God" [Rom. 3:21], I soon came to the conclusion that if we, as righteous men, ought to live from faith and if the righteousness of God contributes to the salvation of all who believe, then salvation won't be our merit but God's mercy. My spirit was thereby cheered. For it's by the righteousness of God that we're justified and saved through Christ. These words [which had before terrified me] now became more pleasing to me. The Holy Spirit unveiled the Scriptures for me in this tower.[13]

Not surprisingly, we have here the same thematic structure observed before: Luther starts with fear and punishment and moves to grace and mercy. This move is driven by his realization that the term "righteousness" or "justice of God" can refer not to God's anger but to God's merciful willingness to accept our "faith" in Christ in lieu of our ability to earn or merit God's favor. In theory, all of the activity is done by God; all we have to do is believe that is true.

Luther is feeling powerless; his works have not worked to salve his conscience. Clinicians know that such a strategy of works never works; you can never do enough to satisfy a demanding conscience. That psychological reality is at the core of Luther's doctrine. Luther embraces this experience of powerlessness, affirming that indeed we can do nothing. This acceptance of the reality of his powerlessness to salve his tormenting conscience opens up the possibility of a new perspective: I cannot do it, but I do not have to do it, for Christ has done it for me.

Again, my question concerns the psychological condition that this theology arises from and speaks to. Luther's experience here is of passivity, even helplessness, on his part. He can do nothing; God must do it all. As he says in

---

13. LW 54:192 (Table Talk no. 3232c: "Description of Luther's 'Tower Experience' "; between June 9 and July 21, 1531).

the "Sermon on Preparing to Die" (1519), "God gives you nothing because of your worthiness, nor does he build his Word and sacraments on your worthiness, but out of sheer grace he establishes you, unworthy one, on the foundation of his Word and signs."[14] This understanding appears congruent with what biographers have pieced together about his life: that Luther tried to deal with his tormenting conscience through performing pious works in accordance with the teaching of the medieval Catholic Church. But as any clinician or pastor knows, a tormenting conscience is not so easily bought off. Rather, the result is more often an intensification of scrupulosity—something Luther reports as true of his experience. Finally, it appears, he "hit bottom" (to use the phrase popularized by Alcoholics Anonymous). Experiences of transformation very often have exactly this thematic-psychological structure: a struggle that leads eventually to psycho-spiritual exhaustion, a hitting bottom and giving up, and a relief experienced as coming from beyond the circle of one's self.

The key to Christian life, for Luther, becomes the ability to say, "I believe that is true," or "I trust that is true." For example, in relation to the absolution of our sins, Luther writes: "When the priest absolves me, I trust in this as in God's Word itself. Since it is God's Word, it must come true. That is my stand, and on that stand I will die. You must trust in the priest's absolution as firmly as though God had sent a special angel or apostle to you, yes, as though Christ himself were absolving you."[15]

Of course, there is a further complication. Such faith and trust are also gifts from God, not something we achieve or deserve. "You must entreat God for faith. This too rests entirely in the hands of God."[16] Here too, the emphasis falls entirely on our passivity and dependence. "Let no one presume to perform such things by his own power, but humbly ask God to create and preserve such faith in and such understanding of his holy sacraments in him. He must practice awe and humility in all this, lest he ascribe these works to himself instead of allowing God the glory."[17]

So psychologically, Luther's theology can be understood as an expression of and an artful response to a certain psychological condition—the tormenting conscience and the concomitant inability of anything we do to satisfy it. Let me be clear that such an analysis is not to reduce Luther's theology to a psychopathology but rather to offer an appreciation of what he achieved psychologically out of his own interior resilience and resources.

---

14. LW 42:109.
15. LW 42:110 ("Sermon on Preparing to Die").
16. LW 42:12 (*A Meditation on Christ's Passion*).
17. LW 42:113.

This analysis does, however, leave me with several questions.

First, one of the dynamics involved with the tormenting conscience is anger. Being constantly criticized from within or without inevitably makes a person furious. And feelings of passivity and helplessness can also potentiate and exacerbate feelings of rage. Often that anger is turned back against the self, hence the connection between such a conscience and depression, understood here as anger turned against the self. Luther's solution of shifting the problem and its solution onto God relieves his inner torment, at least to the extent that he can really accept and believe that, after the cross, God does not condemn him. But it does nothing to deal with the problem of anger. Luther himself acknowledges this: "I am free from avarice, my age and bodily weakness protect me from sensual desire, and I am not afflicted with hate or envy toward anybody. Up to now only anger remains in me, and for the most part this is necessary and just."[18] If this anger is no longer directed against the self, where does it go? The answer seems clear: it is projected onto the Jews, the peasants, the Catholic Church, and so on. Psychologically speaking, Luther's polemical writings are not simply the ravings of a grumpy old man. They are the price paid for Luther's solution to the theology of the wrathful God and the punitive conscience.

And since a concern these days is the connection between religion and violence, a theology that still contains within it the representation of a punitive God of wrath, an image of God associated with violent religions, and that offers no way to transform anger, may not be helpful in breaking the connection between religion and violence.

Second, Luther's distress exemplifies what the Hungarian-American psychoanalyst Heinz Kohut calls "guilty man," the person characterized by what Freud would call a punitive superego. This was the typical patient in Freud's practice. For different reasons, both Luther and Freud consider this character structure *the* universal human condition. But is that the case? Empirically, the answer would appear to be no. Kohut also describes what he calls "tragic man," the person who suffers less from a tormenting conscience and more from a weak and diffused sense of self. Such people often feel empty and disconnected, their lives often feel diffuse and protean, and they seem unable to make lasting commitments.[19] Many times, they overidealize another person, ideology, or institution and then fall into a rage when their over-idealizations are disappointed. Such people are less in need of a more forgiving and accepting

18. LW 54:26 (Table Talk no. 197: "Luther's Analysis of Himself"; end of March, 1532).
19. Heinz Kohut, *The Search for the Self: Selected Writings of Heinz Kohut (1978-1981)*, vol. 2, ed. Paul H. Ornstein (New York: International Universities Press, 1991), 737–70.

God representation and more in need of a solid and empathically experiential relationship. Reports from the clinical field suggest—and this is certainly my experience—that while patients tormented by a punitive superego are still seen, more and more one encounters patients with a more diffused and empty sense of self. For them a theology of sacrificial expiation and divine forgiveness will have less and less psychological relevance and transforming power regardless of how hard they believe it intellectually.

Does Luther's theology contain resources that might address the psychological problem of the diffused self with as much power as it addresses the psychological problem of the guilty conscience, even though that was not the context in which this theology was originally formulated? I leave that question to the Lutheran theologians, but I offer one suggestion in the form of a question: must Luther's theology follow the same trajectory as his development did? That is, must it begin with the wrathful God and the guilty conscience and then move from there to the God-Christ of mercy? Or can it go directly to, or start from, the Christ of mercy? I ask that because it is the merciful Christ, not the wrathful God, that the diffused self can connect with. Or, to put it another way, the psychological situation of the diffused self longing for an empathic other cries out for the merciful God and the Christ who shared the vicissitudes of our life rather than the sacrificial victim that purchases our freedom from a tormenting conscience. I quote Luther's words again:

> See his friendly heart and how this heart beats with such love for you that it impels him to bear with pain your conscience and your sin. Then your heart will be filled with love for him, and the confidence of your faith will be strengthened. Now continue and rise beyond Christ's heart to God's heart and you will see that Christ would not have shown this love for you if God in his eternal love had not wanted this, for Christ's love for you is due to his obedience to God. Thus you will find the divine and kind paternal heart, and, as Christ says, you will be drawn to the Father through him. Then you will understand the words of Christ, "For God so loved the world that he gave his only Son, etc." [John 3:16] We know God aright when we grasp him not in his might or wisdom (for then he proves terrifying), but in his kindness and love. Then faith and confidence are able to exist, and then man is truly born anew in God.[20]

Here is an image of God that, if embraced, might catalyze the transformation of the self.

---

20. LW 42:12 (*A Meditation on Christ's Passion*).

Does this mean the law no longer serves any important psychological function? Of course not. Psychoanalysts like Heinz Hartmann and Erik Erikson, who came after Freud and who expanded on the functions of the ego, insisted that the ego needs the collective traditions of wisdom and moral guidance to facilitate its adjustment to the world. Whereas for Freud the ego was almost exclusively the carrier of scientific rationality, for "ego-psychologists" like Hartmann and Erikson, the ego was also the seat of moral agency, and it needed the support and guidance of the moral law. For Heinz Kohut, the self needs ideals with which to identify and a sense of being a part of something greater than itself. Such theorizing on the part of Kohut and the ego-psychologists leads them to a much more positive assessment of the function of religion than Freud held. The moral law proffered by religion is affirmed by these post-Freudian analysts as a source of ideals to embrace and of guidance and support for human development.[21]

Third and finally, as Luther would say, it all depends on faith. But what are the psychological preconditions and ramifications of the kind of faith Luther calls for? Luther says, "Faith justifies not as a work, or as a quality, or as knowledge, but as assent of the will and firm confidence in the mercy of God . . . It is assent."[22] He recommends that those facing death should "Hold fast to that and say, 'He who gives and has given me his signs and his Word, which assure me that Christ's life, grace, and heaven have kept my sin, death, and hell from harming me, is truly God, who will surely preserve these things for me.'"[23] To illustrate the meaning of faith, Luther tells the following story:

> In Torgau a wretched little woman once came to me and said, "Ah, dear Doctor, I have the idea that I'm lost and can't be saved because I can't believe." Then I replied, "Do you believe, dear lady, that what you pray in the Creed is true?" She answered with clasped hands, "Oh yes, I believe it; it's most certainly true!" I replied, "Then go in God's name, dear lady." . . . We should hold to the Word and let ourselves drag along in this way.[24]

In all these texts, the emphasis falls on the will, on assent, on "holding on to the word of God."

---

21. For more on ego psychology's and Kohut's understanding of religion, see James W. Jones, *Terror and Transformation: The Ambiguity of Religion in Psychoanalytic Perspective* (London/New York: Brunner-Routledge, 2002), 25–27.

22. LW 54:359 (Table Talk no. 4655: "The Faith That Justifies Is Not Knowledge"; June 16, 1539).

23. LW 42:109 ("Sermon on Preparing to Die").

24. LW 54:452 (Table Talk no. 5562: "To Believe and to Comprehend Are Not the Same"; spring 1543).

But did this really work as a solution to the problem of a tormenting conscience and the concomitant depression? The answer is ambiguous at best. Much of Luther's Table Talk portrays a lifelong struggle with melancholy.[25] When describing the necessity of holding fast to God's proclamation of forgiveness, Luther comments, "But I preach to others what I don't do myself."[26] And Erikson reports that toward the end of his life, Luther required people to remind him constantly that God forgave him[27] and even to shout the Lord's Prayer in his ear,[28] to drown out his demonic inner voices. As Luther himself said, "It's very difficult for a man to believe that God is gracious to him. The human heart can't grasp this."[29]

What is the problem here? In the tower, Luther had a profound experiential realization of the truth of justification by faith. But as William James pointed out, such transforming moments are always transitory. That by itself a powerful conversion experience and a realization of the truth of the human condition produced little lasting transformation is no surprise at all to the clinician. We should not blame Luther's theology for his continued suffering. The problem is psychological, not theological. Luther has the theology right. But psychologically speaking, assenting to truth claims—however true they may be—is rarely if ever transformative or curative by itself. It is commonplace to hear patients say, "I understand my problem, where it came from, how irrational it is to think and feel this way, how it affects me. But I still suffer." Agreement, understanding, and assent are rather powerless in the face of deep-seated, often unconscious, emotional currents, habits of mind, wishes, and fears.

In my experience both clinically and spiritually, it is not faith in the sense of thinking or assenting but rather experience and disciplined practice that catalyze lasting psychological and religious transformation. Given the ingrained suspicion of anything that smells of justification by works, could Lutheran spirituality incorporate into itself this doctor's prescription for a life disciplined by spiritual practice as the primary means of internalizing and deepening the truth of justification by faith?

---

25. LW 54:15, 174 (Table Talk nos. 122, 461).
26. LW 54:74 (Table Talk no. 461: "Beware of Melancholy and Trust God"; Feb. 19, 1533).
27. Erikson, *Young Man Luther*, 241.
28. Erikson, *Young Man Luther*, 244.
29. LW 54:19 (Table Talk no. 137: "God's Grace Is Hard to Believe"; between Nov. 30 and Dec. 14, 1531).

CHAPTER 6

God in Luther's Life and Thought
– The Lasting Ambivalence –
Volker Leppin

erman Luther research seems to be terrified by Erik Erikson's *Young Man Luther*.[1] When the book was first published in Germany, most established Luther scholars vehemently rejected it.[2] The book made too many controversial associations. Particularly vexing were the allusions to older Roman Catholic polemics against Luther as a man whose theology was not primarily inspired by the Bible but by his own problematic psychological disposition. Erikson's *Young Man Luther* seemed too close to Denifle's "Luther" for comfort.[3] Denifle's own study of Luther focused on the scrupulous monk who was not able to accept his spiritual father's advice. Erikson took one step back to Luther's own family of origins and turned Luther into an immature adolescent who could never work out his parental issues successfully. If Luther was unable to grow up, then neither have many Lutherans, who seem to suffer perpetually at the hands of a harsh Godfather.

---

1. Erik H. Erikson, *Young Man Luther: A Study in Psychoanalysis and History* (New York: Norton, 1958).
2. See, for example, Heinrich Bornkamm, "Luther und sein Vater: Bemerkungen zu Erik H. Erikson, *Young Man Luther: A Study in Psychoanalysis and History*," *Zeitschrift fuer Theologie und Kirche* 66 (1969): 38–61. On page 50, Bornkamm writes, "It is too bad that Erikson piled up exaggerations and groundless speculations on the true picture of Luther's parents." (Trans. C. H.)
3. Heinrich Suso Denifle, *Luther und das Luthertum in der ersten Entwicklung quellenmässig dargestellet*, 2nd edn. (Mainz: Kirchheim, 1904–1906).

Erikson was not accepted, perhaps not even read, by many German scholars, for another reason. Psychological discourse generally had not been accepted in theology in the sixties when Erikson's book arrived on the literary scene. It then took a long time in Germany for pastoral theology to incorporate psychological concepts into its theorizing, and it took much longer for historians of Christianity to make use of psychological theories in their studies. Gerd Theissen may be one of the first German historians in this tradition.[4] As far as I can tell, church historians and theologians are still not entirely convinced of the theological legitimacy of psychological studies.

I am hopeful, however, that theological attitudes toward psychology will change and that we can think in new ways, with or without definite answers, about the questions Erik Erikson posed for us. By this I mean that we should think about how Luther's early religious socialization in his parental home shaped his later psychological and theological development in different ways, not only negatively. I will not follow Erikson in laying Luther down on the psychologist's couch. In fact, I am, as a "non-psychologist," very skeptical about using the memories documented by Luther or his followers in the same way that feelings and dreams are analyzed in long-term psychoanalysis. I adopt an approach to Luther that Erikson used, which is to see Luther as a human being who grows and develops as others do.

Luther was not only the hero of a struggle against Rome and a discoverer of theological truths. He was someone who had both a childhood and a period of youth when the world was first introduced to him by his parents. A less sharp systematic-theological picture emerges when Luther is studied in view of the factors shaping his early years and how these factors were stamped on his whole life.[5] In my study, I replace doctrinal precision with an exploration of a particular image connecting Luther's childhood experiences to his later theology. This focus allows me to tease out new aspects and nuances of Luther's psychological, religious, and theological development and to look at his "reformation breakthrough" in terms that are more anthropologically robust—for example, psychological, emotional, and intellectual states—than the doctrinal terms specified by the formula "justification by faith." The image I explore in this chapter is, as Erikson proposed, the "punishing God." The punishing God haunted Luther's childhood and also the later Luther's spiritual horizon and

---

4. Gerd Theissen, *Psychological Aspects of Pauline Theology*, trans. John P. Calvin (Philadelphia: Fortress Press, 1987).

5. See my own reconstruction of Luther's life and thought with this argument in mind: Volker Leppin, *Martin Luther*, Gestalten des Mittelalters und der Renaissance (Darmstadt: Wissenschaftliche Buchgesellschaft, 2006).

theology. I look at how this image is in tension with the God Luther would come to know in Christ.

Luther's Religious Education

Little is known about Luther's religious education. What we have are sparse hints in retrospections from the later Luther that we can try to piece together. I look first at Luther's relationship to his parents before turning to the particular implications this relationship had on his theology.

Luther reports that his education was harsh. Let us keep Erikson's negative evaluation of Luther's report in mind as we interpret Luther's recollections of his childhood. Luther's statement should not be read as a rejection of his father, as Erikson had understood it. Other persons besides Hans Luther were responsible for Luther's education. Luther mentions that, in addition to his father, who "whipped him so severely,"[6] his mother also once beat him "until the blood flowed" because he had stolen a mere nut.[7] We must conclude that Luther's mother and father were both severe.

Another dimension to Luther's statement softens the impact. When Luther tells the story in simple pictures, he paints a more sympathetic portrait of his father. The American Edition of Luther's Works translates the beating story as follows: "My father once whipped me so severely that I ran away from him, and he was worried that he might not win me back again."[8] I interpret Luther's reminiscence as a positive evaluation of his father. Luther admits that his father had tender feelings for his son and strove to win his love. It is a loving father, not only a harsh one, that we hear about. It is then not surprising that Veit Dietrich, Luther's companion at the Coburg Castle during the Augsburg debates of 1530, writes in a letter to Luther's wife, Katherina von Bora, that Luther broke out in tears at news of his father's death.[9] More tenderness, less fear and harshness, should help us relativize Erikson's negative judgment of the father-son relationship.

Objections to Erikson's interpretation give the impression that the harsh manner in which Luther was treated by his parents was usual for the times. It was not. If the treatment were widespread, Luther would have had no

---

6. LW 54:156 (Table Talk no. 1559: "Severe Whipping Makes Children Resentful"; between May 20 and May 27, 1532), WATr 2:134, 5–7.
7. LW 54:234 (Table Talk no. 3566a: "Children Must Be Disciplined with Understanding"; between March 28 and May 27, 1537), WATr 3:415, 29–416, 1.
8. LW 54:156, WATr 2:134, 5–7.
9. WABr 5:379, 17–19 (supplement to no. 1595; June 19, 1530).

reason to criticize it as much as he did. The two memories of his parents cited above both employ a critical tone. Luther does not think of "beating until the blood flowed" as the normal treatment of his time. He uses these two incidents as negative examples to show how he would later want to treat his own children.

Luther hints at his religious education, like his general education, with a few snippets of information. Luther mentions in his later years that the catechism was one teaching of his childhood that he still needed to learn and repeat as an adult.[10] Does this recollection mean that Luther's parents taught him the catechism? Did his basic religious education at home consist of learning the Ten Commandments, the Creed, and the Our Father? To answer these questions, consider an incident that involved Luther's father at the occasion of Luther's celebration of his first mass. Luther was terrified throughout the entire service at Christ's real nearness to the mass. Luther then looked up and saw his new brothers in the faith ask his father why the latter had wanted to prevent his son from entering the monastery. At this point the father burst out in rage and cried, "Don't you know that it is written, 'You should honor your father and mother'?"[11] The historical significance of the father's outburst is that it was a matter of course to know the Ten Commandments. We can assume that father had taught son the catechism.

The outburst reveals other dimensions to the religious ethos of Hans Luther's home. It reflects what later Lutheranism calls "legalistic thinking." The father recalls a commandment that his son had found impossible to obey. There was no possibility for Martin to escape the legalistic verdict of "guilty."

Another and very important determining religious factor is the way Luther's father recalls the incident at Stotternheim.[12] During the thunderstorm, Luther feared death and promised Saint Anne he would enter the Augustinian order. Luther reports in a letter to Philipp Melanchthon that Hans Luther had questioned whether Martin's resolve was not just a trick

---

10. LW 54:8 (Table Talk no. 81: "What It Takes to Understand the Scriptures"; fall 1531), WATr 1:30, 26–31, 2.

11. WA 44:712, 4–5 (*Lectures on Genesis*; to Gen 48:20; 1535–45); see also LW 54:109 (Table Talk no. 623; "Father Criticizes Luther for Becoming Monk"; fall 1533), WATr 1:294, 9–12.

12. See Angelika Dörfler-Dierken, "Luther und die heilige Anna: Zum Gelübde von Stotternheim," *Luther-Jahrbuch* 64 (1997): 19–46; Leppin, *Martin Luther*, 28–34; Andreas Lindner, "Was geschah in Stotternheim? Eine problematische Geschichte und ihre problematische Rezeption," 93–100, in *Martin Luther und das monastische Erbe*, ed. Christoph Bultmann, Volker Leppin, and Andreas Lindner, Spätmittelalter, Humanismus, Reformation 39 (Tübingen: Mohr Siebeck, 2007); see also Risto Saarinen's perspective of this incident in "Luther the Urban Legend," ch. 2 of this volume.

of the devil.[13] Hans's question seems to have burned in Luther's soul. Luther
was obsessed with the devil's accusing and tempting presence throughout his
entire life. There is even another text, *The Judgment of Luther on Monastic Vows*
(1521), in which Luther casts his whole life, from childhood on, as a struggle
with the devil.[14] In the same text, Luther writes that the devil left him alone
for only one year after he had entered the monastery.[15] By this report, Luther
implies that he had experienced the full extent of the devil's temptations
before and then after his turn to the monastic life.

We can go one step further. Although the young Luther struggled constantly with the devil, another figure loomed large in Luther's spirituality. This
figure was Christ. The picture Luther paints of Christ in some key texts is as
a menacing person in his own right, not as a friendly antithesis to the devil. It
is rather difficult to understand Luther on this point. We are used to understanding Luther's reformation breakthrough as a clash with his monastic vocation. This presumed clash frames the common interpretation of Luther's "dark
ages" in the monastery that later give way to enlightenment. In this regard,
Luther research has tended to avoid the clues Luther gives about his spiritual
development. Luther alludes to a strict spirituality that does not begin with
the monastery but before. Luther even recalls that the monastic experience
helped him deal with his spiritual rigorism, even if he could not appreciate it
fully during the years in the monastery.[16] When looking back at his early experiences, Luther states in the *Commentary on Galatians* from the 1530s that he
learned from a young age to be frightened at the pronouncement of Christ's
name and to be in awe of Christ as the great judge.[17] In another text, Luther
compares his fear of Christ to the fear of the devil. The legalistic education
is transposed here into the register of Jesus Christ as judge at "asking [me]:
'how have you obeyed the Ten Commandments?' "[18] The question Luther puts
in Christ's mouth captures the entire panorama of his childhood's religion.
Christ appears as a threatening judge together with a threatening devil; both
perceptions are joined by the same duty to obey God's commandments.

It is important to note that Luther situates his fearful spirituality in his
parents' home and not in the monastery. I underline this difference because I
use it to point out a new consensus emerging around the idea of reformation.

---

13. WABr 2:385, 1–3 (no. 428; Sept. 9, 1521).
14. LW 44:299, WA 8:574, 22–25.
15. LW 44:386, WA 8:660, 31–32.
16. Luther can also claim that his monastic faith perceived Christ as a harsh judge: WA
10/3:357, 25–26 ("Sermon on Saint Michael"; on faith and works; Oct. 21, 1522).
17. WA 40/I:298, 28–30 (to Gal 2:20; 1531/1535).
18. WA 41:198, 1-2 ("Sermon on Psalm 110"; June 5, 1535).

New scholarship on Luther moves beyond the line of thinking that sees Luther's development as a rejection of the monastery catapulting him into an enlightened modernity. Rather, the newer view contextualizes Luther's theology in the spirituality of his childhood by taking seriously Luther's own portrayals of his monastic experience as spiritually restorative. The master of the novices kept trying to explain to Luther during his first few years in the monastery that the right disposition toward God was a happy, hopeful, and trusting heart—not fear.[19]

Luther's Reformation Discovery: Its Origins in Love, Not Fear

Luther's reformation development is usually cast as a sharp break. There is a quantum leap between the young Luther toddling through the darkness of medieval piety and the mature Luther who is struck by the gospel's lightning upon reading Paul's Letter to the Romans. In the tower, upstairs in his study, Luther dramatically leaps to his reformation faith. Some Luther scholars, however, beginning with Heiko Oberman, have called the dramatic interpretation of a radical breakthrough into question. Oberman showed that Luther's account was shaped by a long tradition of recounting "tower-experiences" (*Turmerlebnisse*), starting with the Apostle Paul and then passed along to the middle ages, mainly by Augustine.[20] Not surprisingly, Luther, as an Augustinian monk, was familiar with this tradition and also explicitly mentions it. Critical reconstruction of Luther's biography requires taking his own recollections of a dramatic conversion with a grain of salt.

A closer look at Luther's own testimony helps determine the psychological and spiritual dimensions of the alleged breakthrough. One interesting report gives us an important insight into Luther's inner life. Along with the "Resolutions," which Luther published as lengthy commentaries to his theses against the indulgences (1518), Luther wrote a dedicational letter to Johann of Staupitz.[21] This text can easily be read together with Luther's famous testi-

---

19. LW 12:378 (*Exposition of Psalm 51*; to verse 10; 1532), WA 40/2:411, 14–412, 1; see also WATr 5:439, 35 (no. 6017; Table Talk from various years) that can be considered a report of the same event.
20. Heiko A. Oberman, " 'Iustitia Christi' und 'Iustitia Dei': Luther und die scholastischen Lehren von der Rechtfertigung," in *Der Durchbruch der reformatorischen Erkenntnis bei Luther*, ed. Bernhard Lohse (Darmstadt: Wissenschaftliche Buchgesellschaft, 1968), 424.
21. WA 1:525, 1–527, 15. A debate in Germany has focused on this text: see Berndt Hamm, "Von der Gottesliebe des Mittelalters zum Glauben Luthers: Ein Beitrag zur Bußgeschichte," *Luther-Jahrbuch* 65 (1998): 19–52; Richard Wetzel, "Staupitz und Luther," 75–87, in *Martin Luther: Probleme seiner Zeit*, ed. Volker Press and Dieter Stievermann, Spätmittelalter und

mony of 1545, the *Preface* to the complete edition of his Latin works.[22] Luther relates a kind of revelation experience in both texts (1518 and 1545), and in both cases, it is precisely one word in the Bible that offends him. The same word is subsequently lit up by a new understanding that illuminates the entire Bible, and, last but not least, Luther narrates in both cases a traversing of the boundary between heaven and earth. The later text of 1545 uses the terminology of "entering paradise," while the earlier text speaks of "a voice coming from heaven."

But does the coincidence between both texts guarantee the accuracy of the reports? That would be too convenient for scholars! Just one difference complicates an easy convergence. The word on which both reports focus is not the same. The later Luther in the 1545 *Preface* gives to twenty-first-century Lutherans what they want to hear: the Latin word *iustitia*, translated into English as righteousness.[23] The younger Luther does not cast his 1518 recollection in terms of justification. Rather, he inconveniently uses the Latin term for penance, *poenitentia*.[24]

The difference is significant because it gives two different ways of casting a fundamental shift in the understanding of God. We concentrate here particularly on the early text because it gives quite a different spin to Luther's development of the familiar view of "justification." In the earlier text, Luther recalls that it was Staupitz who had shown Luther a new way of experiencing penance. Luther's spiritual experience would be shaped from this point on by the love of God. Luther leaves out the contrasting state, the fear of God, from this 1518 report. Luther had used the term "fear" to describe his experience of God, particularly of Christ as judge. Now with the help of Staupitz, he could leave behind the terrifying image from his father's house.

If we think in images and not in doctrinal concepts, we can see this new view of Christ as the turning point of Luther's spirituality. The spiritual dimension of Luther's biography challenges Luther scholarship that construes a dramatic "reformation breakthrough" around 1520. Staupitz's advice can be dated to about 1515. Luther cannot be regarded at this early date as a Reformation

---

Frühe Neuzeit 16 (Stuttgart: Klett-Cotta, 1986); Volker Leppin, "'omnem vitam fidelium penitentiam esse voluit': Zur Aufnahme mystischer Traditionen in Luthers erster Ablaßthese," *Archiv für Reformationsgeschichte* 93 (2002): 7–25; Martin Brecht, "Luthers neues Verständnis der Buße und die reformatorische Entdeckung," *Zeitschrift fuer Theologie und Kirche* 101 (2004): 281–91.
22. LW 34:326–38 (*Preface to the Complete Edition of Luther's Latin Writings*; 1545), WA 54:179, 27–28.
23. LW 34:337.
24. WA 1:525, 7.

theologian in the full sense of the word, yet this date marks the beginning of a spirituality of comfort in Christ alone. The reformation phrase *solus Christus* is appropriate here, though not yet *sola gratia*, *sola fide*, or *sola scriptura*. Luther begins a longer journey of working out in more precise ways the theological insights of *solus Christus*. The spiritual biographical shift, whether it is chalked up to the Reformation or not, must be contextualized in a monastic theology of piety, not as a shift out from monasticism, as the current consensus claims. When Luther arrives at a new image of God, he does not break abruptly with his medieval roots. Rather, he finds another way to God within the medieval constraints of penitential piety. I go one step further: Luther's spiritual biography reveals how he tries to replace the religious image of God inherited from his natural father with a new image of Christ given by his spiritual father.

Luther experienced the love of Christ that frees human beings from sin and from the duty to save themselves. The new experience did not get rid of the devil; it did not even soften the harsher contours of God. Luther had to struggle his entire life with his natural father's harsh legacy.

The Lasting Ambivalence: The Loving God Who Punishes

The glaring ambivalence between punishing God and freeing God is the distinctive characteristic of Luther's spirituality and theology. Luther cultivated both sides throughout his spiritual biography. Both sides are worked into his theology in different ways. The profound tension shapes the theological ambivalence that Luther could never resolve.

One way of working out the ambivalence is to project the harsh side onto a power other than God. A second way is to drive a wedge directly into God, either through God's actions or metaphysically.

Ambivalence and Projection

The first option—the projection of the harsh side of God onto an entirely different power—is relevant for framing the many vitriolic claims Luther makes in his later years. In Luther's worldview, there was not just one evil power outside of God but an entire array of powers: devil, Antichrist, and Jews. All three are distinguished in some way from each other but in Luther's mind are not really separated from each other either. A favorite combination of Luther's is to separate out the devil and to place Antichrist and Jews close together. While the devil seems to be part of the baggage Luther took from his parents' home, Antichrist and Jews seem to have entered Luther's worldview as a consequence of his reformation theology. Luther's anti-Jewish vitriol cannot be chalked up merely to his being a child of his times. Rather, the disastrous polemic is consistent with his theology, which is indeed a devastating claim. Luther's theology is generated from within the framework of anti-Jewish statements. But let me make this argument in a few steps.

Firstly, Luther knows only one power that works against God: the devil. Luther's father had asked if the Stotternheim experience could not be the devil's trick, and Luther looked back on his life to note that he had struggled with the devil from his youth on. For Luther, the lives of human beings stand "between God and the devil" (to allude to the famous biography of Luther by Oberman[25]). The most famous image for this in-between status is the human being as a beast of burden. Luther writes in *The Bondage of the Will* that the human has no choice. Either he is ridden by God or by the devil.[26] This image is not ever resolved. There is no hint of God's final triumph, and the devil incessantly threatens human life.

The devil is construed as a power threatening the Reformation. In this context, Luther establishes a connection to the Antichrist. Luther came to think about the Antichrist only around the time of the Leipzig disputation in 1519. When challenged by the Catholic theologian Johannes Eck, Luther acknowledged that not only the popes could err but also the councils. From this point on, Luther first cautiously, then later more forcefully, identified the papacy with the Antichrist. Luther did not construe the Antichrist as a person, as consensus at the time would have it, but following some hints of John Wycliffe, he supposed that the Antichrist was something like a system of humans suppressing other humans. If one considers Luther's polemic in the matrix of theology, religious imagery, and psychological development, then the Antichrist emerges as a powerful image threatening the very life of the church. Luther's biblical warrant was 2 Thessalonians 2:4; the counterpart to God who "takes his seat in the temple of God, declaring himself to be God" is the Antichrist at the very center of the church.

Luther's understanding of the Antichrist has enormous implications for the relationship between his psychology and his theology. Soon after having found Christ as loving and freeing God, Luther located the cause for fear in the religious dimension of his world. The object of fear was no longer heaven but the earthly representatives of God, the popes. The fear, divorced from the reformation image of God, was projected back into the church. There,

---

25. Heiko A. Oberman, *Luther: Man between God and the Devil*, trans. Eileen Walliser-Schwarzbart (New Haven: Yale University Press, 1989).
26. LW 33:65 (1525).

fear connected devil to papacy, as Luther's late and cruel tract on the papacy reveals.[27] The psychological dimension of Luther's theology cannot be any clearer. Luther traversed a path to confidence in a loving God. The former fear of God did not disappear but was reimagined in terms of the church of his day. The former threat was now projected onto the ecclesiastical powers with such a force that they took on the most violent religious imagery Luther could locate in the world. While the devil was still part of the heavenly realm, the devil's incarnation—the Antichrist—became the world's cruelest power.

There is another dire consequence of Luther's reorientation of his religious worldview. Luther construed the Antichrist according to the distinction between spirit and flesh. He cast the spiritual Antichrist as the pope, while he identified the carnal Antichrist with the "Turks." This distinction allowed Luther to give a name to the military and cultural threat from the Ottoman Empire during the sixteenth century without diminishing the negative role he had assigned to the papacy.

By far the most discussed topic of this "projection" motif, particularly since the twentieth century is Luther's understanding of Jews. There is no good reason to apologize for Luther. Although he could not personally predict what later Lutherans in the Third Reich would do with his writings, Luther was very well aware of what he did to and wrote about Jews in his own time. One need only look at the late-medieval patterns of anti-Jewish prejudices that Luther explicitly invoked to blame Jews. The common fifteenth-century reproof of sacrilege against the Eucharistic host does not appear in Luther's writings—the only late-medieval pattern that Luther did not appropriate. It is not clear from a theological perspective why this is the case. Luther did not teach that the body of Christ remained in the bread after the celebration of the Eucharist, as was the Catholic theological position. Hence, there is no theological reason why the host could be desecrated outside of the Eucharistic service.

The unsettling and dangerous aspect of Luther's theology is its intimate connection to harsh polemic against Jews. Critical questions must be asked as to whether Luther's theological framework requires an anti-Jewish perspective. One particular case in which Luther connects Jews to the Antichrist is his view of salvation history. For Luther, Jews were envoys of the devil, not really a part of the concept of the Antichrist. Whereas the Antichrist was set up as a reaction to the birth and reign of Jesus Christ, Jews, according to Luther, were enemies of Christ from the beginning of history on. Jews participated in

---

27. LW 41:263–376 (*Against the Roman Papacy, an Institution of the Devil*; 1545).

the array of powers directed against God. Insofar as Luther struggled with the devil throughout his life, so too did he connect devil, Antichrist, and Jews, as a persistent factor in his theology.

What then happened to the threatening parts of God that Luther had known since early childhood? The theological problem is particularly vexing. If God, as the Creed claims, is considered to be almighty in the robust sense that God alone effects all that happens in the world, then God cannot really have any rivals.[28] If effects can be attributed to evil powers as their causes, then all effects according to the definition of "almighty" must also be attributed to God. Luther does not solve this theological problem. The image of a battle between God and devil is too dynamic to be domesticated by a theological explanation that God controls the devil. An abstract theology could harmonize the two opposing forces, but only at the expense of disregarding the deep tension at the heart of Luther's living theology.

Ambivalence in God

The second option—the option that posits ambivalence in God—is as intriguing as it is metaphysically dangerous. Luther in some places can be read as splitting God into two parts, all the while trying to hold the two pieces together. Luther entertains two possible ways of dividing God: either in terms of God's action or in the metaphysical terms of God's essence.

Ambivalence in God's Action

Luther's pre-reformation view of the punishing God is transposed into his reformation understanding of God's action by the concept of law. Luther's whole theology and Lutheran theology would be greatly diminished if it were concentrated solely on the freeing action of God. God's word in Luther's theology is twofold. The first word about human beings is not the word that effects human freedom but the destructive word of law. In classic terms of Lutheran theology, the word of law means the accusing function of law according to Luther's reading of Paul in Romans 1:18, rather than the discrete laws that govern civil society.

Recent reflections on Luther's development have contextualized Luther's view of the law as a transformation of medieval mystical piety. Mystics often speak of the mystical process as self-renunciation; the human being is reduced to pure nothing before being filled up by Christ. Luther was very familiar

---

28. LW 21:327–28 (*The Magnificat*; to Lk 1:49; 1521), WA 7:574, 8–13, 27–34.

with mystical theology and its twofold structure of the self's destruction and reconstruction. Luther developed this mystical concept by binding the process to God's word as law and gospel. Law is intended to reduce the self's efforts at salvation to nothing, and gospel is the word of reconstructing the self on the foundation of Christ's freedom.

The concept of law, derived from the mystical action of self-renunciation, was further extended into the domain of God's agency. Law was more than a mere word. It referred to the entire sphere of God's action in the world. Luther, together with many other interpreters of Paul's first chapter in the Letter to the Romans, knew that the Gentiles were guilty for not having done the will of God in spite of God having "shown it to them" (Rom 1:19). On the basis of this passage, Luther understood the happenings in nature as more than natural occurrences. They were expressions of God's will, often a punishing will that brought catastrophe when humans failed. Stotternheim immediately comes to mind. Luther's vow to Saint Anne presupposes God as agent immediately acting in the thunderstorm. Luther's deep belief in God's agency in and through nature was configured in his reformation theology according to his doctrine of the law. Luther's reformation understanding of a freeing God was connected through the concept of law to a punishing God. The new concept of God was not completely new but integrated both destructive and constructive dimensions. The fear of God that Luther had learned in his youth did not disappear but took on a new role in God's dealings with human beings. Fear was a necessary step in the process of freedom.

Division in God's Essence

A division in God's activity is not deep enough to conceptualize the ambivalence in Luther's understanding of God. Luther casts a metaphysical division in terms of a separation between two aspects of God's own essence: the hidden God (*deus absconditus*) and the revealed God (*deus revelatus*). Much has been written about Luther's famous and compelling distinction. Important for my purpose here is the sense in Luther that the very being of God is considered to be working cruelly against the loving side of God in Christ.

The first step in Luther's articulation of the distinction between hidden and revealed God is, surprisingly, Luther's relationship with Staupitz. Luther ascribed the distinction to Staupitz, who suggested that Luther look to the revealed God for comfort instead of speculating on the hidden God. The terminal spiritual point of Luther's quest to correct the religious education of his youth was to concentrate solely on Christ without interference from a punishing God. Although Staupitz's spiritual advice should not be misconstrued as the theological positing of a destructive part to God, it does seem to sensitize the conceptual backdrop to a distinction that would later run through Luther's theology.

The destructive elements of Luther's picture of God are as terrifying for us as they were to him. The terrifying aspect rests with the fact that they cannot be rationalized. From my reflections on the images—not the doctrinal concepts—that Luther uses to portray God, we see that Luther does not cast the hidden God in terms of an image. Rather, this aspect of God is conveyed as a particular kind of "not-image." Luther cannot draw a picture of the hidden God because the hidden God is a blank void into which all the destructive parts are thrown. The question remains: Is this solution necessary to picture the other, freeing side of God?

A robust ambivalence characterizes Luther's punishing and freeing God. Images connect both sides that are sometimes disjointed from, and sometimes in intimate relation with, each other. The punishing dimension is detected in God's rivals both within and outside the church. God's punishing actions in the law are extended into all areas of life. But the split in God's own nature, mostly concealed by the revealed and freeing side of God, is testimony to the psychological and religious struggles Luther experienced from his youth.

Conclusion

The discussion of robust ambivalence in Luther does not help in making easy assessments of Luther's life and theology. Modern religiosity privileges a friendly sweet Jesus over a harsh punishing God. Even Lutherans seem to prefer the third use of the law—the laws given to believers to act in a manner corresponding to God's will—over the second use of the law, which accuses humans of their sins. But if we think through the various dimensions of a world that is far from perfect, a world that daily is plunged into violence and degradation, then we must admit that the dark sides of reality must have a place in our religious imagination.

The devil may not be the modern theologians' favorite candidate for configuring a more robust religious image of the world in relation to God, but some contemporary Christian traditions do account for the devil in their ontologies. Devil or no devil, modern theology must take seriously the question of relating the world's deep distress and demonic powers to God. It is not easy to find responsible terminology and to articulate adequate concepts for experiences of the threatening and hopeful sides of reality. The various ways Luther proposed to integrate the two sides may not stand the test of the present time, but his articulation of the problem is at least a good starting point. If God is to be honored as the "Almighty," or as the "all-determining reality," to use the term of German theologians Rudolf Bultmann and Wolfhart Pannenberg,[29] God must be conceived in relation to the reality that God determines through God's power. Luther was not afraid to wrestle with this relation, even to the point of making some dangerous claims about God and God's enemies. Our contemporary theological task is courageously and critically to take Luther's important questions one step further.

---

29. "Alles bestimmende Wirklichkeit": Rudolf Bultmann, *Glauben und Verstehen*, vol. 1, 8th edn. (Tübingen: Mohr Siebeck, 1980), 26, and Wolfhart Pannenberg, *Wissenschaftstheorie und Theologie* (Frankfurt: Suhrkamp, 1973), 304.

CHAPTER 7
Suffering and Love
— Martin Luther, Simone Weil, and the Hidden God —
Krista Duttenhaver

Few thinkers have grappled as significantly and profoundly with the stark presence of suffering in the world as Martin Luther and Simone Weil, and both view suffering as one of the most fundamental of human experiences. What is more, while both Luther and Weil acknowledge suffering's capacity to destroy and debase, they maintain that suffering possesses a certain disclosive capacity as well. In some circumstances, the experience of genuine and profound suffering may reveal certain crucial truths about God, the self, and the nature of the universe. This shared focus on human experience is at the center of their similar orientation toward suffering, and behind it lies a similar backdrop: God's hiddenness or absence. Indeed, it is no coincidence that David Tracy, in his essay "The Hidden God: The Divine Other of Liberation," brings Luther together with Weil as the proponents and expositors of a God whom Tracy calls the transgressive, hidden Other.[1] But these similarities—which make Luther and Weil apt interlocutors—are in fact the manifestations of rather different underlying structures.

My intention in this chapter is to examine the role that suffering plays for Luther and Weil, paying attention to their shared perspectives as well as their differences. By putting them into dialogue with one another, it will become

---

1. David Tracy, "The Hidden God: The Divine Other of Liberation," *Cross Currents* 46/1 (Spring 1996): 5–16.

easier to see the potential hazards inherent in their views of suffering and to develop a position that takes seriously the ubiquity and significance of suffering without underrating the damaging effects it can have. Luther and Weil represent two important and valuable approaches through which Christians can contend with both the meaning and the destructive capacity of suffering. Luther's approach permits us to criticize Weil's tendency toward an aesthetic formalization of suffering, while Weil's political mysticism of suffering helps us see the danger of Luther's existential, individualized interpretation of suffering.

Anfechtung and Affliction: The Cruciform Experience of Suffering

Luther maintains that study alone is insufficient training for one who wishes to become a theologian and a good Christian. More important than study are the three Psalms-derived rules of *oratio, meditatio,* and *tentatio.* It is the last rule, *tentatio*—or *Anfechtung,* translated variously as trial, attack, or tribulation— that Luther calls "the touchstone which teaches you not only to know and understand but also to experience how right, how true, how sweet, how lovely, how mighty, how comforting God's Word is."[2] This touchstone—something that cannot be acquired from books but only through experience—is at the center of Luther's theological anthropology. No Christian endeavor can bear fruit without prayer, meditation on Scripture, and, importantly, the experience of suffering and tribulation.

This is so, Luther explains, because only through the experience of suffering will the Christian be forced absolutely to rely upon God's word. Without such a goad, it is easy to become complacent or dependent upon facile consolations. Luther offers a caution to Christians: "For as soon as God's Word takes root and grows in you, the devil will harry you, and . . . by his assaults will teach you to seek and love God's Word."[3] According to Luther, the presence and growth of God's word within us leads inevitably to an experience of suffering. If in these circumstances we occupy ourselves with God's word, then this experience of suffering can lead us onward toward a greater love of God. In similar language, Weil writes of the suffering we experience as a result of the divine seed of grace that takes root within the soul:

---

2. LW 34:286–87 (*Preface to the Wittenberg Edition of Luther's German Writings;* 1539).
3. LW 34:287.

Over the infinity of space and time, the infinitely more infinite love of God comes to possess us . . . If we consent, God puts a little seed in us and he goes away again. From that moment, God has no more to do; neither have we, except to wait . . . It is not as easy as it seems, for the growth of the seed within us is painful. Moreover, from the very fact that we accept this growth, we cannot avoid destroying whatever gets in its way, pulling up the weeds, cutting the good grass, and unfortunately the good grass is part of our very own flesh . . . We know quite well in what likeness this [growth] is made, this tree that has grown within us . . . Something a little more frightening than a gibbet—that is the most beautiful of all trees. It was the seed of this tree that God placed within us, without our knowing what seed it was.[4]

As Weil here makes plain, grace leads unavoidably to an experience of suffering and wretchedness. Like Luther, who insists that the advent of faith may bring with it worse trials than those that afflict unbelievers,[5] Weil understands the divine gift as a disruption of the illusions we harbor concerning ourselves and the worldly things we desire.

For both Weil and Luther, then, grace has little to do with glory, success, comfort, and worldly advantage. While neither would argue that there is no place in life for consolation or triumph, both thinkers place experiential encounters with affliction at the core of their theologies. Employing a pedagogical trope, Luther writes that, when it comes to God's word, "no one can receive it from the Holy Spirit without experiencing, proving, and feeling it. In such experience, the Holy Spirit instructs us as in His own school, outside of which nothing is learned but empty words and prattle."[6] Theology, for Luther, concerns experience—and not just any experience but the

---

4. Simone Weil, *Waiting for God*, trans. Emma Craufurd (New York: Harper, 1992), 133.
5. Indeed, it is after the believer has come to know and experience God's love that the true *Anfechtung* begins: "In the experience of tribulation (*Anfechtung*), the opposition between the Word of God and the feeling of the conscience is intensified. After God reveals God's grace and mercy to the conscience through the Word and Spirit, God again hides, so that the believer is no longer aware of the mercy of God, but only of the wrath . . . In *Anfechtung*, the God who consoled the conscience with the promise of forgiveness now terrifies the conscience with the appearance of wrath." Randall C. Zachman, *The Assurance of Faith: Conscience in the Theology of Martin Luther and John Calvin* (Minneapolis: Fortress Press, 1993), 63. Weil has a similar explanation for this fact: "Saints . . . are more exposed to the devil than other people, because the genuine knowledge they possess of their wretchedness renders the light almost unbearable for them." Simone Weil, *The Notebooks of Simone Weil*, trans. Arthur Wills (London: Routledge & Kegan Paul, 1956, 1976), vol. 1, 299.
6. LW 21:299 (*The Magnificat*; 1521).

experience of suffering.[7] True understanding of God's word is something that must be acquired in the midst of trials and difficulties, or else its lessons will not enter deep within us in ways that actually change us. In similar fashion, Weil argues that it is only when we have experienced affliction ourselves that we can approach some understanding of what Christ's cross truly does. Moreover, for Weil as for Luther, the experience of suffering is connected with the experience of prayer and meditation, since all of these things lay bare for us the limits of our understanding, humility, and patience. Indeed, it comes as no surprise that, in the context of discussing prayer, meditation, and suffering, Weil and Luther both refer to Jesus' instruction on the proper way to pray in Matthew 6:5-14.[8] Prayer, meditation, and—preeminently—suffering are techniques that do violence to our self-satisfied presumption. For both Luther and Weil, this experience of suffering is cruciform: it is the experience of the cross in our own lives.

Such experiential knowledge of the cross differs from an understanding of the cross gained by other means. It alters those who have passed through it and conforms them to the cross. Luther describes his own encounters with *Anfechtungen*, encounters that brought him not *to* the cross but rather *onto* the cross with Christ: "All that remains is the stark-naked desire for help and a terrible groaning. . . . In this situation, the soul is stretched out with Christ so that all of its bones may be counted. Nor is any corner in the soul not filled with the greatest bitterness, with dread, trembling and sorrow . . . Just so the soul, at the point where it is touched by a passing eternal flood, feels and imbibes nothing except eternal punishment."[9] Luther's vivid account leaves no room for doubt that his experience of suffering changed him. He describes neither distance nor detachment from Christ's cross. The bitterness and dread of the cross have become part of him. He has been stretched out on the cross with Christ.

---

7. "The inexperienced have no clue. They cannot do theology (the true theology of the cross) but can only imagine they walk a glory road, from one pinnacle of success, victory, healing, liberation, and works to another. For Luther, the theology of the cross is strictly a matter of experience." Timothy J. Wengert, "Peace, Peace . . . Cross, Cross: Reflections on How Martin Luther Relates the Theology of the Cross to Suffering," *Theology Today* 59/2 (July 2002): 196.

8. Weil writes, "We should pray εν τω κρυφαίω, even with regard to ourselves. It is not my 'I' which prays. If a prayer takes place within me, I must hardly be aware of it. I have no other Father than He εν τω κρυφαίω." *Notebooks*, vol. 1, 173. Luther, also alluding to Matthew 6, writes, "But kneel down in your little room and pray to God with real humility and earnestness, that he through his dear Son may give you his Holy Spirit . . .": LW 34:285–86.

9. LW 31:129–30 (*Explanations of the Ninety-Five Theses*; 1518).

Weil also argues that the experience of suffering has the power to place humans on the cross with Christ: "When we hit a nail with a hammer, the whole of the shock received by the large head of the nail passes into the point without any of it being lost, although it is only a point. . . . [T]he soul, without leaving the place and the instant where the body to which it is united is situated, can cross the totality of space and time and come into the very presence of God. . . . [This] is the point of intersection of the arms of the cross."[10] For Weil as for Luther, the experience of suffering stretches the sufferer upon the cross with Christ. For both authors, the cross is the point of intersection between God's love and the suffering of humans, and its meaning is best grasped in and through an experience of suffering that conforms us to the cross.

The most prominent aspect of this cruciform experience according to Luther and Weil is the sense of abandonment and desolation it causes. Christ's cry of dereliction—"My God, my God, why have you forsaken me?" (Matt 15:34)—becomes the cry of everyone who, like Christ, has been overcome by suffering. For the believer, this is perhaps the most terrible thing of all: to find that after all God does not exist, or if God does exist then God is demonic. Both Weil and Luther attempt to work out a double-valenced approach to the transgressive or hidden God; that is, this aspect of God is made manifest at times as pure absence and at times in the guise of cruel devourer. This is the God that, as Tracy says, "is sometimes experienced as purely frightening, not tender: sometimes as an impersonal 'It' of sheer power and energy signified by such metaphors as abyss, chasm, chaos, even horror; sometimes even as a violent personal reality."[11] It is this God that appears most like the grinding, impartial mechanism of fate. Under the dominion of such a force, it matters not whether one is just or unjust, good or evil. Any sign of providence vanishes in the overwhelming experience of an impersonal necessity. Luther identifies this as a kind of divine retreat: "He hides His face and withdraws the rays of His goodness, leaving [inconstant believers] bare and in misery, their love and praise . . . at an end. They are unable to love and praise the bare, unfelt goodness that is hidden in God."[12] God's desertion denudes the world and seems to leave only misery in its wake. Weil puts it more simply still: "[H]e whom we must love is absent."[13] God has gone from the world, leaving it to the

---

10. Weil, *Waiting for God*, 134–35, 136.
11. Tracy, "The Hidden God," 10.
12. LW 21:309 (*The Magnificat*).
13. Simone Weil, *Gravity and Grace*, trans. Emma Craufurd (London: Routledge, 1995), 99.

devastating force of necessity, which mortifies and afflicts with a disinterested, relentless impunity.

But for Luther and Weil, God's withdrawal from the world does not abrogate the command to love God. The important thing is to continue loving a God who has abandoned the world to its sufferings, who has wholly disappeared into the pulverizing mechanism of the forces that govern the universe, even a God who seems to have become merciless. As Weil writes, "When you, steadfastly clinging to love, sink to the point where you can no longer suppress the cry, 'My God, my God, why have you forsaken me?' but then hold out there without ceasing to suffer, you will finally touch something that is no longer affliction and not joy either, but the pure, supra-sensual, most inward essential being common to both joy and suffering."[14] Weil represents this movement—a movement in love toward a God who by all indications has abandoned or even afflicted the sufferer—in mystical terms. For Weil, to love an absent God in the midst of affliction results in an experience that exceeds language and categories. Such an experience ends in a mode of existence that participates in joy and suffering alike but that in some manner transcends affect. Luther makes the same demand of believers: "Take note what sharp eyes the heart must have, for it is surrounded by nothing but tokens of God's anger and punishment and yet beholds and feels no punishment and anger but only kindness and grace. . . . Penetrating to Him through His wrath, His punishment, and His displeasure is like making your way through a wall of thorns, yes, through nothing but spears and swords. The crying of faith must feel in its heart that it is making contact with God."[15]

Like Weil, Luther here veers toward mysticism. The believer must acknowledge as real the experience of punishment, anger, and suffering, all the while believing only in the reality of God's kindness and grace. For Luther as for Weil, the attempt to continue loving the absent or wrathful God requires the capacity to hold these two experiences in tension: we must, as Weil enjoins, learn to attend unreservedly and lovingly to the reality of something that does not exist.[16] The sufferer must believe that suffering operates as

---

14. Simone Weil, *Das Unglück und die Gottesliebe* (Munich: Kösel, 1953), 79. As cited in Dorothee Soelle, *The Silent Cry: Mysticism and Resistance*, trans. Barbara and Martin Rumscheidt (Minneapolis: Fortress Press, 2001), 151.

15. LW 19:73–74 (*Lectures on Jonah*; to Jonah 2:2; 1526).

16. "Affliction causes God to be absent for a time, more absent than a dead man, more absent than light in the utter darkness of a cell. A kind of horror submerges the whole soul. During this absence there is nothing to love. What is terrible is that if, in this darkness where there is nothing to love, the soul ceases to love, God's absence becomes final. The soul has to go on loving in the void, or at least go on wanting to love, though it may be only with an

a point of contact with God, even while refusing to accept the consolation that such contact might offer. This act of loving God in the void (as Weil phrases it) is a part of the cruciform and christomorphic experience of human suffering. It is just what Christ does in the midst of his own cry of dereliction.

Suffering, the Self, and the God Who Devours

This injunction to love a God who seems bent on torture is disturbing in the extreme. Indeed, it appears counterintuitive or cruel: surely it is good news that lies at the center of the Christian faith? What sort of good news is it that proclaims suffering and trials as the effects—indirect or direct—of grace working within the soul? How can the God of love and mercy whom Jesus proclaims have anything to do with this God who "wants to eat our flesh"[17] or who abandons us to our suffering?

We must tread carefully here. There can be no question that the command to persist in loving God in the midst of suffering has had damaging consequences throughout Christian history for those who have lacked power or who have been forced to live in political and religious situations in which humanity, dignity, the means to survive, and even life have been denied them. Feminist theologians in particular have offered significant and persuasive critiques of Christianity's tendency to glorify suffering, arguing that this tendency—centered upon a macabre celebration of Christ's abasement on the cross—has served time and again to maintain women in positions of passivity and subordination. As Elisabeth Moltmann-Wendel notes, "'Taking up one's cross' could mean patiently tolerating a violent husband, social injustice, and other wrongs that need to be remedied."[18]

Furthermore, the claim that, regardless of status or power, all human beings possess the ego-driven desire for self-aggrandizement at the expense of others has been questioned by feminist theologians who argue that such a claim is valid only for masculine forms of sin—pride and the desire to dominate—and not for feminine forms of sin, which are far more likely to consist of illegitimate, dehumanizing self-effacement. Indeed, the claim made by Weil and Luther—namely, that we should understand our experience of suffering

infinitesimal part of itself." Simone Weil, "The Love of God and Affliction," in *The Simone Weil Reader*, ed. George Panichas (Wakefield: Moyer Bell, 1977), 442.

17. Alec Irwin, "Devoured by God: Cannibalism, Mysticism, and Ethics in Simone Weil," *Cross Currents* 51/2 (Summer 2001): 257.

18. Elisabeth Moltmann-Wendel, "Is There a Feminist Theology of the Cross?" in *The Scandal of a Crucified World: Perspectives on the Cross and Suffering*, ed. Yacob Tesfai (Maryknoll: Orbis, 1994), 87.

as a point of contact with a God who loves us—veers disturbingly near to assertions often made by many battered women that their partners only hit them out of love and that their bruises are marks that demonstrate the jealous affection of their abusers. The notion that affliction can be appropriated and employed as a tool to cut away a swollen, diseased ego leaves Weil and Luther open to serious and justifiable criticism: "While Luther and some theologians may embrace a theology of the cross because it can be *descriptive* and honest in terms of suffering in the world and God's presence therein, the symbol itself is vulnerable to being used *performatively*, enacting the suffering it describes."[19] On the whole, both Luther and Weil focus on suffering and the cross in an attempt to describe and contend with the reality of suffering in human experience. Nevertheless, one cannot deny that for both the experience of suffering also possesses a functional aspect.

Weil in particular, however, would agree with the criticisms of feminist theologians who find in the Christian tradition all too little compassion for outsiders and the oppressed. And it is, of course, an understatement to say that Luther himself is a first-rate critic when it comes to Christianity's wrong turnings and abuses of power. But curiously, neither thinker allows for an exemption for any human being under any conditions from the charge of sinful egoism. While the language Luther employs in exposing this drive for self-aggrandizement sounds more explicitly theological than Weil's language—that is, he couches this claim in terms of original sin, lustful flesh, and pride—both thinkers agree on this fundamental point: human beings are, *without exception*, caught up in a formidable striving for self-realization at the expense of others. No one is entirely or permanently immune to the lure of self-aggrandizement or the instrumentalization of fellow humans. This drive to consume others and avoid anything that brings us displeasure—in short, the ego's drive to take center stage—is precisely the thing that must be undone if grace is to have room to work within us. What is more, the working of grace within us is also precisely that thing that unseats the ego, as both Luther and Weil contend. This process nearly always involves pain and suffering, since the self does not readily yield its place.

For both thinkers, the notion that suffering necessarily accompanies the presence of grace at work in human beings follows from the notion that human beings without grace are inclined to view the world and everything in it as their own to command. The self uses others for its own purposes and refuses

---

19. Marit Trelstad, "Lavish Love: A Covenantal Ontology," in *Cross Examinations: Readings on the Meaning of the Cross Today*, ed. Marit Trelstad (Minneapolis: Fortress Press, 2006), 114.

to acknowledge this fact, choosing instead to create justifications for its harmful behaviors. For Luther, this is the consequence of original sin—the great "uncleanness or fault of our nature"[20]—and its omnipresent reality among all human beings means that human beings are unable to do anything *but* sin. This is the case not only for the powerful and the great but even among those who are seemingly without worldly power, without wealth, without the means to inflict much measurable damage on others. For as Luther observes, "The eyes of the world and of men . . . look only above them and are lifted up with pride, as it is said in Proverbs 30:13: 'There is a people whose eyes are lofty, and their eyelids lifted up on high.' This we experience every day. Everyone strives after that which is above him, after honor, power, wealth, knowledge, a life of ease, and whatever is lofty and great."[21]

It would be a romantic fallacy to believe that poverty and lack of status or prestige in themselves offer an immunity to the desire for selfish gain at others' expense. Weil agrees with Luther on this point, and opposes this universal human tendency toward egoistic self-expansion to God's own loving act of self-diminishment in the act of creation. Weil writes that: "Creation is contradiction, self-limitation, abdication . . . Hence the creation by no means involves, for God, an extension of His being . . . ; rather, by withdrawing, God enables a part of being to be 'other than God.' "[22] In creating, God abdicates power. This abdication is a gesture of love through which God allows others to exist on their own terms. Weil enjoins us to imitate God's generous and life-giving love. But she recognizes that doing so will involve suffering on the part of the self, which so often seeks the annexation and instrumentalization of others in its quest for power and privilege and so rarely cedes place to the needs of others.

Weil does not welcome this kind of suffering, nor is she quick to move past its misery in order to look for some sort of "blessing in disguise."[23] Nevertheless, many of Weil's critics are profoundly uncomfortable with the positive function of suffering in her thought. Despite Weil's realistic evaluation of the dangers and degradations present in the experience of suffering, her critics have accused her of introducing "contemplation in physical suffering [which]

---

20. LW 12:351 (*Commentary on Psalm 51*; to Ps 51:5; 1532).
21. LW 21:300 (*The Magnificat*).
22. Sylvie Courtine-Denamy, *Three Women in Dark Times: Edith Stein, Hannah Arendt, Simone Weil*, trans. G. M. Goshgarian (London: Cornell University Press, 2000), 213.
23. Indeed, Weil disapproves of the masochism that invites affliction: "It is wrong to desire affliction; it is against nature, and it is a perversion; and moreover it is the essence of affliction that it is suffered unwillingly." Simone Weil, *Gateway to God*, ed. David Raper et al. (New York: Crossroad, 1982), 88.

results in a kind of aestheticism. Affliction, Simone Weil claims, reveals [one's] essential wretchedness and thus [one's] spirituality. But is this not to confuse [one's] capacity for moral anguish with the facts of physical pain and social degradation?"[24]

There is truth in this criticism. Weil connects suffering with beauty, and considers them both capable of functioning as levers which, under certain conditions, can hoist us out of our immersion in the world of necessity and its forces. Nevertheless, it is the case that Weil's notion of attention—the element common to her treatment of the leveraging capacity of both beauty and affliction—may lead to depersonalization rather than egolessness, with the result that suffering leaves behind anonymous souls whose resignation in the face of necessity merely helps to sustain the oppressive and unjust status quo. Weil calls for the love of those who have been conformed to the cross to "stretch as widely across all space, and . . . as equally distributed in every portion of it, as is the very light of the sun. Christ has bidden us to attain to the perfection of our heavenly Father by imitating his indiscriminate bestowal of light."[25] It can be difficult to see, though, precisely how such a love, vaulted to a "higher plane" above the quotidian demands of choice and differentiation, retains the friction required for the resistance of injustice when operating on a lower, human plane.

Ironically, in her effort to grapple honestly with the experience of suffering and its effects on the human individual, and despite her lifelong commitment to solidarity with the oppressed, Weil at times seems to be unaware of the potential socio-political ramifications of her treatment of christomorphic suffering. This lack of awareness renders her open to the charge that "her attempt to purify Christian theological symbols from the element of power remains trapped in the social dialectic of domination."[26] Weil's critics are at least partly justified in their fears that Weil has evacuated the particularity, individuality, and gritty *haecceitas* that make the affliction of human beings so profoundly horrifying and immediate.

It is precisely here that Luther's treatment of the experience of suffering can serve as a helpful counterweight to Weil. Unlike Weil, Luther refrains from developing sophisticated underlying thought-structures that might be called metaphysical or cosmological. As theologian Margaret Miles expresses it: "[He] rejected the metaphysical nuances of medieval theological anthropology in order to formulate the primal situation of the human being, the

24. Susan A. Taubes, "The Absent God," *The Journal of Religion* 35/1 (Jan. 1955): 14.
25. Simone Weil, "Last Thoughts," in *The Simone Weil Reader*, 112–13.
26. Taubes, "The Absent God," 15.

confrontation of Adam by God. . . . Luther neglected to draw the careful articulations of earlier thinkers of the exact metaphysical status of the human body and its integration with the human personality because of his strong interest in a simplified anthropology that reinforced his interpretation of the justification event."[27]

For this reason, while Luther does view the cruciform experience of suffering as a "divine technique"[28] for checking the ego's prideful pretensions and prying it away from its complacent hold on the soul, he does not develop any notion of what the soul looks like after the ego has lost its hold. For Luther, there is no "after" the experience of suffering and affliction. As long as there is life, the experience of suffering endures. To speculate about what might take place subsequent to the nailing of the egoistic self to the cross—the shape of love, the manner in which justice is instantiated, the new possibilities for charity—is at best fruitless and at worst misleading.

Luther fears that speculation of this sort invariably leads the human being into a self-regarding, vicious circle at the center of which lies the question of works: Am I really behaving justly? Are my motivations for providing charity pure? Did my experience of the cross go far enough in uprooting my egotistical drives? Weil's concept of a "decreated" soul and the concomitant new possibilities for just and loving actions in the world would be foreign to Luther, for whom all attempts to see through to the other side of the cross are misguided.[29] For Luther, the believer remains permanently in the grip of suffering, in the immediacy of the experience, possessed of an ever-present awareness of sin and misery.

In part because Luther pays less attention to a developed metaphysical apparatus, no structure in his thought serves to lift the human being above the experience of affliction into a mysticism of suffering as we see in Weil. There is a kinship of sorts between Luther and Weil on the epistemological shift required to perceive God's *opus proprium* as the obverse side of the *opus alienum* (or the good and necessity in Weilian terminology). But Luther's distinction operates at the level of perception and does little to mitigate the immediacy or intransigent reality of the experience of suffering.

---

27. Margaret R. Miles, " 'The Rope Breaks When It is Tightest': Luther on the Body, Consciousness, and the Word," *Harvard Theological Review* 77/3,4 (1984): 244.
28. The term is Weil's (see *Waiting for God*, 135), but arguably suits Luther as well.
29. To be sure, it is somewhat artificial to see Weil's notion of decreation as something capable of being schematized temporally; grace's appearance is intermittent, and the process of decreation is in a sense always ongoing. Nevertheless, she pays a great deal of attention to the possible outcomes of decreation, and to the state and subsequent actions of the human being who has had such an experience.

Luther's theology of the cross—and the assurance of salvation that lies hidden beneath its manifest misery and weakness—offers the person of faith an authentic experience of grace and consolation, but this encounter with grace is necessarily fleeting. With an almost dizzying dialectical swing, Luther immediately returns the believer to an experience of suffering and despair that exceeds the one that came before it. Moreover, he discourages the sufferer from seeking meaning or purpose in the experience of suffering, since that would force the gaze inward, onto the self, instead of outward, to the cross and to the neighbor. He advises that "it would be neither good nor useful for man to know what great blessings lie hidden under such trials. Some have wanted to fathom this and have thereby done themselves much harm. Therefore, we should willingly endure the hand of God in this and in all suffering. Do not be worried; indeed, such a trial is the very best sign of God's grace and love for man."[30]

For Luther, consolation in the midst of suffering cannot be gained through speculation or introspection. It is rather a grace that God bestows or withholds as God sees fit. At most, we may interpret suffering as a sign of God's particular favor. To look for something beneath or beyond this simple precept of faith is to become mired in pointless self-absorption. Suffering certainly is not aestheticized in Luther's theology; it cannot become something for us to contemplate, since we never truly gain any distance from our experience of it. For this reason, Luther's treatment of suffering provides a helpful contrast to Weil's, which may be open to the charge that it elides the distinction between beauty and affliction, and that, in reducing the sphere of human freedom to mere acceptance of suffering or to a Stoic *amor fati*, it has succumbed to a fatalism that universalizes and flattens the human capacity to struggle with affliction.

Despair, Suffering, and Love of Neighbor

Luther's dialectical wrestling with the all-pervasive immediacy of despair and suffering shines a spotlight on the contours of individual experience. While work has been done in recent years to shift Luther's theology of suffering from an individual to a communal register, it is still the case that for Luther the "Word of God is not a general communication; it is the word that confronts a particular individual in his/her life, the Word of God 'for you.'"[31] Despite

---

30. LW 42:183–84 ("Comfort When Facing Grave Temptations"; 1521).
31. Miles, "'The Rope Breaks When It Is Tightest,'" 241.

Luther's frequent injunctions to avoid self-preoccupation and the despair that results from dwelling on one's sins, his understanding of the cruciform experience of suffering focuses intently on the individual conscience.

It is not surprising then that Luther's discussions of suffering often contend prominently with psychological suffering. Physical and social sufferings appear to be something of an afterthought for Luther. For Weil, all three kinds of sufferings must be present in order for true affliction to exist. Suffering, for Luther, "is a subjective crisis. . . . The psychological situation in which God will act to redeem is that of a highly intensified and concentrated experience of unbearable tension."[32] This unbearable experience of suffering should drive us to the cross, to seek God's "mercy amid the wrath."[33] Even when we are able to see through the wrath to God's mercy, however, we are unable to retain this perspective for long before something happens that will plunge us once more into fear and despair. This movement of oscillation, though it includes some measure of consolation and comfort, becomes itself an experience of suffering, since the individual conscience "has a natural inclination to see Christ as a judge,"[34] and such an inclination almost always leads from comfort back to despair.

Weil's schematization of suffering can offer a valuable counterpoint to Luther at precisely this point. Ironically, Luther's intense focus on the psychic, spiritual suffering of the individual—coupled with his notion that the believer remains immersed in the immediacy of the experience of suffering throughout life—can lead to just the sort of egoistic self-preoccupation that he decries. For Luther, each human being is the protagonist of her own psychodrama in which the justification event is the high point; everything outside of this event serves as a backdrop to this central occurrence. Every event in life becomes an intelligible part of the personal salvation narrative. Nothing in one's life stands outside this dramatic unfolding.

Even as Luther insists upon the need to remove—sometimes violently— the ego's desire "to ascribe to himself the name of God,"[35] there remains in much of his writing the dramatic figure of the individual who lives at the center of the cosmological battle between God and Satan, each of whom sends *Anfechtungen* in the hope of provoking a response of faith or doubt respectively. In a discussion of the different types and quantities of sufferings borne by saints and sinners, Luther writes, "Whenever you suffer, it is either because

---

32. Ibid, 243.
33. LW 19:73 (*Lectures on Jonah*).
34. Zachman, *The Assurance of Faith*, 64.
35. LW 21:329 (*The Magnificat*).

of your sins or your righteousness. Both kinds of suffering sanctify and save if you will but love them."[36] This theme—the tortured individual's struggle to believe—is present throughout Luther's writings. Even the assurance of faith cannot inoculate the believer from future experiences of doubt, suffering, and tribulation.

This differs substantially from Weil. Although she too sees sinful pride as the principal obstacle to faithful belief, there is little of individual psychodrama in her discussions of how pride is uprooted. In Weil's thought, the affliction that serves as the means for displacing the sinful ego is not visited personally— either from God or from Satan—upon the individual. Nor does it result from the individual's particular form of sinfulness or righteousness. Rather, affliction is the ineluctable outcome of the interplay of necessity's forces, and it falls like rain upon the just and unjust alike (as Weil never tires of reminding us).[37] If God—or Satan, for that matter—send suffering into our lives, they do so only in the mode of absence. Suffering is mediated through the structures of the universe and cannot be interpreted as a sign of our importance or a reflection of our status. Thus, because of her underlying cosmological structures, Weil is able to remove the focus from the individual in a way that Luther cannot. Gone is Luther's dizzying oscillation between comfort and despair; gone is the subterranean but nevertheless real sense of theatricality for the individual at the center of the grand psychodrama; gone too is the tendency to believe oneself more significant than one really is.

For Weil, the point of the ego's decreation is to allow the self to become utterly empty so that God can occupy the position once held by the self. Only then can God's love pass through us to others: "I cannot conceive the necessity for God to love me, when I feel so clearly that even with human beings affection for me can only be a mistake. But I can easily imagine that he loves that perspective of creation which can only be seen from the point where I am. But I act as a screen. I must withdraw so that he may see it . . . If I only knew how to disappear there would be a perfect union of love between God and the earth I tread, the sea I hear."[38] As Weil sees it, the decentering of the self and the capacity to love others are direct correlates. This correlation is built into the very structure of her theological anthropology and cosmology. While her mysticism of suffering enables a decreated individual a degree of self-transcendence—thereby freeing the ego from the immediacy that seductively

---

36. LW 42:140 (*Fourteen Consolations*; 1520).
37. Weil frequently quotes Matthew 5:45 ("[F]or he makes his sun rise on the evil and on the good, and sends rain on the righteous and on the unrighteous") in her writings.
38. Weil, *Gravity and Grace*, 36.

draws the spotlight back upon itself—Luther's immersion in the to-and-fro of suffering at times prevents him from envisioning "a different relation to the ego that . . . perceives the ego in terms of communal participation."[39] Only a self that has become transparent, empty, and free of self-preoccupation possesses the capacity "to love all things equally."[40] Such a self can be present in love to others in a way that Luther's perennially struggling individual cannot. Weil's emptied self begins to operate as a conduit of rather than an obstacle to God's love for created beings.

Indeed, Luther's focus on individual experience renders authentic self-forgetfulness—and the concomitant ability to relate to and love others without instrumentalizing them—exceedingly difficult. Without removing the emphasis on grace and the divine prerogative (it is always God who comes first to us), Weil nevertheless manages to avoid Luther's consuming suspicion of works-based self-justification—a suspicion that at times leads him to appear more indifferent than he really is to charitable works and solidarity with the oppressed. It is not that Weil is naïve about the potential for selfishness to mask itself in sham "selfless" intentions when it comes to good works. Indeed, she is quick to issue warnings about the impurity of most charitable exercises and the fruitlessness of such exercises to determine one's status as a true person of faith: "Those whom Christ recognized as his benefactors are those whose compassion rested upon the knowledge of affliction. The others give capriciously, irregularly, or else too regularly, or from habit imposed by training, or in conformity with social convention, or from vanity or emotional pity, or for the sake of good conscience—in a word, from self-regarding motives."[41]

One hears echoes of Luther in Weil's refusal to allow the conscience to be soothed spuriously by good works. Yet Weil recognizes the possibility—when the individual has been decreated in and through her own experience of suffering—for genuinely good actions to be performed. She writes, "Those who have not seen the face of affliction, or are not prepared to, can only approach the afflicted behind a veil of illusion or falsehood. . . . The benefactor of Christ, when he meets the afflicted man, does not feel any distance between himself and the other. He projects all his own being into him."[42] In so doing, the afflicted soul is relieved for a time of the burden of affliction and is able to enjoy a temporary respite from the experiences of torment. Weil's language in this passage makes it clear that she has in mind Jesus' words in Matthew

---

39. Soelle, *The Silent Cry*, 213.
40. Weil, *Notebooks*, vol. 1, 267.
41. Weil, *The Simone Weil Reader*, 459.
42. Ibid.

25:31-46. She alludes to this discourse to show how the decreated soul is simultaneously serving Christ (in serving the least of these as Christ himself says) and imitating Christ (in accepting suffering on behalf of others). Luther certainly enjoins Christians to engage in charitable works "freely and only for the good of one's neighbor."[43] But his intense focus on the event of justification and the dialectical experience of the individual makes it difficult for him to develop a fully-realized schema of love for the neighbor. Love for the other is of secondary importance; personal salvation takes precedence.

For Luther, of course, this kind of transcendent self-forgetfulness is not only partly undesirable but also plainly impossible—a kind of pie-in-the-sky delusion that rests upon speculation and a dangerous tendency to overvalue the works one performs. To be sure, Luther makes a connection between our imitation of Christ (in freely bearing burdens on behalf of others) and our service of Christ (in freely serving and sharing Christ's blessings with our neighbors). He explains that, because we are ourselves the beneficiaries of grace, "the good things we have from God should flow from one to the other and be common to all, so that everyone should 'put on' his neighbor and so conduct himself toward him as if he himself were in the other's place. From Christ the good things have flowed and are flowing into us. . . . From us they flow on to those who have need of them. . . . That is what Christ did for us. This is true love and the genuine rule of a Christian life."[44]

Nevertheless, Luther peremptorily reverts to an admonitory posture and sounds the familiar refrain of faith: "Enough now of freedom. As you see, it is a spiritual and true freedom and makes our hearts free."[45] Indeed, for Luther true freedom does not entail self-forgetfulness at all, even if it *does* entail the removal of selfish pride: "Freedom from the law does not mean freedom from the feeling of sin and wrath in the conscience, but rather freedom from the condemnation that the law threatens against those who feel their sins."[46] Freedom for Luther is, if anything, an intensification of self-awareness—both the awareness of suffering and of sin and the awareness of redemption and of grace.

Once again, it is the individual who can never—at least in this life—escape the dialectical tension that is Luther's hallmark: *simul iustus et peccator*. And perhaps this is Luther's greatest contribution to theology, since his understanding of the immediacy of suffering makes it impossible to escape

---

43. LW 44:299 (*The Judgment of Martin Luther on Monastic Vows*; 1521).
44. LW 31:371 (*The Freedom of a Christian*; 1520).
45. Ibid.
46. Zachman, *The Assurance of Faith*, 72.

into aestheticism, complacency, or fatalism. Weil reminds us that such a heightened self-consciousness—even a self-consciousness that opens itself to the experience of suffering—risks becoming consolatory if it locates itself at the center of a soteriology that concludes triumphantly in redemption. Weil abstains from constructing such a narrative and abstains from the comfort such a narrative might offer: "The principal effect of affliction is to force the soul to cry out 'why,' as did the Christ himself. . . . There is no reply. When one finds a comforting reply . . . one has constructed it oneself. . . . This whole universe is empty of finality."[47] In rejecting the temptation to transmute suffering into triumph and affliction into glory, Weil stands as a twentieth-century theologian of the cross who, like Luther before her, prophetically seeks to call a thing what it actually is.

---

47. Simone Weil, "The Pythagorean Doctrine," *Intimations of Immortality among the Ancient Greeks* (London: Routledge, 1987), 198.

CHAPTER 8

Luther's Hope for the World
— Responsible Christian Discourse Today —
Jacqueline A. Bussie

For those Christians with eyes to see, the twenty-first century is a newborn's face ravaged by incongruous scars. Though many global Christians hoped the birth of the new millennium might induce a much-awaited renewal and transformation, to our disappointment the new era delivered into our expectant arms unprecedented violence, terrorism, warmongering, human pain, intolerance, and political and religious divisiveness. In the midst of such human suffering and fear, perennial questions regarding hope resurface in our souls and minds with new poignancy. What should we, global Christians of the twenty-first century, hope for? Does God hope? What is the source of our hope? Is Christian hope confined to eschatology? What are hope's dangers and limits? How can responsible Christians safeguard our hope-language from obscenity and quietism?

Writing five hundred years before our own struggles of faith and life, Martin Luther wrote often of hope. He also confessed his ongoing struggle with both divine and epistemic opacity, once observing: "Our Lord God treats people too horribly. . . . Who can serve him as long as he strikes people down right and left?"[1] Luther, a theologian who expounds conflict, paradox, despair, fear, and the pain of lived experience, provides unique theological insights to

---

1. LW 54:11 (Table Talk no. 94; early Nov., 1531). The term "epistemic opacity" comes from Christine Helmer.

help believers grapple with our hope-questions. In particular, reading Luther answers how twenty-first-century Christians with a global perspective can speak, without obscenity or quietism, a word of genuine hope to the radical negativity and human suffering of our time.

Why does the world need to hear from Christians a word of hope? According to Luther, we need hope because the world is a wilderness and because God's apparent injustice causes us incomparable spiritual anguish. Luther argues that a Christian's life on earth is analogous to the lives of the early Hebrews, who had not yet entered the promised land: "As [the Hebrews] were led about in the wilderness, always still in hope, since they had not yet taken possession of the land in fact, so also we are always still led in this wilderness in hope."[2] We are in possession of the promises but not yet their fulfillment.

The existential tension we feel between God's just *eschaton* and "this present winter,"[3] as Luther calls our life on earth, is hope. The wilderness is without, but Luther reminds us it is also within: "Behold, then, what great miseries we are filled with. . . . He who does not feel this is dead, and as I have said, he who really feels it is certainly one of the disciples who wakens Jesus and says, 'Save, Lord; we are perishing.' "[4] The world is a wilderness to all who have eyes to see the desolation, ears to hear the groans, and tongues to experience the thirst. Christians must therefore walk and speak in hope.

How is the world a wilderness? The answer is obvious but by no means simple. The answer is dizzyingly myriad. Waking up in the twenty-first century to our collective memory and media depictions of past and present is much like confronting a gruesome mosaic that functions as a wall in our own house. We need to speak hope and need to hear a word of hope spoken, because this mosaic exhibits the following words: Darfur, Enron, anthrax, cancer, AIDS, Auschwitz, Hiroshima, Oklahoma City, September 11, pedophilia, separation barriers, thousands of children dead each day of simple infections and hunger, racism, sexism, nationalism, terror, apartheid, violence, earthquakes, tsunamis, Columbine, murdered monks in Myanmar, Guantanamo Bay, genocide, chronic depression, mental illness, domestic abuse, Alzheimer's, anti-Semitism, climate change, carbon footprints, Islamophobia, three million tons of oil in the sea annually, seventy-one tons of topsoil erode daily, Edith Isabel

---

2. LW 11:85 (to Ps 78:53; 1513–1515).
3. "Out of this present winter in which everything is dead and buried he [God] will make a beautiful, eternal summer and bring forth the flesh, which lies buried and decayed, far more beautiful and glorious than it ever was before": LW 51:254–55 (to 1 Thess 4:13-18; Aug. 22, 1532, "Second Sermon at the Funeral of the Elector, Duke John of Saxony").
4. LW 51:25 ("Sermon on the Fourth Sunday after the Epiphany"; to Matt 8:23-27; Feb. 1, 1517).

Rodriguez,[5] widening gaps between rich and poor, 1.2 billion people without access to clean drinking water and sanitation, 10.7 million children do not live to see their fifth birthday, more than one billion people live in abject poverty, military expenditures grossly exceeding development assistance.[6] Save, Lord, we are perishing.

Luther's Definition of Hope

In the face of this hideous and grotesque mosaic, what is hope? And how can responsible global citizens breathing in the polluted air of the twenty-first century speak our hope to the people behind this mosaic in a way that is not platitudinous, quietist, or obscene? On a preliminary level, Luther's answer to this question is exactly what we would expect of an orthodox Christian theologian.

Hope is, first and foremost for Luther, an eschatological question, which will receive a divine answer at the *eschaton*. As believers in the gospel, hearers of the good news, we hope in the end to receive redemption, resurrection of the body, and life everlasting in God's presence. We hope that our present suffering will one day cease. Luther writes, "For after all, that is the goal of our faith in Christ, of Baptism, of sermon, and of Sacrament, that we hope for a new life, that we come to Christ, that we rule eternally with Him, delivered from sin, devil, death, and every evil. . . . For what would it amount to if we had received nothing better from Him than this wretched life and if we relied on Him in vain and suffered all that devil and world can inflict on us."[7] Again in this passage, Luther is unafraid to acknowledge the wretched, opaque, wilderness-like attributes of our life on earth. In a manner that resonates with modern and even postmodern preoccupations with theodicy, Luther is very much concerned with and very honest about the ostensible injustice and "hiddenness" of God with regard to God's relationship with creation. "But under the cross which we experience, eternal life lies hidden. If it did not lie hidden, it would be the present life. Therefore we have it in hope . . . Hope means to expect life in the midst of death, and righteousness in the midst of sins."[8]

---

5. Rodriguez, ignored by staff and 911 dispatchers, died on the ER floor of an inadequately funded, now-closed Los Angeles hospital for the poor and uninsured.
6. Statistics are from the U.N. Development Report 2006–2007.
7. LW 28:60 (*Commentary on 1 Corinthians 15*; 1534).
8. LW 29:10 (*Lectures on Titus*; to Titus 1:1; 1527).

Many, including myself, would count Luther's theological honesty about
the ostensible prosperity of evil and the poverty of God's justice among his finest theological strengths. I would argue, however, that Luther can slide much
too quickly into a facile resolution to the very real challenge posed by radical
evil, to God's presumed goodness, omnipotence, and justice. In *The Bondage of
the Will* (1525), Luther explains the three lights by which evil and the problem of human suffering can be viewed: the light of nature (human rationality),
the light of grace (the divine perspective of love for creation), and the light
of glory (the reality of the *eschaton*). "By the light of nature it is an insoluble
problem how it can be just that a good man should suffer and a bad man pros-
per; but this problem is solved by the light of grace."[9] Luther then proposes his
own theodicy and refers to it as a "quick solution" to the problem of evil that
the light of grace provides. Luther argues that "this whole insoluble problem
[of God's injustice] finds a quick solution in one short sentence, namely, that
there is a life after this life, and whatever has not been punished and rewarded
here will be punished and rewarded there, since this life is nothing but an
anticipation, or rather, the beginning of the life to come."[10] For Luther, this
solution renders the perennial problem of evil both "easily settled and put
aside."

Luther's Theodicy

Luther's snappy theodicy rings hollow in the bloody cave of modern atrocities.
Set against our grisly mosaic, Luther's cavalier words of eschatological hope
become cruel platitudes. How can Christians say that the matter of human
suffering should ever be set aside, let alone *easily* settled? It may be true that
Christians believe in God's redemption and justice in the afterlife. But Luther's
quick solution of eschatological postponement fails to address neither our nor
the psalmist's lament: "How long, O Lord, will you look on?" (Ps 35:17). The
question of human suffering is not only about "when?" but about "why?" and
"how could you?"—Luther's short answer only confounds further those theologically honest enough to ask the latter two. Luther's words acknowledge
the truth of redemption but do not sufficiently confess the irascible world-
rupturing truth of human suffering.

Moreover, Luther's theodicy shuns the fact that Christians, following
Jesus, understand redemption to be proleptic, not only "not yet" but somehow also "already." Because of the cross something definitive in the world has

---

9. LW 33:293.
10. LW 33:293.

changed that is not mere sham or show. Luther, usually unafraid to embrace paradox, fails in this passage to address the "already." He fails to express any desire to combat social injustice and to heed the persistent biblical injunction to care for the poor, the widow, and the oppressed. Luther's quietist solution is akin to saying to an orphaned Sudanese refugee or to any of the world's poorest: "Rest assured, in the next life your oppressors and the world's richest people will lose everything too. Just wait to die in order for God's justice to kick in at last." Does anyone think it appropriate for wealthy nations to say to developing nations, "Believe that God loves you, because in the next life our roles will be reversed"? Such bizarre claims portray God not as one who loves the redemption and equality of all but as one who conceives of justice as a retributive hourglass. No matter which end of the hourglass is up, God appears to accept or even savor the reality of untold numbers of people lost in their own languishing.

I am not the first to shoot holes in this theodicy of eschatological retribution, holes that bleed quietism and opiates intoxicating us to accept the status quo—two characteristics for which Luther's own thought is criticized. My colloquial translations reveal the pastoral failure of Luther's discourse. While such theodicies undoubtedly still persist in the twenty-first century, they fail to satisfy the sufferer just as they failed to satisfy the likes of Job, Ecclesiastes, and the Psalmist, to name only a few.

As a biblical rebuttal to Luther's theodicy, we need only remember that even YHWH referred to Job's friends, who found strength and recourse in these exact same claims, as those who "have not spoken of me what is right, as my servant Job has" (Job 42:7). We must acknowledge that such theodicies too often are the luxurious rational thought experiments of those who are not presently suffering, victimized, or dead. Only survivors do theodicy, though we often forget this fact. Are the non-survivors, the already dead, according to Luther's line of reasoning the only ones tasting God's justice? The so-called "light of grace" seems like it is anything but grace. Or if it is such a free gift given in love, it is one that many among us would rather return unopened. Luther's theological sleight-of-hand legitimizes suffering. It allows us to exonerate ourselves of the guilt or shame caused by our complicity with present injustice. Thus Luther inadvertently forecloses the possibility of repentance. Twenty-first-century Christian discourse on hope must be both *coram deo* and *coram hominibus*. It must take into consideration the reality of the cross that exemplifies the reality of radical negativity as well as the radical imminence of redemption. Like Luther's *simul iustus et peccator*, Christian hope must speak at the same time of calamity and redemption without slighting either. "Rejoice in your hope, because you can surely be sad over the things that are seen and are past, while rejoicing over future and unseen things."[11]

Hope Is Communal

When we speak of hope in the twenty-first century, we should remember that we hope with, and not for, others. For us to ascribe meaning to our own suffering is one thing. To assign it to another is something else entirely. The same goes for hope. Hope in the global context means that we must ask other communities what *they* hope for. We must listen to their narratives to hear the answer. Christian hope is not a passive redemption that happens *to* us but an active redemption that happens *with* us and *through* us.

In Luther's writings, hope is paradoxically conceived as both prevenient and an act of human volition.[12] At times Luther asserts that authentic hope comes only from God, which for Luther is a great comfort because the world's misery tends to beat hope out of us. "Nothing has exhausted me so much as sorrow, especially at night."[13] In other writings, I would argue, Luther gives us a means for addressing the concerns raised with his *Bondage of the Will* theodicy. In other words, as is so often true to the delight of Luther scholars, we can use Luther to critique Luther on this issue. Luther takes human suffering seriously when he acknowledges that sometimes negativity eclipses promise and we are no longer able to hope for ourselves. "Therefore the 'God of hope' is the same as the God of those who hope. . . . And in short He is the 'God of hope' because He is the one who bestows hope. He is that even more because hope alone worships Him."[14]

Hope Is a Struggle

Nonetheless, Luther acknowledges that hope is a struggle. Hoping in a hidden God, a *sub contrario* God, is no easy task. "Hence it is a great power of the Holy Spirit to trust the grace of God and to hope that God is gracious and favorably disposed. Nor can this confidence be preserved without the most bitter struggles, aroused in our flesh by our daily occasions for trouble and sadness."[15] Here, hope is likened to trust and confidence, and Luther makes a claim that

---

11. LW 25:106 (*Lectures on Romans*; to Rom 12:6; 1515–1517).
12. Luther refers to hope as a choice in LW 15:146 (*Notes on Ecclesiastes*; to Eccl 9:4; 1526).
13. Quoted in James M. Kittelson, *Luther the Reformer* (Minneapolis: Fortress Press, 1986), 285.
14. LW 25:517 (to Rom 15:13).
15. LW 12:376 (*Commentary on Psalm 51*; to Ps 51:9; 1532).

might surprise many. In this passage, Luther relegates God's grace—including God's forgiveness and mercy—to the domain of hope. Thus we hope for and do not presume sure knowledge of God's grace. Even though the Scriptures speak of divine grace unambiguously, human experience must also be taken into account. In this world, the hiddenness of God eclipses our certainty in the fulfillment of God's promises.

In the midst of radical evil, which often hides God's face from us, hope is often the only thin, frayed cord that binds us to God in relationship. Luther describes it this way: "They [the faithful] at least retain an unformed faith and also hope in some way, and thus like a last thread they still cling to Him as long as they are in this life."[16] In an exposition of the Psalms, Luther's favorite biblical book, Luther poignantly explains: "When He speaks to them [his followers], they will hear Him perfectly. That will happen 'then,' however, not now, as we hope, to whom every delay under the cross seems long. We therefore wish that God would speak now, but He does not will to do so. He wills to speak then, namely, when we, almost despairing, decide that He will keep silence forever."[17] When Luther interprets the Psalms, we find no facile theodicies, because the text demands him to address the cry of "how long" and not just the "when." And while Luther does promise that God eventually will speak, he offers us no reason for God's painful deferment.

Hope Addresses Concrete Suffering

Living in that tension, characterized by what Cornel West has termed "revolutionary patience," is the life of hope, properly understood, and Luther confesses its grievousness. "To us indeed, who are suffering in the meantime, the wrath seems to be delayed a long time and to be very slow. For a hope which is slow in coming afflicts the heart."[18] Theology must be informed by more than just Scripture; theology must be informed also by life. Luther's is an experiential theology that seeks to speak of the two simultaneously even if they cannot now be reconciled. In this way, he speaks to twenty-first-century Christians seeking a mad reconciliation between the gospel and CNN. Luther concludes: "In the midst of a feeling of death, he [David] acquired a hope in life. . . . We are taught . . . to hope for life and grace amid death and the wrath of God. This theology must be learned through experience."[19]

---

16. LW 10:435 (*First Lectures on the Psalms*; to Ps 74:2; 1513–1515).
17. LW 12:31 (*Commentary on Psalm 2*; to Ps 2:5; 1532).
18. LW 12:91 (to Ps 2:12).
19. LW 12:406 (to Ps 51:17; 1532).

Again in the poignant devotional piece, "Comfort for Women Who Have
Had a Miscarriage" (1542), Luther departs from the classic retributive theodicy and reassures the mother that the loss was neither her fault nor a punishment from God for sin. In this pastoral response, Luther again abandons the
when-question of eschatology and focuses on the more immediate why-ques-
tion of grief. In response to the aggrieved mother's "why" regarding the child's
failed birth and hence unrealized baptism, Luther offers the following words
of solace: "It is true that a Christian in deepest despair does not dare to name,
wish, or hope for the help (as it seems to him) which he would wholeheartedly and gladly purchase with his own life were that possible, and in doing so
thus find comfort. However, the words of Paul, Romans 8 [:26-27], properly
apply here: 'Likewise the Spirit helps us in our weakness; for we do not know
how to pray as we ought (that is, as was said above, we dare not express our
wishes), rather the Spirit himself intercedes for us mightily with sighs too
deep for words.'"[20] Luther concludes this section with the remarkable claim
that when we feel most hopeless, often our tears and our silence are all the
hope we have to proffer God.

> Whatever he [the Christian] sincerely prays for, especially in the unex-
> pressed yearning of his heart, becomes a great, unbearable cry in God's
> ears. God must listen, as he did to Moses, Exodus 14 [:15], "Why do you
> cry to me?" even though Moses couldn't whisper, so great was his anxiety
> and trembling in the terrible troubles that beset him. His sighs and the
> deep cry of his heart divided the Red Sea and dried it up, led the children
> of Israel across, and drowned Pharaoh with all his army, etc. This and even
> more can be accomplished by a true, spiritual longing. Even Moses did
> not know how or for what he should pray—not knowing how the deliv-
> erance would be accomplished—but his cry came from his heart.[21]

Here we notice a substantive difference with the quick-solution theodicy
Luther offers in *The Bondage of the Will*. At last we discover words of comfort,
which could be spoken while staring without blinking into the face of our
twenty-first-century mosaic of human pain. According to Luther in this passage, hope is not found in eschatological postponement of justice but instead
in our very own heartache, tears, and groans, signifying an implicit hope that
God is imminent and present with eyes and ears wide open to see and hear
them.

---

20. LW 43:248.
21. LW 43:248.

Hope Evokes Change

Astonishingly, note above that Luther credits Moses's hope, in the form of his sighs and heart-cry, with accomplishing the dividing of the Red Sea. In an unexpected hermeneutical twist, this passage in effect argues that without Moses's cries, evil might have triumphed. Luther echoes this same thought in the *Explanations of the Ninety-Five Theses* (1518), where he states: "So those who have such temptations in this life do not know whether to hope or despair. Indeed, they appear to despair with only a groan for help remaining. By this sign, others, but not they, know that they still have hope. But I am not going to speak more extensively about this matter which is really most abstruse."[22] Luther could have continued his thought here to the logical outcome of social activism, but at least he gets us started on this road by claiming that sincere hope, in the form of a "true spiritual longing," changes the outcomes of history.

Luther correlates hope with activism in the form of charity in thesis 24 of the *Disputation against Scholastic Theology* (1517): "For hope is not contrary to charity, which seeks and desires only that which is of God."[23] Given that God desires justice, surely our hope should also bear the fruit of working to overcome systemic injustice in the world. Luther's most powerful statement of this activist facet of hope occurs in his lectures on the Psalms, where he writes: "So also no one can love (according to the spirit) worthily, except one who takes on the attitude of the Lord Jesus, that is, one who thinks as follows. If he were the highest, noblest, richest, most powerful, and filled with the greatest love, he would give himself over into every evil and death for his enemy or the most loathsome criminal. The more earnestly you do this, the more you will understand the love of Christ."[24] We must push Luther here beyond his own boundaries. But he has planted the seeds for our own contemporary commitment to social activism on behalf of the marginalized.

Just as we are changed by God's hope for us and for the world, Luther claims that our hope changes God, even when our hope is as inchoate as Moses's, as formless as a tear slipping down a child's cheek. And that is not all. Luther argues that though we hope that our hope will change the world, we are certain that our hope changes ourselves. In his interpretation of Romans, Luther notes, "It happens that the thing hoped for and the person hoping become one through the tenseness of the hoping, as blessed Augustine says:

---

22. LW 31:131.
23. LW 31:10.
24. LW 10:374 (to Ps 69:16).

'The soul is more where it loves than where it lives.' "[25] By implication, if we hope for justice, peace, and human flourishing, we become one with these longings. This means not only that they become a part of our identity, and in this we share in God's identity, but also that we strive without ceasing to realize these ideals in the world. The delay in their coming should make us love these things more, not less. Luther continues: "In general potentiality and its object become one. . . . Thus hope changes the one who hopes into what is hoped for, but what is hoped for does not appear. Therefore hope transfers him into the unknown, the hidden, and the dark shadows, so that he does not even know what he hopes for, and yet he knows what he does not hope for."[26]

Hope Is Contrarational

In this passage, Luther makes two important statements that beg for theological analysis. First, Luther argues that hope is contrarational, meaning "excruciating in its incongruity with the present reality."[27] For Christians, as we know from Paul in Romans, we are to hope against hope. Luther interprets Paul thus: "And this beautifully suggests the difference between the hope of people generally and the hope of Christians. For the hope of people in general is not contrary to hope but according to hope, that is, what can reasonably be expected to happen."[28] Christians do not hope according to what reasonably can be expected to happen. Here again, Luther takes seriously the grotesque reality of human suffering. Without the promises of God, who could possibly look at this world and expect redemption? Luther makes clear the both-and character of hope. Both the world is filled with inexplicable suffering and the world is filled with inexplicable grace. God appears both forcefully present and at times excruciatingly absent. God is love and life is horror; the Christian life is a curious admixture of terror and triumph, embrace and absence, laughter and loss.[29] "We have to learn that a Christian should walk in the midst of death . . . in the midst of the devil's teeth and of hell, and yet should keep the Word of grace. . . . We believe that God is favorably disposed to us even when we seem to ourselves to be forsaken."[30]

---

25. LW 25:364 (to Rom 16:24).
26. LW 25:364.
27. The term "contrarationality" comes from Miguel de Unamono, *Tragic Sense of Life* (New York: Dover, 1954).
28. LW 25:283 (to Rom 4:18).
29. For a more in-depth discussion, see Jacqueline A. Bussie, *The Laughter of the Oppressed* (New York: T & T Clark, 2007).
30. LW 12:405 (to Ps 51:17; 1532).

Hope Is Apophatic

Second, Luther makes the fascinating insinuation that even when we are so defeated by life's mosaic of pain that we do not even know what to hope for, and thus feel hopeless, it is enough in God's eyes to know what we do not hope for. Just as a tear of a mother who has miscarried might appeal to God's sense of justice, an angry apophatic prayer also might become an "unbearable great cry in God's ears." Luther says here to twenty-first-century readers that when you feel you have lost all hope, consider this: your hopelessness paradoxically still implies all for which you still so desperately yearn and hope.

Perhaps this is what Luther (and Paul) mean when they make the strange assertion that suffering produces hope (cf. Rom 4:18). Luther introduces us to the idea of what we might call apophatic hope. Just to know what you do *not* hope for in such situations is enough. In the face of radical negativity, are we not often reduced to just knowing what we do not hope for? If you do not hope for destruction, decay, death, and despair, then in your heart of hearts you really love the opposites of these even more fervently—life, justice, presence, and flourishing, even if your pain is so great that this flip-side of your not-hoping cannot be spoken. Maybe the best we can do is to hope for hope. Not only God but hope too resides *sub contrario*, hiding as it does under its opposites: despair and lament. This is what Luther means when he relates, "It is in sorrow, when we are closest to despair, that hope rises the highest."[31] Luther reinterprets sorrow and yearning to be a counterintuitive manifestation of hope, a sign of a summons for God to at last be truly God.

Hope Is Deeply Theological and Deeply Personal

We observe that *The Bondage of the Will* is riddled with Luther's retributive eschatological theology, which borders on contempt for our life in this world. Yet when Luther dons his pastoral hat rather than his apologetic academic one, he avoids such a specious response to life's glaring injustices. Luther unabashedly acknowledges life's often ludicrous wretchedness in his sermons and devotional writings, though he holds out hope of the resurrection in the midst of such human suffering.[32] In these writings as well as in Luther's interpretation of the Psalms, the resurrection is not a "quick solution"; it is longing and lament, and we wait in hope, not in rationality.[33] To be sure, I often won-

---

31. LW 12:220 (to Ps 45:4; 1532).
32. As noted, see especially Luther's "Second Sermon at the Funeral of the Elector, Duke John of Saxony," in LW 51:243–55; and the devotional writing, "Comfort for Women Who Have Had a Miscarriage," in LW 43:247–50.
33. See especially all of LW 12, *Selected Psalms* (1532).

der when reading Luther if he believes in the comfort of apocalyptic justice, or if he just says it because he wants to believe it, preaching it aloud out of evangelical duty and also because to say it enough times is a way of coming to believe it himself. Luther confesses the disjunction to colleagues as recorded in the Table Talk: "But I preach to others what I don't do myself."[34] Perhaps Luther himself is the intended audience for his own sermons.

We can learn much then from Luther the person and pastoral theologian in juxtaposition with Luther the academic theologian. If Luther the man truly did believe in his own theodicy, would his fits of *Anfechtung* not have ceased or never occurred? Does Luther not find the phrase "the righteousness of God" the most disturbing of all scriptural phrases, because God's hiddenness in the world screams into our ears with a deafening, soul-piercing silence? Yet aren't the *Anfechtungen* the very places within Luther where contemporary Lutherans paradoxically find comfort, because none of us who allow human suffering to move us are a stranger to them? Christians in the twenty-first century, when speaking of hope and redemption, must avoid the trap of *negatio negationis*, to use Meister Eckhart's term. Redemption is more than just negating the negativity, sweeping the ashes of human corpses under heaven's plush carpets. Listening to voices such as Holocaust survivor Elie Wiesel, we learn that heaven must be more than mere forgetting. Otherwise our talk of redemption alienates and wounds those who have borne a ghastly share of the gashes of history and those who urge us to remember their pain. History has shown us ad nauseam that those who are complicit in dehumanization and oppression are the very people who encourage forgetting as a form of redemption.

Hope Remembers Forward

For Luther, eschatological hope is a kind of remembering forward. Most of the time, Luther eschews any precise description of the resurrection and what eternal life will beget, honoring the Scriptures' relative imprecision on this oxymoronic memory. A notable exception to this pattern occurs when Luther interprets 1 Corinthians 15:39, and we discover his most vivid explanation of the resurrection of the body: "Then we need no longer eat, drink, sleep, walk, stand, etc., but will live without any creatural necessities. The entire body will be as pure and bright as the sun and as light as the air, and, finally, so healthy, so blissful, and filled with such heavenly, eternal joy in God that it will never hunger, thirst, grow weary, or decline. That will indeed be a far different and

---

34. LW 54:76 (no. 461: "Beware of Melancholy and Trust God"; Feb. 19, 1533).

an immeasurably more glorious image than the present one. And what we bear there will be far different from what we bear here."[35]

Luther elaborates with a poetic agricultural metaphor, reimagining the resurrection as the coming summer to our present winter:

> Thus when a person dies, he must not be regarded otherwise than as a kernel cast into the ground. If this kernel could see and feel what is happening to it, it would also be constrained to think that it is lost forever. But the husbandman would tell it a far different story. He would picture or portray it as already standing and growing there nicely, with beautiful stalk and ears. And we, too, must let ourselves be pictured thus when we are cast into the ground. We must have it impressed on us that this is a matter not of dying and decaying but of sowing and planting and that in this very act there is to be a coming forth again and a growing into a new, everlasting, and perfect life and existence. In the future we will have to learn a new speech and language when referring to death and the grave. When we die, this does not really mean death but seed sown for the coming summer.[36]

These passages are some of Luther at his best, promising redemption and promising also that Luther has heard the cries of the sorrowful and dying. The hope-discourse of twenty-first-century Christians must be characterized not by dichotomous thought and the traditional rationalist either-or but instead by a new both-and language that honors both narratives. It must preserve what Paul Tillich has termed the "in-spite-of" character of our faith and what in Luther we might call the "nevertheless" factor: "Christ always hoped. Nevertheless, these words testify that he was not altogether without grief."[37] Our hope discourse is an interrupted discourse, punctuated as it is with tears, sighs, silence, embrace, acts of accompaniment, and countless other alingual expressions of a "solidarity culture."[38]

A New Hope for Today

The problem with Christian hope in the twenty-first century is that it all too often becomes glib and platitudinous. This is particularly true in the mouths of the privileged, who fail to recognize that their own privilege and empowerment

---

35. LW 28:196 (to 1 Cor 15:48-49).
36. LW 28:177 (to 1 Cor 15:35-38).
37. LW 10:114 (to Ps 18:5).
38. The term "solidarity culture" comes from Dorothee Soelle, *On Earth as in Heaven: A Liberation Spirituality of Sharing*, trans. Marc Batko (Louisville: Westminster John Knox, 1993).

are the real sources of their hope, rather than God. This is my twenty-first-century interpretation of Luther's comment: "One who has not yet lost hope in mammon and all the world and himself cannot hope in God."[39] Many would argue hope is quixotic: a starving HIV-positive child in Ethiopia, after all, every-day hopes against hope for a piece of bread and a nourishing meal or a cure for AIDS, but as we know such hope does not now save the life of the child.

To pretend otherwise is to blaspheme against the reality of human suffering. Is hope therefore a worthless or empty enterprise, a pursuit of the rich or the Pollyannaish or the quixotic? Is hope a word that has contrary meanings depending on who is saying it? Does the assertion "I hope" mean the same if uttered by a Sudanese refugee, by Bill Gates, by Benazir Bhutto, by a diabetic child denied health care, by Mahmoud Ahmadinejad, by George Bush? Can the word's meaning be changed or sullied by the mouth that says it? What is to be done with disingenuous hope? What is our world in the twenty-first century if not a battlefield of hopes, yours against mine, ours against theirs, my nation's against others'? Luther helps us unmask the aching ambiguity of our hopes when he observes: "We were never worse than when we appeared the best."[40]

A first step to take, then, is to recognize the narcissism, ambiguity, and fear behind many of our hopes and to engage in prophetic critique of such "hope." Reading Luther has helped me understand that hope's opposite is not doubt but fear, the quintessential mood of the twenty-first century. For Luther, only God is to be feared, but arguably most of our developed world fears are grown and sown in pursuit of ideology and wealth. "For as such people love where there is no love, so they fear where there is no fear."[41] Hope and fear, Luther recognizes, exist in dialectical relationship, as twins in our spiritual womb vying for birth and shared resources. Luther admonishes, "For wherever there is hope, there is also fear and love and hatred and joy and sadness."[42]

Fear too is *sub contrario, coram hominibus*—it masquerades as hope. On the one hand, hope can be quietist, surly, childish, irascible, obstinate, and dehumanizing. It also can be liberating, flexible, mature, dialogical, and humanizing. History reveals that if left to boil in the pot unsupervised, hope distills swiftly into ideology and imperialism. All the same, a person who has moved the world closer to a just peace cannot be said to have had anything at her foundation other than hope. Despite ambiguity, hope must not be aban-

---

39. LW 10:395 (to Ps 71:1).
40. LW 28:241 (*Lectures on 1 Timothy*; 1527–1528).
41. LW 11:384 (to Ps 112:1).
42. LW 10:260 (to Ps 56:11).

doned. World-transforming hope faces the ultimate battle as it collides with the world-shattering reality of attrition. The world needs more people whose hope is not narcissistic but relational and universal, aimed at the objective life-fulfillment and flourishing of all. In an age of fear and demonization of alterity, Christians must summon the world to such capacious hope. Christian hope, grounded in love and relational lament, must jettison the fears of scarcity and security as well as the fear of failure and the label "idealistic."

For the future, we twenty-first-century Christians hope both with and against Luther. And we can use Luther's own thought to do the latter. With Luther, we hope and pray for spiritual discernment to help us distinguish in sociopolitical realms between genuine and disingenuous expressions of hope for God's justice and mercy, disingenuous expressions merely veiling ideology, materialism, and rapacious power-mongering. We hope to incarnate a hope that at long last rejects double standards, the sure hallmark of ideology donning hope's veil in order to secure a naïve bridegroom. We hope for the strength to hope for others what we hope for ourselves, which entails a willingness to share and sacrifice. In the future, we hope, in the words of Isaiah 58:12, for courage to act in such a way that one day we will be called "the repairer of the breach, the restorer of streets to live in." Against Luther, we hope to call out perverted hope, we hope to hear the cries of those whose hope is thwarted, such as that of the starving child or the refugee, whether those cries are down the street or across the globe. We then pray and hope with Luther that those groans will become an unbearable cry in both God's and our own ears, compelling us to act. We hope with Luther that, for the long run, we will not allow our fear to overcome our hope, even though we know that it sometimes will. We pray that we will overcome the disjunction between our preaching and our actions. We hope for life and grace amidst death and wrath, and pray that we will sustain both narratives over and against one another.

For what must Lutherans in particular, because of their unique heritage, hope? Lutherans of all people must recognize the slippery ease with which hope can become perversion and speciousness, as evidenced when Luther's frustrated hope that Jews would all convert to Christianity evolved into staunch anti-Judaism. Lutherans should ask why Luther did not hope that the peasants could liberate themselves from oppression and become empowered instead of impoverished. Why didn't Luther hope for more than second-class status for his wife Katherina von Bora? Lutherans must reject much of Luther, and hope while so doing that their criticisms of Luther are in keeping with the relentless prophetic social critique that Luther himself brought against authoritative religious voices in his own day. Indeed, one may even hope that in the "light of glory" Luther himself recognizes the ugliness and the parochial-ism of much of his own thinking, just as we hope by the light of grace to dis-cern the parochialism in our own present thinking—or at the very least listen when others reveal these aporias to us.

Whatever hope is, it begins in grief, blood, and terror and in the same breath, denounces these very things. Everyday we are surrounded with events that evoke hope—"already" events such as a baby's laugh, the green sprout of the spring's first daffodil, the mother with Alzheimer's who remembers a loved one's name. But our word of hope must remember the "not yet," for what preceded all of these if not a baby's tears, winter, forgetting, disease? Because of Luther, we know to call things by their right names, even when this means the absence of God where the face of God should be. Reading Luther reveals that if inauthenticity pervades our discourse about human suffering, inauthenticity likewise will taint our Christian discourse of redemption and resurrection. Twenty-first-century hope reclaims lament as its twin sister and gives her twin room enough to breathe in the crib where they lie side by side, both wakeful until the dawn.

Whenever contemporary Christians speak of the light of grace, therefore, they must also speak of the light of Darfur, abject poverty, Auschwitz, and Hiroshima. The twenty-first-century Christian word of hope takes suffering and injustice as seriously as it takes redemption. It expresses the truth about human experience, both the calamity and the joy. Luther gives us the theological resources not to eschew this paradox but instead to confront with the necessary theological honesty the lived tension induced by hope's contrarationality. Our hope yearns, bleeds, struggles, and loves in relation, not in isolation, and will continue to do so until, like Moses, we receive our deliverance. There are silence, tears, and groans within our hope because the twenty-first-century Christian word of hope is an interrupted discourse, and it listens as much to the global, interfaith hopes of others as it speaks in its own voice. This hope is vigilant, with one ear to the ground listening for narratives of injustice and the other ear to the wind listening for narratives of grace and divine mercy. Hope resists horror and insists on a vision of the "already" without which we perish. It is my prayer that twenty-first-century Christians will speak and live in such a way that hope will not remain "a mere dream with a sequel"[43] but instead will transform into a mode-of-being-in-the-world with summer consequences for ourselves and others.

---

43. "For if the resurrection is nothing and yet I believe in it, what is that but a mere dream with a sequel? If it were true . . . that this article is false and that there is nothing to a life beyond, this would constitute the greatest deception ever perpetrated on earth": LW 28:101 (*Commentary on 1 Corinthians 15*; 1534).

Part Three

Language, Emotion, and Reason

E motion and reason are key dimensions of being human. They correlate with the fundamental dispositions, voluntarism and rationalism, as two ways of being in the world and in relation to God. From medievals to moderns, emotion and reason are seen as distinct and related elements of a robust anthropology.

This section considers Luther's contributions to the West's interest in emotion and reason. Luther insisted on faith created by God as the all-determining disposition of the human being. When the self is set free by faith from the uncertain vacillating of the emotions and from the falsehoods constructed by reason, the self is truly free to love God and neighbor. Luther never tires of highlighting faith's exclusive role. Yet understanding Luther on faith requires paying attention to his descriptions of faith experiences that appeal to the language of emotion in order to capture the joy of new freedom in Christ. Luther also employs reason to explain the mechanism by which faith is created and the doctrinal apparatus of faith, such as Trinity and Christology, that explains faith's power to "raise the dead."

One way emotion and reason are conveyed to others is through language. Language was Luther's fascination. His theology of God's word is his great contribution to theology. His Bible translation is remarkably sensitive to language's capacity to describe reality. This is one of his great gifts to the Christian religion and German culture. Birgit Stolt focuses her essay on Luther's language from the perspective of the literary-linguistic discipline. By looking at Luther's translation practices, Stolt shows how deeply Luther cared about choosing specific terms to pinpoint precise emotions, particularly the emotions attached to the experience of justification. Hans-Peter Grosshans studies Luther's texts on reason in order to show that Luther considered reason, like music, to be a gift from God, indispensable for advancing communication and understanding in Luther's time as well as today.

The study of language to work out the emotive and reason-related aspects of Luther's theology takes into account the medieval tradition of the liberal arts. Luther was intellectually formed in the tradition of the *trivium*, which included rhetoric and grammar, and the *quadrivium*, which included mathematics and music. Luther's contributions to Western liturgy and hymnody speak to his appreciation for the preceding medieval tradition. Through Luther, even the famous Protestant tradition of J. S. Bach reaches back into medieval times. Paul Helmer uncovers important connections between Luther and the musicological theories of his predecessors and contemporaries and sets Luther's liturgical reforms against the backdrop of Catholic practices. One implication of this analysis is that current and ongoing reforms in Roman Catholic liturgy cannot disregard the importance of the Lutheran tradition that has preserved medieval traditions of liturgy and hymns, keeping faith with Luther's insistence on continuity. The recording included in this volume illustrates this continuity by a medieval tradition of reworking the Latin sequence, *Victimae paschali laudes*. The sequence, one of only four medieval sequences retained in the Tridentine Mass, is appropriated in Luther's hymn composition that eventually finds its way into Bach's chorale preludes.

CHAPTER 9

Luther's Faith of "the Heart"
— Experience, Emotion, and Reason —
Birgit Stolt

T he person and work of Martin Luther still provoke us today. He can seem surprisingly modern in many ways and at the same time medieval in other ways. It is impossible to label or classify him as, for example, a mystic or a humanist or a renaissance personality or a forerunner of the Enlightenment, although he has characteristics of them all. Luther was a man of immense learning. He followed the biblical advice of putting everything to the test and holding on to what was good (1 Thess 5:21), often transforming it and integrating it into his theology. In our dealings with his writings, we risk treating him as a man of our times—"What would Luther say about this issue if he lived today?" But we also risk seeing him merely as the medieval ex-monk, caught in the superstitions of his time.

The saying goes that "the truth often lies in between." This saying is, however, not entirely accurate in Luther's case: he was "both/and" rather than "in between." He was modern, for example, in his theories and practice of Bible translation—which are still very much admired—but was altogether medieval in his outlook on life and the world. A recommendation in his Table Talk on how to deal with the devil and temptation is a perfect example of his medieval outlook: "I was often pestered [by the devil] when I was imprisoned in my Patmos, high up in the fortress in the kingdom of the birds. I resisted him in faith and confronted him with this verse: God, who created man, is mine, and all things are under his feet. If you have any power over him, try it!"[1] We must never forget that five hundred years separate us from him.

Luther had an extraordinary impact on his own epoch, and his teachings continue to influence today's theology, theories, and religious practices. Luther's transhistorical significance is a major reason why Luther research must be reviewed critically from time to time. This chapter observes Luther as a linguistic-literary phenomenon. Luther's Bible translation has had an enormous global impact. Scholars today date the beginning of modern Swedish from the translation of the Luther Bible into Swedish. Its translation into Finnish by Luther's student Mikael Agricola gave the Finnish people their literary language.

Intellectus and *Affectus*

Luther's translation is distinguished from all later Bible translations by its emotional depth. I think of this intimate relation between language and emotion as Luther's "heart-felt" understanding of the biblical text. "Heart" for Luther comprises *intellectus et affectus*, reason and emotion, and this relationship will be the focus of this chapter. The rendering of emotion in distinctive language is consistent with biblical and Augustinian ideas and is also an important topic in modern thought—for example, in Martha Nussbaum's book *Upheavals of Thought*.[2] I use this evidence to offer an alternative to a common interpretation of Luther that tends to stress to a large extent the *intellectus* (reason) and misses the strong *affectus* (emotional) element in Luther's theology, Bible translation, and preaching. The chapter corrects this one-sided view by discussing the balance between *intellectus* and *affectus* in Luther's person and work.

An Ancient and Modern Issue

In March 2002, Swedish poet and literary critic Kay Glans started a journal with high cultural ambitions called *Axess*. The theme of the first issue was globalization. One article was an extensive review by Professor Inga Sanner

---

1. LW 54:279 (no. 3814: "How to Deal with Specters and Poltergeists"; April 5, 1538). Another example, among many others: "Almost every night when I wake up the devil is there and wants to dispute with me. . . . I instantly chase him away with a fart": LW 54:78 (no. 469: "Do Not Debate with Satan When Alone"; spring 1533).
2. Martha C. Nussbaum, *Upheavals of Thought: The Intelligence of Emotions* (Cambridge: Cambridge University Press, 2001).

of Martha C. Nussbaum's *Upheavals of Thought: The Intelligence of Emotions*.[3] A main concern in Nussbaum's book is the relationship between thought and emotion. Emotions have a cognitive content and are not to be seen as blind forces that turn their bearers into passive victims. Nussbaum sees emotions as intimately connected to intelligence, to the process of rational and moral deliberating, and to decision-making.

Nussbaum is not the only scholar—or the first—to hold this view. In the last few decades, theories of emotion have taken what is called a cognitivist turn.[4] A major trend in contemporary philosophical discussion of emotion is the emphasis on the rationality of emotions. This stress on the cognitive element of emotion as a reaction against earlier theories has, in turn, been criticized for over-intellectualization and neglect of bodily feeling.[5] For Nussbaum, feeling (or "affect") is mental. The current discussion of emotion contrasts with Nussbaum's position and distinguishes between bodily feelings, associated with ideas, and mental feelings, or "feelings toward."[6]

The vast amount of literature on this issue can be referred to here only in passing. My focus is on modern thinking as a bridge to Luther. The new and radical insights of Nussbaum's phrase "upheavals of thought" show remarkable affinity to Luther's ideas about the emotions. Furthermore, Luther's ideas are related to his use of language, as is evident when looking at the rhetorical traditions of his time. The key concept of Luther's religious endeavors—the "faith of the heart" (Rom 10:9, 10)—is at the center of Luther's writings on faith, his Bible translation, his teaching, and his preaching.[7] Here, we look specifically at Luther's treatment of faith and his Bible translation.

Luther translated the Bible so that everyone would be able to understand it. He was a preacher and a professor, actively engaged in daily preaching and teaching. Luther's emphasis on the importance of "the word" makes it easy to cast Lutheranism as a religion of the mind. The Catechisms, too—so intimately connected with Martin Luther's name—convey the air of a classroom.

---

3. Inga Sanner, "Filosofi som försöker tränga sig ur sitt förlegade skal," *Axess* (March 1, 2002): 45. (The journal is available in English online since 2003: http://www.axess.se/english/index.htm.)

4. John Deigh, "Cognitivism in the Theory of Emotion," *Ethics* 104 (1994): 824–54; Åsa Carlson, ed., *Philosophical Aspects on Emotions* (Stockholm: Thales, 2005).

5. Carlson, ed., *Philosophical Aspects*, 263-64; see also the section, "Rethinking Emotion," by Jane F. Thrailkill in *Affecting Fictions: Mind, Body, and Emotion in American Literary Realism* (Cambridge: Harvard University Press, 2007), 15–17.

6. Peter Goldie, *The Emotions* (Oxford: Oxford University Press 2000); see also the discussion in Carlson, ed., *Philosophical Aspects*, 267, 273.

7. See Birgit Stolt, *Martin Luthers Rhetorik des Herzens*, Uni-Taschenbücher 2141 (Tübingen: Mohr Siebeck, 2000).

Luther's followers, primarily Philipp Melanchthon, seem to have emphasized the intellectual, cognitive aspect of Luther's theology. Melanchthon, who was the leader of the Reformation movement after Luther's death, has been called *Praeceptor Germaniae*, or "Germany's Teacher." This honorary title reveals in this case a deficiency: Melanchthon was an intellectual and a learned humanist, but no priest. For him the church's primary task was teaching, and he saw no great difference between church and school. He even imagined paradise as a school with Christ as the great teacher. Unlike Luther, Melanchthon had no interest in the mystical dimensions of faith. As Bengt Hoffman puts it: "The danger in many interpretations of Luther's Reformation thought is that the inner dimension . . . recedes under the impact of attempts to render the entire evangelical faith a cognitive undertaking, a mere ordering of concepts."[8]

Luther on Language and Speech

In his *Preface on the Psalter*, Luther writes that a person without speech is like someone who is half dead.[9] Speech is the human being's most important faculty. Speech, more than any other faculty or capacity, distinguishes humans from animals. Languages have been endowed with a divine quality since the Holy Spirit used them as the word of God in the Bible. Hebrew, Greek, and Latin have been "brought from heaven" by the Holy Spirit himself and are sacred as shrine, vessel, and basket for the gospel.[10] Luther gave his mother tongue the same status as the original biblical languages by translating the Bible into German, although he did not at first want German to replace the three original languages in worship.

For Luther, speech is more powerful than the written text. It is the human voice that gives life to words or text: "Letters are dead words, oral speech is living words."[11] The voice is "the soul of the word." Today, "orality" is a rather

---

8. Bengt Hoffman, *Luther and the Mystics: A Re-Examination of Luther's Spiritual Experience and His Relationship to the Mystics* (Minneapolis: Augsburg, 1976), 158; see also Bengt Hoffman, *Theology of the Heart: The Role of Mysticism in the Theology of Martin Luther*, ed. Pearl Hoffman (Minneapolis: Kirk, 1998). Hoffman concentrates on the "feeling" side of the heart concept, while I stress the balance and interdependence between thinking and feeling in Luther's work.

9. LW 35:254, WADB 10/I:101; see Stolt, *Martin Luthers Rhetorik*, 44–45.

10. WA 15:38–39 (*To the Councilmen of All Cities in Germany That They Establish and Maintain Christian Schools*; 1524), LW 45:358–61.

11. WA 54:74, 17–18 (*Treatise on the Last Words of David*; to 2 Sam 23:3; 1543; translation B. S.), LW 15:322. (All subsequent translations from the WA are by B. S., unless otherwise indicated.)

new realm of research in linguistics.[12] Linguists agree that the sound of the living voice transmits the "feeling" of the message, the attitude and personality of the speaker, and the contact between speaker and hearer. These transmissions are important clues that help the hearer understand *how* what has been said is actually meant, whether friendly, or reproving, or sarcastic, or as a joke. Luther points out that Christ did not leave any written books to posterity. Only his spoken words are transmitted to us.[13] The written text poses to the reader the challenge of imaginatively supplying the prosody or the "melody" in interpreting the text, as well as its intonation and emphasis.

The famous Roman Jakobson (1896–1982) once illustrated the degree of meaning conveyed by intonation. He called this function of language "the so-called *emotive* or 'expressive' function." He arrived at this conclusion by conducting an experiment that he originally carried out at the Stanislavskij's Moscow Theater, and then repeated for research purposes under the auspices of the Rockefeller Foundation. In the original experiment, an actor was asked to create forty different messages out of the phrase, "this evening." In the experiment repeated under research conditions, the actor made up a list of some forty emotional situations and then made up messages for a tape recorder that corresponded to the emotional situation. Listeners correctly decoded most of the messages.[14]

Luther was far ahead of his time in recognizing that the emotions were a necessary ingredient in the process of understanding verbal messages. His Bible translation was meant to be read aloud.

Luther on Thoughts and Emotions: "The Heart"

For Luther, thought is intimately connected to emotion. The mutual connection between thought and emotion is a major presupposition of Luther's anthropology. The same idea can be found in the Bible and in Augustine's writings, as well as in the rhetorical tradition since Quintilian.[15] This classic conception of the human heart has a very wide range of meaning from thinking to feeling. Today, the metaphorical sense of "heart" is restricted to mere "feeling."

---

12. See, for example, Walter J. Ong, *Orality and Literacy: The Technologizing of the Word* (London: Routledge, 1987).
13. LW 52:205 (*Church Postil*; "The Gospel for the Festival of the Epiphany [Matt 2:1–2]"; 1522), WA I/1:17, 7–12.
14. Roman Jakobson, "Closing Statement: Linguistics and Poetics," in *Style in Language*, ed. Thomas A. Sebeok (Cambridge: MIT Press, 1960), 354–55.
15. See Stolt, *Martin Luthers Rhetorik*, 64–83.

The heart is used in the Bible to refer to the center of personality and
the seat of all human faculties: reason, understanding, willpower, memory,
decision-making, and emotions. Luther is familiar with this range of meaning, as is clear from his exposition of Psalm 51:10, which in Latin is: *Cor
mundus crea in me* ("Create in me a clean heart"). Luther writes that the
German word for heart, *Herz* (*cor*, in Latin), is a translation of a number
of Latin terms: soul (*anima*), mind (*intellectus*), will (*voluntas*), and feeling
(*affectus*).[16] In the Bible, the mind is described as inseparable from the heart's
other faculties. All human faculties are infused with the heart. A phrase often
found in the Bible is that somebody is "thinking in his heart." The reference
to "heart" is, in this case, not a metaphor for emotional thinking but can
sometimes refer to hidden thoughts that are known only to God and Christ
(Matt 9:4; Mark 7:21). The human being meets God in the heart. In his particular version of the parable of the sower, Luke says that the word is sown
in the "heart" (Luke 8:15). Augustine's writings allude to this metaphor in
Luke's parable.[17]

Luther too alludes to the heart's intimate connection between thought
and feeling in the *Preface on the Psalter*. The Psalter illustrates for us the hearts
of the saints in their prayers to God. This biblical book shows us "their very
hearts and the inmost treasure of their souls, so we can look down to the foundation and source of their words and deeds. We can look into their hearts and
see what kind of thoughts they had, how their hearts were disposed, and how
they acted in all kinds of situations, in danger and in need."[18] Talking to God
in prayer means "speaking with earnestness, open[ing] the heart and pour[ing]
out what lies at the bottom of it."[19]

Thus thoughts and feelings are closely connected, interdependent, and
stimulate each another. Luther often speaks of the "heart" as *intellectus et affectus*. An example is his interpretation of Psalm 119:10, which reads, "With my
whole heart I seek you," in the NRSV and, "With all my heart I strive to find
thee," in the NEB. Luther writes that the philosophers (or the scholastics) only
seek God with half of their hearts, since they seek only with their intellect,
not with their feeling.[20] In a commentary on Psalm 27:8-9, Luther writes that
"the heart" can seek God only by turning to him "by intellectual and emo-

16. WA 40/II:425, 17 (*Commentary on Psalm 51*; 1532). The LW translates the phrase a bit
differently, as "mind, intellect, will, affections" (LW 12:379).
17. For detailed treatment and additional references, see my "Luther on God as a Father,"
Lutheran Quarterly 8/4 (Winter 1994): 385–95, esp. 385–88.
18. LW 35:254.
19. Ibid.
20. LW 11:418 (*First Lectures on the Psalms*; 1513–1516), WA 4:282, 8–9.

tional means."[21] The heart is a key concept in Luther's writings that brings the intellect into intimate connection with the emotions.

Affectus refers to all kinds of emotions. There are warm and soft emotions (*ethos*), like joy and love, as well as strong and harsh emotions (*pathos*). Luther carefully cultivated his emotional life during his young years in the monastery. Prayer, meditation, and Bible study were important tools in educating the young monks, particularly in introducing them to the complexities of emotional life.[22] The art of rhetoric, an important subject in the late medieval school and university, also stressed the importance of the emotions. Rhetoric dealt exclusively with the methods of alternately exciting the emotions and then calming them down. For Quintilian, the author of a famous textbook for orators, rhetoric deals with many aspects of speech. Yet "it is in its power over the emotions that the life and soul of oratory is to be found," without which all else "was bare, meager, and weak."[23] Luther praised Quintilian repeatedly in his Table Talk and recommended that his students study the classic theorist of rhetoric "because he moves your heart."[24]

It is important to remember that feeling, for Luther, is never a case of sentimentality, nor is feeling to be sought for its own sake. *Affectus* is linked to *intellectus*; feeling is a way to knowledge. The heart is not only hot and passionate but also wise.

Luther's ways of thinking may seem strange to us and can cause us interpretative difficulties. Our modern separation of feeling from thinking is, perhaps, a serious impediment to understanding Luther. Intellectual faculties have, since the Enlightenment, been associated with the brain, while feeling is still located in the heart. Understanding is regarded as the sole work of the mind. Emotions are considered from our modern perspective to hinder clear reasoning. From the 1960s on, great importance was attached to the "IQ," a quotient for intelligence quantifying a series of tests varying in degrees of difficulty. Then it was shown that occasionally people with a low IQ were quite successful at a job, while people with a high IQ could make a mess of things. Today there is even talk of an EQ, an emotional quotient, as well as of a "social competence."

---

21. "Per intellectum et affectum" (WA 3:151, 5–13). The LW translation differs slightly: see LW 10:125.
22. Günther Metzger, *Gelebter Glaube: Die Formulierung reformatorischen Denkens in Luthers erster Psalmenvorlesung, dargestellt am Begriff des Affekts* (Göttingen: Vandenhoeck & Ruprecht, 1964), 60–61.
23. Quintilian, *Institutio Oratoria* 6, 2, 7, trans. H. E. Butler, Loeb Classical Library 125 (London: Heinemann, 1966).
24. WATr 2:411, 19–21 (no. 2299; between Aug. 18 and Dec. 26, 1531).

If there had been an IQ and an EQ in Luther's time, I think he would have had a high score on both tests. Luther was a person of strong feelings and had an exceptional gift for expressing them. An often-quoted Table Talk clearly illustrates the close interdependence of *intellectus* and *affectus*. Its theme is wrath (*ira*, in Latin), and it is usually used as an example of Luther's irascibility. This Table Talk is recorded in a characteristic mixture of German and Latin and can be translated as: "I can never preach, pray, or write better than when I am irate. Wrath refreshes all my blood, sharpens the mind, drives temptations away."[25] Wrath, for Luther, does not cloud the mind but actually "sharpens" it (*acuit ingenium*, in Latin).

We have one example of Luther's expression of feeling "in both soul and body." The text is a polemical pamphlet from 1541, *Against Hanswurst*. Luther defends his lord, the elector of Saxony John Frederick, against a libel that is also directed at himself. Luther describes his feelings as being provoked by wrath, using the same aggressive language characterizing the libelous text to which he is responding. Luther writes that Duke Henry (whom Luther nicknames Harry) of Braunschweig-Wolfenbüttel "curses, blasphemes, shrieks, struggles, bellows, and spits . . . just as if . . . he were possessed by a legion of devils and had to be seized and bound."[26] The next excerpt is charged to the brim with *affectus* and expresses both the intense heat of the dispute and the triumphant joy of his Christian faith's certainty:

> Speaking for myself, I am very glad that such books are written against me, for it makes me tingle with pleasure *not only in my heart but down to my knees and toes*[27] when I see that through me, poor wretched man that I am, God the Lord maddens and exasperates both the hellish and worldly princes, so that in their spite they would burst and tear themselves to pieces—while I sit under the shade of *the Creed*[28] and the Lord's Prayer, laughing at the devils and their crew as they blubber and struggle in their great fury . . . How better could I plague them? For thus I become young and vigorous, strong and gay.[29]

25. WATr 2:455, 33–35 (no. 2410a; between Jan. 10 and Jan. 22, 1532).
26. LW 41:185–86, WA 51:469, 10, 12–13.
27. The italicized phrase is translated by B. S. The LW translates the italicized phrase with "from head to toe" (LW 41:185). This translation is a worn-out colloquialism; Luther's expression is not.
28. The italicized phrase is translated by B. S. The LW mistakenly translates the Latin as "faith" (LW 41:185). For Luther the recitation of the Creed and the Our Father served as a defense, like a charm, against the devil.
29. LW 41:185, WA 51:469, 17–23, 29–30.

Luther wrote this text in 1541, when he was almost sixty years of age! Thoughts are reciprocally related to emotions, and emotions are interdependent with mind and body. Mind and body are one and belong to God as a whole. The center of the mind-body unity is the all-permeating faith of the heart.

The "Faith of the Heart"

The importance of the concept of the heart for Christian faith is wonderfully expressed in Luther's "House Sermon" (*Hauspredigt*) on the Apostles' Creed (1537). There is no belief in God without "feeling it in the heart."[30] In the third part of the sermon, which deals with the Holy Spirit, Luther refers to the heart no less than fifteen times. Just hearing and knowing is not enough: "a human being might be saved, but as long as he or she does not believe it, does not feel it, it does not exist in his or her heart. . . . A lazy, cold soul may speak with its mouth: 'I believe in God,' but it neither knows nor feels in its heart what it is saying. . . . The pope and his followers may have it in their books, but because they do not feel it in their hearts, they despise it." It is the work of the Holy Spirit, poured by God into the heart that enables the heart to grasp the gospel. Luther describes this work, which includes an active response by the hearer's heart, in a picture: "for a flame is kindled in those who hear it so that their heart says: That is most certainly true, even if I should die a hundred times over for it."[31] Receptive listening that leads to faith is an active reaction to, not a passive reception of, the work of the Holy Spirit. Luther can even speak of faith in the context of the Holy Spirit's work as the first of all "works."[32]

In his teachings on the Creed, Luther repeatedly stresses the difference between believing *that* something we have been told has happened and believing *in* God. The first kind of belief is devoid of feeling. It is more a kind of knowledge, a taking notice of a message, but is not real faith. Real faith is "not just that I believe that what is said about God is true, but that I put all my trust in him, that I make the venture and take the risk to deal with him, believing beyond doubt that what he will be toward me or do with me will be just as [the Scriptures] say."[33] Only this kind of trust is a living faith that makes a Christian.

True, living faith enters the heart and creates love and hope in it. Luther compares this kind of faith to the kind of "knowing" in Genesis 4:1: "Now [Adam] knew his wife Eve." This kind of knowing does not come about through

---

30. WA 45:12, 1–2 (Feb. 11, 1537; in Schmalcald).
31. WA 45:22, 12–13, 20–21; 23, 14–15, 10–12.
32. WA 6:206, 35–38 (*On Good Works*; 1520).
33. LW 43:24 (*Personal Prayer Book*; 1522), WA 10/2:389, 1–22 (*Betbüchlein*).

speculation or storytelling but through personal experience.[34] For Luther, the necessity of experience for true faith assumes that thinking is tied to experience in the concrete situation. The feeling of mind is intimately linked to the body in concrete experience. The result of this interconnection between both is a knowledge deeply felt in one's innermost being. This particular knowledge is an "erudition of the heart" that, to a certain extent, can be associated with mystical thinking. Bengt Hoffman has underlined that, for Luther, "the feeling component of faith did not spell emotionalism. . . . Feeling-in-faith was rather an experience of God's comforting presence."[35] However, this experience could, in turn, rouse strong emotions.

No Real Understanding without Feeling

The Latin writings sometimes articulate a more precise understanding of Luther's thoughts on knowledge and experience. Luther's exposition of the phrase *iniquitatem meam cognosco* in Psalm 51:3 ("For I know my transgressions") is a key text in this regard. Luther discusses the difference between intellectual knowing, or *cognoscere*, and experiencing, or feeling in the heart. The Hebrew term for *knowing*, Luther writes, does not mean merely considering what one has done, "as the pope teaches," but "feeling and experiencing the intolerable burden of God's wrath." The knowledge of having sinned is the feeling of sin itself. Thus Luther translates the Latin word *agnosco*, which is usually rendered with "perceive," as "feeling": "Agnosco means rightly 'feeling.'"[36] Luther explains that this knowledge—*cognitio* in Psalm 51:3—should not be only theoretical but wholly practical and felt knowledge.

This claim rings true especially for the forgiveness of sins. Luther admits he had been told and had understood intellectually that his sins were forgiven by God's grace without his own merits. Yet it was necessary for him to begin to feel it so that he could truly grasp it in some measure.[37] Luther's emphasis on feeling was the result of his experiences in the monastery. He had studied Augustine, Bonaventure, and Hugo of St. Victor, who all had stressed the importance of emotional conformity to theoretical knowledge;

---

34. WA 40/3:738, 7–20 (*Commentary on Isaiah 53*; to verse 11; 1544 [published 1550]).
35. Hoffman, *Luther and the Mystics*, 219.
36. WA 40/2:326, 10–11, 16; 328, 30–33 (*Commentary on Psalm 51*; 1532), LW 12:332–33; on this subject, see Oswald Bayer, "Oratio, Meditatio, Tentatio: Eine Besinnung auf Martin Luthers Theologieverständnis," *Luther-Jahrbuch* 55 (1988): 34–35.
37. WA 40/2:422, 3–4 (to Ps 51:8), LW 12:373; see also Stolt, *Martin Luthers Rhetorik*, 56, 182–83.

feeling deepened real and personal understanding of forgiveness.[38] Luther
makes a similar point in his "Sermon on Genesis" (1523). The correct evaluation of a text's emotional content is equally as important as the intellectual
understanding of its meaning: "You must correctly grasp the words and the
emotional content [*den Affekt*], and feel it in your heart. Those who cannot
do this are not allowed to read it."[39]

For Luther, reading and understanding the Bible involve the entire person.
No correct understanding is possible without emotional conformity that, for
Luther, is based on personal experience. The most important dimension of
translation, even of teaching, is the experience of spiritual tribulation, anguish,
doubt, and despair—what Luther calls *Anfechtung*. The well known account
in the Table Talk captures Luther's sentiment: "Yet experience alone makes
the theologian."[40] Luther makes a similar point in his exposition of Psalm 77:
"Nobody who has not experienced such compunctions and anguish of the
conscience can teach so much as one word about this psalm. . . . For no one
is able or competent to speak about parts of scripture, or listen to them with
understanding, if his emotional disposition is not in conformity with them, so
that he feels inside what he speaks or hears outside, and agrees: 'Yes, truly so
it is.' "[41] This kind of experience-based understanding takes place according to
Luther's anthropology "in the heart."

No Bible Translation without "Heart-Felt" Understanding[42]

The "heart" is also important for a Christian who is engaged in translating
the Bible. Luther regards it as a necessary tool in his *On Translating: An Open
Letter* (1530): "Ah, translating is not every man's skill. . . . It requires a right,
devout, honest, sincere, God-fearing, Christian, trained, informed, and experienced heart."[43] He illustrates his method by choosing to translate the Latin
phrase, *ex abundantia cordis os loquitur* (Matt 12:34; Luke 6:45). The literal
translation in English is: "from the abundance of the heart speaks the mouth."
Luther translated the phrase by using a familiar German saying, which in

---

38. See the chapter, "Die Konformität des Affekts als Verstehensweg," in Metzger, *Gelebter
Glaube*, 64–68.
39. WA 12:444, 7–9 ("Sermon on the First Book of Moses"; March 15, 1523).
40. LW 54:7 (no. 46: "Value of Knowledge Gained by Experience"; summer or fall 1531),
WATr 1:16, 13.
41. WA 3:549, 30–35 (*First Lectures on the Psalms*; to Ps 77:21), LW 10:37.
42. For explicit details and references, see ch. 4 of Stolt, *Martin Luthers Rhetorik*, 84–126.
43. LW 35:194, WA 30/2:640, 25–26, 27–28.

English can be rendered as: "What fills the heart, overflows the mouth."[44]
Luther's German wonderfully captures his own dizzying activity as writer,
translator, and preacher—although he might not have been aware of it at the
time.

The intense emotional undercurrent of Luther's Bible translation makes
it stand out from its modern counterparts. Today's scholars keep an objective
distance from the text as they translate the Bible according to modern scientific methods. Luther, on the other hand, kept no such distance. He had an intimate relationship with the Bible; he lived with and in the Bible. He knew large
sections of the Latin Vulgate by heart, particularly the Psalms. He favored
some texts while he cared less about other texts. When speaking of the texts
he held dear, Luther sometimes used the endearing ending, "-ichen," usually
reserved for his children—like Lenichen, Martinichen: *textichen, pselmichen,
versichen*, and so on. There are many examples of Luther's use of the diminu-
tive ending in connection with the Psalms. He writes of Psalm 17: "This is a
fine *pselmichen* [little psalm] and my *gebetlin* [little prayer]"; of Psalm 56: "This
is really a fine *pselmichen*, I love it very much." A striking example of his personal involvement with a specific biblical text is found in a Table Talk on Paul's
letter to the Galatians: "The Epistle to the Galatians is my dear little epistle;
I have entrusted myself to it. It is my Katy von Bora."[45] Love, trust, warmth,
and esteem characterize Luther's dedication to his wife and to the Bible. Both
involve a relationship of "the heart" in every sense of the word or, to use his
own expression: "a Christian, trained, informed, and experienced heart"!

Luther took great care to find appropriate and moving German equivalents in order to arouse the feelings expressed in the Bible, such as love, grief,
and particularly joy. I turn to love and then to joy in the next sections.

Love

An example of Luther's effort to render an expression of feeling in the most
moving terms are his comments on his own practice in an exposition of the
first few words of Psalm 18. He considers the first word in Latin, *diligam*, a
simple word meaning "I love." The usual translation in modern German versions is the phrase "Ich liebe dich," which is in English, "I love you." The NRSV

---

44. LW 35:189–90. The German saying is: "Wes das hertz vol ist, des gehet der mund über"
(WA 30/2:637, 32).
45. WATr 1:69, 18–19 (no. 146: "The Epistle to the Galatians"; between Dec. 14, 1531 and Jan.
22, 1532). Luther uses the endearing form "mein Epistelcha." The LW translates the original's
"mich anvertraut habe" with the less intimate English sentence: "I have put my confidence in
it" (LW 53:20).

translates accordingly: "I love you, O LORD, my strength" as does the King James Version: "I will love thee. . . ." But for Luther, this is no simple matter. He consults the Hebrew text and detects a problem: the Hebrew word for the Latin *diligam* is exclusively used in the Bible to denote God's special love for the human. A translation of this phrase must take this very special case into account. Luther's comments show how he plumbs the depths of feeling in order to find adequate synonyms in both Latin and German. I reproduce the original text: " *'Diligam': Paternabo, maternabo, filiabo te.* Ich habe dich hertz-lich lieb, wie 'bin ich dir so hold.' Er meinet *viscera*, mutter hertz. Ich habe ein hertz zu dem, Je, wie hertze ich dich."[46] It is difficult to translate Luther's remarks adequately. Luther begins by constructing Latin verbs from the Latin words for father, mother, and child. This grammatical conversion could be rendered in English as, "You are dear to me like a father/mother/child." Luther then tries out expressions in German, such as, "I hold you heartily dear," or "I am so devoted to you." Luther continues: "He means [by the term] *viscera*, a mother's heart." And then concludes with more attempts: "I have lost my heart to you," or "Oh, how I embrace you." After more experimental variations, Luther hits on the formulation: *Herzlich lieb habe ich dich*, which means, "I hold you heartily dear," although Luther inverts the two phrases (to render literally "heartily dear I hold you"), which adds emphasis to the "heart." Luther's German rendition is still used in modern German Bibles.

In another striking example, this time in *On Translation* (1530), Luther discusses his translation of the angel Gabriel's address to Mary: in Latin, *Ave Maria, gratia plena* (Luke 1:28).[47] The problematic term is the Latin *Ave*, which precipitates a discussion of the appropriate greeting in terms of the salutation in German, *liebe*, which in English means "dear" or the noun "love." The translation for Gabriel's greeting from the Latin is, "Hail, Mary, full of grace." Luther's extensive and careful discussion of the term *Ave* demonstrates his medieval, palpable concept of the angel, his humanist training of going "back to the sources," and how he is far ahead of his time in linguistics. The angel Gabriel is presented in very human terms while addressing a human being on behalf of God. The angel, Luther remarks, must have spoken Hebrew, the language of paradise. Luther finds three examples in the Book of Daniel in which Gabriel greets a person on behalf of God (Dan 9:23; 10:11, 19). These he identifies fully in accord with modern speech act analysis as

---

46. WADB 3, XLI (*Protocol of Meeting on Psalm Translation*; to Ps 18:2; 1531).
47. WA 30/2:638, 13–639, 23, LW 35:190–91. See my criticism of the LW translation in "On Translating Ave Maria as 'Hello there, Mary,'" *Lutheran Quarterly* 12/1 (Spring 1998): 105–7.

a respectful and friendly greeting. Luther decides on an appropriate translation: in this particular situation, a German would say, *Du liebe Maria*, or in
English, "You dear Mary." Luther concludes, "And this is how the angel would
have expressed himself if he would have greeted her in German." The angel
would have addressed her with the German *liebe*, because this precise word
"pierces and rings through the heart, through all the senses."[48] The word *liebe*,
for Luther, does not only have an effect on the mind but also vibrates in the
body (especially when spoken!).

Closely Connected to "Love" Is "Joy"[49]

Luther, as perhaps no other theologian of his time, stressed joy and gladness
as the predominant feeling of the human being's contact with God. "Before
God there is the place of happiness," a joy and peace of mind independent of
the external conditions of life.[50] The heart's faith creates happiness and trust.
Luther's remarks about the way he decides on specific words to translate the
Bible give insights into his translation practice and his theology. Luther takes
special care to choose words that tease out different nuances to portray his
particular relationship with God. An example of theological insight is found
in Luther's annotations to the revised translation of the Psalter (1531), specifically to Psalm 54:6: "With a freewill offering I will sacrifice to you." Luther
comments on the sacrifice David promises to God in exchange for divine
rescue from his enemies. Modern German versions uniformly stress David's
willingness to offer a sacrifice. Luther translates in such a way as to emphasize
sacrifice in terms of joy: the sacrifice is *ein Freudenopfer*, rendered in English
as "I will offer you a sacrifice of joy." Luther justifies his choice: "To offer a
sacrifice of laughter and joy, because our God likes it when we rejoice in him,
because he is so good, kind, comforting, fills the heart with joy."[51]

This passage presents an endearing image of God the Father. It contrasts
sharply with the harsh and awe-inspiring conception of God the young monk
had in the monastery. Now in the early 1530s, God fills Luther's heart with joy!
A comforting image of God in a Table Talk gives another example of Luther's
experience of God from the same time. Luther stresses the importance of his

---

48. "Daß es dringe und klinge ins Herz, durch alle Sinne": WA 30/2:639, 2, LW 35:192. For
a detailed account, see Stolt, *Martin Luthers Rhetorik*, 91–95.
49. For the following, see Stolt, *Martin Luthers Rhetorik*, 104–10.
50. "Coram deo, ubi est locus laetitiae" (cited in Metzger, *Gelebter Glaube*, 195–96). A recent
study shows that the Reformers advocated a joyful and confident approach to death and
dying: see Austra Reinis, *Reforming the Art of Dying: The ars moriendi in the German Reformation (1519–1528)*, St Andrews Studies in Reformation History (Aldershot: Ashgate, 2007).
51. WADB 3:56, 20–24.

daily prayer. Whenever the day's tasks prevent him from his morning prayer, he feels terrible all day long: "Prayer helps us very much and fills the heart with joy, not on account of any merit in the work, but because we have talked with our Lord and entrusted everything to his care."[52] The change in his "God-Father-image" is notable after Luther became a father himself and experienced the tender feelings of a father toward his children. He was amazed by the intensity and tenderness of this emotion.[53]

Significant cultural changes since Luther's times can be tracked by changes in language. Luther's favorite word for happiness and joy, *fröhlich*, denotes a less intense emotion in German usage today than it did for Luther. In Luther's time, it meant a joy that expressed itself by jumping, dancing, clapping hands, trampling of feet, and so on. In the Vulgate, it corresponds to *exultatio* ("to exult"). Adults in the Bible and in Luther's time expressed overflowing joy by leaping, dancing, and clapping hands, a behavior that today is restricted to children (with a few exceptions, mainly in the domain of sports). Luther repeatedly described great joy as "a heart hopping and dancing." The other sense of *fröhlich* is an inner joy that is not exhibited noisily or ostentatiously. This sense is rendered in the Vulgate as *laetari*, or "gladness," and it corresponds to modern German usage. Modern German Bible translations use expressions like *jubeln*, which means "jubilate" or "exult," instead of Luther's *fröhlich*, which today is too weak.

By using *fröhlich* in its modern sense, modern translations often do not convey the same emotional intensity as Luther's original. This linguistic shift has serious implications for understanding the word as it appears today; there is no indication that a change in meaning has taken place.[54] As a result, an important aspect of Luther's theology—overflowing, exultant joy—does not reach us in its abundant freshness but only in a more subdued form.

This is a serious problem, since it seems to me that the attitude of joy and thankfulness is an important part of Lutheranism and is not fully appreciated today. Luther—at least as he is portrayed in Sweden today—is altogether too harsh and stern. People seem to have forgotten a Luther who taught that a

---

52. WATr 1:49, 24–26 (no. 122: "Treatment of Melancholy, Despair, Etc."; Nov. 30, 1531). The LW translation, "found everything to be in order" (54:16), does not adequately capture the original German: "ihm alles haben [an]heim gestellt."
53. See Stolt, "Martin Luther on God as a Father," 29–31.
54. Ethnolinguistics today deals with questions of cultural differences expressed in languages. See also Stolt, "Mit fröhlichem springenden Geist: ethnolinguistische und sprachhistorische Notizen zu Ausdrücken für 'Freude' in Martin Luthers Bibelübersetzung," in *Sprache als lebendiger Kulturspiegel: Festschrift für Astrid Stedje*, ed. Martin Todtenhaupt and Ingela Valfridsson, Umeå Studies in the Humanities 119 (Umeå: Acta Universitatis Umensis, 1994), 185–93.

Christian has a duty to be glad and thankful for God's grace in Christ, while
the devil is the *spiritus tristitiae*, the evil spirit of depression and an enemy of
all true joy. "Therefore God has told us to be glad in his presence and does
not want a gloomy sacrifice, as it says so often in the Books of Moses," Luther
writes to Joachim von Anhalt in a letter of consolation. Luther continues the
letter with seven lines about the commandment of joy.[55]

Luther knew at a deep level that this joy can arise in the midst of daily
obedience to one's duties. Confidence in God and the awareness of God's loving care convey the experience of joy amidst one's "calling in life." For Luther,
knowledge of the great value of one's vocation in God's eyes, no less than
the vocation of the monks, precipitates joyful existence. He remarks on the
Fourth Commandment in his Large Catechism: "Must not your heart leap and
overflow with joy when you go to your daily tasks, and say: 'Look, this is better
than the holiness of all Carthusian monks, even if they are fasting themselves
to death and incessantly pray on their knees.'"[56] The Small Catechism gives
another example of Luther's insistence that joy characterizes daily existence.
Luther instructs the "housefather" (*Hausvater*) how to help his family and servants start a new day: first, by making the holy sign of the cross "in the name
of God the Father, Son, and Holy Spirit," then by reciting the Creed and Our
Father, and—"If you want to"—another prayer by Luther. "And thereafter go
with joy to your duties, and maybe with a song." For evening, Luther suggests
similar prayers and then "immediately go gladly to sleep."[57] Thus the whole day
is framed by cheerfulness in being aware of the dignity and blessing of one's
vocation in God's eyes.

The enjoyment of daily life in times of peace is a gift of God that should
be appreciated in gratitude. In remarks to his translation of Psalm 65:8 ("You
make the gateways of the morning and the evening shout for joy"), Luther
paints a delightful picture of the "outgoings" and "homecomings":

> "You fill with joy all who go forth and move about, both in the morn-
> ing and in the evening." That means: It is your gift, that all beings, both
> humans and animals, rise in the early morning in good peace, and every-
> one goes forth with joy to their nurture and their work. There the birds
> are singing, the beasts are lowing, servants and maids go out to the fields
> with a song. Likewise in the evening they all come home again singing

55. WABr 7:66, 11–25 (no. 2113; May 23, 1534).
56. WA 30/1:149, 32–35. The German differs slightly from the English translation (BoC, 403, 120).
57. The German, "flugs und fröhlich geschlafen" (WA 30/1:262, 21), differs slightly from the English translation (BoC, 363, 3; 364, 5).

and lowing. In short: The Psalm praises God for peace and good times. Because where peace reigns and times are good there is singing and rejoicing. . . . This is a great blessing and gift from God, the giver of all joy.[58]

The intimate connection between the experience of God, love, and "leaping and dancing joy" is a consistent theme in Luther's works. Luther's commentary on the Magnificat offers a powerful description of Mary's feelings when praising God (Luke 1:46-55): Mary, "the tender Mother of Christ," rejoices and praises God *mit fröhlichem, springendem Geist*, or "with a soul dancing for happiness at having been regarded tenderly by the Lord."[59] I quote one more important section in the English translation, but have changed the LW's terms "gladness" and "pleasure" to note more passionate expressions of joy:

> And this is the source of men's love and praise of God. For no one can praise God without first loving Him. No one can love Him unless He makes Himself known to him in the most lovable and intimate fashion. And He can make Himself known only through those works of His which He reveals in us, and which we feel and experience within ourselves. But where there is this experience, namely, that He is a God who looks into the depths and helps only the poor, despised, afflicted, miserable, forsaken, and those who are nothing, there a hearty love for Him is born. The heart overflows with joy[60] and goes leaping and dancing for the great happiness[61] it has found in God. There the Holy Spirit is present and has taught us in a moment such exceeding great knowledge and exultation[62] through this experience.[63]

"The Happy Exchange"

To conclude this chapter, I return to the question of the forgiveness of sins that is so predominant in Luther's theology. The following is a famous passage from the treatise *The Freedom of a Christian* (1520). The passage illustrates Luther's treatment of the forgiveness of sins as a matter of overflowing joy and points to the language difficulty triggered by both translation choices and changes in mentality (as mentioned above). Most translations available today follow the

---

58. WA 38:11, 1–9 (1531–1533).
59. WA 7:548, 29, 31–33. The LW translates as follows: "For since she boasts, with heart leaping for joy and praising God, that He regarded her despite her low estate and nothingness" (LW 21:301).
60. "gladness" (LW 21:300, WA 7:548, 8–9).
61. "pleasure" (LW 21:300, WA 7:548, 9).
62. "gladness" (LW 21:300, WA 7:548, 11).
63. WA 7, 528, 1–11.

Latin version, written for theologians and longer than the German version. The section in the *Freedom* treatise that famously addresses what has come to be known as "the happy exchange" (*der fröhliche Wechsel*) is found only in the German version addressed to lay people. I quote Bertram Lee Woolf's translation from 1953,[64] with some tweaking as I deem necessary.

Luther associates the process of the forgiveness of sins with the most joyful event in human life: a wedding. Christ the bridegroom takes the soul as his bride. They exchange wedding gifts. The celebration is characterized by overflowing joy. Luther captures his view of faith's accomplishment with the words:

> It also unites the soul with Christ, like a bride with the bridegroom, and, from this marriage, Christ and the soul become one body as St. Paul says [Eph 5:30]. Then the possessions of both are in common, whether fortune, misfortune, or anything else; so that what Christ has, also belongs to the believing soul, and what the soul has, will belong to Christ. As[65] Christ is the owner of all good things, including blessedness, these will also belong to the soul. The soul is full of trespasses and sins: these will now belong to Christ. At this point a contest of happy exchanges takes place. Because Christ is God and man, and has never sinned, and because His sanctity is unconquerable, eternal, and almighty, He takes possession of the sins of the believing soul by virtue of her wedding ring, her faith, and acts just as if He had committed those sins Himself. As His unconquerable righteousness is stronger than any sin whatever all the soul's sins are swallowed up and drowned in Him. Thus the soul is cleansed from all her sins by virtue of her dowry, thạt is her faith. . . . Is that not a happy wedding feast,[66] when Christ, the rich, noble, and good bridegroom, takes the poor, despised, bad little harlot in marriage, sets her free from all evil, and graces her with all good things?

One of the changes I made to Woolf's text may seem insignificant. Woolf's translation: "If Christ has all good things. . . . If the soul is full of trespasses . . . ," conveys the content as hypothetical figures of thought. Luther, however, does not use "[i]f," but a triumphant, demonstrative "[t]hus." Luther is interested in portraying a glorious event celebrating the wonderful bridegroom and the "poor little harlot." Who but Luther could convey this event with such wonder, admiration, and warmth?

---

64. *Reformation Writings of Martin Luther*, vol. 1 (New York: Philosophical Library, 1953), 363–64.
65. Woolf's text uses "if" twice, here as well as in the next sentence.
66. Woolf here translates "Luther's "eine fröhliche Wirtschaft" as "a happy household."

Another perhaps more tangible example of a misunderstanding conveyed by the English translation is Woolf's rendering of the German, *eine fröhliche Wirtschaft*. Woolf translates this phrase as "a happy household" according to the modern meaning of *Wirtschaft*. The term should much rather be translated as "a happy wedding feast," given the older German meaning of a feast, or a sumptuous meal celebrating a wedding with many guests.[67] In fact, Luther might possibly have in mind the sumptuous eating of the fatted calf and the drinking, music, singing, and dancing heard by the elder brother at the return of the Prodigal Son in Luke 15:23-24. In Woolf's translation, Luther's text loses its fundamental quality of overflowing joy. All gone, the festivity is changed into domesticity. Feelings of joy, wonder, and deep gratitude, all like sunshine on a text, are changed very subtly into intellectual rationality with just a few insipid flavors left.

This is only a handful of the many examples that could illustrate the changes Luther's texts have undergone. The accumulated result is a definite loss of vitality, often in the case of positive emotions. These impressions are reflected back on the author, coloring our picture of him.

Conclusion

I stated in the beginning that Luther was "both/and": both medieval and modern, both intellectual and emotional. I argued that Luther's work is a striking balance of *intellectus et affectus*, an "erudition of the heart." Luther taught that faith must be lived in body and soul, not just understood theoretically. He stated in view of the Psalms: "By living, even by dying and being damned, one becomes a theologian, not by intellectual understanding, reading and speculating."[68] No strict border separates everyday life, *vita activa*, from religious life, *vita contemplativa*; they are interdependent. The center for both everyday and religious life is the "heart," in Luther's sense of the word. In this chapter I chose to concentrate on the heart's joy rather than on Luther's stormier and perhaps more famous moments of *Anfechtung*. Luther's theology of the heart is infused with the happiness he found in his dealings with God in prayer and meditation: a heart "leaping and dancing for joy," in gratefulness and love.

---

67. See Jacob and Wilhelm Grimm, *Deutsches Wörterbuch* (Leipzig: S. Hirzel, 1854–1960), vol. 14/II:666.
68. "Vivendo, immo moriendo et damnando fit theologus, non intelligendo, legendo aut speculando": WA 5:163, 28–29 (*Operationes in Psalmos*; 1519–1521).

Luther's experience-based spirituality may be one of the most relevant dimensions of his word to us today. Sociologists have called the society we live in an *Erlebnisgesellschaft*, or experience-based society. Tourists do not want to see sights necessarily but want to experience new and strange forms of life. More and more people today long for a deeply felt and "lived" spirituality, instead of a theoretical religion.[69] Luther has much to teach us about the wholehearted passion for God and life, for heart-felt love and joy.

69. Gerhard Schulze, *Die Erlebnisgesellschaft: Kultursoziologie der Gegenwart*, 2nd edn. (Frankfurt: Campus, 2005); Peter Zimmerling, "Die Spiritualität Martin Luthers als Herausforderung," *Luther-Jahrbuch* 73 (2006): 19.

CHAPTER 10
The Catholic Luther and Worship Music
Paul Helmer

A mutually productive relationship existed between Martin Luther and the Catholic Church in the realm of worship music. As an Augustinian monk, Luther inherited a rich tradition of music theory, aesthetics, and practice that he passed on in word and tone to his fellow Christians. Acknowledged as the "father" of what has come to be known as the "Reformation," his "break" with the Catholic Church has been seen as the beginning of the modern age. Here, another side of Luther will be stressed. Luther's adherence to the received musical legacy of the universal catholic church allows us to study him as a most faithful son of Holy Mother Church. In light of the extremely close relationship between Luther's views of worship music and those of the Catholic Church, I propose to use the term re-alignment, rather than reformation, to describe Luther's contributions to worship music.

Luther's Debt to Rome

Luther professed faith with all of his fellow Christians in one holy, catholic (universal, global), and apostolic church (*unam sanctam catholicam et apostolicam ecclesiam*). The words of the Niceo-Constantinopolitan Creed articulated for Luther the object of faith, while the words Luther wrote for his own creedal hymn from 1524, "We All Believe in One True God" (*Wyr gleuben all an eynen Gott*), were modeled on a fifteenth-century German devotional song.[1] Luther's commitment to the creed in its various forms witnesses to his belief that the universal church of Christ on earth was founded on the Petrine rock of Catholicism. The Reformer further adhered to the plural form, "*We all believe*," as the Nicene Creed's subject of recitation. The "we" was used in pre-Tridentine times by the entire congregation when it professed the symbol (or creed) of the faith.[2] During the middle ages, the role of the "we" gradually was taken over by priest and choir, who spoke on behalf of the assembled laity. Joseph Jungmann would applaud Luther's intentions to have the creed professed again by the entire congregation: "The plain recitation of the creed by the whole congregation, as is done in the dialogue Mass, is far more in harmony with the original design of the *Credo* and with its place in the plan of the Mass-liturgy, far more in harmony than such and similar residua of a musical culture that is past."[3]

Music as a Gift of God

Luther was deeply indebted to pre-Tridentine theologians who saw music as a divine gift. When music is used to praise and worship God, it actualizes its divine function. Luther's own writing on music, his *Preface to Georg Rhau's Symphoniae iucundae* (1538), gives great insight into how he agreed with medieval consensus on the divine origin of music. The treatise begins with a thesis familiar to many medieval writers, including Luther's own monastic patron, Saint Augustine. Music is "that most excellent gift of God."[4] For medieval musicians, the particular music that was deemed a gift of God was

---

1. LW 53:272–73. The individual volume 53 of Luther's Works—American Edition, entitled *Liturgy and Hymns*, is edited by Ulrich S. Leupold. Leupold was a fugitive from Nazi Germany, at risk both because he was Jewish on his mother's side and because he was a Christian pastor in the Confessing Church, which had early on rejected National Socialist propaganda. He came to Kitchener, Ontario, in 1939 and became dean of the Lutheran seminary there. See Paul Helmer, *Growing with Canada* (Montreal and Kingston: McGill-Queen's University Press, 2009).
2. Joseph Jungmann, *The Mass of the Roman Rite: Its Origins and Development (Missarum Sollemnia)*, trans. Francis A. Brunner, Westminster: Christian Classics 2 vols. (New York: Benziger, 1951–1955), vol. 1, 472; see also David Hiley, *Western Plainchant: A Handbook* (Oxford: Clarendon, 1995), 170.
3. Jungman, *The Mass of the Roman Rite*, vol. 1, 474.
4. "Donum illud divinum et excellentissimum": WA 50, 368. The English translation of Luther's preface is by Leupold in LW 53:321–24. There are two German versions of the preface: WA 50:368–74 publishes Johann Walther's 1564 translation from the Latin original, and Robin A. Leaver (in his *Luther's Liturgical Music: Principles and Implications*, Lutheran Quarterly Books [Grand Rapids: Eerdmans, 2007], 320–24) reproduces a version that is the

Gregory the Great, 13th c.

Gregorian chant. There are numerous portrayals of this claim from the eighth century on. The heavenly inspiration for chant was represented visually by a dove, the symbol in the New Testament for the third person of the Trinity. The dove, perched on the ear of Pope Gregory the Great (pontificate 540–604), dictates to him the melodies and texts that Gregory later transmitted—with raised index finger—to a waiting scribe for inscription in the codex. Gregorian chant is the music par excellence of the Catholic Church and a gift that Luther, along with his colleagues, treasured greatly.

Music as Sounding Number

What attributes did music have that led thinkers to deem it a gift of God? The answer for Catholic, pre-Tridentine intellectuals was unambiguous. Music was "sounding number." Music for the medievals was intimately correlated with mathematics, not with emotions or language as the modern West tends to think. "Sounding number" referred to God's creation of music by precisely correlating the creation of each tone with a specific number. The exegetical warrant in this tradition of interpreting the creation story was the Wisdom of Solomon 11:20: God created order out of chaos by "arrang[ing] all things by measure and number and weight." Luther alludes to this entire tradition when he claims in the previously mentioned preface that music consists of "numero sonoro." "Sounding number" is a concept fundamental to Luther's

---

ostensible draft for Luther's Latin version as published by Wolfgang Figulus in 1575. The Latin is more precise and is preferred here.

understanding of music and one that seems to have eluded Luther scholars to this day.[5]

Quadrivial Thinking around Luther's Time

Like all prospective theologians, doctors, and lawyers, Luther would have studied music as part of his university education. The medieval university prescribed music along with arithmetic, geometry, and astronomy as the four parts of the *quadrivium* of compulsory education in the liberal arts (*artes liberales*).[6] The *quadrivium* can be divided up as four different ways of studying number. Arithmetic is the theory of number, geometry is the study of number in space, music studies number in sound, and astronomy studies number in motion.

As an arts student at the university of Erfurt (1501–1505), Luther surely would have come into contact with an important medieval treatise dealing with music and number: Jean de Muris's redaction (1323–1325) of Boethius's text *Musica speculativa*. Muris's redaction was the obligatory text used in Oxford, Paris, and in German universities in the fifteenth and sixteenth centuries. This work discusses music according to the Pythagorean system of numbers, a system based on the premise that mathematical proportions govern both musical consonances and dissonances and give order to the entire world of organized sound. Pythagoras was a Greek music theorist (c. 560–480 B.C.E.) and medieval writers constantly cite the story of his discovery of the mathematical foundation for musical consonance when he compared the sounds emitted by proportionally varying weights of hammer heads striking an anvil. The justification for correlating music with number has to do with analyzing the geometrical proportions on the monochord, a medieval instrument composed of a single string. When the string is divided up according to a specific proportion—for example, divided into one half—the string sounds the octave in either half. The following chart from Muris's treatise illustrates the geometric and arithmetic justification for the medieval musical consonances of the octave, fifth, and fourth. The mathematical ratios are 1:2 (octave); 2:3 (fifth); and 3:4 (fourth).

All intervals used in music are founded upon mathematical ratios. The Pythagorean system gives prominence to the prime numbers as consonant intervals. Hence the fifth and fourth are consonant in medieval music, but not the

---

5. Leupold translates *Nihil enim est sine sono, seu numero sonoro* as "For nothing is without sound or harmony," and consigns the alternate reading "literally sounding number" to a footnote (LW 53:322). Leaver renders the Latin as "There is nothing on earth that is without its sound and its harmony" (Leaver, *Luther's Liturgical Music*, 314).

6. The three parts of the *trivium* are rhetoric, logic, and dialectic. The *trivium* and the *quadrivium* together make up the seven liberal arts.

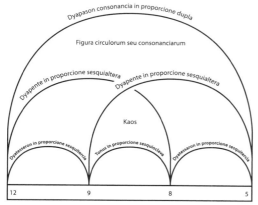

Johannes de Muris,
*Musica speculativa
secundum Boetium,* 14th c.

third or sixth. Why did Muris transpose the 1:2, 2:3, and 3:4 ratios of the consonant intervals to the higher equivalents 6:12, 8:12, and 9:12? He could show
by these equivalents that the consonances were symmetrically ordered around a
center, the tone produced by the ratio of 8:9. This dissonant tone was considered
Kaos, the formless void out of which God fashioned the order of creation. Muris
then locates the various harmonies (or musical intervals) around the center as
they are each correlated with a specific mathematical ratio. The center is surrounded by the interlocking and adjacent symmetries of the consonant fifth and
fourth, which are equal to the ratios of 12:9:8:6 in the Pythagorean system and
which can further be reduced to the ratios for octave, fifth, and fourth:

6:12=1:2
8:12 and 6:9=2:3
9:12 and 6:8=3:4.

The diagram also includes Muris's terminology for the ratios. The "dyapa-
son" is the octave, the "dyapente" is the fifth, the "dyatesseron" the fourth. The
"proportio dupla" is 1:2; "proportio sesquialtera" is 2:3; "proportio sesquitercia"
is 3:4; and "tonus" in "proportio sesquioctava" is 8:9.

The diagram's architectonic beauty relates geometry, music, and mathematics to each other in a stunningly coherent manner. A similar pattern can
be found in the successively higher tones produced by blowing through a
mouthpiece into a length of tubing. The system of increasingly smaller intervals exactly parallels the Pythagorean ratios. In music this is known as the
overtone series.[7]

---

7. A description of the notes is available online at http://smu.edu/totw/overtone.htm.

The correlation between music and proportion was demonstrated for music students in the medieval period on the monochord. Medieval scholars also related the proportion to the metaphysical order in the universe. The *Timaeus*, Plato's famous dialogue treating the creation of the world by the Demiurge, was known throughout the middle ages in the short version—until passage 53c—translated into Latin by Calcidius in the fourth century.

> Here it is explained how the demiurge (easily transmuted by later writers into the Christian God) created the world-soul from a substance which combined that which is indivisible and unchanging (eternal verities) and that which is divisible, material, and subject to change. This substance was divided into sections whose lengths were in strict proportional relationship with each other, 1:2, 2:3, 3:4 and so on. Since the proportions were those of Pythagorean harmonic theory, music could be understood as a reflection of the creation of the world and its divine order. The divine order was reflected not only in the ordering of the Earth and heavenly bodies, the macrocosm, but also in man, the microcosm, in the balance between his spiritual and physical being. Hence the influence of music on the state of his soul and behavior.[8]

The Pythagorean proportions were precisely those that Plato's Demiurge had calculated when creating the universe.[9]

The sixteenth century saw the rise of tuning systems that divided the musical "space" between notes in a manner differently than Pythagoras and Muris. "Mean-tone tuning," with its numerous subtypes, became the foundation of Western music from the sixteenth to the nineteenth centuries. It was based on the third as a consonance. "Equal temperament," with antecedents in the sixteenth century, became the norm in the nineteenth and twentieth centuries. It was based on an equidistant space between each of the twelve notes of the chromatic scale and was particularly apt for dodecaphonic (twelve-tone) music.

Luther and his Wittenberg colleagues, however, held fast to the older system. Luther's good friend, Martin Agricola (1486–1556), wrote an instrumental treatise, the *Musica instrumentalis deudsch*, which was published by the enterprising Wittenberg printer Georg Rhau. Agricola's work is based on the Pythagorean-Muris system but expands it in the 1545 edition by adding (1) the varying sizes of hammers that Pythagoras had originally used to construct his system; (2) a musical staff that included the corresponding notes of the

---

8. *Timaeus Commentary of Calcidius* as cited in Hiley, *Western Plainchant*, 444.
9. See Plato, *Timaeus*, VI, 36a–37a.

scale (F-Bflat-C-F, which comprise the fourth, tone, and fourth with over-lapping fifths F-C and Bflat-F); and (3) the various mathematical ratios from Muris's fifteenth-century model. The Wittenberg tradition of music theory is consistent with what we know about how deeply Luther was embedded in the Catholic intellectual tradition.

It is tantalizing to speculate on other literary works that Luther might have read as a student in Erfurt and later as an Augustinian monk. Was he aware of Plato's *Timaeus* as transmitted through neo-Platonic thought, or of Saint Augustine's copious notes on music and its relation to mathematics? Well-known in the middle ages was Augustine's *De musica*, a treatise on num-ber, equality, and inequality in poetic verse. For Augustine, music pleases by proportion, that is, number.[10] Was Luther aware of Augustine's *De trinitate*, in which the author points to the duple proportion 1:2 as an analogy to Christ's atoning for the human's twofold death in body and soul? "This match . . . or whatever the right word is for the proportion of one to two . . . is what the Greeks call *harmonia*."[11] Augustine correlates musical harmony with the

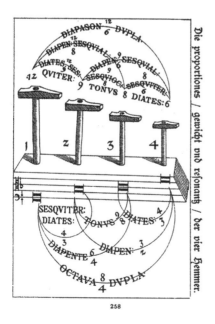

Martin Agricola, *Musica instrumentalis deudsch*, Wittenberg, 1545

---

10. "Haec igitur pulchra numero placent": Aurelius Augustinus, *De musica*, ed. Giovanni Marzi (Florence: Sansoni, 1969), 596.

11. *De trin*. IV, 2:4; cited in Saint Augustine, *The Trinity*, trans. Edmund Hill, O.P., ed. John E. Rotelle, O.S.A., The Works of Saint Augustine: A Translation for the Twenty-First Century (Brooklyn: New City, 1991), 155 (italics in original).

theology of salvation. "As for our present concern . . . is how the single of
our Lord Jesus Christ matches our double, and in some fashion enters into a
harmony of salvation with it."[12] Countless medieval theorists—among them
Boethius, Johann Scotus Erigena, Roger Bacon, and Nicholas of Cusa—would
echo Augustine's sentiments.[13] Whether Luther was explicitly familiar with
these theories of music or not, he demonstrated knowledge of the great tradition in pre-Tridentine thought of arithmetic-geometrical-musical proportions
that underlie the divine order of music.

The tradition of quadrivial thinking has an exciting history even after
Luther. Its culmination was achieved in Johannes Kepler's *The Harmony of the
World* (*Harmonices mundi*), published in Latin in 1619. Kepler (1571–1630)
was educated at the seminary school in Maulbronn that was established by the
Württemberg reformer Johannes Brenz (1499–1570). Kepler went on to study
at the University of Tübingen, where he intended to become a Lutheran pastor. Kepler's treatise, which contains major sections devoted to musical theory,
is generally recognized as the beginning of modern astronomy.[14] The author
adduced that the six known planets circumnavigate the sun in elliptical orbits
and that the mathematical relation between the point at which the planets
are closest to the sun, compared with the point furthest away from the sun,
reveals a divine metaphysical order based on number that could be attributed
only to a divine Creator. For Kepler, such mathematical relations were a demonstration of God's order in creation: his treatise concludes with a personal *Te
Deum*: "Great is our Lord, and great is His excellence and there is no count of
His wisdom. Praise Him heavens, praise Him, Sun, Moon, and Planets, with
whatever sense you use to perceive . . . praise Him, heavenly harmonies, praise
Him judges of the harmonies which have been disclosed; and you also, my
soul, praise the Lord your Creator."[15]

The following chart by Kepler diagrams the relation between planetary
orbits and musical proportions. The movements of planets are correlated

---

12. *De trin*. IV, 2:5; cited in Saint Augustine, *The Trinity*, 155.
13. Heinrich Hüschen, "Augustinus," in *Die Musik in Geschichte und Gegenwart*, 1st edn.
(Kassel: Bärenreiter, 1989), vol. 1:855.
14. It is revealing that Kepler quotes the sequence *Victimae paschali laudes* as an example
of well-constructed melody (see recording included with this volume). Kepler's treatise also
includes a description of the rise and fall of this tune based upon the pauses and stresses
on consonant notes as well as the brief passing over dissonant ones. See Johannes Kepler,
The Harmony of the World, trans. E. J. Aiton, A. M. Duncan, and J. V. Field, Memoirs of the
American Philosophical Society 209 (Philadelphia: American Philosophical Society, 1997),
217–19. Kepler uses the analogy of the human skeleton (consonances), which is covered by
flesh (dissonances).
15. Kepler, *The Harmony of the World*, 498.

Harmonia binorum		*Apparentes diurni*	diurni. Prim Sec.	*Harmonie singulorum propria* Prim. Sec.
Diver.	Conv.			
a 1	b 1	♄ Aphelius 1.46.a. Perihelius 2.15.b.	Inter 1.48 & 2.15.	eſt $\frac{4}{5}$ Terria major.
d 3	c 2	♃ Aphelius 4.30.c. Perihelius 5.30.d.	Inter 4.35. & 5.30.	eſt $\frac{5}{6}$ Terria minor.
e 8	d 1			
f 1	e 5	♂ Aphelius 26.14.e. Perihelius 3.81.f.	Inter 25.21. & 38.1.	eſt $\frac{2}{3}$ Diapente
e 5	f 2			
h 12	g 3	Tel.Aphelius 57.3.g Perihelius 61.18.h	Inter 57.28. &61.18.	eſt $\frac{15}{16}$ Semitonis
g 3	h 5			
k 5	i 8	♀ Aphelius 94.50.i. Perihelius 97.37.k.	Inter 94.50. & 98.47.	eſt $\frac{24}{25}$ Diesis
i 1	k 3			
m 4	l 5	☿ Aphelius 164.0.l. Perihelius 384.0.m.	Inter 164. o. & 394. o:	eſt $\frac{5}{12}$ Diapaſon cum tercia minore

Johannes Kepler, *Harmonices mundi*, 1619

with specific mathematical ratios that are equivalent to particular musical harmonies. Saturn's orbit, for example, is correlated with the ratio 4:5, hence a major third; Jupiter with 5:6 (minor third); Mercury with 2:3 (fifth); Earth with 15:16 (semitone); Venus with 24:25 (a chromatic sharp); and Mars with 5:12 (minor tenth). The work is a perfect synthesis of the arts of mathematics, music, geometry, and astronomy, the culmination of medieval quadrivial thinking and at the same time the path breaker to our modern world.

Developments in "Sounding Number" around Luther's Time

The theory of music as sounding number was developed around Luther's time to represent the height of quadrivial thinking. This tradition began with pre-Tridentine composers, who extended mathematical relations to the temporal aspect of the art of music. This tradition of *mensura*, the idea of dividing up time into measurable units, was a fundamental concept in Augustine's *De musica*. *Mensura* took on musical shape in the metrically-organized polyphonic *clausulae* (a type of musical composition) of the Notre Dame School in the late twelfth century. Composers added metrically-organized companion voices to a segment of Gregorian chant in the tenor. In this specific case, the triple meter, the long plus a short beat, presented metric "perfection" and predominated in the *clausulae*. The duple meter, a short plus a short beat that displayed "imperfection," was later added. The interplay between both triple and duple meter became an important compositional device.

The length of musical phrases could also be divided temporally. Numerical principles were seen as the organizational features of entire works. This

idea flourished in the medieval isorhythmic motet and was a common practice during the fifteenth century. A representative example is the isorhythmic
motet that the Renaissance composer Guillaume Dufay (1397–1474) composed to commemorate the dedication of the Florence Cathedral Santa Maria
del Fiore on March 25, 1436. As Craig Wright has shown, Dufay's *Nuper rosarum flores* ("Lately Roses Bloomed") exactly replicates in its musical layout the
dimensions of the Solomonic Temple as given by God to King Solomon. The
dimensions of the Temple according to 1 Kings 6:2 are a total length of sixty
cubits, the nave length of forty cubits, a width of twenty cubits, and a height
of thirty cubits. When these dimensions are reduced to the lowest common
denominator, they give the musical ratios of 6:4:2:3 that Dufay used in his
motet.[16] As an admirer of the Franco-Flemish school of musical theory, Luther
would definitely have been exposed to such ideas.

Musicians could superimpose the mathematical foundation of music with
various levels of emotional, linguistic, or dramatic meaning and develop theories to support the new readings. Luther's pastoral advice relating music to the
emotions is often read in light of this trajectory. A famous example is his claim
that music's function is "to comfort the sad, to terrify the happy, to encourage
the despairing, to humble the proud, to calm the passionate, or to appease
those full of hate."[17] Luther alludes to David's banishing of Saul's foul moods
through the gift of music (1 Sam 16:23). Yet the explicit association of music
to emotions would be left to others. Only later development began to view
music as one of the language arts. Music would become part of a new *trivium*
along with logic (the meaning of ideas), grammar (how ideas hang together),
and rhetoric (how one presents these ideas to others). The new view that had
displaced music from *quadrivium* to *trivium* would be treated intellectually
in *Figurenlehre*, the theory of the figures, and later *Affektenlehre*, the theory of
affects. These concepts were elaborated intellectually and musically in the
Baroque period.

Music as Divine Gift for Worship

As a gift of God, music was a significant part of the worship service. Luther
advocated his own changes to the Mass, first in 1523 and then again with the

---

16. Craig Wright, "Dufay's *nuper rosarum flores*, King's Solomon's Temple and the Venera-
tion of the Virgin," *Journal of the American Musicological Society* 47 (1994): 395–441. The 1
Kings 6:2 passage reads: "The house that King Solomon built for the Lord was sixty cubits
long, twenty cubits wide, and thirty cubits high."
17. LW 53:322 (*Preface to Georg Rhau's Symphoniae iucundae*; 1538).

turn to the vernacular in the German Mass (*Deutsche Messe*) of 1526. I discuss Luther's re-alignment of the Mass in this section by contextualizing it in the late middle ages.

Criticisms of Abuse

Luther's indebtedness to Catholicism is revealed by his quadrivial thinking. But his Mass reforms were also in substantial agreement with pre-sixteenth-century theologians who found elements that needed to be changed. Peter Cantor, John Gerson, and Nicholas of Cusa were among the late medieval theologians who had already inveighed against the custom of endowing private Masses. The practice was widespread throughout the middle ages. In some churches, more than fifty private Masses needed to be said (or sung) during the day. This led to the practice known as the "Boxed Mass." In the words of Jungmann, "one Mass was sung to the offertory or to the *Sanctus*, then continued as a low (spoken) Mass while at another altar a second Mass was begun. . . . The complaints raised by the Reformers, especially by Luther, were aimed accurately and quite relentlessly against questionable points in ecclesiastical praxis regarding the Mass: the fruits of the Mass, the Votive masses with their various values, the commerce in stipends."[18] Luther's criticisms of abuses of the Mass may refer back to the fourteenth century. In the epic *Premier livre de fauvel*, the major protagonist, Chaillou de Pesstain, is a Luther-like figure who rails against the abuses within the established church and longs for a reform of its practices, advocating even apostolic poverty.[19]

The church building is an important aspect of studying the liturgical transitions of the sixteenth century. Church architecture in particular directly affected the hearing of the Mass. Worship services were performed behind a rood screen that separated the clergy and choir at the front of the church from the laity in the nave of the church. The rood screens in cathedral, collegiate, and monastic churches were substantial, often made of stone, and sometimes more than ten feet deep. The Mass was celebrated by the clergy on the principal altar that was placed on the eastern wall beyond the rood screen. The choir would sit behind the screen in the often ornately carved choir stalls on either side of the apse. The sights and sounds of the Mass were virtually unseen and unheard by the laity. Even small parish churches were divided by a screen so that the eastern end of the church where the priest celebrated the Mass and

---

18. Jungmann, *The Mass of the Roman Rite*, vol. 1, 131.
19. Paul Helmer, *Le premier et le secont livre de fauvel in the version preserved in B.N. fonds français 146* (Ottawa: Institute of Mediaeval Music, 1997).

said the Office was only partly visible, if at all, from the nave. Jungmann sums up a major subject of reform: "the line of separation . . . between those whose duty it was to perform the sacramental action and those who formed the celebrating congregation . . . was now made into a broad line of demarcation . . . which became a real wall separating the *presbyterium* (sanctuary) from the nave of the church."[20]

The lay faithful would stand throughout the service, occasionally bowing or kneeling. There was "no provision for the laity to sit down."[21] Only in those churches that had instituted a service of the word, a *Predigtgottesdienst*, might there have been fixed pews on which the congregation could sit. The core of the Mass, the Canon, would hardly have been noticed by the laity since the priest recited it in a very quiet voice at the altar in a presumably incomprehensible language. At the Elevation, bells would be rung so that the faithful could view the moment of the transubstantiation of the host. The whole office was a "service" performed for the faithful, a sacrifice offered by the clergy on behalf of the laity.

Luther's ire was inflamed by the separation of clergy from laity and the general feeling that the clergy was there to perform a "service" or meritorious "work" on behalf of the faithful. In particular, the Canon and Offertory of the Mass spoke of a sacrifice being offered up to God.[22] In his revisions of the Mass, Luther excised both Canon and Offertory in order to delete a work for which one presumably derived merit.[23] Anything that did not seem to be prompted by the Spirit should be purged—the sequences, the *Sanctorale* (the liturgical book devoted to the services of the saints), the proliferation of feast days devoted to the saints, and the tropes.[24] Luther also wished to purge the "tomfoolery" of Holy Week: no "Lenten veils, throwing of palms, veiling of pictures, and whatever else there is of tomfoolery."[25] "Nor is it proper to distinguish Lent, Holy Week, or Good Friday from other days, lest we seem to mock and ridicule Christ with half of a mass and the one part of the sacrament. For the Alleluia is the perpetual voice of the church, just as the memorial of

20. Jungmann, *The Mass of the Roman Rite*, vol. 1, 83–84.
21. Jungmann, *The Mass of the Roman Rite*, vol. 1, 241.
22. A vivid example of Luther's vintage rhetoric is: "What I am speaking of is the canon, that abominable concoction drawn from everyone's sewer and cesspool. The mass became a sacrifice": LW 53:21 (*An Order of Mass and Communion for the Church at Wittenberg*, 1523).
23. On Luther's excision of Canon and Offertory: "Let us, therefore, repudiate everything that smacks of sacrifice, together with the entire canon and retain only that which is pure and holy, and so order our mass": LW 53:26.
24. LW 53:13–14 (*Concerning the Order of Public Worship*, 1523).
25. LW 53:90 (*The German Mass and Order of Service*, 1526).

Charles Henri Toussaint, *The Rood Screen of St. Etienne du Mont*, Paris, 1881

His passion and victory is perpetual."[26] An Alleluia during Holy Week is true freedom!

The Freedom of the Mass

Luther's re-alignment of worship music can best be captured by the title of his famous theological treatise *The Freedom of a Christian* in regard to the worship practices of the faithful. His recommendations for renewal of the liturgical services are available in three publications: a revised daily Matins and Vespers entitled *Concerning the Order of Public Worship* (1523)[27]; an order for the Latin Mass entitled *An Order of Mass and Communion for the Church at Wittenberg* (1523)[28]; and *The German Mass and Order of Service* (1526) for his revised German Mass.[29] In addition, there were a number of Visitation articles and Wittenberg Church Orders from 1533.[30] Luther makes the theme of freedom clear as the overarching rubric for alignment: reforms are the prerogative of every individual congregation and cannot be mandated from above.

Luther was at first reluctant to commit himself to reforms of the Mass. He was aware of the dangers of a new tradition that might take on a life of its own. He kept the freedom of conscience in non-essential items at the forefront of

26. LW 53:24 (*An Order of Mass and Communion*; 1523).
27. LW 53:11–14.
28. LW 53:19–40.
29. LW 53:53–90.
30. Leaver, *Luther's Liturgical Music*, 260. See also LW 40:262-320 ("Instructions for the Visitors of Parish Pastors in Electoral Saxony"; 1528).

his recommendations. He writes in *Against the Heavenly Prophets* (1525) that either German or Latin in the Mass is fine, but he underlines that the most important thing is clear communication of content.[31] His reforms do not insist upon uniformity: "I do not propose that all of Germany should uniformly follow our Wittenberg order. Even heretofore the chapters, monasteries, and parishes were not alike in every rite."[32] When prodded by Nicholas Hausmann of Zwickau to prepare a German version in 1524, the Reformer replied that he did "not consider it sufficiently safe to call a council of our party for establishing unity in the ceremonies. . . . Of its own accord a congregation should, therefore, follow one another, or else be allowed to enjoy its own customs."[33] Luther was guided by the desire to preserve freedom in the non-essential orders, to allow the believers the right to preserve, reform, or create new liturgies as the Spirit moved them. To the Livonians (of current day Estonia) he advised, "for even though from the viewpoint of faith, the external orders are free and can without scruples be changed by anyone at any time, yet from the viewpoint of love, you are not free to use this liberty, but bound to consider the edification of the common people."[34] Freedom tempered by love was the touchstone.

Freedom within Tradition

Luther's advocacy of freedom at the local parish level was tempered by his own love for the Catholic tradition. By recommending change, Luther insisted on continuity with Gregorian chant and the magnificent Latin polyphonic repertoire.

The balance of freedom within tradition was cast differently between two distinct services. Luther clearly distinguished between collegiate and cathedral churches with a choir or Latin school, in which services were held in Latin, and parish churches without choir, in which the unlettered laity would be brought gradually to participate in the services. He intended his early reform, the *Formula Missae* of 1523, for the first group. His main consideration was to retain the Latin service for the boys and the learned. As Luther writes: "It is not now my intention to abrogate or to change the service. . . . For in no wise would I want to discontinue the service in the Latin language, because the young

---

31. LW 40:141–42.
32. LW 53:62 (Luther's "Preface" to *The German Mass*; 1526).
33. LW 49:87 (no. 148: "To Nicolas Hausmann"; Witttenberg; Nov. 17, 1524).
34. LW 53:47 ("A Christian Exhortation to the Livonians Concerning Public Worship and Concord"; 1525).

are my chief concern."[35] Luther's *German Mass* of 1526 was intended as a German service for the unlettered, as well as for those "who do not believe and are not yet Christians . . . to move them to believe and become Christians."[36] The two services are identical to their Roman counterparts with the exception of the omission of the Canon and Offertory.[37] Mass could be sung at eight or nine o'clock in the morning. In addition, Luther provided for a simplified (measured against the monastic counterpart) daily Matins and Vespers, the former sung at five or six in the morning, the latter in the afternoon. The Reformation's alignment with the Catholic Mass is aptly summarized by Philipp Melanchthon in the Augsburg Confession of 1530: "Our churches are falsely accused of abolishing the Mass. In fact, the Mass is retained among us and is celebrated with the highest reverence. Almost all the customary ceremonies are also retained, except that German hymns, added for the instruction of the people, are interspersed here and there among the Latin ones."[38]

Luther mentions a third worship service as subject of reform. It seems to be intended as private worship for those more advanced in the faith. Luther writes of "a truly evangelical order" that is "not held in a public place for all sorts of people. But those who want to be Christians in earnest and who profess the gospel with hand and mouth should sign their names and meet alone in a house somewhere to pray, to read, to baptize, to receive the sacrament, and to do other Christian works. . . . Here one could also solicit benevolent gifts to be willingly given and distributed to the poor, according to St. Paul's example, II Corinthians 9. Here would be no need of much and elaborate singing."[39] Frank Senn sees this innovation as a forerunner of the *collegia pietatis*, formed under the Pietist movement, some one hundred and fifty years later, with the key difference that the sacraments were not celebrated by the Pietists.[40]

The renewal of worship services in the 1520s and 1530s proceeded in the German states on a church-by-church basis. Hence, it is difficult to give a general picture of exactly what happened. Individual churches presumably would have removed the rood screen at different times and under different circumstances. In the church in which I worship in Germany, Saint Amandus in Bad Urach, there are remnants of a previous rood screen that either has been

35. LW 53:62–63 (Luther's "Preface" to *The German Mass*; 1526).
36. LW 53:63.
37. Synoptic tables in Siegfried Bräuer, *Thomas Müntzer: Deutsche Evangelische Messe 1524* (Berlin: Evangelische Verlagsanstalt, 1988), 130–33.
38. BoC, 69, 1–3 (section 24).
39. LW 53:63–64.
40. Frank C. Senn, *Christian Liturgy: Catholic and Evangelical* (Minneapolis: Fortress Press, 1997), 282.

dismantled in the meantime or was never actually built; the severed stumps of prospective supporting arches are still evident on the two pillars closest to the choir.[41] In the areas reformed by Martin Bucer and Johannes Brenz, the choir screen was dismantled by local decision. The dismantling of the screen in Bad Urach probably occurred on the "day of idols," the *Götzentag*, September 10, 1537. In England rood screens were the norm even in small parish churches.[42] They were removed by parliamentary act, particularly Edward VI's injunction in 1547. Some screens were restored during the Catholic interim under Mary I (1553–1558). Later, under Protestant Elizabeth I (1558–1603), they were again removed. The dismantling of this barrier meant that the "priesthood of the laity" of which Luther spoke became a real possibility.[43]

When clergy and choir were relocated to the nave to reinforce the singing of the congregation, the polarity between clergy and laity broke down. Later Baroque architecture continued the new tradition by leaving the apse uncluttered with choir screens. The preferred visual context required a dramatic sweep down the nave to an impressive high altar.

Continuity and Change

The Catholic traditions of the performance of worship music that Luther received and desired to be continued are briefly outlined in this section.

Ornamentation by Soloists and Choir

Choirs in the sixteenth century were male- or female-only organizations and probably were confined to collegiate and cathedral foundations. It is difficult today to imagine that the norm for choral singing prior to the eighteenth century was soloistic, that is, one singer per part. This type of performance allowed for a purer intonation and a more flexible style of singing that included a highly developed ornamentation technique. Hermann Finck documents the technique for mid-century Wittenberg in his 1556 *Practica musica*, Book V: "De arte eleganter et suaviter cantandi" ("On the Art of Singing More Elegantly and Sweetly"). Using the term *coloraturae* ("coloring"), he demonstrates that singers should judiciously add turns, neighboring tones, *passaggi*, and so on, to

---

41. Monika Ingenhoff-Danhäuser, "Das Altargitter," in *Die Amandus Kirche in Bad Urach*, ed. Friedrich Schmid (Sigmaringen: Thorbecke, 1990), 123.
42. John Harper, *The Forms and Orders of Western Liturgy from the Tenth to the Eighteenth Century* (Oxford: Clarendon, 1991), 36 and diagram on page 37.
43. See Allen G. Jorgenson's essay, "Contours of the Common Priesthood," ch. 15 in this volume.

the printed notes in order to beautify the music. He illustrates the technique by coloring a motet with words by Philipp Melanchthon, *Te maneat semper* ("You remain always"), and Finck states that embellishment can be done successfully only when one voice per part is used: "[I]n choirs *coloraturae* cannot be used without detriment to the music, for when one part is given to several singers it follows that the *coloraturae* will be very different, which means that the sweetness and character of the mode will be obscured."[44] The technique of vocal ornamentation was even more highly developed in the Italian sources of the period. Sylvestro Ganassi, Girolamo della Casa, and Giovanni Battista Bovicelli, chapel singer at the Milan cathedral, applied the technique to a large repertoire that included madrigals, motets, and liturgical intonations, including works by Palestrina. The practice of one voice per polyphonic part continued into the Baroque period.

Organ and Instruments

Luther had no reservations regarding the use of instruments to support and accompany liturgical vocal music. The development of organs and organ music was spurred on by the increasing need to support congregational singing. In the northern German states in the seventeenth and eighteenth centuries, a golden age of organ composition would ensue. Hand in hand with new composition was the development of organ technology to take on a more brilliant tone: four foot and two foot stops were added, as well as a host of mixtures and a stronger pedal register.

The way hymns were performed during the service is also important to consider. In general, all verses of a particular hymn were performed, since each verse was just part of a greater whole.[45] Each strophe, however, could be performed in various ways. Following the fifteenth-century tradition of organ Masses and organ versets, various *alternatim* practices were in use. Hymn verses could alternate between organ and choir (congregation), and if the organist played a verse, the congregation would mentally sing the strophe. In the sixteenth century, the congregation presumably would have sung unaccompanied and in unison. If a choir were present, it could sing a verse monophonically or in a polyphonic setting using elaborate Franco-Flemish techniques of point-by-point imitation. The core of composers drawn to Wittenberg in Luther's time had mastered the art of the Northerner composers to a high degree, and

---

44. Frank E. Kirby, "Hermann Finck on Methods of Performance," *Music and Letters* 42 (1961): 218.
45. Friedrich Blume, *Geschichte der evangelischen Kirchenmusik*, 2nd edn. (Kassel: Bärenreiter, 1965), 63.

their works were published by Georg Rhau. The choir could sing *a cappella* (unaccompanied), accompanied by other instruments—lute, fiddles, recorders, crumhorns, cornettos, and sackbuts (perhaps drawn from the town's *Stadt-pfeifer*), or supported by the organ. Latin hymns, sequences, or canticles were performed and often coupled with successive presentation of the appropriate German strophe in unison. Performance possibilities were extensive.

The tempo was undoubtedly a stately one.[46] The beat, or *tactus* in six-teenth-century terminology, was a complex balance among the various time units of half note, quarter note, and eighth note (in modern equivalents).[47] The beat was, therefore, variable and dependent on the musical syntax within a particular piece, although in general theorists distinguished between church, court, and private traditions of tempos. Ecclesiastical architecture usually demanded a more majestic tempo. Furthermore, techniques of ornamenta-tion developed during this period were increasingly applied to all vocal and instrumental works. This practice would have had a moderating effect on the *tactus*.

Latin and Vernacular

Luther's Reformation is commonly associated with a sudden turn to the vernacular. Yet this idea of instant transformation is a stubborn misinterpre-tation. Friedrich Blume's magisterial survey of Protestant Church music con-tains substantial sections regarding the use of Latin liturgical service music in Protestant churches in the periods of the Counter Reformation, Orthodoxy and Mysticism, and J. S. Bach.[48] The Leipzig church orders of 1710, to offer a specific example, included Latin for Sundays and festival days throughout the year. Latin was also used for Mass ordinaries, introits, Magnificats, priestly intonations, prefaces, and the words of institution. The use of Latin continued unabated through the middle of the eighteenth century in Lutheran areas.

Contrafact and Parody

The reuse of preexisting material, both text and music, was a hallowed tra-dition prior to and after the sixteenth century. The practice of borrowing, known as contrafact, was applied to the reuse of a single melody or could be extended to the practice of parody, in which all the voices in a previously composed polyphonic piece could be reused. This tradition was used in vocal

---

46. *Pace* the introduction by Leupold to the section on Luther's hymns in LW 53:205 that claims: "the beat of the music was fairly rapid."
47. In the words of the theorists: "tactus tardior," "maior," "celerior," or "minor."
48. Blume, *Geschichte der evangelischen Kirchenmusik*.

and instrumental music from the thirteenth to the nineteenth century. Long before the advent of intellectual property legislation, composers could "borrow" from their own material or that of others if the text, instrumentation, voicing, tempo, and so on, could be applied appropriately to a parallel passage. In the Lutheran tradition, recycling was done on a large scale from previous Latin or German (*Leisen*) devotional songs or from secular songs. Of the thirty-seven hymns generally attributed to Luther, a significant number are contrafacts of Latin or German devotional songs.

Borrowing from the secular sphere for devotional songs was also a frequent practice. Sermisy's chanson, "Il me suffit" of 1529, was transformed into Herzog Albrecht's "Was mein Gott will"; Heinrich Isaac's sixteenth century "Innsbruck ich muss dich lassen," into three different songs: "O Welt, ich muss dich lassen," Paul Gerhardt's "Nun ruhen alle Wälder," and Matthias Claudius's eighteenth-century "Der Mond ist aufgegangen." Luther was probably opposed to lascivious, carnal songs, but when the melodies were dressed in suitable texts, he took no offense. In the fifteenth and sixteenth centuries, the *chanson* mass, based on a secular French song, proved to be a popular means of using well-known material in ceremonial garb. Although clerics from time to time might rail against the practice, the persistence of their admonitions implies that the practice was indeed very widespread. Musicians moved with ease from appointment to appointment, from court to church or vice versa, and hence would carry techniques used in one domain to the new one. Prominent musicians such as Guillaume de Machaut, Guillaume Dufay, Josquin des Prez, and Claudio Monteverdi on the Catholic side, had taken minor orders and could be members of chapel choirs or equally *maestro di cappella* in secular appointments. On the Protestant side, the same tradition held. Heinrich Schütz as court composer in Dresden was responsible for the court's ecclesiastical music. J. S. Bach's positions embraced both court and church and ensured that worship music was constantly being nourished and refreshed by developments outside the church.

Manuscript and Printing Press

The sixteenth century saw the increased use of the printing press as a means of disseminating text and music. The difficulties of printing music by mechanical means stymied printers for a while, since the alignment of horizontal staff lines with vertical notes was problematic. If one considers the expense of early printed materials and the low level of literacy among the general populace, one can easily infer that the new technology did not supplant traditional notation by hand. Rote learning and oral transmission, which had served the vast repertoire of Gregorian chant and traditional (folk) music, would continue unabated, and a flourishing manuscript tradition would ensure the vigorous cultivation of local traditions.

Rome's Debt to Luther

Although Luther was prevented by his death from attending the Council of Trent (1545–1563), his thinking cast a long shadow over that august assembly. Worship music was dealt with by the Council in the twenty-second to twenty-fourth sessions. Cardinal Karl Borromeo of Milan, Cardinal Vitellozzi, and Cardinal Otto Truchsess of Augsburg were among those in charge of the musical reforms undertaken by the Council. Each was noted for his substantial knowledge of liturgical music. It is inconceivable that Luther's writings on worship music were unknown to these theologians, as the discussions at the Council substantially affirmed Luther's re-alignment of service music.

The reform Breviary and Missal published subsequently to Trent in 1568 and 1570, respectively, vindicated Luther's call for a cleansing of the church calendar. Some one hundred and fifty days of the church year were freed from sanctoral commemorations. Yet the liturgical books were also freed from much medieval tradition. The vast repertoire of proses, prosulas, and other textual and musical additions that had invigorated service music across Europe for a thousand years was expunged in one fell swoop. Thousands of sequences were likewise purged. Fortunately for posterity, one of Luther's favorite sequences, *Veni sancte spiritus*, was retained for Pentecost as were *Lauda Sion* for Corpus Christi, and *Dies irae* for Requiem Masses. *Stabat mater* was added in the eighteenth century.

Certainly the Council's desire to use all liturgical means to impress the faithful—the traditional Latin chant and polyphony, which reflected the latest developments of the Franco-Flemish school—would have pleased Luther greatly, since he too was of the same opinion. Latin choir schools and the use of instruments in worship were also retained, as well as the rich pre-Tridentine tradition of vernacular hymns supplemented by a continuous stream of new ones. Judging by publications of vernacular hymns in Catholic German regions, Rome-centered composers were every bit as concerned with vernacular hymns as evangelical composers. Johannes Leisentrit's *Geistliche Lieder und Psalmen* of 1567, with some two hundred and fifty hymns on four hundred and eighty published pages, complete with illustrative woodcuts, was known throughout Germany and was a worthy counterpart to any Lutheran publication.

Joseph Jungmann concedes Luther's right to demand an end to the abuses in liturgical services,[49] but he would, at the same time, lament the response of the Roman church to those complaints:

> After fifteen hundred years of unbroken development in the rite of the Roman Mass, after the rushing and streaming from every height and out of every valley, the Missal of Pius V was indeed a powerful dam holding back the waters or permitting them to flow through only in firm, well-built canals. At one blow all arbitrary meandering to one side or another was cut off, all floods prevented, and a safe, regular, and useful flow assured. But the price paid was this, that the beautiful river valley now lay barren and the forces of future evolution were often channeled into the narrow bed of a very inadequate devotional life instead of gathering strength for new forms of liturgical expression.[50]

To oversee compliance of the Council of Trent's recommendations for reform, a Congregation of Rites was instituted, centralizing the decision-making process for liturgical music to an unprecedented degree. A reform Gradual that included the music to accompany the Missal, the so-called Medicean edition, was published in 1614–1615, but was not made binding. Local congregations were left with the enormous task of rewriting their service books in order to make them conform to Tridentine norms. Ecclesiastical communities that could demonstrate a two-hundred-year tradition were exempt from the new regulations, and in France, neo-Gallican chant emerged.[51] Polyphonic composition was now restricted to canticles or the *Ordinarium*, but composition of new Propers virtually ceased.

Did the church named after Luther fare any better? Once *cuius regio, eius religio* ("whose realm, his religion") had been adopted by the Peace of Augsburg for the German territories in 1555, the freedom envisioned by our theologian would apply only to the territorial lords; the local participation that Luther had declared all-important was now lost. A brilliant but brief period of religious freedom in the 1520s and 1530s would soon be eclipsed by political developments. Individual German states soon would adopt a system of church polity that would closely reflect the new Rome-centered bureaucracy. The grassroots movement of a lay priesthood that Luther had found in Scripture and tradition, and which had been the normal practice up to that time, would

---

49. Jungmann, *The Mass of the Roman Rite*, vol. 1, 132–41.
50. Jungmann, *The Mass of the Roman Rite*, vol. 1, 140–41.
51. Hiley, *Western Plainchant*, 618.

come to an abrupt end in both the Evangelical and Catholic institutions. The schisms that began to pervade Christendom—Mennonites, Anabaptists, Presbyterians, Anglicans, and Calvinists, among others—would be an expression of local religious fervor that could not be suppressed, though they previously had been allowed within a more tolerant church order. Each denomination, by separating itself from Holy Mother Church, would construct ever more insurmountable barriers to differentiate itself from the universal church. The unity that they professed with the creedal symbols would in many ways be lost.

Luther was very much a product of the theological and music-theoretical traditions of his time. He respected and cherished the musical heritage of the universal catholic church as expressed in Gregorian chant and the rich polyphonic repertoire that the church had so faithfully promoted. His suggestions for changing a worship service to reflect more adequately the personal piety of the faithful were accepted by the Council of Trent and instituted by subsequent church orders emanating from Rome. There was no hiatus in divine worship services beginning on October 31, 1517, but there was a continuing cross-fertilization between Wittenberg and the greater musical-ecclesiastical community around that university town. It is perhaps a tragedy that the symbiotic relationship between the members of the church universal in the 1520s and 1530s was co-opted by political developments and that Luther's ideas on music and liturgy were not seen for what they were—an improvement of something that was very precious.

CHAPTER 11

Luther on Faith and Reason
— The Light of Reason at the Twilight
of the World —

Hans-Peter Grosshans

We live now in a global world with a global understanding of how we live together. Our present condition leads us to question the high value we once gave to reason in the project of modernity. The idea that reason might be capable of improving our lives and facilitating our interactions with each other through different social and political institutions is widely contested today. Whether we esteem reason highly, care little for it, or see it as the cause of much evil in our world, we approach problems today without modernity's confidence in reason's capacity to better human lives. Rather than placing our trust in the unity of reason, as was the case in the modern West, we highlight in our "postmodern" West the differences in tradition, culture, human feeling, aesthetics, authority, the execution of power, religion, and how religion shapes morality.

Arguments in current public debates demonstrate this shift away from the unifying force of a universal reason. Worldwide church organizations—for example, the World Council of Churches (WCC) or the Lutheran World Federation (LWF)—shape arguments by privileging various traditions, circumstances, and situations in which people live rather than basing them on reason. The appeal to universal reason for establishing consensus is not usually the favored argument by which religious leaders find solutions to the church's internal problems or its problems with the world. The same situation exists in politics. The political realm is characterized today by the interests of various ethnic, religious, ideological, social, or other particular determinations of groups in a society. The various interests are weighed against each other according to the power that each group has in its respective society. In politics, as in churches, people do not typically use a universal form of reasoning to solve problems. Universal reason is oriented to the common good and does not necessarily mediate between the various group or party interests in a society.

The current rhetoric against reason is surprising. At least in the modern West, reason has been deployed historically as the universal tool to facilitate public and respectful interaction between people of different viewpoints. During the Enlightenment in the seventeenth and eighteenth centuries, reason became the means by which differences in tradition could be appreciated and individual lives could be mustered to pursue the common good. "Listen to the call of reason" is the philosopher John Locke's famous summons. Reason was called on to establish peace among previously warring religious and political groups, and it did so by providing ways to articulate the universal common good in the midst of competing particular interests. The first—and probably best—example of reason's potential to establish truthful consensus is Socrates. Socrates dedicated his life to striving for the good of society on the basis of reason, and his vision contained an implicit criticism of his own particular culture and morality, which precipitated his death sentence.

Today, the intellectual current is similar to Socrates's own time. The local is favored when it comes to solving problems of cultural, religious, political, and legal differences; the particular, not the universal, dictates the rules according to which people should live their lives. Current problems tend to be solved by referring to traditional answers from the past. This look to the past may be safer in terms of preserving group identity. But the result of underlining identity is that real communication between groups is not fostered. By placing various cultures, traditions, and contexts next to each other, real interaction between them is avoided.

How should we proceed when past traditions and ways of life do not provide solutions to current problems? This question is particularly pertinent in today's context of radical global change. Martin Luther lived in a time that also experienced great religious, political, and social upheaval. In order to work through the various dimensions of my question, I turn to Luther as a productive dialogue partner.

Luther and Reason

Luther's theology displays a surprisingly modern and inspiring understanding of reason and its role in public and private life. Luther thought very highly of human reason in almost all earthly affairs. He considered reason the God-given means to *explore* the psychic, social, and physical reality and to *shape* the natural, social, and moral world.

In spite of his high estimation of reason, it is Luther's criticism of reason that has received all the attention. Reason, for Luther, is a faculty of the human soul and is therefore a part of nature. It is bound to the created world, to time and space. When it respects its own limitations, it fulfills its God-given vocation. When it overextends itself beyond the empirical world, reason gets it wrong. Reason is woefully inadequate, even stubbornly sinful, in religious and spiritual matters. For Luther, reason deployed in religion always misses the true God and ends up constructing idols of its own fabrication. Luther's sharp criticism of reason as it relates to true religion and the true God is behind his famous condemnation of reason as a "whore" who sells itself to anyone—and every religious endeavor—that pays well.

We must consider both aspects—the appreciation for reason and the critical restriction of reason—in Luther's evaluation of human reason.[1] Both sides will help us explore how reason can be considered an invaluable tool for making arguments in discussions today.

Reason in Biblical Interpretation

An important area of contemporary debate is the interpretation of the Bible. How can reason play a role in interpreting this important text? My dialogue with Luther on this issue explores how Luther uses reason as an essential tool in his biblical hermeneutics. In fact, Luther can be seen primarily as a biblical scholar who assigns a particular and important role to reason in this task. The interpretation of biblical texts today is sometimes like a guessing game. The

---

1. The following are a few exemplary monographs—apart from discrete sections on reason in systematic-theological reconstructions of Luther's overall theology—that address Luther's understanding of reason: Gerhard Ebeling, *Lutherstudien*, vol. 2, *Disputatio de Homine*, 3 vols. (Tübingen: Mohr Siebeck, 1977, 1982, 1989); Wilfried Joest, *Ontologie der Person bei Luther* (Göttingen: Vandenhoeck & Ruprecht, 1967); Graham White, *Luther as Nominalist: A Study of the Logical Methods Used in Martin Luther's Disputations in the Light of Their Medieval Background*, Schriften der Luther-Agricola-Gesellschaft 30 (Helsinki: Luther-Agricola-Society, 1994).

Bible often is read to reassure people about their present or past practices, or as a starting point for contemplating one's inner self or social situation. The biblical texts are also used often as recipes from a cookbook that guide the "cooking" of one's own life. If the Bible is taken as a set of individual prescriptions from which to pick and choose, it is not taken seriously as the Holy Scriptures for today.

Luther's basic approach to the Bible is governed by the principle that Scripture is "self-authenticating." This phrase means that the Bible neither has nor requires any other guarantor for its truth other than itself. Luther articulated this principle as an alternative to other methods of biblical interpretation that introduced other sources and other authorities beside the Bible to make sense of biblical texts. The method of using different sources to help mediate between competing interpretations was used in Luther's time, particularly in Catholic and Anabaptist traditions.

The term "self-authenticating" is very important in Luther's understanding of how the Bible discloses the essence of its status as "Holy Scripture." It does not mean that the Bible must necessarily be inspired by God simply because "the Bible says so." One must keep in mind that Luther's understanding of biblical inspiration is quite different from the literal doctrine of inspiration that is prevalent in fundamentalist Christianity today. For Luther, literal inspiration is a weak circular argument. There must be a real reason why the Bible is "self-authenticating." Luther was a realist, and this meant that he understood the Bible's authority to rest entirely on its content. The Bible's reality derives from its referent: Jesus Christ and the divine activity of human salvation. The Bible's truth depends on its content, not the other way around. Its authority does not depend on the fact that the church has selected and combined the biblical texts into one large volume. The authority of the church depends rather on the truth of the Bible's content. Luther claims that the Bible is "totally certain . . . quite easy to understand, completely revealed, its own interpreter."[2] "It is splendid when Scripture interprets itself."[3] The Bible "interprets itself" by successfully conveying its content of divine mercy in Christ. This content alone has the capacity to guarantee the Bible's truth. No other inspiration, whether of person or church, can usurp this capacity.

---

2. "Ipso per sese certissmima, facillima, apertissmime, sui ipsius interpres": WA 7:97, 23 (*Assertio omnium articulorum M. Luther per bullam Leonis X. novissimam damnatorum*; Dec. 1520). (Translation H.-P. G.)
3. "Also ist die schrifftt jr selbs ain aigen liecht. Das ist dann fein, wenn sich die schrifft selbs außlegt": WA 10/3:238, 10-11 ("Sermon on Saint James Day"; 1532).

Luther's understanding of biblical interpretation can be contrasted with the reading of Scripture proposed by the sixteenth-century Anabaptist movement. The Anabaptists stressed the inward and spiritual side of Christian life and set the Holy Spirit in opposition to the letter of Scripture. They made the experience of the Holy Spirit the necessary qualification for church membership. Church leadership of religious communities fell to those who were spirit-filled, whether they were clergy or laity. Thomas Müntzer articulated his view of the Spirit's role in biblical interpretation: "God discloses himself in the inner word in the abyss of the soul. The man who has not received the living witness of God knows really nothing about God, though he may have swallowed one hundred thousand bibles. God comes in dreams to his beloved as he did to the patriarchs, prophets, and apostles. . . . God pours out his Spirit upon all flesh, and now the Spirit reveals to the elect a mighty and irresistible reformation to come."[4]

For Anabaptists, true interpretation of biblical texts required a spiritual talent that God gives to particular people. Luther agreed with the view that the Holy Spirit is indispensable in interpreting Scripture, but he differed from the Anabaptists by claiming that the Spirit is conveyed exclusively in the words of the Bible. Luther was in fundamental disagreement with the theological position of "enthusiasm," by which he meant the imposition of interpretational rules onto Scripture that were not in line with the spirit of the Bible. He put both Catholics and Anabaptists into the enthusiast camp because he was suspicious of their allegorical, pictorial interpretations of biblical texts. Luther's own hermeneutic advocated a literal interpretation, which he deemed was the sole vehicle of biblical meaning. At the literal level, the Bible was clear enough for human reason to interpret.

Luther's *The Bondage of the Will* (1525) articulates in part his understanding of biblical interpretation. One aspect to Luther's discussion with Erasmus of Rotterdam is Luther's evaluation of the human mind's capacity to understand Scripture clearly. Luther introduces his new distinction between the external and the internal clarity of Scripture in this discussion:

> To put it briefly, there are two kinds of clarity in Scripture, just as there are also two kinds of obscurity: one external and pertaining to the ministry of the Word, the other located in the understanding of the heart. If you speak of internal clarity, no man perceives one iota of what is in the Scriptures unless he has the Spirit of God. All men have a darkened heart,

---

4. Cited in Roland H. Bainton, *Here I Stand: A Life of Martin Luther* (Nashville: Abingdon, 1990), 204.

so that even if they can recite everything in Scripture . . . yet they apprehend and truly understand nothing of it. . . . For the Spirit is required for
the understanding of Scripture. . . . If, on the other hand, you speak of the
external clarity, nothing at all is left obscure or ambiguous.[5]

Luther puts forward the distinction as a response to Erasmus's claim that
Scripture contains obscure passages that make it necessary for their interpretation to be decided by church authorities or church tradition.

Luther's distinction aims to contradict Erasmus's position. For Luther,
the Bible has an external clarity, which refers to human reason's capacity to
understand clearly the literary signs—words, punctuation, grammar, and syntax—that explain the text's meaning. There is nothing "obscure or ambiguous"
about the biblical text's external character. The Bible also has an inner clarity,
by which Luther means that the Bible's religious meaning must be understood
by the heart. This inner perception of the Bible by the human heart requires
the activity of the Holy Spirit. Only the Spirit can disclose the Bible's content,
Christ and salvation, to the individual reader (or hearer) of the text. When the
Holy Spirit acts, the Bible's inner clarity is apprehended. In view of both inner
and external clarity, external authorities or sources are not necessary for the
task of interpretation.

Luther's distinction seems to privilege human reason highly in interpreting the biblical text independently of established sources. A sound mind and
faithful heart can access the full and true extent of what the Bible has to say.
Some philosophers have noticed Luther's defense of the human mind's capacity to interpret the Bible and have applauded Luther's freedom of the human
mind over Erasmus's tendency to abdicate interpretation to church authority.
The contemporary Croatian philosopher, Jure Zovko, shows in a recent article
that Luther's call to employ reason in biblical interpretation is a characteristic
mainstay of the Luther tradition. Particularly the second-generation Lutheran
theologian, Matthias Flacius Illyricus, develops Luther's view in a text that is
considered foundational in the history of hermeneutics, the *Clavis sacrae scrip-
turae* (*The Keys of Holy Scripture*). Zovko shows that Flacius shared Luther's
idea that a reader can correctly and faithfully understand the biblical text by
following generally acknowledged rules—rules of reading and interpretation
that proceed from human reason.[6]

---

5. LW 33:28 (*Bondage of the Will*; 1525).
6. Jure Zovko, "Die Bibelinterpretation bei Flacius und ihre Bedeutung für die moderne
Hermeneutik," *Theologische Literaturzeitung* 132 (2007): 1169–80.

Luther's position, however, also notes the limits of human reason. Human reason can discover the meaning of biblical texts, but it has no access to their inner clarity. Reason cannot convince the human heart to trust in the Bible's message—especially in the promise of the gospel.

Reason in Theology

The distinction Luther makes in his biblical hermeneutics between reason and the understanding of the heart is also relevant to Luther's use of reason in theology.

In Luther's opinion, it is an important element of reason's capacity to make clear distinctions. It is necessary to make distinctions everyday in order to clarify issues and actions. To distinguish is an act of human reason. Reason distinguishes between different objects and events. It also distinguishes between the different ways in which human beings relate to objects, to themselves, to others, and to God. Luther appeals to reason to understand the external aspect of Scripture because reason distinguishes correct from incorrect interpretations. With reason, a human being can distinguish between its reason, which seeks understanding, and its heart, which seeks to trust. Reason cannot create trust. Questions of the heart cannot be decided by reason. The heart should consider the jurisdiction of reason, but it is not by reason that the human heart comes to trust or distrust. Luther captures this idea in his explanation of the Third Article of the Creed in his Small Catechism: "I believe that by my own understanding or strength I cannot believe in Jesus Christ my Lord or come to him."[7]

The twilight is the time of day when we cannot clearly distinguish between light and dark, between objects and events. Sometimes we have trouble distinguishing between good and evil, between responsibility and risk, between individual agency and global accountability. When must we act on the basis of trust and when must we act on the basis of reason? People contribute to the world's twilight when they confuse reason and trust in their lives. Some people try to use reason to cultivate trust in others and in God—and in doing so lose the essence of trust. Some people operate with a trust that is not justified rationally in areas in which they should use reason. One can see daily this confusion in politics and, quite often, in economics: when people do not act in these areas on the basis of reason but on the basis of speculative trust.

---

7. BoC, 355, 6.

The current post-Enlightenment view of reason rehearses Luther's disparagement of reason. The Lutheran tradition has also followed this line of thinking. But it has overlooked Luther's own distinction between reason and trust in particular matters of the heart. In this regard, the postmodern appeal to Luther as an ally is a misunderstanding of his positive view of reason in human thought and action.

Reason in Life

How did Martin Luther understand the positive capacities of reason? A classic point of departure for exploring this question is Luther's explanation to the First Article of the Creed in the Large Catechism. Here Luther writes: "I hold and believe that I am God's creature, that is, that he has given me and constantly sustains my body, soul, and life, my members great and small, all my senses, my reason and understanding, and the like."[8]

Another key text is the 1536 disputation, *Concerning the Human*. Luther makes a strong case for reason in this disputation. Reason is part of God's good creation. Luther's fourth thesis admits reason's divine origin: "And it is certainly true that reason is the most important and the highest in rank among all things and, in comparison with other things of this life, the best and something divine."[9] Luther praises reason's achievements. Reason is "the inventor and mentor of all the arts, medicines, laws, and of whatever wisdom, power, virtue, and glory men possess in this life."[10] Culture, art, science, medicine, and law are under reason's jurisdiction.

Luther's disputation clearly assigns reason to tasks that are strictly located in this world, to what we can empirically grasp. Yet Luther insinuates that reason has a quality that is akin to godlike majesty. This "image of God" has as its God-given task to order the human being's earthly life. Luther articulates this high estimation of reason in thesis 8 of the disputation: Reason "is a sun and a kind of god appointed to administer these things in this life."[11] Thesis 8 alludes to Aristotle's discussion of the same subject in *On the Soul*, while

---

8. BoC, 432, 13.
9. LW 34:137 (*The Disputation concerning Man*; 1536). (The English title given in the LW translation is "man," although the term, "human," is a more appropriate translation of the Latin, "homo." [C. H.])
10. LW 34:137 (thesis 5).
11. LW 34:137. According to Aristotle, "thought is, no doubt, something more divine and impassible": Aristotle, *De anima* I:4 (408b29-30); cited from Aristotle, "On the Soul," trans. J. A. Smith, in *The Complete Works of Aristotle: The Revised Oxford Translation*, 2 vols., ed. Jonathan Barnes, Bollingen Series 71–72 (Princeton: Princeton University Press, 1984), vol. 1, 651; for further discussion, see Ebeling, *Disputatio de Homine*, vol. 2, 189.

establishing a difference. According to Aristotle, reason shows its divine status in the philosophical way of life. Aristotle calls this way of life the "theoretical life." Luther, in contrast, sees the divine dimension of human reason in the "active life" of human beings; reason is capable of making sound decisions about economy, politics, and the sciences. Theology must respect reason's competence in earthly affairs by allowing reason to make political, economic, and scientific judgments.

Luther's discussion surprisingly does not appeal to an important classic distinction in the concept of reason. Augustine and later the Scholastics distinguished between two parts of reason: a superior part and an inferior part (a *portio superior* and a *portio inferior*).[12] This distinction reflects two different directions of reason: the superior part of reason is directed toward the *aeterna*, or eternal things, and the inferior part is directed toward the *temporalia*, the temporal objects. This distinction also reflects two different acts of knowledge: the superior part of reason is intellectual (*intelligere*), knowing something in its simple wholeness, and the inferior part employs discursive thinking (*ratiocinari*). This distinction in others words is the distinction between wisdom and science. The Scholastics, like Augustine, distinguished between use (*uti*) and enjoyment (*frui*), which means that all *temporalia* are meant to be used by us, and all *aeterna* are meant to be enjoyed by us—and not to be used. The inferior part of reason deals with all temporal creatures; the superior part of reason deals with God, who is the only one that human beings can really enjoy.

Instead of the classic distinction between a superior and an inferior part of reason, Luther distinguishes between reason (*ratio*) and faith (*fides*). This distinction has new possibilities for determining specific roles that reason might play in today's twilight of the world.

The first implication is that any relationship between human beings and God (and all eternal things) is not conceived by reason—not even by a superior part of reason. Faith alone is the vehicle and instrument by which the human person is related to the triune God. Only by faith can the human being apprehend God's self-giving and self-revealing essence in Jesus Christ. The human person is given faith to connect to God in a relationship with God. Reason is, thereby, freed by faith from any illusions of attaining God on its own capacity. Once freed from the *aeterna*, reason becomes the vehicle and instrument by which human beings are related to all the *temporalia*.

A second implication of Luther's distinction is a new concept of the human person. Traditionally, the human being was defined as a rational animal

---

12. Augustine, *De trin.* XII, 3:4.

(*animal rationale*). Rationality is the essential characteristic of human nature. The human being is then identified with its rationality. Consequently, a human person—in this tradition—is not the subject of her own determination.

Luther's distinction between reason and faith has an important consequence for the philosophical tradition that regards the human person as subordinate to a given general determination of reason. In fact, Luther's distinction makes it possible to conceive the human being as the subject of her rationality. A human person is related to God by faith. Within this relationship, she perceives herself to be the subject of her own life in the temporal world. The human person can use reason within the sphere of personal responsibility to exercise her own subjectivity in the world. The human person is free to use her reason to exercise her own subjectivity and to deal exclusively with worldly things.

One very relevant implication of Luther's abandoning of the older distinction between the two parts of reason is the issue of gender. The superior part of reason was traditionally perceived as dominating in men and the inferior part dominating in women. By abandoning this distinction, Luther acknowledges that the capacity for reason is equal in women and men, as is the human capacity to know God. Unfortunately, it took Lutheran churches several hundred years to embrace the equal rationality of both men and women and allow women to be ordained to the ministry. The ordination of women reflects Luther's concept of reason: men and women are equal before God and in their ability to relate to God, to know God and all eternal things, and to serve God at the altar and everywhere in the world.

Reason and Faith at the Twilight of the World

We can now develop an idea of the complementary activity between faith and reason on Luther's terms. Reason equips human beings to bring light to the twilight of the world. One might, however, acknowledge that reason has contributed to the twilight. Reason has precipitated some of modernity's ills, as postmodern thinkers propound. But reason is one of the only capacities in human nature that can bring clarity to the self-produced twilight. Reason has been characterized since Immanuel Kant by "critique." Reason is able to reflect critically on the self and on others. Reason's struggle for truth makes its critical reflections valuable. Reason's critical capacity shows that it communicates—critically and dialectically—with one's own thinking, one's past, the contributions of others, and their pasts.

Faith also can shed light on the twilight produced by human reason. Faith informs reason about its own role, limits, and dignity. Faith, as faith, is responsible for religious matters. By limiting its jurisdiction to things of the spirit, faith opens up the world to reason. The use of human reason, free from illusions or "higher" ambitions and expectations, is characteristic of Lutheran theology. This position is not identical to the concept of secularized reason: that human reason, as it relates to all earthly things and affairs, is completely separate from theology. Rather, reason is considered to be God-given; its origins authorize its jurisdiction as part of the God-given order. Reason is to be used in all worldly affairs, including the articulation of theology. Yet human beings—who are generally understood as sinners in Lutheran theology—are always tempted to misuse reason and to ascribe to reason more value than it actually has. Theology must employ reason in order to safeguard it from making claims that overextend the limits of reason.

Luther's understanding of Adam's fall is relevant in this context of discussing the capacities and limits of reason. Luther did not claim that reason was entirely incapacitated as a result of Adam's fall. All people are able to order and govern their earthly affairs rightly by using the rational capacities that God has given them. Luther writes, "Nor did God after the fall of Adam take away this majesty of reason, but rather confirmed it."[13] But reason "loses its way" after Adam's fall. By this Luther means that reason no longer recognizes its own God-given dignity, and by not attributing reason to its divine source, reason is also unable to determine its own limits. Reason's God-given jurisdiction is the natural, moral, and social world. But reason's drive to overextend its jurisdiction might be the result of refusing to acknowledge God as the source of setting the limits of reason. Reason's lure to overextend itself might also be due to its lack of respect for other capacities of the human soul. In this regard, reason should allow these other capacities their rightful place in a person's life.

We can learn from Luther that a right use of reason in today's world is an exercise of freedom. When we are confronted with the task of solving the many problems we have on a daily basis in the various areas of life, we find that preestablished answers, laws, norms, values, or ways to order the world are not helpful or applicable. In these instances, we can appeal to reason to develop in freedom our own answers, laws, norms, values, or ways of ordering the world (or, in other words, of determining the way the world is ordered). God places

---

13. LW 34:137 (*Concerning the Human*).

us in a free space that God has created for us in the natural, moral, and social world. It is a world in which we can orient ourselves and create our own ways to order. To use a formulation from Friedrich Nietzsche: the orders we assign to the world so that we can live in it are the responses to the very freedom that is our birthright.

Today's Ecumenical Discussion

How can reason help us to know God? This question addresses the classic relationship between theology and philosophy, and it is particularly pertinent in light of the contemporary discussion of the relationship between faith and reason.

Pope Benedict XVI can be credited for putting reason and its role in theology back on the ecumenical agenda. Perhaps one of his most controversial lectures to date was held on this topic in 2006 at the University of Regensburg in Germany.[14] In his address, Benedict XVI reiterates a familiar criticism of the theology of the sixteenth-century Reformation: the theology of the Reformation was historically, according to Benedict, the first major attack on the alliance between faith and reason. The complementarity between faith and reason was developed in the first five centuries of the Christian church. For Benedict, early Christianity was characterized by marrying biblical religion to Greek philosophy as a historically necessary development. The theology of the Reformation turned out to be a regression to the antithesis between the two. God was thought of as utterly transcendent and beyond the limits of reason. God could only be known through revelation in biblical texts.

But as Benedict XVI argues, if reason cannot grasp God, then God is beyond reason's control, and much can be claimed in God's name that is entirely unreasonable. The suspicion is that the emphasis on God's utter transcendence opens the door to violence in God's name. The implicit claim in Benedict's considerations is that Protestant Christianity falls into this trap. The Protestant difficulty is avoided by relating God to reason for the sake of a peaceful life. For peace, Benedict's argument continues, a synthesis between faith and reason is needed in a Christian conception of God. A rational order in nature, morals, and the social world can then be derived from this concept of God. Perhaps it is not surprising that some representatives of modern

---

14. Benedict XVI, *Glaube und Vernunft: Die Regensburger Vorlesung: Vollständige Ausgabe*, with commentaries by Gesine Schwan, Adel Theodor Khoury, and Karl Lehmann (Freiburg: Herder, 2006).

Roman Catholic theology claim to know the fundamental order of the cosmos and of human life.[15]

The complementarity between faith and reason follows from the presupposition that a fixed natural and moral order in our world is given by God and accessible to human beings. Luther's reformation theology is based on another presupposition and has different implications. The Reformation understands the natural and moral world to be a space given to humans by God. God has equipped humans with reason to explore and shape the world in ways that promote life. Thus reason emerges in reformation theology as the new horizon of both order and communication in most, if not all, aspects of life. This horizon is embedded in an original relationship between God, the world, and humankind by virtue of God's creative activity. This original relationship is "beyond" reason; reason cannot explain or justify this relationship because it is grounded in the mercy, grace, and love of God. As such, reformation theology preserves God's transcendence in the sense of distinguishing sharply between creator and creature. But with respect to both this world and human life, all competence is given to human reason. This competence includes the possibility of redefining the order of nature and of the social world. While some Roman Catholic theologians conceive the natural and social world as given by God with a fixed order that human beings must explore, the Lutheran concept of the world's social and natural order is that order is always a result of human activity. The best ways of ordering the social and natural world stem from the activity of human reason that does not instantiate an exercise of power.

Reason can contribute to an analysis of the relation between God and world. Natural theology and philosophy of religion are useful critical tools in a theological perspective that sets particular limits to both. Reason is fully capable of making claims concerning the existence of God and of predicating the attributes of transcendence, omnipotence, and eternity of God. But on Luther's terms, trust cannot be produced by reason. Consequently, reason cannot provide the foundation of a person's relationship to the God revealed in Jesus Christ. Reason *is* necessary to define both its own limits and the difference between reason and faith, between knowing and believing, between the responsibilities of human beings and the responsibilities of God, and between the problems we have to solve and the problems that are not ours—because they are God's.

---

15. For a criticism of the Roman Catholic concept of faith and reason, see Hans-Peter Grosshans, "And the Truth Will Make You Free: On the Relationship between Religion, Truth, and Power," *Studies in Interreligious Dialogue* 17 (2007): 184–204.

Part Four

Luther's Theology for Today

Two ideas are practically synonymous with Luther's name: the doctrine of justification and the theology of the cross. These are the foundation of Luther's thought. They have also generated an abundance of theological reflection after Luther. This volume has approached the heart of Luther's theology through interdisciplinary discussions of what it means to be a human person. By taking this specific route to the doctrine of justification, the theological claim is made that even Luther's own theology must be contextualized by broader issues informing the explicit description of theology's subject. Theology as a discipline is articulated by the human subject, who bears witness to experiences attributed to God as their cause. Justification is a doctrine about the divine subject who creates a new relationship of freedom for the sinner.

Ideas inevitably take concrete shape in daily life. If justification is the message of freedom, then it is made relevant by its reception in different social realities. If God addresses persons through people, then God's address is conveyed amid social circumstances. In view of the economic and political realities of his own time, Luther took the welfare of the poor very seriously. Luther's theology was marked from its very beginnings by his commitment to social issues. The intimate weave in Luther's own life between his theological convictions and his social action is crucial as we explore the question of justification's relevance to contemporary life.

The importance of Luther's doctrine of justification is discussed in this section by Theodor Dieter. Dieter's question—is the doctrine of justification at all relevant for today?—is daring, particularly as it goes to the heart of Lutheran identity. The very raison d'être of Christianity is at issue. Yet this question must be asked if Luther's theology is to be a "living tradition." Dieter offers an answer to the question and in the process gives a multidimensional account of this key doctrine. Antti Raunio addresses the social and ethical implications of justification in the political reality of the Nordic welfare states. Ronald F. Thiemann takes Luther's theology of the cross into the contemporary context of religious pluralism. All three authors pull the doctrine of justification into areas of current concern. They give examples of how Luther's theology, even its very foundation, ought to be tested for its merits. This work of testing is a key aspect of theology as a creative, critical, and living enterprise.

CHAPTER 12

Why Does Luther's Doctrine of Justification Matter Today?

Theodor Dieter

Translated by Christine Helmer

Problem and Possible Solutions

"When I preach on the article of justification, the congregation sleeps and coughs. When I begin to tell stories and give examples, the people perk up their ears, are quiet, and listen intently."[1] These are not the words of a frustrated pastor at the beginning of the twenty-first century. They are Luther's comments in 1532 on the reactions of his parishioners to sermons on justification. Even in Luther's day, ordinary people understood "justification" to mean something very different from the grand meaning assigned to it by Lutheran theologians, namely, the article by which the church stands or falls.[2] Three hundred years after Luther, on the anniversary of the Reformation in 1817, Johann Wolfgang von Goethe commented in a letter to Karl Ludwig von Knebel that justification had completely lost its relevance. "The only thing worth mentioning [about the Reformation] is Luther's personality. Luther is about the only thing that really makes an impression on people. Everything else is confused nonsense, and we must contend with this burden on a daily basis."[3] And in 1963, a document entitled "Justification Today" was circulated

---

1. WATr 2:454, 17–19 (no. 2408b; between January 10 and 22, 1532). (Translation C. H.)
2. See Theodor Mahlmann, "Articulus stantis et (vel) cadentis ecclesiae," in *RGG* 1:799–800.
3. Cited in Heinrich Bornkamm, *Luther im Spiegel der deutschen Geistesgeschichte: Mit ausgewählten Texten von Lessing bis zur Gegenwart*, 2nd rev. edn. (Göttingen: Vandenhoeck & Ruprecht, 1970), 216.

at the General Assembly of the Lutheran World Federation in Helsinki. The document attracted widespread attention and, although it was not deemed binding for the church at the time, it represents the sentiments of the day:

> The Reformation witness to justification by faith alone was the answer to the existential questions: "How do I find a gracious God?" Almost no one asks this question in the world in which we live today. But the question persists: "How do I find meaning for my life?" When man seeks for meaning in his life he is impelled to justify his existence in his own eyes and before his fellow men. He then proceeds to judge his fellow men by these same standards. This is why men are confident of their own accomplishments and avid for recognition and fame. It also explains why there is so much mutual accusation and condemnation. Do men not all compulsively pursue dreams of the future which they expect will give validity to their lives?[4]

Countless discussions of the doctrine of justification in Lutheran churches all around the world were inspired by the 1999 signing of the *Joint Declaration on the Doctrine of Justification* in Augsburg by representatives of the Lutheran World Federation and the Roman Catholic Church. Yet often the actual significance of the doctrine of justification remains unclear. The many discussions of the topic circulate repetitive formulas about "the" doctrine of justification without really dealing seriously with the subject matter. The doctrine's motto as "the article by which the church stands or falls" is taken as an unquestioned and unexamined authority in many Lutheran circles. But what is the doctrine of justification, and why does it matter to us today?

There are a few ways to answer the two parts of this question. The first is to diagnose the issues troubling human life today and then to prescribe the doctrine of justification as the solution for one of the problems, hopefully the most important of them. Such a diagnostic procedure takes place without presupposing that the doctrine of justification is the solution. Justification is drawn in as the solution only after the analysis is complete. This way highlights the argument's strength: the doctrine of justification is relevant for today because it is, or rather its actuality in human lives is, the answer to pressing human questions.

The difficulty with this method, however, is that the answer purports to have a key insight into the human condition; without justification, no such

---

4. *Proceedings of the Fourth Assembly of the Lutheran World Federation Helsinki, July 30 to August 11, 1963* (Berlin and Hamburg: Lutherisches Verlagshaus, 1965), 478.

insight is to be had. If this way of arguing were adequate, then a diagnosis of the human condition not oriented to justification would be only partially correct. If one then claimed that justification were the solution to a basic problem defined by diagnosing the human condition, then the understanding of justification would be compromised. Furthermore, diagnosis allows for a variety of solutions. By this token, justification could not be mustered as the only solution to the human problem. An exclusive argument for justification could not be made in this case to solve a real and pressing problem.

The second way begins by exploring a few elementary aspects of human life, such as the foundational problems of doubt and certainty, of meaning and meaninglessness. The doctrine of justification is then brought into these explorations in order to plumb their depth-dimensions and to identify something akin to "justification" in the meaning available in meaninglessness, or certainty in doubt, and joy in sorrow. This method applies a general meaning of justification for comparative purposes and thereby abstracts from justification's unique theological content. In order to demonstrate its relevance broadly to contemporary experience, justification pays a heavy price. Justification moves away from the specifics of "Christ alone," witnessed in "Scripture alone," so that the correlated terms "by grace alone," "by word/sacrament alone," and "by faith alone" are altered at a fundamental level. All that is left of the classic Lutheran doctrine of justification are structural similarities.

The third way is actually to begin with the doctrine of justification, in spite of the fact that the significance of this doctrine for modern human beings has been called into question. The doctrine of justification here is taken as the answer to a question that has yet to be posed. If justification is determined in this round-about way, it becomes suspect for first creating a problem that it then afterwards promises to solve. A defense of this method claims that justification simply discovers a problem that already exists in the depths of the human soul. If the claim is advanced that justification is indeed a helpful tool in making sense of human existence, then it must show how justification can both disclose humanity's deepest needs and fulfill them by establishing a new relationship to God. The underlying argument of this third way is that plausibility for justification is charted step by step in the movement from need to fulfillment and vice versa. Its advantage is that it deliberately reveals what is alien in the doctrine of justification to contemporary people. If justification is to be appropriated as exciting and pertinent, then it must be treated as a unique challenge for us today.

The Doctrine of Justification

Human Destiny and the Sin of Unbelief

Humans are aware that they are not their own creation. They recognize that personal existence, prior to every temporal moment or action, is given to them by others, most immediately by their parents. Existence in its deepest sense is confessed by Christians as given by God. According to Christian theology, humans, like all other beings, are found in the world: we are all creatures of God. Creatures are created through the word, as the first page of the Bible tells us. God, who creates human persons, also assigns them their destiny. Humans are destined to hear God speak to them and to respond.

Martin Luther recognized that serious and wonderful consequences follow from the recognition that God speaks in many ways with humans: "Where and with whomever God speaks, whether in anger or in grace, that person is surely immortal. The Person of God, who speaks, and the Word point out that we are the kind of creatures with whom God would want to speak eternally and in an immortal manner."[5] Luther's recognition, articulated in his *Lectures on Genesis* (1535–1545), is striking. God has no beginning or end because God is God. When God begins to speak to a human being, when God creates that person, God never stops talking with her. God enters into a relationship with the created person that never ends. Nor does God's speech with the person terminate with death. Rather, God overcomes the death of the body with resurrection. Luther accounts for the immortality of the mortal human being from the perspective of God's speech. God's eternal speech with the human person creates her immortality. Luther applies this argument to human destiny. Humans are destined to be *a* conversation (that is, not only *in*) with God. Community with God is humanity's eternal calling.

Luther has human immortality in mind when he distinguishes between philosophy and theology in his disputation *Concerning the Human* (1536).[6] Philosophy is preoccupied with the human being in this present life, meaning the mortal human (thesis 3), whereas theology "defines man as whole and perfect" (thesis 20).[7] A human being is created in the image of God and thus destined to eternal life.[8] In the words of Dietrich Bonhoeffer, philosophy is

---

5. LW 5:76 (to Gen 26:24), WA 43:481, 32–35.
6. LW 34:135 (*The Disputation concerning Man*; 1536). (The English title given in the LW translation is "man," although the term "human" is a more appropriate translation of the Latin "homo." [C. H.])
7. LW 34:135, 137, WA 39/I:175, 7–8, 176, 5–6.
8. LW 34:137, WA 39/I:176, 7–8, 12–13.

concerned with the penultimate, theology with the ultimate. The penultimate is not untrue simply because it precedes the ultimate; the penultimate is only false when it desires to be the ultimate. Luther makes the important distinction between the mortal human, who exists from birth to death, and the human, made in the image of God and destined for immortal community with God. There is a difference between any human judgment—even my own judgment—over me and my life and God's judgment over me and my life. We humans usually confuse this distinction, to our great misfortune.

Sometimes human beings are aware of their destiny to be in communicative community with God. But even if they have knowledge *about* God, they may not know *who* God is. Luther loves to highlight this important point in his interpretation of Jonah. Jonah the prophet escapes God's call and gains passage on a ship that runs into a terrible storm. The mariners fear for their lives and all cry out to their own respective god (Jonah 1:5-6). They know *that* God is a being from whom they can expect every good, but they do not know *who* God is. In the explanation to the First Commandment in his Large Catechism, Luther writes,

> What does "to have a god" mean, or what is God? Answer: A "god" is the term for that to which we are to look for all good and in which we are to find refuge in all need. Therefore, to have a god is nothing else than to trust and believe in that one with your whole heart. As I have often said, it is the trust and faith of the heart alone that make both God and an idol. If your faith and trust are right, then your God is the true one. Conversely, where your trust is false and wrong, there you do not have the true God. For these two belong together, faith and God. Anything on which your heart relies and depends, I say, that is really your God.[9]

If human beings do not know who God is, then they trust in a false god and anticipate good gifts from this god. The First Commandment, "You are to have no other gods," is broken.[10] For Luther the "original sin" is that human beings do not know who to trust; they trust in false gods. Original sin's perversion exists before humans actually encounter the word of God—as both the word about God and the word of God's promise. When God's word is encountered against the background of original sin, a controversy emerges concerning who the true God is. Which god is worthy of human trust?

---

9. BoC, 386, 2–3.
10. Cited according to BoC, 386, 28.

Sin: To Seek One's Own in All Things[11]

The existential corollary of the lack of trust in the true God (or in other words, trust in a false god) is a perverse orientation of human will, striving, and desire. The person who doesn't trust the one who is the giver of all good things must struggle toward the good by himself. It can be said with Luther: sin consists of seeking one's own good in all things.

Sin is not just selfish behavior, hoarding more than what rightly belongs to you or giving to someone else less than she deserves. Sin is much more serious than this. The sinner is like King Midas in Greek mythology, who strives to fulfill his insatiable desire for wealth: everything he touches turns to gold, including food and drink. Similarly, the sinner hoards every good he does or receives. He does everything with his own good in mind. He may act morally by giving other people what they deserve, acting morally precisely because it is good and commanded by right reason. Yet when he recognizes his good deed, he pats himself on the back and applauds his moral superiority. Perhaps this sinner has pious intentions. But he exhibits his superior piety by showing off with devout actions and dutiful meditating, with prayers and fasting, and with acts of charity to others. He compares himself to others who are not as spiritually advanced as he is, and he despises them. Religious folk sometimes fight about which ways to serve God are the best and who is the most pious. We may infer from the intensity of many of these debates that they have nothing to do with loving and serving God. This form of religiosity has to do, first, foremost, and last, with the human alone.

Luther took seriously the task of the human to love God and neighbor (Matt 22:37-40).[12] All capacities and functions of the human soul must be focused on loving God. Only one action truly can satisfy this commandment: the self-giving of the entire person to God. The will can control only acts of will, however, not the affects or sensuous desires. The will is directed only to the cultivation of virtue. Yet the person is constituted by much more than the will. The giving of the entire self to God cannot be an object of the will because the will only takes specific acts, not the whole person, as its object. There is an insoluble dilemma that the law requires the very thing that humans are not capable of. How can this difficulty be solved?

---

11. On this topic, see my *Der junge Luther und Aristoteles: Eine historisch-systematische Untersuchung zum Verhältnis von Theologie und Philosophie*, Theologische Bibliothek Töpelmann 105 (Berlin: de Gruyter, 2001), 80–107.

12. The New Testament double love commandment has Deuteronomy 6:5 in view: "You shall love the LORD your God with all your heart, and with all your soul, and with all your might."

The scholastic theologians of the middle ages resolved the difficulty with the axiom: "No one is obliged above and beyond his capacities" (*ultra posse nemo obligatur*). For the medievals, the command in Deuteronomy 6:5 is satisfied when the human loves God above all. The fulfillment of the command is taken by the medievals as an act of the will. Luther, on the contrary, did not use human capacity to measure God's demand, but rather he used God's demand to evaluate the whole human condition: the human, incapable of fulfilling God's commandment, is a sinner. Luther's early *Lectures on Romans* (1515–1516) appealed to experience in their exposure of sin: "For willy-nilly they recognize the evil lusts in themselves. For this reason I say: 'Hah! Get busy now, I beg you. Be men! Work with all your might, so that these lusts may no longer be in you. Prove that it is possible by nature to love God, as you say, "with all your strength" (Luke 10:27) and without any grace. If you are without concupiscence, we will believe you. But if you live with and in these lusts, then you are no longer fulfilling the Law.' Does not the Law say, 'You shall not covet' (Ex. 20:17), but rather, 'You shall love God' (Deut. 6:5)?"[13] The capacity to give the entire self to God does not lie in the will's power, and here Luther's position agrees with scholastic theology. Luther concludes that the human person does not have the freedom to love God as God requires. Where Luther differs from his medieval predecessors is to identify who the human is—a sinner—by judging the human according to a standard that has not been crafted to human possibility.

If this were all Luther had to say on the matter, the human situation would be desperate. Luther's radical understanding of the law is a challenge to the contemporary reader. The dominant discourse regarding the inner life today is psychology, and from a psychological perspective, Luther on the law presents an impossible ideal that makes humans anxious, even unbalanced. Many people today are already burdened by multiple demands. A humane psychology would aim to ease the impact of life's stresses. Yet now, we come with Luther and place a new demand on people's shoulders that surpasses all the demands of daily life. Many contemporary Christians would exclaim, "This bleak understanding of law must be criticized in the name of the gospel." Such a reaction brings today's ideas about law and gospel to light. The gospel is seen as recasting the law's demands for the purpose of a more tolerable life. Gone is Luther's understanding of gospel as deliverance from a desperate situation.

---

13. LW 25:262 (to Rom 16:27), WA 56:275, 4–10.

The Christian response I have described can be seen in some Roman-Catholic ways of thinking. If one agrees today with this response, one will not be able to understand the first thesis of the Ninety-Five Theses on indulgences that famously declares "the entire life of believers to be one of repentance."[14] This thesis, foundational for all subsequent theses in the text, presupposes that the law's demand is to love God completely and entirely.

Luther's solution is a new configuration of the relation between law and gospel. In the *Lectures on Romans*, Luther relates law and gospel (using the terminology of old and new law) in this way: "The real difference between the old and the new law is this, that the old law says to those who are proud in their own righteousness: 'You must have Christ and His Spirit'; the new law says to those who humbly admit their spiritual poverty and seek Christ: 'Behold, here is Christ and His Spirit.'"[15] The law's spiritual sense does not list imperatives that place an unbearable burden on a person. Rather, it confronts a person with the desperation of her situation and points to Christ as the way out. The appropriate reaction to this news is to desire "to have" Christ.

Luther's new configuration does not compromise the law's demand to give the entire self to God. Neither should it be misunderstood today as an amplified ideal. The law's spiritual sense might be more accessible today if it were described as a critical theory of morals, even though Luther was not explicitly preoccupied with moral deeds. A moral act is an act of will that has in its purview the knowledge of the good in a specific situation and does the good on account of the good. When Luther writes that the sinner seeks his own in all things, he does not dismiss the claim that the human, in respect of the will's intention, can do the good on account of the good. Luther is, however, more interested in *how* humans deal with their moral actions. Humans struggle with conflicting desires, thus they might be content when they manage to perform moral actions. Conversely, they are unmerciful and even scornful when they notice immoral behavior in someone else. How humans relate to their moral actions is evidence that they seek their own in all things. Although a person might give to another what she deserves, he aims to serve himself by this act. Much conflict is caused by such self-serving intention.

The law's spiritual sense is part and parcel of human experience. The law sheds light in the depths of the human condition. The desperation remains shrouded in darkness if the light is not turned on.

---

14. LW 31:25 (*Ninety-Five Theses or Disputation on the Power and Efficacy of Indulgences*; 1517), WA 1:233, 10–11.
15. LW 25:327 (to Rom 16:27), WA 56:338, 27–30.

Overcoming Sin by Justification

The sinful human, curved in upon himself, runs around in circles. The sinner's lack of faith and his perversion of love have to be broken up by a divine double strategy. Luther emphasizes both aspects at different times of his life, but they actually belong together.

The theology of the cross captures one dimension of God's plan. Luther writes in the *Heidelberg Disputation* of 1518: "A theologian of glory calls evil good and good evil. A theologian of the cross calls the thing what it actually is."[16] Luther's explanation of this famous thesis 21 is surprising and provocative: suffering is to be called good and acting is to be called bad. Human actions are not able to overcome the human's concern with his or her own good, rather actions intensify this concern. Everything that the human wills is willed from the perspective of the good (*sub specie bonitatis*). The culmination of the human situation occurs when the human, who seeks his own in all things, is oriented to God, the highest good (*summum bonum*). Human desire should be satisfied at its core by this orientation.

But the sinner does not seek God; the human only seeks God in order to fulfill his own needs. At this point, and here Luther is at his most radical, sin is maximized. God encounters the universal human quest to acquire all things by appearing not as strong, wise, and good but, as Luther highlights, under the opposite—as weak, foolish, evil.[17] The person, who seeks his own in everything, does not love this God who appears contrary to expectations of divinity. Human striving is "frustrated" by the God crucified on the cross of Christ. It is "destroyed" through God's suffering.[18] "For this reason true theology and recognition of God are in the crucified Christ."[19] True knowledge of God is attained only when the striving for one's own gain is overcome.

A second part to God's strategy is related to the spiritual sense of the law mentioned in the preceding section. In his *Lectures on Galatians* (1531/1535), Luther recounts how human beings can be "doers of the law." He thus hones in on justification as the main theme of the *Lectures*. "First, through the forgiveness of sins and the imputation of righteousness, on account of faith in Christ; secondly, through the gift and the Holy Spirit, who creates a new life and new impulses in us, so that we may keep the Law also in a formal sense. Whatever is not kept is forgiven for the sake of Christ."[20] Luther explains in this pas-

---

16. LW 31:53 (thesis 21; translation altered by T. D.), WA 1:362, 21–22.
17. See LW 31:52–53, WA 1:362, 4–14.
18. See LW 31:53 (translation altered by T. D.), WA 1:362, 23–33.
19. LW 31:53, WA 1:362, 18–19.
20. LW 26:260 (to Gal 3:10), WA 40/I:408, 29–409, 12.

sage that the person is transformed into a "doer of the law." Luther thus adds another dimension to human agency that is much more, something other than just an expansion of human possibilities for action.

Justification as Righteousness of Christ

This transformation has two aspects. First, the person's sin is forgiven and Christ's righteousness is attributed to him. The sinner is made righteous through Christ's alien righteousness. This alien righteousness becomes the believer's righteousness by faith.

Why does this attribution of righteousness matter? Martin Heidegger formulated the foundational question of metaphysics for today: "Why is there something rather than nothing?"[21] When a person poses this question to herself, it has a different resonance than when it is posed of any contingent being. In view of themselves, human beings ask the question why *their* being is privileged over nonbeing. The important question comes to the fore, "what is the justification for *my* existence?" We ask, "What justifies my saying to someone else: 'It is good that you exist'?" When you say to someone else, "It is good that you exist," you love this person.[22]

The question concerning the reason for existence can now be posed in view of God, although in a much more radical way.[23] What justifies God telling a person, "It is good that you exist," even though she, in her unbelief, might not expect any good thing from God and may be seeking her own in all things? How can God accept her?

The question was at the forefront in Luther's day. "How do I find a gracious God?" The "how" presupposes that human beings must act in order for God to react in mercy—meaning, to forgive their sins. When Luther says that Christ's righteousness is attributed to human beings, he stresses that they can never attain God's acceptance or love by their own actions. The classic formulation for Luther's claim is thesis 28 in the *Heidelberg Disputation*: "The love of God does not find, but creates, that which is pleasing to it. The love of man comes into being through that which is pleasing to it."[24] God acknowledges the person whom he designates righteous. Christ is righteous because he fulfilled the law. He never was in conflict with God's will, always in agreement with it. But the believer is righteous when he accepts in faith that he is united

---

21. Martin Heidegger, *Einführung in die Metaphysik* (Tübingen: Niemeyer, 1966), 1.
22. See the wonderful book on love by Josef Pieper, *Über die Liebe* (Munich: Kösel, 1972), 67–91.
23. Note that "radical" has a Latin root, namely *radix*, which means "root."
24. LW 31:57, WA 1:354, 35–36.

with Christ. By faith, the believer participates in Christ's righteousness. Thus the question of the real Luther of the Reformation is not, "How do I find a gracious God?" but "Where do I find a gracious God?" The answer can only be "in the gospel."

The righteousness of Christ is attributed to the believer, as Luther says with Paul in Romans 4:5. Theologians today sometimes say that the believer is *only seen* by God as righteous but cannot admit that the believer *is* righteous. This distinction reflects an all-too-human approach to God's way of seeing things. Our looking at someone from one angle or another does not elicit any change in the person we see. When God sees the person as righteous, then God's looking changes everything. What can be more "real" than God seeing a person as righteous? The "Magnificat" in Luke's Gospel expresses God's way of seeing. "For he has looked with favor on the lowliness of his servant," Mary exclaims, and goes on, "Surely, from now on all generations will call me blessed" (Luke 1:48).[25] Mary's words must be taken seriously in order to avoid saying, as Luther sometimes does: "If you look at yourself, all you see is sin; if you look at God, then you will be *regarded* as righteous." Actually, a human could never look at himself apart from God and see sin. And a human should never look at himself while ignoring the fact that he believes in Christ. Everything else is the view of unbelief. Thus even Luther's position can be unhelpful in grasping the believer as a sinner.

Justification as Gift of the Holy Spirit

The second aspect of justification focuses on the Holy Spirit, who is given to the believer as gift. The Holy Spirit produces new movements of the soul, new desires and affections, in the believer. The reality of the believer's righteousness is not the same as the reality of these new movements of the soul. Both are different levels of reality, although they are intimately bound together. Christ's righteousness is attributed to the human by faith as one reality. The Holy Spirit's action transforms the substance of the believer's will, her desires, and her actions as another reality of justification.

The renewal process does not grasp a person in its entirety before death. Hence the law's demand for complete fulfillment is not completed in this life, and the human remains a sinner before God's law.

There is, for Luther, no contradiction between the two realities of justification. Luther views the person from two perspectives. The human is situated

---

25. See also Luther's interpretation of this passage in LW 21:321–24 (*The Magnificat*, 1521), WA 7:567, 24–570, 27.

in two relations: *in relation to the gospel's promise*, the believer believes that he is righteous, and *in relation to the law's demand*, he confesses himself to be sinner. His sins are forgiven on account of his faith in Christ's gospel, even when he is unable to fulfill the law.

The reformation formula, "the believer is simultaneously righteous and a sinner" (*simul iustus et peccator*), can be interpreted as follows. The whole person is accepted unconditionally by God. This claim of unconditional acceptance is of extraordinary importance. Every person, even the believer, suffers the brokenness of sin until the end of his earthly life. He does not give God, the giver of all good things, his undivided trust. He does not give God his undivided love, but God expects undivided love from his beloved humans.

Luther's doctrine of justification is of relevance here because it specifically addresses this concern for wholeness. God's way of seeing encompasses the whole person by attributing to the believer the righteousness of Christ. The Holy Spirit lives in the believer, awakening new expressions of life. The believer's new movements correspond to God's law, even when she does not fulfill the law in its entirety. Unconditional acceptance is bound up intimately with transformation at the very core of the person's being.

The Communication of the Gospel

How is Christ's righteousness made available to humans? When the gospel is preached; when the gospel, even as the specific words that constitutively belong to the sacraments, is communicated to humans. Luther understands the gospel's communication in a special way. For Luther, the gospel is particular phrases, words, and sentences that create in reality what they say. Sentences such as "Your sins are forgiven," or "I am with you," create the state of affairs to which they refer. This property of the gospel's communicability differs from other phrases, words, and sentences that declare an already existing state of affairs (as in, for example, "This table is brown") or that convey a demand (for example, "You must speak the truth"). The gospel's words do not point to an already existing or a future state of affairs; they effect in reality what they mean. It is faith that corresponds to the creative action of these words by trusting them.

The gospel's words are creative. They do not refer to a disposition present in the human or an act performed by the human. The cause of the gospel's words is God's mercy. Human trust directed to these words is, in fact, faith in God as their origin. A person should not regard her disposition or acts as worthy of God's attention; rather she must look solely to God's promise. A person's certainty in being accepted unconditionally by God is only possible when she trusts in God's external word (*verbum externum*). If God's acceptance were to depend on something already existing in the person, she could never be certain of God's acceptance. A person can have no certainty because she is never fully transparent to herself. The burden of attaining certainty would exhaust any introspection. No one can definitively reach the bottom of self-certainty by introspection.

A passage by the apostle Paul was well known in the middle ages for referring to the difficulty of attaining certainty. "I am not aware of anything against myself, but I am not thereby acquitted. It is the Lord who judges me. Therefore do not pronounce judgment before the time, before the Lord comes, who will bring to light the things now hidden in darkness and will disclose the purposes of the heart." (1 Cor 4:4-5) Medieval theologians never could resolve a lingering uncertainty as to whether the human could be deemed in the state of grace or not. People could not be sure as to whether the sacrament offering grace was efficacious for themselves personally. Medieval theologians recognized the objective efficacy of the sacraments, they also held that a correct disposition in the human subject was required for the worthy reception of the sacraments. Given the inability of any person to attain complete introspection—the human is opaque to herself—she can never be certain as to whether she is worthy enough to receive the sacraments efficaciously. Luther's new understanding of sacramental efficacy placed all certainty on the side of the gospel's promise communicated in the sacraments.

Psychological introspection into self-development plays a huge role in people's lives today. Luther's doctrine of justification has special relevance in view of the contemporary fascination with psychology. Luther stresses that the certainty of one's acceptance by God does not result from a detailed analysis of the self. Rather, certainty is a gift that comes "from outside" the self. The only place where certainty concerning the gift of grace is available is in the communication of the gospel. For Luther, this word is "external" because it is spoken by another who is external to the self. This word communicates God's acceptance to the person and by communication the word really creates the acceptance that is communicated. The word neither describes nor judges the already existing state of affairs in which a person finds herself. Rather, the word effects God's acceptance that then becomes the sole basis for certainty.

In the sacraments, the words are concise expressions of the gospel, spoken in particular situations. "I call you by your name, you are mine!" "Your sins are forgiven." "Christ's body, broken for you." The goal for these sacramental words is that they take root in and gradually permeate the human person. The word continues to have deep effects in its hearers. One way in which words act in human lives is through regular immersion in the Holy Scriptures. The Bible is the multivalent witness both to God's acts and words addressed to humans and to human encounters with God. The biblical texts disclose the world as it appears from the perspective of God's speech and action. When Scripture is read, it is interpreted. Yet for Luther, daily meditation on the Bible also effects the reverse: the Bible interprets its readers. When this occurs, human destiny to be in conversation with God, even to be a conversation with God, is attained.

Many people today think that the doctrine of justification has nothing to do with real life. It is a collection of formulas all containing the word "alone": "by grace alone"; "by faith alone"; "through Christ alone"; "through word/sacrament alone"; "by Scripture alone."

Luther would address this in the following way. If we take the Holy Scriptures seriously, allowing the words truly to work on us and in us, whether alone or in community, the words come to be related in a deep way to our individual life circumstances. By this process of living "from" and "in" the Bible, we gain a deeper understanding of justification and figure out why justification is necessary for life. Luther describes the correct way to study theology—and in this sense, every Christian can study theology—by intimately connecting three exercises with the reading of Scripture. His famous text, the *Preface to the Wittenberg Edition of Luther's German Writings* (1539), shows how *oratio* (prayer), *meditatio* (meditation), and *tentatio* (*Anfechtung*) necessarily belong together.[26] Scripture is the focal point of all three. Luther first advises his reader to begin with prayer: "You should know that the Holy Scriptures constitute a book which turns the wisdom of all other books into foolishness, because not one teaches about eternal life except this one alone. Therefore you should straightaway despair of your reason and understanding . . . But kneel down in your little room [Matt 6:6] and pray to God with real humility and earnestness, that he through his dear Son may give you his Holy Spirit, who will enlighten you, lead you, and give you understanding."[27] The second exercise is meditation. By this Luther does not only mean something that occurs in the inner depths of the soul.

> You should meditate, that is, not only in your heart, but also externally, by actually repeating and comparing oral speech and literal words of the book, reading and rereading them with diligent attention and reflection, so that you may see what the Holy Spirit means by them. And take care

---

26. LW 34:283–88, WA 50:657–61.
27. LW 34:285–86, WA 50:569, 5–12.

that you do not grow weary or think that you have done enough when you have read, heard, and spoken them once or twice, and that you then have complete understanding. You will never be a particularly good theologian if you do that, for you will be like untimely fruit which falls to the ground before it is half ripe.[28]

The third exercise is, in Latin, *tentatio*, in German, *Anfechtung*. The term, which can be translated into a number of English words, such as attack, trial, and temptation, is used to describe a power that attacks humans to the extreme point that they despair of their lives. It is the "touchstone which teaches you not only to know and understand, but also to experience how right, how true, how sweet, how lovely, how mighty, how comforting God's Word is, wisdom beyond all wisdom."[29] Trials and temptations are the experiential proving-grounds of faith. Faith is experienced as real only through *tentatio*. Luther's view is often misconstrued as referring to the psychological strength of faith under attack. Yet Luther makes it clear that Christians experience the comfort and power of God's word when they are burned in the forge of *Anfechtung*. The word's power is known when it overcomes the attack. Attack drives Christians more deeply into the experience of the word's power.

The meaning and relevance of justification cannot be demonstrated in abstraction from reality. For Luther, justification has to do with profound experiences of God that are forged in the midst of trials and attacks. And this experience of justification is bound together with immersion in Scripture.

Receiving the Gospel: The Passivity and Activity of Faith

Luther understands faith to have two sides, the objective and the subjective. He emphasizes on the objective side that there is a givenness of the object, which is Christ, the gospel, the Holy Scriptures, and the sacraments. On the subjective side, faith is the presence in the human of these objects given by God. "If you believe, you shall have all things [grace, righteousness, peace, liberty]; if you do not believe, you shall lack all things."[30] Both sides of faith are intimately bound together. As Luther writes in the context of his discussions of the Lord's Supper: "For anyone can easily see that these two, promise and faith, must necessarily go together. For without the promise there is nothing to be believed; while without faith the promise is useless, since it is carried out

---

28. LW 34:286, WA 50:659, 22–29.
29. LW 34:286–87, WA 50:660, 1–4.
30. LW 31:348–49 (*The Freedom of a Christian*; 1520), WA 7:53, 6–7.

and fulfilled through faith."[31] Faith cannot create the object of belief; the object must be given to it. Faith must also have a subjective side. If something is given to me and I do not accept it, the object remains outside of me.

One area of serious concern for Christians is the question of how to celebrate the Lord's Supper in a worthy manner. The apostle Paul's warning in 1 Corinthians 11:27-29 is taken as the biblical warrant for this concern.[32] Paul's injunction to self-examination has goaded Christians to take seriously, time and time again, their preparation of contrition, confession of sin, absolution, and fasting. Luther too was preoccupied with this problem. He taught that faith is the correct preparation. Faith is trust in Christ's promise, "This is my body, given for you." Luther makes the point by considering a person who is unable to believe in Christ's promise because this person thinks he has not adequately made the required contrition. This person would—and this is Luther's key argument—turn Christ into a liar, for here, Christ is taken as someone who promises something that he cannot deliver. The highest dishonor one can have towards God or Christ is to take Christ as a highly untrustworthy person.[33] Faith does the exact opposite. Faith

> attributes glory to God, which is the highest thing that can be attributed to Him. To attribute glory to God is to believe in Him, to regard Him as truthful, wise, righteous, merciful, and almighty, in short, to acknowledge Him as the Author and Donor of every good. Reason does not do this, but faith does. It consummates the Deity; and, if I may put it this way, it is the creator of the Deity, *not in the substance of God but in us.* For without faith God loses His glory, wisdom, righteousness, truthfulness, mercy, etc., *in us*; in short, God has none of His majesty or divinity where faith is absent. Nor does God require anything greater of man than that he attribute to Him His glory and His divinity; that is, that he regard Him, not as an idol but as God, who has regard for him, listens to him, shows mercy to him, helps him, etc. When He has obtained this, God retains His divinity sound and unblemished; that is, He has whatever a believing heart is able to attribute to Him. To be able to attribute such glory to God is wisdom beyond wisdom, righteousness beyond righteousness, religion beyond religion, and sacrifice beyond sacrifice. From this it can

---

31. LW 36:42 (*The Babylonian Captivity of the Church*; 1520; LW translation altered by T. D.), WA 6:517, 8–10.
32. "Whoever, therefore, eats the bread or drinks the cup of the Lord in an unworthy manner will be answerable for the body and blood of the Lord. Examine yourselves, and only then eat of the bread and drink of the cup. For all who eat and drink without discerning the body, eat and drink judgment against themselves." (1 Cor 11:27-29)
33. See, for example, LW 36:43, WA 6:517, 22–33.

be understood what great righteousness faith is and, by antithesis, what a great sin unbelief is.[34]

Faith's subjective dimension lets the life-giving gifts that God gives become present to humans; its objectivity lies in the givenness of word and sacraments. Luther emphasizes objective givenness because he wants to prevent an understanding of faith as producing the object of its trust by its own creative power. Faith, in this case, would be a human work, and justification by faith would be the master formula for justification by works.

Another important distinction informing our interpretation of Luther's understanding of faith is the distinction between passivity and activity. Luther often understands faith in a passive sense. He can even go so far as to underline the "pure passivity" of faith that receives the passive righteousness of God. Faith passively endures the justifying action of God who acts in us.[35] Yet an understanding of faith as receiving God's action can also be taken in an active sense, as the above citation from Luther shows by speaking about what faith does. Luther makes clear that in the context of justification, faith's activity is not carried out as works on behalf of the neighbor, but vis-à-vis God. How can we make sense of the contradiction between a passive and an active aspect of faith? First, faith is passive because it receives God's righteousness and does not produce it. Second, faith is passive because even its reception is caused by God. Luther writes in the explanation to the Third Article of the Creed in the Small Catechism, "I believe that by my own understanding or strength I cannot believe in Jesus Christ my LORD or come to him, but instead the Holy Spirit has called me through the gospel, enlightened me with his gifts, made me holy and kept me in true faith."[36] Faith believes in God's promise, and as such, faith is not an act of will. Will is the human faculty that allows men and women to make choices about what they do. Trust has to do with whether or not a promise—or better, with whether someone who makes a promise—is trustworthy. The will cannot make its object trustworthy; this trustworthiness must disclose itself as trustworthy to humans. God's promise is above reason (*supra rationem*). Hence the Holy Spirit has the task of disclosing the promise as trustworthy to humans. When taken in this sense, faith is passive.

---

34. LW 26, 227 (*Lectures on Galatians*; 1535 [italics added]), WA 40/I:360, 2–35.

35. "For here [in the righteousness of faith] we work nothing, render nothing to God; we only receive and permit someone else to work in us, namely God": LW 26:5, WA 40/I:41, 18–20.

36. BoC, 355, 6.

Christians are struck by faith's passivity, often painfully so, when they are confronted with the terms of faith. There are many people today who are interested in the Christian religion. Yet when you ask them, "Do you believe in the things that capture your interest?" they reply, "No, I am tone-deaf to religion."

When we are asked to describe the inner structure of the receptivity of faith, then we see that this structure has an active aspect, or can even be deemed an activity, as Luther demonstrates in the quote above. Let us describe this active dimension of receptivity by looking at an anthropological phenomenon. When we hear music, we do not produce what is heard in the act of hearing; rather, we receive it. Even as reception, hearing is an activity. Whoever wants to "receive" Bach's Mass in B Minor must also practice the activity of hearing well and understanding correctly.

We can go one step further. When one person loves another person, then the beloved does not simply receive the love passively from the first. This "passivity" would be a catastrophe for love. Love would remain external to the beloved, and the beloved would not have received the love at all. When the beloved perceives that she is loved by another, she might then receive the love. This reception occurs in the fullest sense when she returns the love. The return of love is the highest form of receiving love offered in the first place. The point is that reception always includes activity: reception's activity is not just a reaction to the action, but belongs essentially to the nature of reception.

Faith, on Luther's own terms, can also be understood as the activity of reception. Faith is active when it receives—in a deep and transformative sense—God's work in the human person. The theological implication of this twofold understanding of faith is that faith in terms of an either/or is inappropriate: faith is not either passivity or activity. Rather, even when the description of "pure passivity" is attributed to faith, faith should also be taken as active in the sense of the activity of reception. As God's work, the reception of faith is effected by the Holy Spirit; thus any talk of faith's activity according to its receptivity has absolutely nothing to do with meritorious works.

Trust in God's promise includes the honoring of God as trustworthy and merciful. Faith inscribes God's image in the human being. The image of God in the human corresponds to the reality of God's righteousness. When God is considered in light of the correspondence between real image in the human and divine reality, the two sides of God—who God is in God's self and who God is for humans—come together. God is honored when God's image in humans—God for us—corresponds to God's reality—God for God's self. For Luther, human beings are destined to honor God. They fulfill their destiny when they receive—passively and actively—God's righteousness. Luther's *Galatians Commentary* (1531/1535) is famous for its discussion of faith. A passage in this text appeals surprisingly to the universal concept of righteousness, namely, to give to each his or her own. While Luther had often rejected this concept from theological discussions of justification, the concept appears here in the context of the human-divine relationship: "Therefore faith justifies because it renders to God what is due Him; whoever does this is righteous. The laws also define what it means to be righteous in this way: to render to each what is his. For faith speaks as follows: 'I believe Thee, God, when Thou dost speak.'"[37]

Ecumenical Aspects of the Doctrine of Justification

Luther's doctrine of justification comes down to one thing: the communication of the biblical gospel. When Lutherans speak of *Luther's* doctrine of justification, they are making a mistake. It is not *his* doctrine of justification, but a biblical doctrine, and as such it has an ecumenical aspect. The ecumenical aspect is crystallized in the *Joint Declaration on the Doctrine of Justification* from 1999. The work leading up to the *Declaration* intended to heal the most important source of confessional division since the sixteenth century between the Roman Catholic and Lutheran churches. The document articulates a consensus on the doctrine of justification, yet its formulations of consensus are carefully differentiated. There are common points of agreements as well as points of difference. The decisive passage is: "Justification . . . means that Christ himself is our righteousness, in which we share through the Holy Spirit in accord with the will of the Father. Together we confess: By grace alone, in faith in Christ's saving work and not because of any merit on our part, we are accepted by God and receive the Holy Spirit, who renews our hearts while equipping and calling us to good works."[38]

An important realization took place among ecumenists during the course of working out a differentiated consensus. Dialogue partners acknowledged the significant fact that both churches sometimes spoke different languages and made use of different conceptual models. An important avenue to con-

---

37. LW 26:226 (to Gal 3:6), WA 40/I:361, 121–24. See also Bo Kristian Holm, *Gabe und Geben bei Luther: Das Verhältnis zwischen Reziprozität und reformatorischer Rechtfertigungslehre*, Theologische Bibliothek Töpelmann 134 (Berlin: de Gruyter, 2006); and Wolfgang Simon, "Worship and Eucharist in Luther Studies," *Dialog* 27/2 (Summer 2008): 143–56.
38. *Joint Declaration on the Doctrine of Justification by the Lutheran World Federation and the Roman Catholic Church* (Grand Rapids: Eerdmans, 2000), 15.

sensus was acknowledging that both churches use different languages but that they nevertheless are capable of expressing the "same" content. Would translations be even possible without some dimension of "sameness"?

I illustrate this point with one example (although there are many others). Luther was summoned to Augsburg to appear before Cardinal Cajetan in 1518. Cajetan's task was to get Luther to recant his positions. Cajetan was familiar with all of Luther's texts available to him at the time. Upon being presented with Luther's understanding of the certainty of salvation (see section "The Communication of the Gospel" above), Cajetan exclaimed, "This would mean to build a new church!"[39] Cajetan employed concepts and distinctions that differed from Luther's. Although Cajetan had studied Luther in detail, the Cardinal seriously misunderstood the Reformer. Roman Catholic theologians today take Luther's way of thinking seriously, even though it differs from their usual ways of thinking, maybe even using Luther to think in new ways for themselves. The *Joint Declaration* sums up this point: "Catholics can share the concern of the Reformers to ground faith in the objective reality of God's promise, to look away from one's own experience, and to trust in Christ's forgiving word alone."[40] Look how far we have come! Not any more, "This would mean to build a new church," but "Catholics can share the concern of the Reformers!"

There are many tasks remaining for ecumenical work. Contemporary biblical scholarship is different from the scholarship of the sixteenth century. One question today for both Protestant and Roman Catholic theologians is how to relate the results of modern critical scholarship with the classic doctrines of representative traditions, particularly as these traditions are based on premodern exegesis.

Another, perhaps even more difficult task, is expressed in the "Official Common Statement."[41] "Lutherans and Catholics will continue their efforts ecumenically in their common witness to interpret the message of justification in language relevant for human beings today, and with reference both to individual and social concerns of our times."

---

39. Charles Morerod, *Cajetan et Luther en 1518: Edition, Traduction et Commentaire des Opuscules d'Augsbourg de Cajetan*, vol. 1 (Fribourg: Universitaires Fribourg, 1994), 336.
40. *Joint Declaration*, 36.
41. The "Official Common Statement" is a short text to which the signatures of representatives of the Roman Catholic and Lutheran Churches are appended. The signatures, appended in Augsburg in 1999, signify the acceptance of the *Joint Declaration*. The last sentence of the statement reads: "By this act of signing the Catholic Church and the Lutheran World Federation confirm the Joint Declaration on the Doctrine of Justification in its entirety."

In these times of rapid change and deep uncertainty, the doctrine of justification opens up the promise of God's wholeness in the midst of brokenness, and faith in the midst of *Anfechtung*. In these times of introspection and even self-absorption, the doctrine of justification is a challenge to look beyond the self by opening up the self to other human beings and to God. Justification is Luther's contribution to understanding life that contains the promise of joyful abundance. For Luther, true life is available in the midst of life's manifold ambiguities by faith, by trust in Christ's promise.

CHAPTER 13

Luther's Social Theology in the Contemporary World

—Searching for the Neighbor's Good —

Antti Raunio

Lutheranism and the Good Society

Is Lutheranism Socially Passive?

Does Lutheran theology have anything substantive to contribute to the discussion of a good society? The most likely answer to this question is that Lutheranism has enjoyed some success in promoting a safe, stable, and peaceful society because it teaches people to obey the law and worldly authorities. One could say also that Lutheranism has promoted learning, since it teaches people to read the Bible. Its influences on politics and society are, however, less obvious in reality than the answers on the surface suggest. If one presses the question and asks whether Lutheranism has taken an active role in seeking a good society, one will likely be met with a negative response. Charles Curran, for example, recently described the "classic Lutheran position" as one that ascribes a minimal and negative function to the role of the state. The Lutheran position sees the state as assuming solely a coercive function in preserving human life and in preventing humans from harming each other. The political use of the civil law is Lutheranism's sole means of achieving these social goals.[1]

---

1. Charles E. Curran, *Catholic Social Teaching 1891–Present: A Historical, Theological, and Ethical Analysis* (Washington: Georgetown University Press, 2002).

The consensus regarding the limited social and political effects of Lutheranism is still dominated by the interpretations of Ernst Troeltsch, Max Weber, and Ludwig Feuchtwanger.[2] These scholars introduced the view at the beginning of the twentieth century that Lutheranism is politically and socially passive. Many other Lutheran scholars have since criticized and revised this basic position. But new developments in acknowledging Lutheranism's important social and political engagement have not succeeded in reaching an audience beyond the narrow confines of Lutheran theology. The way ahead requires creative and interdisciplinary dialogue. The recent example of John Witte Jr.'s book *Legal Teachings of the Lutheran Reformation* is a step in the right direction because it pays close attention to the positive, innovative impact of Lutheran theology in the spheres of legislation and justice.[3] I begin my study of Lutheranism's impact on society and politics with a turn to the Reformation and its particular contextualization in Nordic society and politics.

Lutheran Social Renewal

The historical sources of the sixteenth-century Reformation do not provide any evidence for a socially passive Lutheranism.[4] The Reformation was a broad movement that included major efforts to improve the social circumstances and welfare of the poor, to promote health care, and to institutionalize education. For these purposes, the Reformation cities, for example, Leisnig, together with nearby villages initiated the practice of collecting funds in communal chests.[5] Parish and town worked closely together to organize the common

---

2. Feuchtwanger wrote a dissertation on social politics and the care for the poor during the Reformation. He used the work as the basis of a later essay that was published in two parts: "Geschichte der sozialen Politik und des Armenwesens im Zeitalter der Reformation," *Jahrbuch für Gesetzgebung, Verwaltung, und Volkswirkschaft im Deutschen Reich* 32 (1908): 167–204; 33 (1909): 191–228. See also a recent interpretation in line with Weber and Troeltsch by Andrew Bradstock, "The Reformation," in *The Blackwell Companion to Political Theology*, ed. Peter Scott and William T. Cavanaugh (Malden, Mass: Blackwell, 2004), 62–75.

3. John Witte Jr., *Law and Protestantism: The Legal Teachings of the Lutheran Reformation* (Cambridge: Cambridge University Press, 2002).

4. See Carter Lindberg, *Beyond Charity: Reformation Initiatives for the Poor* (Minneapolis: Fortress Press, 1993); Samuel Torvend, *Luther and the Hungry Poor: Gathered Fragments* (Minneapolis: Fortress Press, 2008); and the "Christians and the Social Good" section of this chapter.

5. Lindberg, *Beyond Charity*, 125–27. The Finnish church historian, Kaarlo Arffman, has recently published a study of the development of Lutheran welfare in the Reformation cities and Nordic countries. See Kaarlo Arffman, *Auttamisen vallankumous: Luterilaisuuden yritys ratkaista köyhyyden aiheuttamat ongelmat* (Helsinki: Suomen Kirkkohistoriallinen Seura/ Suomen Historiallinen Seura, 2008) [*Revolution of Helping: The Lutheran Attempt to Solve the Problems Caused by Poverty*]. Arffman summarizes the results of his study in an English

funds. No sharp distinction between church and state was made during the Reformation. Consequently, social responsibility was not divided between church and state.

After the Reformation, many of the social tasks for which the Lutheran churches were responsible were taken over by the public authorities. As European Lutheranism reshuffled its social responsibilities in the face of political developments, its relations to respective social contexts took on distinctive character. Lutheranism did not establish an explicitly Christian (specifically Lutheran) political society. Rather than influencing the political realm directly, Lutheranism tends to rely on people's "natural" moral capacities in addressing "worldly" issues. Lutheranism occupies a unique position in Christian social ethics by basing its view on a specific understanding of the love of neighbor. For Lutheranism, love of neighbor is both a major preoccupation of the church and the deepest moral and social challenge of all human beings. The proclamation of the gospel and the exercise of love of neighbor are not consigned to private religion but are available with their social and political dimensions. An ethos of social influence rather than an explicit political program characterizes Lutheran social influence that is common to all Nordic Lutheran countries.

Nordic countries are known throughout the world for having developed a distinctive type of welfare state. This model's social success can be measured in a number of ways. The majority of Nordic citizens clearly support the welfare model. Most political parties are willing to maintain it, even though there is debate concerning the ways in which it can be sustained and adapted to new political and global circumstances. Although the Nordic countries have regional differences in implementing social and political solutions, they share one important feature: the broad social responsibilities of both municipality and state. Yet this common feature has been under fire since the end of the twentieth century. The idea of broad, public, social responsibility does not fit into the dominant tendencies of contemporary economic and political thinking. Although many people appreciate the concrete social achievements of the Nordic welfare states, others call its viability into question and ask whether such a thing as a welfare state can exist in the world today.

Lutheranism as the "people's church"[6] of the Nordic countries can be regarded as a significant cultural presupposition of the welfare state. Lutheranism's emphasis on the community's social responsibility can be linked to

---

essay, "The Lutheran Reform of Poor Relief: A Historical and Legal Viewpoint," in *Lutheran Reformation and the Law*, ed. Virpi Mäkinen (Leiden: Brill, 2006), 205–230.

6. The term "people's church" is used currently by Nordic churches to designate themselves. The term "state church" is used officially only for the Lutheran Church in Denmark.

the welfare state's responsibilities for its citizens. From a scholarly perspective, however, it is difficult to specify precisely how and where the Lutheran church has had an impact on society. It is clear that the Lutheran ethos does not explain all features of the Nordic welfare state, although many researchers see some connection between the Lutheran cultural heritage and the Nordic social model.[7] In this chapter, I will not address how Lutheranism has influenced the Nordic welfare model. My primary concern is to show how some social aspects in Luther's theology can be relevant to today's discussion concerning a good society.

One more observation is needed by way of introduction. A strong case can be made for Lutheranism's contribution to establishing a welfare state, but Lutheran theology and Lutheran churches often are ambivalent in their embrace of this kind of society. Lutheran churches generally support the idea of broad, public, social responsibility. Yet one must remember that the idea of broad social responsibility was historically introduced during the Reformation when the church was still intimately connected to the state. Once the separation occurred, social responsibility was transferred to the state, inevitably diminishing the need for the church's diaconal work. One can say that the less a society takes care of its people, the more the church and its diaconal services are needed. This inverse linear equation poses difficulties in today's global context. There are plenty of tasks in many parts of the world that can be assigned to both a socially responsible public welfare system and to diaconally active religious groups.

What Is a Basic Social Good?

Individual Human Activity as the Basic Social Good

An important question of social theology concerns how social responsibility is divided between public institutions, individual citizens, and religious organizations. The frequent criticism of the welfare state is that it takes on too much responsibility, consequently weakening the role of voluntary charity organizations and creating socially passive and irresponsible citizens.[8] Many supporters

---

7. See, for example, Tim Knudsen, ed., *Den nordiske protestantisem og velfærdstaten* (Århus: Århus Universitetsforlag, 2000); Carl-Henrik Grenholm, "Politisk moral i en luthersk kontekst," in *Etisk pluralisme i Norden*, ed. Lars Østnor (Kristiansand: Høyskole, 2001), 239–64; Gunnar Heiene, "Velferdsstat och sivilsamfunn. En skandinavisk debatt," in *Kirke, protestantisme og samfunn: Festskrift til professor dr. Ingun Montgomery*, ed. R. Jensen, D. Thorkildsen, and A. V. Tønnesen (Trondheim: Tapir Akademisk, 2006), 211–27.

8. Recent Finnish studies concerning citizens' willingness to take on voluntary work do not support this critical view. Perhaps a more accurate way of diagnosing the problem of

of economical liberalism or libertarianism have reiterated this critical position that, surprisingly, can be found also in social encyclicals of the Roman Catholic Church.

The question of social responsibility has different answers concerning the basic good of each individual in society. A basic good is commonly defined as the good needed to attain other (secondary) goods. Here we observe three alternative understandings of the basic good. Two ways of understanding basic goods, let us call them, respectively, the "Catholic" view and the "modern liberal" view, are similar because both consider the person's basic good to reside in her agency for responsible action. This kind of thinking is known in theological terms as a "teleological anthropology." According to this view, a human being is created with the goal of actualizing possibilities of human nature with which she is originally endowed. She strives to actualize the goal to perfection during the course of her life. The "Catholic" view, in particular, presupposes that all human beings have a universal human nature and are created for a common end. It is informed philosophically by classic Aristotelian and Thomistic anthropology and tends to be represented today by Roman Catholic ethical and social teaching.

The Catholic view holds that the teleological basic good guiding the development of all human beings is derived from universal human nature. Two different examples can be mentioned here: political authorities may prescribe how a person can best reach his or her natural and social goals, while the church communicates the way a person can attain his or her eternal end. The issue is where responsibility for striving toward one's divinely appointed end is located. Catholic social teaching locates responsibility first and foremost with the person. Her good is promoted when her agency in attaining natural and supernatural goals is supported. This way of thinking emphasizes that a person has positive freedom to both follow a common model of good life and to reach a given end. This position is also critical of a negative understanding of freedom, which asserts that a person is independent from any given social models for living.

The second view, the "modern liberal" view, picks up where the critical outlook of the Catholic view leaves off. The liberal view emphasizes the negative dimension of human freedom. Modern liberal democracies presuppose that human nature is individualized in human persons. The presupposition leads to the idea that, in most cases, a human person knows what is good for her because she is the best judge of her individual goals and preferences. Some

---

"passivity" in the welfare state is to consider how the legal conditions for receiving welfare restrict personal agency in improving one's personal situation.

of her closest peers may also be able to determine what is good for her, but most people are not in a position to make this determination, not to mention public institutions. The ideal society leaves the decision regarding the good to individual persons. By refusing to prescribe given ends and models for the good life, society sets a negative boundary to human freedom. Human persons are free to make individual choices; society cannot intervene. Apart from the law, society has no right to require individuals to adhere to prescribed choices in order to achieve specified aims.

These two views concerning the basic good promote a robust sense of personal agency and individual responsibility. But they differ as to their arguments for personal accountability. The Catholic view takes a classic Aristotelian position to argue for the cultivation of personal virtues. The modern liberal view guarantees freedom for individual decision-making by arguing on the anthropological basis of individual free agency.

Meeting Human Needs as the Basic Social Good

The third view, the "decency of life" view, considers the specific needs a person must have to live with individual human dignity. Needs are not only material but also intellectual and spiritual. A good society must provide and guarantee access to these goods for each and every member of society. The "decency of life" view insists that the basic social good consists in meeting the needs required for living a decent and modest life and thereby differs from the first two models that privilege personal human agency. Furthermore, the third view regards a person's right to access the goods conducive to a decent life independently of her capacity to act for her own good and the good of the community. A critical question surfaces at this point: Does this model lead to passivity? In response, the point must be made that the "decency of life" model does not intend to render persons passive but to secure the conditions for active participation in the life of the community. This view is fundamental to Nordic thinking on welfare.

So far, I have described three different ways of understanding a person's basic good within a social context. I emphasize that theoretical differences between the models concern the basic or primary good, not the inevitable secondary goods. I also recognize that the three models seldom exist in "pure" forms. There are in reality a diversity of social models; each is a unique combination of individual negative freedom, personal positive freedom, and basic human needs. One may ask: Does the fulfillment of basic needs presuppose personal freedom? Or is maximal (negative or positive) freedom a necessary or sufficient condition for meeting individual needs?

The Neighbor's Good in Luther's Theology

The Goodness of the Object of Love

Lutheranism is often seen as socially disinterested, but this stereotype cannot hold true. Lutheranism is known for the idea that faith frees the human being to serve the neighbor in love. Luther defines the love of neighbor as a striving for the good of another. The self is freed from striving for personal good and gain. Luther often describes neighborly love as a love that aims solely to fulfill the neighbor's need. The neighbor's need is precisely the point at which Luther begins to determine the good. Luther does not start with the person's effort to attain and guarantee her own good but turns his attention to the neighbor. Important questions emerge from Luther's distinctive focus on neighbor: How can one recognize what the neighbor needs? What is the relation of this determination of need to the neighbor's negative and positive freedom?

It is best to begin with an explanation of how Luther understands the concepts of "good" and "goodness." All goodness is based on the goodness of God who is goodness itself. Luther, however, does not determine goodness to be the fundamental divine attribute. God is not only goodness, but God is love. God is goodness because God does good works, yet this goodness flows delightfully from God's love.[9] Luther's writings suggest that God's love cannot be conflated with God's goodness, even though both attributes belong close together.[10] Luther's privileging of love over goodness perhaps may be a theological clue to his understanding of love as the fundamental principle of reality.[11]

Luther scholars agree that Luther distinguishes between two types of love: divine love and human love. This interpretation is based on the famous thesis 28 of the *Heidelberg Disputation* (1518): "The love of God does not find, but creates, that which is pleasing to it. The love of man comes into being through that which is pleasing to it."[12] God does not desire an object that is good and valuable in and of itself. Rather, God's love creates value and goodness in the

---

9. "God is love. Indeed, God is nothing else than love. For even though He is also goodness, yet all His blessings flow from love. These words are of great importance, and they are believed by few, yes, by very few": LW 30:300 (*Lectures on 1 John*; to 1 John 4:16; 1527), WA 20:755, 31–33.

10. The distinction between love and goodness is significant for Luther's political theology as well.

11. On this topic, see Adrian Pabst, "Partizipation durch Relationalität," *Ökumenische Rundschau* 57 (2008): 205–213.

12. LW 31:41, WA 1:365, 2–17 (discussion to thesis 28).

object. Human love contrasts sharply with divine love. Human love is directed to an object that is already determined as good in and of itself.

Anders Nygren, an early twentieth-century Lutheran theologian, agreed with Luther's thesis and argued for the strict opposition between divine and human love. In his famous book *Eros and Agape*, Nygren claimed that all forms of human love are characterized by sinful egocentric human love (*eros*). The love that Christians show neighbor is the effect of divine love (*agape*) alone.[13] Recent theological treatments of love and desire have criticized Nygren's characterization as too reductionist. The Finnish theologian Tuomo Mannermaa, for example, suggests that Luther did not see all of human love as sinful *eros*.[14] If human love is not to be blanketed entirely as sinful, then it must be related in some way to goodness. We are concerned here precisely with this relation.

Luther's view that God's love creates goodness in its object is a key to his theology and a starting point to his social theology. In addition to creating the goodness of its object, divine love also creates and sustains the object. Luther casts God's creative love in Trinitarian terms. God's work of creation takes place through the divine word or second person of the Trinity, the Son who is eternally begotten of the Father. The triune God's work involves creating individual beings and wholeheartedly accepting them. The Father speaks objects into being; they receive their existence through the Son, and the Holy Spirit sees and accepts them.[15] "God saw everything that he had made, and indeed, it was very good" (Gen. 1:31). Luther takes the Spirit's seeing and acceptance of creation as good to mean that the triune God loves and preserves God's own creation.[16] God's love is the explanation for God's creation of good things and, furthermore, God's love is the reason for accepting and sustaining creation's goodness. For Luther, divine love is more than a love that gives goodness; it accepts the given goodness. Goodness is seen as a gift of love; the existing goodness in an object is not taken in opposition to its existence as an object of God's love. The same love has two aspects: divine love creates goodness and divine love is directed to a good object.

One small difference exists between the two aspects of love. For Luther, divine acceptance presupposes creative giving. Luther's emphasis on divine giving is an important aspect of his doctrine of God. God always acts in

13. Anders Nygren, *Eros and Agape*, trans. Philip S. Watson (London: SPCK, 1932; reprint: New York: Harper, 1969), 681–741.
14. Tuomo Mannermaa, *Christ Present in Faith: Luther's View of Justification*, ed. and introduced by Kirsi Stjerna (Minneapolis: Fortress Press, 2005), 63–71.
15. David Löfgren, *Die Theologie der Schöpfung bei Luther*, Forschungen zur Kirchen- und Dogmengeschichte 10 (Göttingen: Vandenhoeck & Ruprecht, 1960), 34–35.
16. LW 1:49 (*Lectures on Genesis*; to Gen 1:20; 1535–1545), WA 42:38, 7–12.

accordance with God's nature to give, even when it means God's giving of God's very self.[17] Luther's text *Confession Concerning Christ's Supper* (1528) summarizes his view of the self-giving nature of the triune God: "These are the three persons and one God, who has given himself to us all wholly and completely, with all that he is and has. The Father gives himself to us, with heaven and earth and all the creatures. . . . Therefore the Son himself subsequently gave himself and bestowed all his works . . . . [And] the Holy Spirit comes and gives himself to us also, wholly and completely."[18]

Luther unfortunately gives very few clues to what he might mean by the following three aspects of divine self-giving: (1) God's self; (2) who God is; and (3) what God has. One possible way of understanding what Luther means is to take the "being of God" (2) to refer to the self-giving love; the "self" of God (1). God's very self is understood in Trinitarian terms of the three divine persons who are united as one God. "What God has" (3) can then be taken as both the divine attributes and all the divine works, for example, creating and sustaining.

The Triune God's Self-Giving

An intriguing aspect of Luther's idea of divine self-giving is that all three persons—Father, Son, and Holy Spirit—give themselves in and through created things. The connection between God's self-giving and created things is crucial to the way Luther sees God's activity together with its success in granting all gifts needed for life. Luther unambiguously makes the connection in the *Confession* from 1528. The Father gives himself together with heaven, earth, and all creatures "so that they may serve us and benefit us."[19] The relation of service by creatures to human beings is not to be interpreted in one direction. No creature, including a human person, exists for itself. All things are created to serve all others.

Luther describes in detail what the triune God gives to human beings in the explanation to the First Article of the Creed in the Large Catechism (1529). The Father "has given me . . . my body, soul, and life, my members great and small, all my senses, my reason and understanding, and the like; my food and drink, clothing, nourishment, spouse and children, servants, house and farm, etc. Besides, he makes all creation help provide the benefits and necessities of life—sun, moon, and stars in the heavens; day and night; air, fire,

---

17. "And so He gives Himself, and He does not give, but is Himself the good and complete blessing of the saints": LW 10:252 (*First Lectures on the Psalms*; to Ps 54:6; 1513–1515), WA 3:303, 20–21.

18. LW 37:366 (*Confession Concerning Christ's Supper*; 1528), WA 26:505, 38–41.

19. LW 37:366, WA 26:505, 38–41.

water, the earth and all that it yields and brings forth; birds, fish, animals, grain, and all sorts of produce. Moreover, he gives all physical and temporal blessings—good government, peace, security."[20] Luther stresses that the Father's good works do not only include giving them to people as gifts but also that God protects and guards these gifts from their destruction by evil. In other words, God preserves the goodness of these created gifts. Luther reiterates in the above passage what we have seen before concerning the two aspects of the one divine love. God's seeing and acceptance of creation as good includes the aspect of preserving creation in its existence. Giving involves accepting, and accepting presupposes giving. By giving and accepting human beings in their goodness, God takes care of their needs.

The difficulty arises in a theological sense when human beings are unable to recognize the divine gifts and their goodness. In a *Postil* from 1526, Luther claims that if we were able to look at all creatures, we would acknowledge a lot of God's goodness in them. His exegetical basis is Christ's words in Matthew: "He makes his sun rise on the evil and on the good, and sends rain on the righteous and on the unrighteous" (Matt 5:45).[21] God gives sunshine and rain to all. The sun illumines the human eye, but no one sees God's gifts or acknowledges these gifts to come from God. If the sun were not to rise on a given morning or would rise three hours too late, this event would cause great misery and distress. All creatures respond with the same ingratitude. There are too many goods, so that we (at least many in the modern West) overdose every day on good works and do not recognize them as good gifts anymore. Only when a person lacks some good does he appreciate the gift he has enjoyed.

The link from gift to self-giving God further complicates the difficulty. If, as Luther claims, the Father gives himself together with all creatures, then any difficulty in recognizing the creature as God's gift would directly relate to the difficulty in acknowledging the Father's intimate involvement with the gift. For Luther, the link between Father and gift multiplies the degree to which human beings have fallen; humanity has lost both God and gift.[22] People have lost the Father's self-giving love, God's acceptance, and God's good works in the sense that they are unable to recognize or receive goodness as it is given by God. While attributing this inability to human agency, Luther holds on to the theological claim that God never ceases to love and to do good works. Yet a difficult issue arises that has specific relevance for today's global context

20. BoC, 432, 13–16, WA 30/I:183, 29–184, 23.
21. WA 10/I.2:384, 8–21 ("Gospel for the Sixteenth Sunday after Trinity"; Luke 7:11-17; *Sommerpostille 1526*).
22. LW 37:366 (*Confession Concerning Christ's Supper*, 1528), WA 26:505, 38–41.

of social injustice: the human inability to recognize goodness inevitably and fundamentally distorts all relations to any good gift.

Luther underscores the same link between God's self-giving nature and gift under the second and third articles of the Creed. The second person of the Trinity, the Son, became human and gave himself to humanity in order that human beings would be able to recognize the Father and his gifts. But people are unable on account of sin to recognize what Christ has given to them, namely, his acceptance of them. So the third person of the Trinity, the Holy Spirit, comes and gives itself entirely to humanity, teaching people to acknowledge Christ's good work of restoring them to both Father and his good gifts. The Spirit also teaches people how to communicate these gifts to others, to multiply them, and to increase their power.[23] The triune God's complete self-giving together with all God's gifts and power is intended to help people appreciate all of God's creatures as God's gifts. And this appreciation is measured by keeping God's commandments.[24] The goal of God's self-giving is for people to live in accordance with God's good will.

God's Two Ways of Actualizing Love

Luther understands God to work according to two "ways" in the world. Both ways presuppose God's ubiquity, namely, the presence of the triune God in all of creation. God is present in creation and works either as unsearchable Majesty or as incarnate God for us. These two ways of expressing the divine power are commonly known in Lutheran circles as worldly and spiritual government. God's aim in both governments is to actualize love that fulfils the creature's needs.

In God's spiritual government, God's word and sacraments are the instruments enabling people to receive God's love. Christians depend on God's love to perform good works. The good deeds performed out of love of neighbor are spontaneous and uncoerced expressions of faith. For Luther, it is important that Christians receive the whole incarnate Christ, who forms them so that they can become "Christs to one another."[25] There are, however, no "perfect" Christians in this sense. All Christians exist together with all other people in God's worldly government.

God makes use of worldly power to influence people outwardly. All aspects of worldly government are instruments of God's worldly government

---

23. LW 37:366, WA 26:505, 42–506, 7.
24. BoC, 440, 69–70.
25. LW 31:367 (*Freedom of a Christian*; 1520), WA 7:66, 25–36.

to meet the needs of human beings and to protect them from evil, such as political authorities, civil laws and punishments, but also the welfare of the poor, schools, and hospitals. Unfortunately, people—even Christians—oppose God's will. Although they are inwardly unwilling, they must be coerced externally by the law to do good works.

Even the imperfect fulfilling of the law is, however, crucial for social justice. Luther's distinction between love and good works is important here. Luther identifies the divine law with the law of love. It is the "law of love in the Spirit, which should govern all the external laws in the world."[26] Luther distinguishes carefully between the "law in the Spirit" and the "external, worldly laws," thereby alluding to his classic distinction between spiritual and worldly government. The "law of the Spirit" refers to the demand of love; the "external laws" refer to diverse, concrete, good acts or deeds. Luther continues the passage by claiming that all laws, namely, legal and political laws, should be given, ordered, and kept in order to exercise and express love. At this point, Luther unites both spiritual and worldly realms on the basis of the "law" of love. The real aim of all external laws is love, not certain precepts or deeds in themselves. Love realizes itself when the neighbor's needs are fulfilled. If the work is not helpful for the neighbor, it should not be performed.[27]

Luther gives an example for the way he understands the relation between the practice of love and external laws. The example was pertinent in the sixteenth century, and its relevance is not diminished five centuries later. What is the right way to feed and clothe one's neighbor? Luther emphasizes that one should not be preoccupied with the particulars of food and clothing. Rather, the question of basic needs should be contextualized by the question of the good of the other. One should stop giving when one sees that the other does not need or cannot receive any more.[28] Luther's point here is that, even though the works are good in themselves, only love makes them good for a certain person in a particular situation. Practicing love is a striving to understand and to meet the real needs—meaning the good—of one's neighbor.

Luther addresses in detail what he means by love in his explanation to the "Golden Rule," which is the commandment of love. The Golden Rule predominant in the major global religions is the command to love neighbor as one's self. Particularly in the Augustinian tradition of Christianity, the command to self-love has been viewed ambivalently. Self-love is considered the original sin

---

26. WA 17/II:94, 17–19 ("Epistle for the Fourth Sunday after Epiphany"; Rom 13:8ff.; *Fastenpostille* 1525).
27. WA 17/II:94, 17–19.
28. WA 17/II:94, 31–35.

that precipitated the Fall; concupiscence is the source of all actual sin. Yet does the commandment of love not require you to love your neighbor as *yourself*?

Luther's interpretation of the Golden Rule differs from the Augustinian tradition. Firstly, Luther regards the double commandment to love self and neighbor as identical in content. The same Spirit writes them continually in the hearts of all human beings.[29] Secondly, the double love commandment exposes the human being's need for self-love. Everyone desires love, acceptance, and good works from other people. The command to love the self considers the self's own heart as representative of how one should love the neighbor. Love's direction should move naturally from self to neighbor. The only aim of neighborly love is to seek and promote the neighbor's good. For Luther, the Golden Rule should be applied: put yourself in the other's position and ask, "What would I need if I were the other?" Luther poses his "version" of the Golden Rule with the aim of really trying to understand the needs of the other, which is much broader than doing what the other wills at that very moment. Luther's idea of the actualization of love is the concrete fulfilling of the neighbor's need; it is much more than a fuzzy feeling or specific desire.

An important dimension of Luther's social theology is his twofold interpretation of the Golden Rule's concretization of love in good works. On the one hand, love does not demand any identifiable work. It is more formal than material (to use the Kantian language of the categorical imperative). Love is the criterion that decides what should be done and what should be left undone. On the other hand, the love commandment contains many particular commands. All of love's work should be "works of love" (to allude to Kierkegaard).[30] At this point, Luther can specify particular works that are contained in the formal command. External laws are required to guide people in knowing love and in actualizing it. Concrete civil and political laws should serve love so that love alone may decide when you should do or not do a work.[31]

If Luther's theology of love is to be relevant in global context, it must address the question of love's command as it pertains to all people. Luther's theological interpretation of the love commandment is of limited relevance because it is addressed primarily to Christians. Yet the important question people are asking today concerns its relevance for non-Christians as well.

Christian theology has classically treated the question of universal relevance as a question of "natural law." Clarity from Luther on this issue must

---

29. WA 2:580, 14–23 (*Lectures on Galatians*; 1519).
30. See Søren Kierkegaard, *Works of Love*, ed. and trans. Howard V. Hong and Edna H. Hong, Kierkegaard's Writings 16 (Princeton: Princeton University Press, 1995).
31. WA 17/II:95, 33–35.

take into account Luther's specific use of the term "natural law." For Luther, natural law is identical with the commandment of love. Human beings have the rational capacity to recognize outward good works. But this recognition does not mean that they understand the natural law correctly. For Luther, the term "natural" does not refer to human nature or to human rational and moral capacities, as it is defined in both the Thomistic tradition of moral theology and in the Lutheran tradition following Philipp Melanchthon. Rather, Luther understands "natural" to refer to the divine nature. God's love means God's self-giving love.[32] By understanding "natural" in this way, Luther makes a move we have already seen concerning the double inability of people to receive the gifts of created goods and to acknowledge their source in God's self-giving. All people know according to reason some aspect of the commandment of love, namely outward good works. Yet they do not grasp the inner dimension of love in terms of the divine nature to love and hence are unable to see the connection to God's love and to receive created goods as gifts to be loved.

Who Promotes the Good?

Worldly and Spiritual Dimensions

Another aspect of the good in society requires our attention, particularly in view of contemporary questions concerning the relation between political and religious interests in striving for a just society. The issue of the individual good's relation to the corporate good is urgent in light of contemporary neo-liberal politics that tend to subsume all interests under the individual. In this section, I address Luther's view that both private (personal) good and common good are required for the concept of the neighbor's good. I deal specifically with Luther's understanding of property in order to show how he envisions the task to serve both individual and common good.

A serious problem in the contemporary world concerns the division of labor between worldly and spiritual governments. It may seem natural to apply Luther's idea of the two governments to the fundamental separation between church and state, and to ask, which is responsible for promoting the common good? The Lutheran distinction, however, is not identical to the separation between state and church. For Luther, both governments are God's two ways of using creatures as instruments of God's power. God uses creatures by giving God's self with and through them. God's power is God's self-giving love.

---

32. See Antti Raunio, "Divine and Natural Law in Luther and Melanchthon," in *Lutheran Reformation and the Law*, ed. Virpi Mäkinen (Leiden: Brill, 2006), 21–61.

Luther calls love "the master and the real righteousness [*Bescheidenheit*[33]]" of the divine good works." Love aims at the good of one's neighbor and, in this sense, it is a "righteousness." Luther sees the righteousness of love as the basis for worldly virtues. Worldly righteousness seeks the common good and ordains the laws in accordance with it.[34] Although Luther distinguishes between the two forms of righteousness, he does not separate them. Both the striving for the neighbor's good and the striving for the common good are required in order to fulfill the neighbor's basic needs. Luther's idea of the two governments combines these two tasks.

The idea of the two governments has often been understood as a radical separation between the two. A liberal democracy, for example, sees personal freedom as the basic good of an individual, but it tends to interpret religious freedom as freedom from all religious aspects of life (at least in the countries of modern Europe). Freedom is thus understood in the negative sense of "freedom from." But how can a society promote positive freedom, the "freedom to" practice religion and to proclaim the gospel of God's love, grace, and good gifts? The Lutheran tradition has an important contribution to make to this conversation, not by dictating political policy, but by contextualizing the question in intimate relation to social and political dimensions.

Luther's explanation to the Creed in the Large Catechism serves as a helpful starting-point. Luther explicitly claims that worldly goods such as good government, peace, and security are God's gifts.[35] God's gifts, such as money, house, land, and—in Luther's sixteenth-century context—servants, are showered on all people. Luther admits that these goods can convey worldly honor and power. Property is a necessary worldly gift because the worldly government cannot function without it. Property is a good that serves its owner, and should also be used to help those who live in poverty.[36]

The idea of property in the service of individual good is, for Luther, a matter of both worldly and spiritual realms. Worldly government should be premised on a responsible community that assures persons the right to work in order to acquire goods and property. Two levels of responsibility help achieve this goal: the relation of individuals to their neighbors and the corporate responsibility of the community for the common good.

---

33. Luther uses the German word "Bescheydenheit" in the sense of righteousness (in Latin, "probitas," and in modern German, "Rechtschaffenheit").
34. WA 17/II:96, 24–27.
35. See above footnote 20.
36. WA 10/I.2:376, 6–21 (*Sommerpostille 1526*).

On this point, Lutheran theology can be critical of the welfare system. The criticism should address a specific misunderstanding, rather than jump to the conclusion that the welfare system immediately implies passivity vis-à-vis social responsibility. From a theological perspective, the misunderstanding concerns the "divinization" of a social or economical model. People misconstrue the welfare system when they see it as the *source* of good, not as a divine gift for guaranteeing and assuring basic social goods for all.[37] The Nordic welfare state can be misunderstood in these terms. People may wait for society to take care of things they have received or should receive as personal goods from God. Passivity can then result from misunderstanding the source of the good. The task of society or the worldly government is to guarantee a particular framework for welfare, security, and justice, but citizens must take on their own responsibility for securing the goods as well.

The flipside of misconstruing the welfare system is when individuals turn a blind eye to the common good and misuse social goods to their own advantage. These folk are not concerned about common welfare, security, and justice, but are solely preoccupied with their individual well-being. The worldly government corrects for individualistic tendencies by using "coercive" measures, such as laws and taxes. The political goal is to coerce unwilling people to promote the common good.

In conclusion, we can distinguish between three different "goods" in Luther's social thinking. Firstly, there is the common good, meaning things that are good for an entire community, for example, justice, peace, and security. Secondly, there is the private or personal good, meaning the things that fulfill the material and spiritual needs required for a decent life. Thirdly, there is one's "own good," meaning both personal and common goods taken in a selfish way. Luther's social theology aims to promote the common and personal good, which benefit the neighbor and include one's personal good. The searching for one's "own good" does not promote the neighbor's good, because the selfishly considered good separates the good from its function to serve all creatures.

Christians and the Social Good

Luther's justification for social action rests on, as we have seen, the law of love as it informs external laws. One issue that remains to be addressed concerns the spiritual realm's function in prescribing specific social actions in the worldly

---

37. Luther writes in the Large Catechism that God gives us our daily bread chiefly through civil authorities and the government (BoC, 450, 73).

realm. Classic Lutheran theology has tended to shy away from the spiritual realm's concrete determination of worldly prescriptions. I look in this section at how Luther makes a case for assigning precise responsibilities to Christians in their vocations as worldly authorities in order to promote social action.

Luther's historical commitment was the drawing up of new ordinances for common chests in towns that had accepted the Reformation. Luther introduced the idea in his *Address to the Christian Nobility* (1520).[38] Luther's intention was to give an impulse for new social ordinances, placing responsibility on towns and surrounding villages to take care of the poor via the common chests.[39] The ordinance of Leisnig, for example, for which Luther himself wrote the introduction, was explicitly based on applying the principle of the Christian love of God and neighbor to the social life. The order begins by stressing that both the inward and outward capacities of Christians should serve to honor God and to love neighbor.[40] The ordinance's emphasis presupposes that the people of Leisnig were aware of the interdependence between inner and outer aspects of living in a community.

Luther was involved in writing the ordinance of Leisnig, yet he later made explicit in his *Exposition of Psalm 82* (1530) his own views concerning the responsibilities of public authorities. For Luther, public authorities are responsible for supporting and promoting the rights of the poor, orphans, and widows.[41] Responsibility for social justice is the mark of a good community. External laws and prescriptions for behavior help to guarantee rights, and see to it that individuals are assigned to particular estates and are kept employed in workshops, stores, and service roles. In the absence of these laws, the poor, orphans, and widows are forgotten, and people destroy, rob, steal from and cheat each other. Luther recognizes that the absence of good laws and social norms affects primarily society's weakest members, while also endangering the community's health. For Luther, the rights of the poor must be promoted as an effective means to support the community's common good.

But is this sufficient to establish justice? Luther is careful to note that there is a distinction between a good work that helps the poor and a notion of justice that is ultimately a divine work concretely available in the community. In the *Exposition of Psalm 82*, Luther compares a just community with a heavenly and divine hospital.[42] It is a divine work to transform the entire land

---

38. LW 44:189.
39. See Torvend, *Luther and the Hungry Poor*, 105–113.
40. WA 12:16, 4–10 (1523).
41. LW 13:52 (to verse 2; 1530), WA 31/I:200, 5–19.
42. LW 13:53 (to verse 2).

into a hospital, which can benefit all, especially the poor. A good work helps a few citizens, but a divine work serves the whole community. A community informed by justice ensures that every member has food and property. If justice is missing, all citizens become beggars and perish. Luther speaks here as a child of his own times, but his message of justice is badly needed today.

Luther's idea of the neighbor's basic good is that each member of a community serves every other member. In order to be a member who serves the neighbor's good, a citizen must first be served by the community in being given temporal goods. In other words, the community must have the common good as its main focus. The common good means that every member has enough for a decent life, where "enough" is measured by real needs. What one does not need is meant to be used by others. In practice, human beings must be content with a modest life. Their needs must be tempered to avoid excesses and consumption must be restricted to moderation. In this sense, the good is common.

At the same time, the community exists to serve the good of each and every member. At this point, the intimate relationship between common and personal good involves the two aspects of worldly and spiritual goods. The good life in a community combines common goods with personal or private goods. The worldly government aims to promote the common good, while the spiritual government of love aims to actualize the personal good of the neighbor.

Yet for Luther, both spiritual and worldly governments are intimately related by virtue of the same reality that informs personal goods and the common good. Personal goods and the common good are two aspects of the same reality. Both are good gifts and works of the loving God, who fulfils the creatures' needs by giving both kinds of goods. A human being cannot separate her personal needs from the community's welfare, even though the tendency in modern Western societies to do so is strong. There are serious social and political consequences for both community and world that arise when the personal is privileged and separated from the communal. In our globalized world, the consequences can be downright disastrous.

Can the vision of a human community of mutual service and love be actualized in reality? Luther recognized that such a community exists in a way that has a beginning in reality but is not yet actualized. His theological commitments compelled him to believe that a reciprocally serving and loving community could be actualized. The ground of human community is God's self-giving love. God's works of love are given generously, in order that they may be continuously received and further distributed to those who are in need. Luther's view may just be the theological justification for a Lutheran vision of social action for the contemporary world.

CHAPTER 14

Luther's Theology of the Cross

— Resource for a Theology of Religions —

Ronald F. Thiemann

artin Luther is one of those figures in the history of Christianity who have been invoked to support every imaginable theological, cultural, and political point of view. Luther has often functioned as a blank screen onto which scholars, politicians, and polemicists have projected their own hopes, fears, illusions, and fantasies. The uses and abuses of Luther's legacy in the German Nazi and Communist regimes are well known, and the late Robert Scribner has documented the myth-making function of Luther images in post-Reformation Germany in his delightful article "Incombustible Luther: The Image of the Reformer in Early Modern Germany."[1] Luther seems to be an inexhaustible resource for polemic, propaganda, and even phantasmagoria.

To propose that Luther's theology of the cross can serve as a resource for a Christian theology of religions might seem just another illusory projection by a Lutheran theologian desperate to invoke the Reformer's authority over his own theological proposals. How might this equal opportunity excoriator—known for his condemnations of Jew, Turk, Catholic, pope, peasant, and pagan alike—serve as a model for our contemporary efforts to engage the challenge of religious diversity and religious conflict? And how might his highly particular christocentric theology of the cross be a theological resource

---

1. *Past and Present* 110/1 (1986): 38–68.

for inter-religious understanding and dialogue? Such a proposal may seem on the face of it counterintuitive and unpersuasive, but I intend to make just such a case in this chapter.

Luther's *Theologia Crucis*

Theological, Existential, and Spiritual Practices

Before I propose Luther's *theologia crucis* as a model for a theology of religions, I need to sketch out my understanding of the conceptual shape of this fundamental theological issue (*theologoumenon*). Following many Luther interpreters, I understand *theologia crucis* not just as one evangelical doctrine among others but as the chief hermeneutical key to Luther's theological orientation.[2] *Theologia crucis* identifies not just Luther's basic theological insight into the gospel but also describes the fundamental spiritual orientation or sensibility[3] of the evangelical theologian. It is no accident that in the *Heidelberg Disputation* (1518), Luther emphasizes not simply the *theology* of the cross but more importantly the stance of the *theologian* of the cross. Luther is simultaneously describing an intellectual approach to the theological task and an existential commitment to an evangelical spiritual practice. *Theologia crucis* is, on this interpretation, a complex set of intellectual and spiritual practices designed to shape the mind, character, and faith of the theologian.[4] *Theologia crucis* invites

---

2. *Theologia crucis* is, I would argue, more fundamental to Luther's understanding of theology than the doctrine of justification, because it is not limited by the forensic conceptuality that circumscribes the latter doctrine. Of the vast literature on Luther's theology of the cross the following have been most useful to me: Walther von Loewenich, *Luther's Theology of the Cross*, trans. Herbert J. A. Bouman (Minneapolis: Augsburg, 1976); Alister E. McGrath, *Luther's Theology of the Cross* (London: Basil Blackwell, 1985); Jürgen Moltmann, *The Crucified God*, trans. R. A. Wilson and John Bowden (New York: Harper, 1974); Horst Beintker, *Die Überwindung der Anfechtung bei Luther: Eine Studie zu seiner Theologie nach den Operationes in Psalmos 1519–1521*, Theologische Arbeiten 1 (Berlin: Evangelische Verlagsanstalt, 1954); Eberhard Jüngel, "Die Welt als Wirklichkeit und Möglichkeit," in *Unterwegs zur Sache* (Munich: Kaiser, 1972), 206–231; Brian A. Gerrish, "To the Unknown God: Luther and Calvin on the Hiddenness of God," *Journal of Religion* 53 (1973): 263–92.

3. By "sensibility" I follow Henry James's notion of imaginative experience as described in his essay "The Art of Fiction" (in *The Art of Criticism: Henry James on the Theory and the Practice of Fiction*, ed. Henry James, William Veeder, and Susan Griffin [Chicago: The University of Chicago Press, 1986], 172): "Experience is never limited and it is never complete; it is an immense sensibility, a kind of huge spider-web, of the finest silken threads, suspended in the chamber of consciousness and catching every air-borne particle in its tissue. It is the very atmosphere of the mind; and when the mind is imaginative—much more when it happens to be that of a man of genius—it takes to itself the faintest hints of life, it converts the very pulses of the air into revelations."

4. To some extent I disagree with Walther von Loewenich when he asserts that Luther's theology of the cross is primarily "a distinctive principle of theological knowledge" rather

the theologian into an evangelical form of life that will continually shape and reshape the believer's orientation toward Christian thought and practice. *Theologia crucis* is thus an invitation to "theology as a way of life."[5] *Theologia crucis* reaffirms Luther's conviction that "living, or rather dying and being damned make a theologian, not understanding, reading, or speculating."[6]

Crux Sola Est Nostra Theologia![7]

The *locus classicus* for Luther's theology of the cross is the *Heidelberg Disputation* over which Luther presided on April 26, 1518 for the chapter meeting of the Augustinian Order at Heidelberg. Luther drew up a series of theological and philosophical theses at the invitation of Johannes von Staupitz and, in so doing, sketched out the shape of a theology that would sustain him throughout his life. The first two sets of theses (1–12 and 13–18) deal respectively with the problem of good works and the will.[8] In the theses on good works, Luther drives home the point that good works, though they appear attractive and comely, are in fact "mortal sins" (thesis 3). Contrariwise, God's works, which often appear unattractive and even evil, are in fact the sole source of our eternal life and merit (thesis 4). As God drives us to the recognition that "there is no form or beauty in us, but our life is hidden in God,"[9] God accomplishes his proper work (*opus proprium*) through its apparent opposite, his alien work (*opus alienum*). Thus there is nothing within human beings that can in any way merit the righteous and saving love of God. Our salvation is accomplished solely through the hidden works of God accomplished in our behalf. In like manner, Luther asserts that human will is unable to accomplish anything that would make us righteous before God. "The person who believes that he can obtain grace by doing what is in him [*quod in se est*] adds sin to sin so that he becomes doubly guilty" (thesis 16).

Our utter inability to achieve righteousness before God should not, Luther stresses, "give cause for despair," but rather should arouse "the desire

---

than an "ideal of humility." In the effort to draw a sharp distinction between the medieval and the early modern Luther, many scholars have lost a sense in which *theologia crucis* constitutes a set of non-monastic spiritual practices. See Loewenich, *Luther's Theology of the Cross*, 13.

5. In this regard, *theologia crucis* constitutes a set of spiritual exercises available to all believers who seek to be followers of the Crucified. For a parallel approach to the philosophical task, see Pierre Hadot, *Philosophy as a Way of Life: Spiritual Exercises from Socrates to Foucault*, trans. Michael Chase, ed. Arnold Davidson (Oxford: Blackwell, 1995).

6. WA 5:163, 28–29 (*Operationes in Psalmos*; 1519–1521).

7. WA 5:176, 32–33.

8. LW 31:39–40.

9. LW 31:44 (to thesis 4).

to humble oneself and seek the grace of Christ" (thesis 17). But even this self-humbling and seeking is not a meritorious human act; the transformation of our wills is itself always and only a work of God. "It is certain that man must utterly despair of his own ability before he is prepared to receive the grace of Christ" (thesis 18). Thus it becomes clear in these early theses that Luther is laying out a set of normative proposals for living a life shaped by the gospel of Jesus Christ. While there are important epistemological consequences of living such a life, the existential and spiritual dimensions of the theology of the cross are front and center from the outset.

It comes as no surprise that in the next set of theses, Luther turns *not* to the abstract question of a *theology* of the cross, but to the concrete issue of the form of life exemplified by the *theologian* of the cross.

> 19. That person does not deserve to be called a theologian who looks upon the invisible things of God as though they were clearly perceptible in those things that have actually happened. [Rom. 1:20] (*Non ille dignus theologus dicitur, qui invisibilia Dei per ea, quae facta sunt, intellecta conspicit.*)
>
> 20. He deserves to be called a theologian, however, who comprehends the visible and manifest things of God seen through suffering and the cross. (*Sed qui visibilia et posteriora Dei per passionem et crucem conspecta intelligit.*)
>
> 21. A theologian of glory calls evil good and good evil. A theologian of the cross calls the thing what it actually is. (*Theologus gloriae dicit malum bonum et bonum malum, Theologus crucis dicit id quod res est.*)[10]

These three theses describe a set of theological practices that characterize the work of one whose life has been shaped by the saving grace of God in Christ. As one saved solely through the gracious action of the crucified God, the theologian deserving of that name adopts those theological practices appropriate to the cruciform nature of God's saving acts. Together these theses sketch out a program of "epistemological realism," an approach to theology that discourages metaphysical speculation and encourages a sober descriptive realism. The goal of theological reflection is not to hypothesize about the invisible attributes of an unknown transcendent God, but to describe the visible and manifest works of a God become flesh and thereby hidden in suffering and the cross. God's reality is not to be found in an invisible realm beyond the

---

10. LW 31:40, WA 1:354, 17–22.

human senses, but in the visible evidence of a suffering and crucified Christ. The God upon whom the theologian ought to reflect is not the invisible things of God (*invisibilia Dei*) perceived through metaphysical speculation, but a God who shows the theologian his backside (*posteriora Dei*) in suffering and the cross. The revealed God is the God who is hidden (*absconditus*) in the cross of Christ. God's reality is thereby revealed precisely in its hiddenness, under the form of its opposite (*abscondita sub contrariis*). As Luther remarked in a sermon delivered on February 24, 1517: "Man hides what is his own in order to conceal it, but God conceals what is his in order to reveal it."[11]

The God who is revealed through the hiddenness of the cross can be known only through faith. Faith alone receives the righteousness of God in Christ, and faith alone opens the eyes of the believer to see the true God hidden in suffering. The theologian of glory expects God to be manifest in power, majesty, and strength, but the theologian of the cross knows through the eyes of faith that God is, in fact, manifest in suffering, death, and a cross. Because God's true nature is always and only revealed under God's opposite, faith cannot rely upon the evidences of reason, nature, or experience for its certitude. Luther was particularly fond of the definition of faith found in the Book of Hebrews (11:1): "Faith is the assurance of things hoped for, the conviction of things not seen." Such a faith is inevitably plagued by doubt and assaulted by uncertainties (*Anfechtungen*). Faith itself undergoes the crucible of suffering and death as the believer/theologian seeks to follow the suffering and crucified Christ. Faith thus shares in the sufferings of the Crucified One as the believer struggles to follow in faithful discipleship.

Because faith itself undergoes such a crisis of confidence, Luther insists that faith's doubts can be assuaged only through the saving work of God in Christ. No amount of contemplation of one's own faith or subjectivity can ever convince the believer that the God revealed in the cross of Christ is the God who makes the sinner righteous. That confidence flows only from the believer's contemplation of the cross of Christ, the act whereby Christ becomes sin so that sinners might become righteous. This theme of the "blessed exchange" receives its most magnificent expression in Luther's *Greater Galatians Commentary* (1535), but it is present in Luther's earlier thought as well. Already in his *Operationes in Psalmos* (1519–1521), Luther asserts that Christ became sin for us in order that his righteousness might become ours as well.[12] Luther's penchant for realist discourse comes to the fore again as he claims that Christ

---

11. LW 51:26 ("Sermon on St. Matthew's Day"; to Matt 11:25-30; Feb. 24, 1517), WA 1:138, 13–15.
12. WA 5:607, 32–37.

became the "greatest sinner" (*maximus peccator*) so that sinners might become the righteous ones of God.

> This is the most joyous of all doctrines and the one that contains the most comfort. It teaches that we have the indescribable and inestimable mercy and love of God. When the merciful Father saw that we were being oppressed through the Law, that we were being held under a curse, and that we could not be liberated from it by anything, He sent His Son into the world, heaped all the sins of all men upon Him, and said to Him, "Be Peter the denier; Paul the persecutor, blasphemer, and assaulter; David, the adulterer; the sinner who ate the apple in paradise; the thief on the cross. In short, be the person of all men, the one who has committed the sins of all men . . ." Now let us see how two such extremely contrary things come together in this Person. Not only my sins and yours, but the sins of the entire world, past, present, and future, attack Him, try to damn Him, and do in fact damn Him. But because in the same Person who is the highest, the greatest, and the only sinner, there is also eternal and invincible righteousness, therefore these two converge: the highest, the greatest, and the only sin; and the highest, the greatest, and the only righteousness. Here one of them must yield and be conquered, since they come together and collide with such powerful impact and fury. What happens? Righteousness is eternal, immortal, and invincible . . . Thus in Christ all sin is conquered, killed, and buried; and righteousness remains the victor and ruler eternally.[13]

The theologian of the cross lives by faith and not by sight. Moreover, such a theologian lives out of the humility and gratitude of one who recognizes that salvation, knowledge of God, and true theology are all gifts of the unmerited, yet free love and mercy of God. The theologian of the cross lives a life of the humility of faith (*humilitas fidei*), a faith born of both humility and confidence, of gratitude and grace. Having seen God's proper work emerge out of God's alien work, the theologian of the cross refuses to avert her eyes from the suffering of the world, knowing that such suffering has been borne and reconciled in the cross of Christ. The theologian of the cross is thus willing to call things what they really are, knowing that no sin or death is so great that it cannot be redeemed by the Crucified. The theologian of the cross engages in a theology of cruciform and realistic hope, always expecting the unexpected from a God whose revelation is hidden within its apparent opposite. The theologian of the cross is realistic yet hopeful, doubting yet faithful, humble yet confident,

---

13. LW 25:280–81 (*Lectures on Galatians*; 1535).

trusting that the grace and mercy of God will enable theological work to discern the visible and manifest things of God through suffering and the cross.

Theologia Crucis and a Cruciform Theology of Religions

One of the greatest needs in today's world is for Christians to develop theological approaches to the engagement with the world's religious traditions—an engagement which holds fast to the deepest convictions of the Christian faith and is yet open to other traditions' own witness to truth.[14] The challenge is to find a way between forms of absolutism and exclusivism which deny *a priori* the validity claims of other religions and forms of relativism which undermine the truth claims of all religions in the name of tolerance and mutual understanding. Fundamentalisms of various stripes assert the truth of their own religious claims to the exclusion of all other claims to truth. Liberalisms of various sorts eschew truth-claiming altogether in order to foster a peaceful rapprochement between the world's religious faiths. Both approaches are, in my judgment, corrosive of the integrity of a faith which is, at once, confident yet modest, faithful yet questing. In this second part of the chapter, I want to argue that a religious sensibility shaped by the virtues of Luther's theology of the cross provides important resources for developing a theology of religions that is both robustly truth-claiming yet genuinely open to the faith claims of others. A theology of the cross can assist communities of faith in recognizing the compatibility between deep and abiding commitment to the truth claims of one's own tradition and an openness to and respect for the claims of another tradition. Truth-claiming and acceptance of religious pluralism are not inconsistent. In the next section, I argue that a necessary prolegomenon to any Christian theology of religion is an understanding of Christian truth-claiming that finds a middle way between exclusivism in truth and absolutism in knowledge, on the one hand, and a truth-eroding relativism, on the other. The rest of the chapter argues that a convergence exists between a non-foundational

---

14. Of the vast literature on a Christian theology of religions the following texts have been most useful to me: Jacques Dupuis, *Toward a Christian Theology of Religious Pluralism* (Maryknoll: Orbis, 1997); S. Mark Heim, *Salvations: Truth and Difference in Religion* (Maryknoll: Orbis, 1995); S. Mark Heim, *The Depth of the Riches: A Trinitarian Theology of Religious Ends* (Grand Rapids: Eerdmans, 2001); Gavin D'Costa, *The Meeting of Religions and the Trinity* (Maryknoll: Orbis, 2000); J. A. DiNoia, "Varieties of Religious Aims: Beyond Exclusivism, Inclusivism and Pluralism," in *Theology and Dialogue* (Notre Dame: University of Notre Dame Press, 1989), 249–74; Francis X. Clooney, *Hindu God, Christian God: How Reason Helps to Break Down the Boundaries between Religions* (New York: Oxford University Press, 2001); Francis X. Clooney, *Divine Mother, Blessed Mother: Hindu Goddesses and the Virgin Mary* (New York: Oxford University Press, 2004).

pragmatist but non-relativist philosophy and a theological and spiritual sensibility shaped by a *theologia crucis*.

Exclusivism and Absolutism: Forms of Religious Intolerance

Exclusivism is the view that only one religious tradition, worldview, or system of belief can be true. In order to assert the truth of one's own religious tradition, it is necessary, exclusivists argue, to deny the truth of all other traditions or worldviews. Exclusivists often argue that since there is only one path to salvation ("I am the way, and the truth, and the life. No one comes to the Father except through me." [John 14:6]), religions that claim salvation through other redeemers, saviors, or paths of enlightenment cannot be true. If Christ is the one way to salvation, then no other claim to salvation can hold validity. Religious revelations are, this view argues, incommensurable. It is impossible consistently to hold more than one view of salvation as valid. The logic of revelation and salvation is inherently exclusivist. To believe, for example, in Christ is perforce to reject the way of Muhammad, Buddha, or Moses.

To some degree, the exclusivist position seems self-evidently true. If a believer is to commit his or her life to a religious tradition or set of practices, it seems obvious that one cannot simultaneously commit one's life to another different, perhaps even conflicting, tradition or set of practices. To serve the God revealed in the cross of Christ is perforce to refuse to follow other gods or other redeemers. In part, the exclusivist claims seem merely to be a comment on the very logic of truth-claiming. Truth-claiming is, in one sense, an inherently exclusivist venture. To say something is "true" means that everything else that conflicts with that assertion must by definition be "false." That is the *meaning* of "true." Or, to put the matter differently: if I hold a belief to be true, I am thereby committed to denying the truth of beliefs that directly conflict with my own. That which conflicts with truth is by definition "false." In this very restrictive and formal sense, then, truth is an absolute and exclusive concept.[15] If one wants to maintain the place of truth-claiming in religion, as I do, then some assertions made by adherents of religious traditions will inevitably conflict with all other sentences that explicitly contradict those assertions.

---

15. The most thorough discussion of truth-claiming in theology is Bruce D. Marshall, *Trinity and Truth* (Cambridge: Cambridge University Press, 2000). "We do have a stable grasp of the concept of truth, [Donald] Davidson argues, for every sentence in our language. Supposing that language is English, our grasp of the concept 'true' as applied to the sentence 'Grass is green,' for example, is expressed in our untroubled assent to the sentence "'Grass is green' is true if and only if grass is green" . . . that is . . . "s is true-in-*L* if and only if *p*" (234). For further background, see Jeffrey Stout, *Democracy and Tradition* (Princeton: Princeton University Press, 2003).

"Truth" is, in the first instance, a property of propositions, beliefs, and assertions. To say that something is "true" is to express commitment to the content of a proposition. "What Wiesel says about the evil of the persecution of Jews is true." In addition, however, to say something is "true" is to assert that "*it is the case that* the persecution of Jews is evil." "S is true if and only if S" is one standard way of expressing this second sense of the word "true." Truth, then, is a property of propositions precisely when propositions correctly state "what is the case." And in stating "what is the case," true propositions also contradict, or determine as false, propositions that directly conflict with true statements. To say that the sentence "the persecution of the Jews is evil" is true, is *necessarily* to assert that the sentence "the persecution of the Jews is good" is false. In that sense, truth always excludes what is false. Our moral language could not function if that were not the case. So if we are not to fall into a mindless and self-defeating form of relativism, we must acknowledge that true propositions do, indeed, exclude false propositions and their associated states of affairs.

But surely the mere fact of truth-claiming in religion cannot constitute exclusivism, that is, the claim that the truth of my religious beliefs requires the denial of the truth of all other religious beliefs. The problem with religious exclusivism in my judgment is not that it functions with a notion of truth that is exclusive, but that it *applies* the notion of truth incorrectly. Exclusivists are wrong, and dangerously so, because they take a notion of truth that belongs to propositions and their associated states of affairs and apply it to entire conceptual frameworks, worldviews, or religions. It would be impossible ever to gather together all the propositions within a worldview and show that without exception every proposition within it is true (or false). But that is the only intelligible way in which one can apply the notion of "truth" to a religion or comprehensive scheme, that is, to the entire set of propositions comprised within that conceptual framework. The problem with many exclusivists is that they apply the term "true" to their entire framework and then believe that they further have the warrant to dismiss all other frameworks as false. It is precisely this double intellectual and moral mistake that leads so easily to fanaticism.

Exclusivists often also claim "absoluteness" for their beliefs. Absoluteness is the assertion that claims to truth cannot be contradicted because they have indubitable, self-evident, and incorrigible grounds upon which they stand. Absolutists believe that they have indubitable grounds for their statements of religious faith. Often they appeal to revelation or doctrines of inspiration, inerrancy, and/or infallibility to support their claims to indubitability. It is precisely this conviction about the infallibility of religious beliefs that breeds the attitude of arrogance and disdain that characterizes far too many believers

today. Absolutist claims assert indubitability based upon the self-evident, reve-
latory grounds adduced for those claims. Certain sentences are indubitable
because the grounds for those claims are derived from the self-evidence of
divine revelation,[16] or so its adherents seek to argue.

In opposing absolutism, one need oppose neither claims to revelation[17]
nor robust strongly held truth claims.[18] The problem with absolutism is that it
is grounded in a foundationalist epistemology that cannot ultimately be given
self-consistent formulation. The foundationalist asserts that truth claims must
be justified through an appeal to self-evident and incorrigible grounds, but can
adduce no such grounds for the foundationalist thesis itself. The claim that
all rationally justified beliefs must ultimately be grounded in self-evident and
incorrigible evidence cannot itself be justified by such evidence. Such claims
appeal to forms of immediate, intuitive, and self-authenticating experiences
which cannot themselves be justified. Attempts to justify these experiences
finally amount to claims like "you had to be there to know it" or "if you shared
the experience you'd know that it was self-authenticating." But such claims are
simply asserted without justifying reasons or arguments. Thus they inevitably
appear to be arbitrary, irrational, or fideist in character. On its own account
of rational justification, the foundationalist claim is found wanting. Wilfred
Sellars identifies this problem as "the myth of the given" and develops an
inconsistent triad to show the inability of foundationalist positions to be given
self-consistent articulation.[19] Donald Davidson develops these ideas further to
suggest that the epistemic division between scheme and content cannot itself

---

16. Among the many accounts of foundationalism, Bruce Marshall's (see footnote 15) is one
of the most succinct. "By 'foundationalism' I mean a set of three claims tightly connected by
adherents of the thesis: (F1) that with regard to at least some of the sentences we hold true,
we have direct or immediate access to states of affairs, events, or experiences in virtue of
which those sentences are true; (F2) that this direct access guarantees the truth of these sentences, and so justifies us in, or serves as the ultimate evidence for, holding them true; (F3)
that the rest of our beliefs must be justified by establishing some suitable kind of warranting
link with those which are directly tied to the world (and thereby serve as the justificatory
'foundations' for the rest)." (*Trinity and Truth*, 54)
17. I seek to develop a non-foundational understanding of revelation in *Revelation and
Theology: The Gospel as Narrated Promise* (Notre Dame: University of Notre Dame Press,
1985).
18. Bruce Marshall, who shares my critique of foundationalism, nonetheless, affirms the
"incorrigibility" of "the Church's central beliefs." "The Christian tradition, however, has generally taken the church's central beliefs to be certain and incorrigible, while explicitly denying that those beliefs are self-evident, empirically evident, or even very widely held . . . We
who hold these beliefs should therefore regard them as certain and incorrigible—incapable
of turning out to be false." (*Trinity and Truth*, 168–69)
19. "Empiricism and the Philosophy of Mind," in *Science, Perception, and Reality* (London:
Routledge & Kegan Paul, 1963), 127–96.

be sustained.[20] In the light of such strong anti-foundationalist arguments, a consensus has formed within much theology and philosophy that absolutist claims grounded in foundational epistemologies simply cannot be sustained. Nonetheless, in practice many Christians and Christian communities continue to employ foundationalist absolutist understandings of their doctrines of revelation. Many believe that without such assertions of indubitable foundations, Christian claims to truth lack their grounding in the revelation of God. Thus foundationalist accounts of revelation have shown remarkable resilience in the face of philosophical and theological critique.

If, however, one is convinced by the anti-foundationalist critique, what becomes of Christian claims to truth? Once the foundationalist basis for absolutism has been swept away, what remains then for the Christian adherent to assert? Does the fall of absolutism require the embrace of relativism? Do Christian theological assertions now reside in a realm where skepticism and even nihilism threaten the truth status of those claims? Such worries exemplify what Richard Bernstein has termed "the Cartesian anxiety," that "grand and seductive Either/Or. *Either* there is some fixed foundation for our knowledge *or* we cannot escape the forces of darkness that envelop us with madness, with intellectual and moral chaos."[21] The demise of foundationalism and its associated demons, exclusivism and absolutism, by no means entails the demise of robust truth-claiming in theology. The challenge remains, however, to show how non-exclusivist and non-absolutist (but also non-relativist) truth claims can be sustained in a religiously plural context. To meet that challenge we need to invoke the convictions and virtues inherent in Luther's theology of the cross.

Theology of the Cross and Religious Pluralism

At stake here is the question of whether there is compatibility between a deep and abiding commitment to the truth claims of one's tradition and an openness to and respect for the claims of another tradition. In the remainder of the chapter, I argue that truth-claiming and an acceptance of religious pluralism are not inconsistent. Nicolas Rescher has stated this issue with special eloquence.

> Pluralism holds that it is rationally intelligible and acceptable that others can hold positions at variance with one's own. But it does not maintain

---

20. "On the Very Idea of a Conceptual Scheme," in *Inquiries into Truth and Interpretation* (Oxford: Oxford University Press, 1984), 183–98.
21. Richard Bernstein, *Beyond Objectivism and Relativism: Science, Hermeneutics, and Praxis* (Philadelphia: University of Pennsylvania Press, 1983), 18.

that a given individual need endorse a plurality of positions—that the fact that others hold a certain position somehow constitutes a reason for doing so oneself. . . . Pluralism is a feature of the collective group; it turns on the fact that different experiences engender different views. But from the standpoint of the individual this cuts no ice. We have no alternative to proceeding as best we can on the basis of what is available to us. That others agree with us is not proof of correctness; that they disagree, no sign of error.[22]

Fundamental to the acceptance of pluralism is the conviction that we have no self-evident, incorrigible means of establishing the truth of our positions. The same grounds that lead us to reject foundationalist absolutism also make it possible for us to embrace pluralism. It does not follow that we have no way at all to establish the truth of our assertions; however, the means at our disposal will not necessarily convince those with whom we disagree. Consequently, we must hold open the possibility that those who disagree with us do so rationally. This position implies neither relativism nor indifferentism to truth. It simply suggests that we cannot coerce others into believing as we do. We can offer our reasons for so believing, but these reasons, even if sufficient to support our claims, will not compel others to accept our beliefs. Thus we need now to turn to a consideration of those "reasons for so believing" and an assessment of whether such beliefs can be formulated so as to avoid the twin dangers of exclusivism and absolutism.

Ludwig Wittgenstein has taught us that "the meaning of a word is its use in the language."[23] If you want to find meaning, look to use. If you want to find the meaning of beliefs, in this case Christian truth-claims, then you need to see how those beliefs are used in the context of Christian practice. I am in agreement with George Lindbeck when he argues, "Christian ontological truth-claims" are made "in the activities of adoration, proclamation, obedience, promise-hearing and promise-keeping which shape individuals and communities into conformity with Christ . . . Truth and falsity characterize ordinary religious language when it is used to mold lives through prayer, praise, and exhortation. It is only on this level that human beings linguistically exhibit their truth or falsity, their correspondence or lack of correspondence to the Ultimate Mystery."[24]

---

22. Nicolas Rescher, *Pluralism: Against the Demand for Consensus* (Oxford: Clarendon, 1993), 89.
23. *Philosophical Investigations*, vol. 1, no. 43 (Oxford: Basil Blackwell, 1958), 20.
24. *The Nature of Doctrine: Religion and Theology in a Postliberal Age* (Philadelphia: Westminster, 1984), 68.

Christian truth claims are located within the complex web of beliefs and practices that constitute the Christian community. Christian identity is shaped and nurtured by belief-ful participation in the communal life of Christianity. While truth claims can be found throughout the Christian web of belief, some beliefs and practices are clearly more decisive for Christian identity than others. Beliefs that are decisive for forming and maintaining Christian communal identity might be called "fundamental beliefs."[25] These are beliefs which, if they were discarded or radically changed, would so fundamentally alter the identity of the community that it would no longer be recognizable as Christian. Or to put it another way: these are beliefs which the community should be least willing to discard in face of opposition or adversity, for if they are discarded it becomes unclear whether the community any longer remains in significant continuity with the historic Christian tradition.

Bruce Marshall has introduced the helpful language of "epistemic primacy" to identify the function of fundamental beliefs when faced with conflicting or incompatible beliefs: "A community regards belief A as central with respect to belief B if and only if, should conflict arise between A and B, the community persists in holding A true, and rejects or modifies B. But this is simply to say that the community regards A as a criterion for deciding about the truth of B. Faced with the incompatibility of the two beliefs—that is, the inconsistency which belongs to logical contradictions—it holds A true, and finds that it must therefore hold B false. The community, we can say, regards A as *epistemically primary* with respect to B."[26] Among the beliefs that the Christian community holds to be epistemically primary are the christological and Trinitarian beliefs that constitute the heart of the Christian vision. Indeed, the claim that in the death and resurrection of Jesus Christ the truth about the relation between the triune God and the cosmos has been revealed is the most central and fundamental claim of the Christian faith.[27] Can such a fun-

---

25. In *Revelation and Theology*, I spoke of these beliefs as "basic," but I now think that this term does not sufficiently signal the strong resistance a community should have to revising such beliefs. Bruce Marshall in *Trinity and Truth* terms such beliefs "essential" and is willing to claim that some of these beliefs are "incorrigible." Because I am unwilling to make the latter claim, I prefer the less essentialist language of "fundamental."
26. *Trinity and Truth*, 45.
27. Marshall claims for this belief and indeed all fundamental Christian beliefs "unrestricted epistemic primacy." "To say that central Christian beliefs have unrestricted epistemic primacy means that any possible belief which contradicts them must be false. Ascribing genuinely *unrestricted* primacy to these particular beliefs, moreover, preempts the application of the category; no other beliefs will be able to enjoy this logical status. From this it follows that no true belief can contradict the narratives which identify Jesus and the Trinity." (*Trinity and Truth*, 120)

damental, identity-shaping, epistemically primary belief be compatible with religious pluralism? Can a Trinitarian theology of the cross be developed in such a way as to avoid the dangers of exclusivism and absolutism? What might a Christian theology of religions focused on a Trinitarian theology of the cross look like? To that question we now turn.

I believe that the appropriate goal of a Christian theology of religions is to understand those religions in and for themselves and to give an account of the grounds within Christian theology itself for being open to the witness of truth that might come from careful listening to those religions. Careful listening, done in a respectful manner, requires a genuine openness to the claims of other religions, an openness that does not prejudge whether those claims confirm, conflict with, or simply differ from the Christian witness. Genuine respect for the religious Other requires Christians to hold open the manifold possibilities that might emerge from genuine interreligious dialogue and mutual examination. Generalizations about the truth of all religions seem no more plausible than generalizations about the falsity of all religions. Genuine respect for the religious Other requires, in my estimation, holding open the possibility that claims of the Other might be true, false, relevant, irrelevant, wise, or foolish. Empty generalizations about the necessary truth within the Other is no more respectful (though probably considerably less dangerous) than empty generalizations about the falsity of the religious Other.

Religious traditions will almost certainly possess different, and possibly incompatible, fundamental epistemic priorities. Religious dialogue should not, in my estimation, have as its goal the attempt to resolve these differences between fundamental identity-shaping epistemic priorities; rather, dialogue should seek to find the many places in the complex bodies of beliefs held by different communities where these traditions have resolvable disagreements. Recent advances in understanding between Roman Catholics and Lutherans on the doctrine of justification give ample evidence that such an approach to dialogue works in the intra-Christian ecumenical discussion. The fundamental changes in Christian beliefs regarding the election of Jews and the rejection of all forms of "supersessionist" doctrines give another instance of such powerfully important dialogical work. While Roman Catholics, Lutherans, and Jews have the advantage of sharing some fundamental epistemic priorities, their differences have been theologically profound. This approach to dialogue can also serve as a model for discussions among religious traditions which share neither fundamental epistemic priorities nor a common history.

Christian theology should eschew all attempts either to assert the necessary superiority of the Christian faith or the necessary equality of other religions' claims to truth. Rather, Christian theology should simply give the grounds within the Christian faith for a respectful hearing of the Other that might alert us to claims of truth should we encounter them in the witness of other religions. I believe that the grounds for this openness are found in the intellectual and spiritual practices of a *theologia crucis*. Thus a Christian theology of religions, modest though it be may,[28] should emerge from the very heart of the Christian witness to the God revealed in the person and work of Jesus Christ.

As we have seen, Martin Luther has given the classic Christian statement of *theologia crucis*.

> *He deserves to be called a theologian . . . who comprehends the visible and manifest things of God, seen through suffering and the cross . . .* The "back and visible things of God" are placed in opposition to the invisible, namely, his human nature, weakness, and foolishness . . . Nor is it sufficient for anyone, and it does him no good, to recognize God in his glory and majesty, unless he recognizes him in the humility and shame of the cross . . . For this reason true theology and recognition of God are in the crucified Christ . . . He who does not know Christ does not know God hidden in suffering . . . God can be found only in suffering and the cross.[29]

Christian doctrines of God's triune reality have traditionally asserted a dialectical relationship between the apophatic and cataphatic aspects of God's revelation. While some theologians stress more the mystery at the heart of God and others emphasize the genuine availability of God's revelation to human knowing, all such doctrines claim a complex relation between God's hiddenness and revelation. Even Karl Barth, the great Protestant theologian of revelation, emphasizes God's inescapable hiddenness. For Barth, God is fundamentally defined as the "One Who Loves in Freedom."[30] For Barth, God's freedom is never "absolute freedom"; rather it is the freedom of divine self-determination. And the wonder of grace is that God uses that unconstrained self-determination to bind God's self eternally to human beings through the person of Jesus Christ. God's freedom is not constrained by this act of binding because God freely determined so to bind God's self. Understanding God's freedom as the self-determination by which God identifies with the human

---

28. The kind of theology of religions I am offering here is "modest" primarily in the sense that it eschews the attempt to provide an overarching theory of religions which claims that all religions have either the same aim or share a common experience.
29. LW 31:52–53 (*Heidelberg Disputation*; to thesis 20; emphasis R. T.).
30. Karl Barth, *Church Dogmatics*, vol. II/1, *The Doctrine of God* (Edinburgh: T & T Clark, 1957), 257–321.

condition in Christ is not, I would argue, a denial of God's freedom but an affirmation of God's freedom under the conditions of a *theologia crucis*.

As one who stands in the tradition of theologians of the cross, Barth claims simultaneously that God has bound God's self eternally in Jesus Christ and is, thereby, available to be known by us and that God remains sovereign Lord always and everywhere in control of God's own self-revelation. For finally God's self-revelation is nothing more or less than the presence of God among us, Immanuel, the divine in human flesh. But the encounter with God's revelation is always itself an "event," an act in which God remains solely in control of God's own self-disclosure. Thus while we do have confidence that God is truly present for us in Jesus Christ, we must recognize that God's presence always exceeds any ability we might have for knowing or grasping it. God's mystery is every bit as much a part of God's self-giving in Jesus Christ as is God's self-revelation. Consequently, a genuine modesty about what we claim to know must be yoked to an appropriate confidence that we do, nonetheless, genuinely know God in the person of Jesus Christ. Barth is characteristically better at asserting the confidence than he is at the modesty, but both are an essential part of his doctrine of God. Nonetheless, one can work within the context of a doctrine of God like Barth's and have ample grounds for asserting the continuing majesty of God's self-giving, a majesty that relies always and only upon God's self-determination and never upon our feeble attempts to understand. The scope and availability of God's self-revelation is limited only by the scope of God's own unconstrained self-determination.

But there are other more centrally christological grounds for asserting Christian openness to the witness to truth within other religions: "The Almighty exists and acts and speaks here in the form of One who is weak and impotent, the eternal as One who is temporal and perishing, the Most High in the deepest humility. The Holy One stands in the place and under the accusation of a sinner with other sinners. The glorious one is covered with shame. The One who lives forever has fallen prey to death. The Creator is subjected to and overcome by the onslaught of that which is not."[31]

At the heart of the gospel narratives is a controversy concerning the identity of Jesus Christ. In the Synoptic Gospels, Jesus is regularly misidentified by those who are closest to him. I have shown in previous work how the Gospel of Matthew is structured around the distinction between "disciples" (*mathetes*)

---

31. Karl Barth, *Church Dogmatics*, vol. IV/1, *The Doctrine of Reconciliation* (Edinburgh: T & T Clark, 1961), 185.

and those who "follow" (*akolouthein* and its variations).[32] The disciples are often those who are physically in proximity to Jesus, but most often misunderstand his words and actions. An epithet Jesus uses of the disciples on a number of occasions in the narrative is "those of little faith" (*oligopistoi*). The ones who most often recognize Jesus' true identity are apparently minor characters in the stories: a leper, a Roman centurion, the Gadarene demoniacs, a paralytic, a hemorrhaging woman, two blind men, a Canaanite woman, and the centurion at the foot of the cross. Within the Passion Narrative itself, the only true followers, the ones who recognize that Jesus' mission and ministry must follow the road to crucifixion, are Joseph of Arimathea and most importantly Jesus' women followers. So the Gospels themselves witness to the fact that Jesus' own identity is most likely to be recognized by those who live on the boundaries, beyond the pale, and on the margins. These stories give no support to those who would assert that "insiders" have a unique and incorrigible grasp of the gospel's truth. On the contrary, those who are apparent "outsiders" recognize Jesus' identity and thereby witness to the truth.[33] *Mutatis mutandis*, we should hardly be surprised if, in our own times, authentic witness to the truth comes not from those who are the apparent insiders within Christianity, but precisely from those religious Others who too often have been consigned a place beyond the pale of truth but may in fact be carriers of it.[34]

It is, finally, the fundamental drama at the heart of the Christian story that gives the strongest warrant for Christian openness to the witness to truth of other religious traditions. Christianity's basic claim is that the truth about God and the world is to be found in the story of the execution of a political prisoner at the hands of the Romans. This itinerant preacher now become the crucified victim of the state is, nonetheless, declared by Christians to reveal the loving being of God. Moreover, Christians further assert that this crucified man now lives through the resurrecting power of God—that the one who died by crucifixion now lives as exalted Lord of the universe. In its more radical christological traditions like *theologia crucis*, Christianity claims that in the

---

32. *Revelation and Theology*, 112–40, and "The Unnamed Woman at Bethany: A Model for Discipleship," in *Constructing a Public Theology: The Church in a Pluralistic Culture* (Louisville: Westminster John Knox, 1991), 63–74.
33. For a discussion of the relationship between insiders and outsiders in narrative interpretation, see my "Radiance and Obscurity in Biblical Narratives," in *Constructing a Public Theology*, 45–62.
34. It is not my intention here to assert the identity of the adherents of non-Christian religions as "outsiders." I am using the term ironically to remind Christians, who have often marginalized that non-Christian Other, that so-called "outsiders" are the bearers of truth in the gospel narratives. And if non-Christians, too, are bearers of such truth, then their marginalization by Christians can no longer be sustained.

death of Jesus Christ God engaged in a remarkable exchange, that in Jesus' death God became a curse for us in order that we might become righteous like God,[35] and further, that through this extraordinary act of exchange, God takes on our fate, the destiny of death, and transforms it into life everlasting in God's own presence.

Now if ever there were a religion founded upon a series of counterintuitive, even paradoxical claims, it is surely Christianity. No simple act of reason can possibly incline Christian believers to commit themselves to the belief that Jesus the Crucified now lives, and that we, too, will live in him. Such a commitment entails an act of faith that contradicts ordinary experience concerning the finality of death. That is why Christians confess in the words of the Book of Hebrews (11:1) that "faith is the assurance of things hoped for, the conviction of things not seen." That is why Christians confess with St. Paul that "now we see through a mirror, dimly" (1 Cor 13:12) and cannot know with absolute certainty that the path of discipleship leads to its promised end. Still believers follow on in hope, awaiting that day when we may "see face to face." But for now, Christians have only faith, the demands of discipleship, and the beckoning presence of One who bids us come and follow. And for some, that is enough.

Such following in faith, hope, and love should instill an attitude of modesty, humility, and gratitude. Far from grasping the truth and extolling the sufficiency and finality of the Christian revelation, followers of the cross recognize that, in Luther's words, God always reveals God's self *sub contrario*, under God's opposite. Faith in the Christian gospel yields a *theologia crucis*, a theology of the cross that seeks the truth of God's revelation wherever the loving self-determining God seeks to make God's self known. The path of Christian discipleship is one of hopeful following, and the life of Christian discipleship is one of loving commitment to the neighbor in need. The theological virtues of faith, hope, and love ought thus to quicken the Christian's awareness of the manifold sources of God's glorious and gracious self-revelation. And knowing God as we do in Jesus Christ, Christians should be the first to acknowledge that God's self-revelation appears in some surprising places indeed.

Not only does the Christian gospel make no a priori denial of the possibility of God's self-revelation to other persons in different times and places, it alerts Christians to the ever-present possibility that God's revelation is likely to appear where we least expect it. But in order to recognize such moments, we must engage in careful and modest listening to the religious Other, neither

---

35. See especially Luther's *Lectures on Galatians* (1535), in LW 26:248–90.

consigning the Other to eternal perdition nor claiming without careful examination that the Other has found the way or the truth. Listening carefully and
making modest, careful, and thoughtful judgments about truth and falsity is
the best way to be faithful to the Christian gospel and to respect the freedom
and integrity of the religious Other. Thus following the spiritual practices of
the theology of the cross might allow a genuine Christian theology of religions
to emerge. And for that, we might have to offer, at the very least, a tip of the
biretta to Martin Luther.

Part Five

Politics and Power

The final section of *The Global Luther* has to do with the reality of politics in church and world. The political is a subject with a long theological history, and Luther's theology in particular had political interests. Luther reached deep into medieval traditions in order to frame the relevance of the "two kingdoms" for his own time.

The terminology of two swords or kingdoms suggests that Luther divides reality into two distinct zones, "two kingdoms" of state and church and two statuses for churchgoers, clergy and laity. The beauty and challenge of Luther is his love of binary opposites. Luther's word was a two-edged sword, and his contribution to posterity rests in part on the crystal clarity of distinct oppositions. The appeal to theological distinctions continues to this day in Lutheran theology—between eros and agape, heaven and hell, hidden God and revealed God, and as such it builds theology's stable structures.

But for the human being existing simultaneously under law and gospel, what can this binary opposition possibly mean? When law and gospel are actualized in social and political realities, their opposition is more nuanced, less sharp. Luther's texts and times expose the dynamic tensions and movements between binary opposites. Indeed, as we have argued throughout this volume, the vitality of Luther's theology is in the tension it sustains between amplitudes of opposing poles. The real mix of power and politics is a test site for the viability of binary oppositions, even as their contrariness is tempered by context.

Language is one area in which Luther deploys and then complicates binary opposites. Peter J. Burgard analyzes Luther's rhetoric from a literary-linguistic perspective to explore not simply binary opposition but its subversion. Luther sides with the nobles against the peasants, as the standard interpretation goes. But does he? A new look at Luther's literary creation opens to another theological possibility. Language is always messier than thought's ideal clarity.

The ambivalence of unresolved binaries is the source of the creativity of Luther's thought. The best place to start is a distinction that Luther himself blurred, with dangerous political consequences. The idea of universal priesthood erased the line dividing clergy from laity. It is a bold and compelling idea that, as Allen G. Jorgenson shows, is rooted in late-medieval ground. Jorgenson takes Luther's theory—wonderfully radical in its own day—and points it forward to its liberative potential today. Vítor Westhelle focuses on the binary opposition of the "two kingdoms" that Luther intended to maintain, at least on one level of his texts, and recontextualizes this theory in view of a Lutheran global population. Where the modern West has domesticated binary opposites, new lines of interpretation, particularly in view of global Christianity, take up the tradition and imbue it with liberating power.

CHAPTER 15
Contours of the Common Priesthood
Allen G. Jorgenson

lthough Martin Luther is often misappropriated in Protestantism, his treatment of the priesthood as applied to all believers is
especially misunderstood. This is not altogether surprising, since
Luther's insights on the common priesthood are only properly
understood in concert with broader themes in his thought and the history of
the tradition. From Luther's vantage point, we see in the common priesthood
particular contours given to questions regarding the location of authority in
the church, the role of both clergy and laity in concretizing that authority,
and the manner in which Christ gains voice in and from the priesthood of all
believers.

This chapter advances the thesis that the "priesthood of all believers"
names Luther's conviction that the *congregatio fidelium*—the community of
the faithful—is concretized by the church's proclamation as the *vox Christi*
(voice of Christ) in the community gathered around word and sacrament for
the sake of the world.[1] I first locate Luther's view of the common priest-

---

1. Timothy J. Wengert notes in "The Priesthood of All Believers and Other Pious Myths"
that the phrase "priesthood of all believers" (in German: "das allgemeine Priestertum aller
Gläubigen") was not penned by Luther (www.valpo.edu/ils/documents/05_wengert.pdf).
See also Wengert, *Priesthood, Pastors, Bishops: Public Ministry for the Reformation and Today*
(Minneapolis: Fortress Press, 2008). The phrase closest to this was "das eynige gemeyne
priesterthum" in WA 8:254, 7 ("Pious Myths," 1, n. 1). Wengert makes a strong case for
eliminating this phrase, but I fear its ubiquity precludes such a possibility.

hood in response to the received fourteenth-century problem of locating the church's authority in either the papal head or the church in council that confers authority on behalf of the *congregatio fidelium*. I then argue that Luther determines the priesthood of all believers as a more faithful way to construe authority. Believers are priests by virtue of participation in Christ and they exercise their priestly ministry through love of neighbor. I finally address Luther's understanding of ordained ministry on the basis of order for the sake of mission. Luther's view challenges us to see the concretization of the church's mission in the *congregatio fidelium* and, more precisely, to pay closer attention to the mandate that the body of Christ be represented in particular instantiations.

The Priesthood of All Believers and the *Congregatio Fidelium*

As is the case with so much of Luther's creative thought, the theme of the priesthood of all believers emerged as he reframed a broader theological question in his context, namely, the fourteenth-century interest in locating authority in the church as the *congregatio fidelium*. It was affirmed that authority resided in the church, but it was up for debate as to the place and means by which that authority was to be exercised. At the center of fourteenth-century discussions regarding the *congregatio fidelium*, two options vied with each other as expressions of Christ's promise to keep the church whole in one true faith: papalism and conciliarism. Between these two extremes lay various hybrids.

Papalism in its most radical form "regarded the papacy as concentrating the whole of the church in its functions, with the fullness of authority subject to no control."[2] Confidence in this solution waned with the Western Schism at Avignon (1378–1417) and brought to the fore the dangers of staking all on the pope. Another means to express the catholicity of the church was needed. The expression was found in a complex of ideas that began to appear in the thirteenth century and came to fuller expression in the aftermath of 1378: in the event of conflict between pope and council, authority resides in a general council composed of all the bishops of the church.[3]

The Council of Constance (1414–1418) advanced the cause of the conciliar theory by asserting the superiority of a council to the will of the pope. But this council's trust in the role of councils as seen in its call for regular

---

2. Odilio Engels, "Council," in *Encylopedia of Theology: The Concise Sacramentum Mundi*, ed. Karl Rahner (New York: Seabury, 1975): 304.
3. See Engels, "Council," 304.

meetings was belied by the non-implementation of this mandate. This led some to propose that the institutionalization of the church rendered regular councils superfluous.[4] Moreover, it was given to the pope in concert with the curia to govern the church in accordance with canons established by the councils.[5] This reflects the development of a church model that follows the wisdom of councils, whose canons are implemented by the papacy, thus concretized as the *congregatio fidelium*. This church model did not solve all problems of locating power, but succeeded in stabilizing the tensions of the "curia versus council" debate. Something of a peace with the "papacy or council" tension was brokered by a "corporation" model of church: "During the fourteenth century the most respected canonists held that in the corporate whole of the Universal Church all power was concentrated in the head by a direct act of the divine will; but they also held that, as a general principle of corporation structure, authority resided with all the members of a church, who conferred upon the head only a limited and conditional right to act on their behalf."[6]

The church into which Luther was baptized and educated embraced the tension of locating the *congregatio fidelium* in either pope or council. This tension displays a trajectory of thought marked by an interest in granting expression to the church's catholicity in a concrete person, or group of persons. Luther rejected this particular way of framing the answer, but the question remained: How is the church's catholicity to be articulated? This was as important to Luther as it was to his opponents.

Luther rejected the two medieval solutions and identified congregations gathered around word and sacrament as concretizations of the whole people of God. This view, of course, did not so much resolve the medieval tension as situate it anew in the relationship between lay and ordered ministry, a concern that will be examined below. In order to explore this tension, however, it is valuable first to explicate three themes that incited Luther to locate the *congregatio fidelium* in the congregation: the failure of councils to initiate reform, the common priesthood as a function of Christ's priesthood, and the marks of the church as pointing to the priesthood of all believers.

---

4. Jaroslav Pelikan, *The Christian Tradition: A History of the Development of Doctrine*, vol. 4, *Reformation of Church and Dogma, 1300–1700* (Chicago: University of Chicago Press, 1984), 102.
5. Brian Tierney, *Foundations of the Conciliar Theory: The Contribution of the Medieval Canonists from Gratian to the Great Schism* (London: Cambridge University Press, 1968), 49. See also James Estes, who notes that the Council of Basel (1431–1449) discredited conciliarism with the claim that the papal curia increasingly exercised authority for the good of Rome (*Peace, Order and the Glory of God* [Leiden: Brill, 2005], 3).
6. Tierney, *Foundations of the Conciliar Theory*, 244.

Luther's assessment of the efficacy of councils changed over time.[7] Earlier in his career, he hoped that Charles V would convene a council for the well being of both church and state.[8] Luther became increasingly negative about such a possibility, especially after repeated disinterest on the part of his Roman interlocutors. His 1539 treatise *On the Councils and the Church* articulates his increasing pessimism. His criticisms became sharper as the Roman church began, after years of disinterest, to make overtures to the Evangelicals (or Protestants) on the possibility of calling a council. Luther questioned the wisdom of an appeal to a council in light of its Trojan horse character. No matter the makeup of a council, its outcome would be shaped by the papacy, which had an unfortunate track record of undermining substantial reform.[9]

Luther's assessment of a council's utility in *On the Councils and the Church* was prefaced by a careful study of the council at Jerusalem (c. 50 C.E.) and the first four ecumenical councils (Nicea in 325 C.E.; Constantinople I in 381 C.E.; Ephesus in 431 C.E.; Chalcedon in 451 C.E.). He concluded that councils, at their best, condensed scriptural themes.[10] One cannot look to councils for fresh revelations from the Holy Spirit, since councils largely deal with contextual issues that are not binding for subsequent communities.[11] In fact, the Christian community does better to look to the Creed or Scripture for counsel in matters of faith. Yet while Luther roundly chastizes councils for both inconsistency and poor judgment—especially evident in decisions such as the commendation of celibacy—he applauds their usefulness when they recognize their limits.[12] Moreover, Luther indirectly affirms the significance of councils by calling both parishes and schools "councils." He thus builds the conceptual bridge to his understanding of the priesthood of all believers and grounds it in

---

7. This assessment contrasts with Luther's pessimism regarding reform through papal initiative.

8. Rome tried to block the election of Charles V. See Estes, *Peace, Order and the Glory of God*, 19.

9. LW 41:32 (*On the Councils and the Church*) and LW 42:263 (*Against the Roman Papacy: An Institution of the Devil*; 1545). Charles Taylor notes that reform was a concern of the age preceding the Reformation. See *A Secular Age* (Cambridge: Harvard University Press, 2007), 76–77. What was new, according to Louis Dupré, was that "Luther did not solve the problems of the past but presented them in a wholly new way, a way that was characteristically modern and that allowed those who followed him to live with the problems rather than being paralyzed by them." (*Passage to Modernity: An Essay in the Hermeneutics of Nature and Culture* [New Haven: Yale University Press, 1993], 206).

10. See the doctrine of the *homoousion* in, for example, LW 41:83.

11. Jaroslav Pelikan, *Obedient Rebels: Catholic Substance and Protestant Principle in Luther's Reformation* (New York: Harper, 1964), 74.

12. See LW 45:147–48 (*An Exhortation to the Knights of the Teutonic Order that They Lay Aside False Chastity and Assume the True Chastity of Wedlock*; 1523), where Luther suggests that councils limit their scope to temporal matters.

his commitment to education for clergy and laity. Schools and parishes are the places in which Christians are educated in the priesthood.

Luther's turn from council and pope to the *congregatio fidelium* as site of reform reflects his theological conviction that the common priesthood is achieved by participation in Christ. In a famous passage from *The Freedom of a Christian*, Luther writes:

> Now just as Christ by his birthright obtained these two prerogatives [to pray and to preach], so he imparts them to and shares them with everyone who believes in him according to the law of the above-mentioned marriage, according to which the wife owns whatever belongs to the husband. Hence all of us who believe in Christ are priests and kings in Christ, as 1 Peter 2 [:9] says: "You are a chosen race, God's own people, a royal priesthood, a priestly kingdom, that you may declare the wonderful deeds of him who called you out of darkness into his marvelous light."[13]

Christian priesthood is, for Luther, a derived reality in which all share by being in Christ. Christians are priests "in Christ" and so priesthood, in the first instance, precludes two possibilities: a priesthood of *some* believers and a priesthood of *each* believer. Participation in Christ means union with Christ that is concretized in the give and take of the Christian community.[14] The community gathers around word and sacrament that make Christ present to each believer. But the community participates in Christ's presence by teaching the word of God, baptizing, consecrating, binding and loosing from sin, sacrificing the self for the good of neighbor, praying for others, and judging and passing on doctrines.[15] Through these actions, Christ constitutes the community as the common priesthood.

The marks of the church identify the priesthood by making Christ present. In *On the Councils and the Church*, Luther notes the following seven marks of the church: the word of God with its infectious holiness, baptism,

---

13. LW 31:354 (1520). The reference to marriage as the benefit of faith is found in LW 31:351: "it unites the soul with Christ as a bride is united with her bridegroom. By this mystery, as the Apostle teaches, Christ and the soul become one flesh [Eph. 5:31-32] . . . . Accordingly the believing soul can boast of and glory in whatever Christ has as though it were its own, and whatever the soul has Christ claims as his own."

14. In contrast to the nominalist understanding of community as contractual, Luther presumes a communal ontology based on *koinonia* and donation. See Reijo Työrinoja, "*Communio Sanctorum*: Remarks on the Ideal Community," in *Lutheran Reformation and the Law*, ed. Virpi Mäkinen (Leiden: Brill, 2006), 122–23.

15. LW 40:21–32 (*Concerning the Ministry*; 1523). Luther is careful to underscore that these tasks are given to all, which in his opinion is a most frightening truth for the "papists," who deem that "the laity are to believe us and not themselves." (LW 40:31-32)

the sacrament of the altar, public exercise of the keys, ministers called by the church,[16] public prayer, thanksgiving and praise, and the sacred cross.[17] The key question at this juncture concerns how these marks of the church are related to mission in the world. Luther looks beyond the church by conceiving these marks in view of the church's relationship with and to the world. The church as common priesthood realizes these marks for the sake of the world. As believers exercise the priestly ministry of loving the neighbor, the church conveys its essence as participation in Christ by its actions. The common priesthood concretizes the *congregatio fidelium*: it is in Christ and from Christ for the world as the *vox Christi*.

The Priesthood of All Believers and the *Vox Christi*

Luther was convinced from early on that the common priesthood was an important means by which the church would engage the world. Yet this relationship for Luther entailed the idea of reformation. Christ would reform his body through the common priesthood that would be his voice in the world. I look in detail at Luther's 1520 treatise *To the Christian Nobility of the German Nation Concerning the Reform of the Christian Estate* as an early pivotal document drawing the connection between common priesthood, reformation, and mission.[18]

In this text, Luther identified three walls erected by the Roman church that were quickly crumbling: the idea that temporal rulers' jurisdiction in no way includes the church, that the pope alone may interpret Scripture, and that the pope alone may summon a council. Luther topples the first wall by asserting that the divorce of temporal authority from spiritual courts is specious. This claim is proved by church history and most clearly undone by the recognition that baptism, according to 1 Peter 2, initiates Christians into the common priesthood. Luther dismantles the second wall by examples demonstrating papal error in interpreting Scripture and by the recognition that Scripture teaches the mutuality of the Christian community. Moreover, the third wall consists of the Roman error of confusing categories in imagining that the keys given Peter grant authority in doctrine and governance of the

---

16. Luther presumes that this precludes women or children, save in an emergency. The danger of this position will be further explored below.

17. LW 41:148–64.

18. LW 44:123–217; see also Peter J. Burgard's article as ch. 16 in this volume, "Masterful Rhetoric: The Logic of Authority and Subjection in Luther," that addresses Luther's text in detail.

church (Matt 18:18) when, in fact, the keys refer to clerical responsibility for the forgiveness of sin. In responding to the claim that only the pope can summon a council, Luther notes that this can neither be substantiated by scripture, nor buttressed by historical precedence. The document then lists a number of conciliar and ecclesial reforms needed that replicate concerns raised in Catholic Germany at the Diet of Augsburg in 1518.[19]

Bernd Moeller notes that the reception of Luther's treatise on the part of Roman Catholics was, without exception, marked by critical reactions to the theme of the common priesthood rather than Luther's criticism of both papacy and conciliar position.[20] The application of vocation to the laity was the novel and revolutionary element in this text. Luther asserts that all Christians are of the spiritual estate and that ordained ministers merely act in place of the community.[21] Elsewhere, Luther challenges the Roman view of ministry by identifying the parish as a treasure that cannot be secured by either pope or council: "Neither an angel nor a pope can give you as much as God gives you in your parish church. The fact is, the pope leads you away from the gifts of God, which are yours without cost, to his gifts, for which you have to pay."[22] For Luther, the parish is the concrete location for Christ's gospel because it participates through the common priesthood in baptizing, proclaiming the word of God, and in distributing holy communion. How do these acts concretize the common priesthood in the parish?

Luther spoke of baptism as the sacrament of Christian initiation into the priesthood of all believers.[23] Although certain members of the community are ordained, all are born priests by the baptismal waters. Ordained ministers serve the church by word and sacrament, whereas all serve the world in neighborly love. The link between ordained and common priesthood is baptism. Luther's justification for cases of emergency at which all can administer baptism[24] is the common priesthood:

> Suppose a group of earnest Christian laymen were taken prisoner and set down in a desert without an episcopally ordained priest among them. And suppose they were to come to a common mind there and then in

19. Estes, *Peace, Order and the Glory of God*, 20.
20. Bernd Moeller, "Klerus und Antiklerikalismus in Luthers Schrift an den Christlichen Adel Deutscher Nation von 1520," in *Anticlericalism in Late Medieval and Early Modern Europe*, ed. Peter A. Dykema and Heiko A. Obermann (Leiden: Brill, 1993), 364.
21. "[W]e must regard their office as one which has a proper and useful place in the Christian community": LW:128.
22. LW 44:189 (*To the Christian Nobility*).
23. LW 40:19 (*Concerning the Ministry*).
24. LW 40:37.

the desert and elect one of their number, whether he was married or not, and charge him to baptize, say mass, pronounce absolution, and preach the gospel. Such a man would be as truly a priest as though he had been ordained by all the bishops and popes in the world.[25]

Luther's generous view of the priesthood is based on his theology of baptism. Baptism renders Christians agents of God by grace so that all Christians are valid instruments through whom God works the divine will. If baptism is what Christians confess it to be—the means of incorporation into the life of God—then it is the primary means by which God calls and uses all for the sake of the gospel. The reign of God is realized as the Spirit effects the presence of Christ in the Christian priesthood for the sake of the world. In sum, baptism grounds the "community of saints" because it is the visible means by which the Spirit incorporates Christians into the community of the faithful. Baptism, as the beginning of Christian life, initiates a journey made possible by the living Spirit. Baptism submerges Christians in the knowledge of the journey's end, the resurrection: baptism for Christians means death with Christ in order that they will be raised as he has been raised. Baptism locates Christians in the interval between birth and death; the promise of resurrection is the condition for the possibility of a journey with God in Christ.[26]

Luther's understanding of the common priesthood is related to one more important element. Christian incorporation into Christ is inclusion into the living word. Christ is present in the community as it communicates the divine promise of incorporation. The living word of promise entails that to which it points: the promise of incorporation effects precisely the action of incorporation.[27] This idea is of immense significance to the believer. By incorporation into the living word, the priesthood of all believers is identified as the "voice of Christ." Christians are not only spoken *to*, but are spoken *as* words of God to the world. The church is spoken into being so that it might be the *vox Christi* bearing word to the world. This word is spoken—according to the classic Lutheran distinction—as law and gospel, although it is but one word. This unity of law and gospel in Christ's speaking the word through all is the concord of the so-called profane and sacred: "God so loved *the world* . . ." (John 3:16). God in Christ speaks Christians to the world and so renders Christians

25. LW 44:128 (*To the Christian Nobility*).
26. Gustaf Wingren, *The Living Word: A Theological Study of Preaching and the Church*, trans. Victor C. Pogue (Philadelphia: Muhlenberg, 1960), 45.
27. See LW 12:32 (*Commentary on Psalm 2*; to Ps 2:5; 1532) and Risto Saarinen, "The Word of God in Luther's Theology," *Lutheran Quarterly* 4/1 (Spring 1990): 35.

priests for the world. The end for which Christians are spoken is the eucharistic consummation of the word.[28]

Holy communion identifies every celebrating community as an instantiation of Christ's real presence.[29] The eucharist is God's promise to include
Christians into Christ's body. Christians gather at every eucharistic celebration
as the body of Christ. Union with Christ takes place through the sacrament. As
such, the incorporation instantiates the congregation of the faithful in its most
inclusive sense. Word and sacrament render the common priesthood precisely
by immersing all in the *congregatio fidelium*. By the happy exchange of faith,
Christians participate in Christ and Christ is present in the community.[30]

We see, then, that Luther holds forth a profoundly catholic vision of the
church that is gathered around both word and sacrament, and constituted as a
common priesthood. But as David Yeago has noted, Luther never entertained
the possibility of lay presidency at the eucharist.[31] Moreover, in his desert congregation scenario above, Luther saw one ordered to meet the need for ministry. How, then, do we relate Luther's assertion of a common priesthood to his
affirmation of an ordered ministry?

The Priesthood of All Believers and the Ordered Ministry

Scholars see in Luther's thought a theology of ordered ministry from both
"below" and "above."[32] I will investigate, in this section, the usefulness of the
spatial metaphors of "below" and "above" for describing Luther's position on
the ministry. But first, I identify some key parameters for looking at Luther's
understanding of ordered ministry in light of his commitment to the priesthood of all believers.

---

28. LW 36:348 (*The Sacrament of the Body and Blood of Christ—Against the Fanatics*;
1526).
29. Through God's Holy Word, "we are called, received and numbered into the host which
is God's communion or church . . ." (LW 12:147 [*Exposition of Psalm 23*; 1536]); see also
LW 23:386 and 36:285.
30. See LW 35:67 (*The Blessed Sacrament of the Holy and True Body of Christ and the Broth-
erhoods*; 1519) and Wingren, *The Living Word*, 162.
31. David Yeago, " 'A Christian Holy People': Martin Luther on Salvation and the Church,"
Modern Theology 13/1 (Jan. 1997): 114.
32. See Paul Althaus, *The Theology of Martin Luther*, trans. Robert C. Schultz (Philadelphia:
Fortress Press, 1966), 326; and Mark Ellingsen, "Luther's Concept of the Ministry: The Creative Tension," *Word and World* 1/4 (1981): 339. Brian Gerrish considers Luther to have a
"pastor from below" model—although Luther fails to fully engage it as such; see Gerrish's
The Old Protestantism and the New: Essays on the Reformation Heritage (Chicago: University
of Chicago Press, 1982), 94, 98.

First, Luther never envisioned that the priesthood of all believers would result in a situation wherein all would publicly minister and teach. Luther's treatment of the priesthood of all believers trades upon a distinction between public and private ministries. All are to engage in private ministry insofar as all are called to pray and teach.[33] To minister publicly is another matter: "Although we are all equally priests, we cannot all publicly minister and teach. We ought not do so even if we could."[34] Even Luther's provisions for public ministry in the event of an emergency are guarded: "For it is one thing to exercise a right publicly; another to use it in time of emergency. Publicly one may not exercise a right without consent of the whole body or of the church. In time of emergency each may use it as he deems best."[35]

On the one hand, then, we clearly see an interest in locating the public exercise of ministry within the order by which a community is already structured. Moreover, under normal circumstances, this order presumes the importance and necessity of the education due one who speaks in the stead of the community. On the other hand, this does not really equate to the Roman Catholic position insofar as: "In this view of ministry, the so-called 'indelible character' vanishes and the perpetuity of the office is shown to be fictitious. A minister may be deposed if he proves unfaithful."[36]

Luther's texts, therefore, can be interpreted as a middle way (*via media*) between a public ministry that arises by virtue of education from the common priesthood and an ordination that confers an "indelible mark" on the priest. But this interpretation too easily assumes the dichotomy of above/below and does not do justice to Luther's more nuanced position. David Yeago considers

---

33. LW 31:355 (*The Freedom of a Christian*).
34. LW 31:356; see also LW 35:12, 16, 22 (*The Sacrament of Penance*; 1519).
35. LW 40:34 (*Concerning the Ministry*).
36. LW 40:35. There is no "essential" difference between lay and clergy apart from the ordered office (see LW 36:159). Luther understood his position to differ from those of both Roman priests and Anabaptist prophets, whom he claimed shared in the sin of pride (Pelikan, *Reformation of Church and Dogma*, 175). In fact, the radical Reformers shared with Luther a view of ministry in which an ordained pastor was to be chosen from the community whose ministry was necessary for the good of the community. See also "The Schleitheim Confession (1527)," in *Creeds of the Churches*, 3rd edn., ed. John Leith (Louisville: John Knox, 1982), 287. An important difference was that many pastors of the radical Reformation were poorly educated. Although this might be attributed to a theology in which an immediate appeal to the Spirit precluded the need for education (see LW 46:209 ["Introduction" by Charles M. Jacobs and Robert C. Schultz to Luther's *A Sermon on Keeping Children in School*; 1530]), it was also the case in certain quarters of the Reformation that this was necessitated by the martyrdom and mistreatment of educated leaders who had embraced the radical Reformation. See also Gary K. Waite, "The Anabaptist Movement in Amsterdam and the Netherlands, 1531–1535: An Initial Investigation into its Genesis and Social Dynamics," *Sixteenth Century Journal* 18/2 (Summer 1987): 253.

the dilemma: "The misunderstanding here lies in the peculiar assumption that communal necessity and divine institution are mutually exclusive; for Luther, the ordained ministry is a divine institution, a gift of Christ to the church, whose *rationale* can be clearly seen in the obvious necessities of common life."[37] Luther's theology of ministry is grounded in the shared nature of day-to-day existence. For this reason, Yeago argues that the common priesthood and created order co-constitute one another.[38]

Further, the ordained ministry is not only a gift to the church but is also a gift of the church to the world. As the church instantiates the common priesthood in concrete situations, it becomes present for the world. This happens in two steps that are linked to each other. The community of saints gathers around word and sacrament. From this perspective, an ordained Christian exercises her pastoral vocation in preaching and teaching. But this instantiation includes, at least in latent form, the individual vocations of each Christian. These hearers and participators in the word are the Christians who exercise their vocations in the world. The community of the faithful is concretized in these two senses. In the primary sense, it is located in the community gathered around word and sacrament; in the second and derived instance, it is located in the community, which distributes the word by loving the neighbor.[39] Both ways are ordered by the same Spirit:

> In God's sight this principle stands firm and unshakeable: all saints live by the same Spirit and by the same faith, and are guided and governed by the same Spirit and the same faith, but they all do different external works. For God does not work through them at the same time, in the same place, in the same work, or in the sight of the same people . . . So that his ways may be hidden and his footsteps unrecognizable [Ps. 77:19], he provides each one with other works in other times and places, just as he did with other saints. . . . This is the true knowledge of faith in which all saints are instructed, each in his own vocation.[40]

The usual interpretation of Luther on the issue of the relation of ordered to common priesthood is cast in terms of a dichotomy between "above" and "below." Yet Luther's own position reveals another tension: the concept of priesthood requires that each believer both occupy an ordered place in the church and be led by the Spirit to serve the world. The exercise of ministry

---

37. Yeago, " 'A Christian Holy People,' " 112.
38. Yeago, " 'A Christian Holy People,' " 114.
39. LW 43:109 ("A Christian Letter of Consolation to the People of Miltenberg"; 1524).
40. LW 44:269 (*The Judgment of Martin Luther on Monastic Vows*; 1521).

drives both lay and ordained to live in both church and world by faith; in both instances, ministry entails being dependent on the Spirit. The tension inherent in the medieval synthesis of pope and council is relocated in Luther's theology in the relationship between pastor and congregation. The dynamic relationship between pastor and congregation involves the exercising of individual vocations for the world. It is this tension, rather than the "above/below" tension, that is most helpful in today's context, which is rather different from Luther's.

The *Priesthood* of All Believers: The *Vox Christi* in the World

Luther lived in a world emerging from medieval Latin Christendom. Lutheranism today is moving south and east. Churches in the lands that hold Luther to be a national hero increasingly struggle to preserve this claim. The lands into which Lutheranism arrived by immigration also need to rethink their sense of mission in their changing world. Lutherans in lands in which Lutheranism is growing face the challenge of adequately addressing the unique questions arising in their respective cultural contexts. In each case, however, there is a need to revisit the relationship between church and world. I describe this relationship in today's global terms and then show how we can use Luther's view of pastor and congregation as a constructive model for the relationship between church and world.

Luther's theology of the world is decidedly different from that of Roman Catholicism, Calvinism, and the radical Reformation. The Catholic church of Luther's day lived with an institutional memory of a brokered sharing of power between pope and emperor. The Calvinist vision of a Geneva under the gospel imagined the possibility of a Christian state in which the third use of the law ordered the land, while the left wing Reformation's experience of *Realpolitik* brought its adherents to believe that the Sermon on the Mount meant that the persecution of the church is inevitable in the world until God's reign comes. Luther's theology of the world, by contrast, emerges from his treatment of the two reigns. Decisive is Luther's affirmation of the world as a gift from God for the church and the church as a gift from God for the world, precisely because God in Christ is Lord of both church and world.

Luther's understanding of the intimate relationship between the two reigns implies a particular posture of church to world. Gustaf Wingren is most helpful here. He envisions that church and world share an end that transcends the immediate ends of both church and world.[41] Both have a higher end, but a church that truly lives as a church lives for the world in the priesthood of all believers.[42] The common priesthood, however, can fail in its relation to the world and, in doing so, mirrors the failure sometimes experienced between pastor and congregation.

Luther's understanding of the relationship between pastor and congregation steers clear of two dangers in the church and in the church's relationship to the world. The first danger is a notion of a common priesthood that fails to perceive the basic and different orders that constitute every community. The second is a hardened structure that fails to recognize the malleability and mutuality of authentic authority. The first danger tends to exist in communities refusing prophetic leadership, and the second danger, in communities where pastors are unable to acknowledge the talents and vocations of the laity. I map these dangers onto the church's engagement with the world. The first danger points to a church that fails to discern its distinctive character and merely mirrors the culture in which it is located. The second danger points to a church that fails to recognize the gift that the world is. In short, the former fails the doctrine of redemption and the latter, the doctrine of creation.[43]

These two dangers continue to haunt Lutheranism as it moves into the twenty-first century. On the one hand, the horrors of the twentieth century call the church to eschew quietism in the exercise of bold prophetic leadership for the sake of world and church. On the other hand, the appearance of parochialism in the history of the mission of the Lutheran church calls the church to repent of an attitude that sees the world as mere fodder for conversion, imagining the engorgement of the church as end of the world. In sum, the church sometimes fails to speak prophetically and sometimes fails to listen pastorally; sometimes it simultaneously fails on both accounts.

As the churches of the north and west enter into the season of Lent, the churches of the south and east enter the season of Pentecost. To both clusters of churches, the task is given to discern the Spirit's call through law and gospel to witness to God's justification of human life by Christ's conversion of the human project. God calls the church to the task of being priest in both a

---

41. Gustaf Wingren, "Welt und Kirche unter Christus, dem Herrn," in *Reich Gottes und Welt: Die Lehre Luthers von den Zwei Reichen*, ed. Heinst-Horst Schrey (Darmstadt: Wissenschaftliche Buchgesellschaft, 1969), 347.
42. "Eine Kirche die wahrhaft kirchlich lebt, lebt für die Welt." (Wingren, "Welt und Kirche," 343)
43. Wingren, "Welt und Kirche," 348–49.

ALLEN G. JORGENSON

prophetic and pastoral mode. There is a time for the common priesthood to call the world to be world, and a time for the church to let the world be world. There is also a time for the church to consider, prophetically and pastorally, the clarity and character of its own voice and to imagine a symphonic *vox Christi*.

The Priesthood of *All Believers*: A Symphonic *Vox Christi*

Any serious consideration of Luther's treatment of the common priesthood cannot avoid mentioning the usual criticisms. This idea of Luther's is one of his best known. It is ubiquitous in Protestant theology and church practice, and it is imbued with a romantic air in some contemporary Roman Catholic circles. In this section, I consider criticisms of Luther's dismissal of monasticism and his affirmation of the ordinary. I then discuss both Luther's and Lutheranism's failure to engage the priesthood of *all* believers on other accounts.

Franz Overbeck wrote a stinging attack on the Christian state of affairs at the beginning of the last century. Overbeck judged the predominant, apologetic Christian theology of his time to be a failure. For Overbeck, authentic Christianity is always at odds with the thought systems of its time. Overbeck considered the reign of God as completely incommensurable with the Christianity comfortable with the salons and parlors of his contemporaries. At the heart of his evaluation was his assessment that the Reformation—with its idea of the priesthood of all believers—gave up one of the most significant weapons in the arsenal against the hegemony of the state, first encountered with Constantine but finally victorious with the Reformation:

> Recognition by the state, however, inevitably involved for the church the loss of the possibility of martyrdom, a loss Origen had foreseen with some concern as early as the third century, but one the church could not accept as definitive. By finding, however, a substitute for martyrdom in the *martyrium quotidianum* [daily martyrdom] of monasticism, the church managed to ensure nothing less than its own survival. A theology, on the other hand, that regards the ascetic view of life as a characteristic connected with Christianity only for a specific period of its history, but fundamentally irrelevant to it, and believes it can, without sapping its strength, reconcile Christianity with secular culture, such a theology will necessarily also consider that the history of the church could be imagined without monasticism.[44]

---

44. Franz Overbeck, *How Christian Is our Present Day Theology?* trans. Martin Henry (New York: Continuum, 2005), 84.

Overbeck considered the monastery to be a place where the brightest and best from the church could be saved from the clutches of empire. There, monks and nuns were habituated in the ways of the reign of God. Moreover, the monastery was the place where the most inventive and provocative ideas of Christianity were cultivated.[45] Overbeck was convinced that Roman Catholicism had lost sight of the explosive potential of this institution and that Protestantism had never understood it in the first place. Luther, of course, was roundly critical of monasticism. The story of Luther's disenchantment with monasticism began with his exit from the monastery, followed by grudging acceptance of the vows for those old enough to make them in good conscience, and ending with a definitive refusal, viewing vows as demonic. For many of Luther's interpreters, the most provocative and potent implication of Luther's critical view of monasticism is the turn to family and daily life. Ordinary life is the place where vocation takes the shape of the cross.[46] But it can be argued that something is lost in an indiscriminate turn to the ordinary insofar as the church in mission sometimes needs to address the ordinary and the possible difficulties associated with it. Overbeck appreciates this very point.

Overbeck's criticism is particularly fitting in North America, not because the church needs more monasteries, although it might,[47] but because the monastic movement at its best was rooted in the church's self-understanding as attentive from the margins. The monastic movement was one of the principal institutions by which the church engaged the world prophetically, albeit with mixed results. Monastic communities are neither immune to inflexibility nor impermeable to borders. Yet it must be recognized that, in certain periods in church history, these groups engaged the gospel at the borders of the church. The demise of the medieval worldview, in which the individual vicariously received the transcendence experienced by communities set apart from world, proffers the need for a different sort of community of mission in

---

45. Overbeck, *How Christian is our Present Day Theology?* 84.
46. Charles Taylor considers Luther's affirmation of the ordinary to be among the most important of the Reformation's developments. This is especially evident in the establishment of vocation as a category applicable to laity. In affirming the ordinary, a criticism of spiritual elitism follows: preferential relationship to the divine is replaced by equidistant proximity to God. See Charles Taylor, *Modern Social Imaginaries* (Durham: Duke University Press, 2005), 102, 158. In this way, Taylor sees Luther's treatment of vocation via the priesthood of all believers as an important stage in the arrival of the secular, which began with the high middle ages (Taylor, *A Secular Age*, 98).
47. See Ian A. McFarland, *The Divine Image: Envisioning the Invisible God* (Minneapolis: Fortress Press, 2005), 109, who notes that the various ways of living out "this desire for the neighbor," which makes possible countercultural practices (103), have historically included living in community.

North America today. The need for alternate local churches still exists. Such movements exploit secularization's discontent by modeling anticipation of the divine among the forsaken.

In contemporary North American Christianity, attention to the border has been too easily forgotten.[48] Moreover, even when the church engages boundaries, it has failed too often to speak to its surrounding world from this location. The church's attention to its identity as people of God—too comfortably understood as family of God—easily eclipses its identity as temple of the prophetic Spirit. It has forgotten that it has a unique role in the plethora of voices that constitute the politics of a people. The church gains voice in the world in two ways: first, as one of many public voices in political discourse and second, in shaping its members in such a manner that their mode of being in the world is formed by the love and justice of which the Bible and the church speak.[49] This way of being in the world enables the church to exist in both prophetic and pastoral modes.[50] Yet one more question remains: has the church done justice to its identity as the body of Christ—that site which hosts, assimilates, and coordinates a variety of members?

Luther's treatment of the priesthood of all believers was dogmatically rich enough to embrace the constitutive, missionary, and mutual identities of the church.[51] In fact, however, the recurrence of familial language in Lutheranism too often reprises patriarchal and parochial patterns of thought. This is sometimes seen in Luther, who denied women a voice at the baptismal font, pulpit, and altar—save in the case of an emergency—and thereby rendered one gender impotent.[52] This proviso is an assault to Luther's own theology of ministry: if all are priests, then that reality should gain visibility and voice in the living word. While not every priest can be ordered, an ordered ministry that fails to mirror the diversity of the priesthood has failed itself. The common priesthood is compromised insofar as the taxonomy of ministry excludes those who are otherwise gifted to concretize the *vox Christi*. Recently, the church has begun to regain the prophetic and pastoral voice of women. In

---

48. There are exceptions to the rule, notably the L'Arché communities: see from February 18, 2008: www.larche.ca.
49. The world gains voice in the church by virtue of context and through the church's members, whose vocations enable them to be the church in the world.
50. Seen, for example, in the base Christian communities of Central and Latin America. As Altmann writes, "Today, this same revolution [of vocation] must be reexperienced in radical new terms." (Walter Altmann, *Luther and Liberation: A Latin American Perspective*, trans. Mary M. Solberg [Minneapolis: Fortress Press, 1992], 145–46)
51. The constitutive, missionary, and mutual identities of the church refer to the dominant biblical metaphors as people of God, temple of the Spirit, and body of Christ.
52. LW 41:154, 156 (*On the Councils and the Church*).

the Evangelical Lutheran Church in Canada, for example, women equal or outnumber men in most incoming seminary classes, with the result that the number of women pastors increases regularly. The Canadian church recently elected a national bishop who is a woman, and 40% of our synodical bishops are women. Yet women ordinands regularly wait longer for first calls and discover an uphill battle in parishes. This example of glacial change is, to mix metaphors, only the tip of the iceberg. Intransigence is, as it were, infectious. In Canada—where one in five people are born elsewhere and where nearly half of the residents in our largest city are born outside of Canada[53]—the faces in Lutheran pulpits are decidedly white and middle class. Further, many in our church now lament the paucity of voices on the margin, wondering how the poor and marginalized can be given voice when education for ordered ministry demands substantial financial investment. Others ponder how gay and lesbian voices can be heard in a church sharply divided on the possibility and conditions of their inclusion. Creative solutions are needed to bring a broader register to an often monotone *vox Christi*. Clearly, much remains to be done in order to ensure that the voices heard from font, pulpit, and altar reflect the diversity of the *vox Christi*. This task can seem daunting, yet sometimes the most creative solutions emerge from rather desperate situations, as God works through this priesthood that we all share.[54]

Although it is not clear, the path forward clearly demands the special creativity and provocative risk that characterize the *congregatio fidelium* as it is justified by grace under the cross. When believers are rendered as the *vox Christi* in the concrete situation, they are suspended between certainty and chaos. There, they practice the common priesthood's vocation of first listening to, and then speaking with and for, the neighbor, who is increasingly global and interested in a global Luther.

---

53. Marina Jiménez, "When Multi Morphs into Plural," *The Globe and Mail*, 8 December 2007, A27.
54. Deanna A. Thompson, *Crossing the Divide: Luther, Feminism, and the Cross* (Minneapolis: Fortress Press, 2004), 98.

CHAPTER 16

Masterful Rhetoric

– The Logic of Authority and Subjection in Luther –

Peter J. Burgard

A t the end of the first part of Dieter Forte's drama *Martin Luther und Thomas Münzer, oder Die Einführung der Buchhaltung*, a window-washer is ironically figured as bringing light and transparency to Luther's trial, which is being held at Fugger's house, and repeatedly declares that Luther "is completely on our side," meaning the common man's.[1] The scene ends with the common folk carrying Luther on their shoulders as a hero of the people and Luther bellowing, "Murder and blood! Murder the bishops! Destroy the monasteries! Kill them! Exterminate them! Wash your hands in their blood! Be dear little children of God! Rebellion! Rebellion!"[2] And the people cry out in joy.

This is the greatest flashpoint for the vehement criticism that was heaped on the play for its misrepresentation of history even as it claims for itself historical truth, for putting words in Luther's mouth even as it claims to use only his words.[3] I would argue, however, that this scene, while technically an

---

1. Dieter Forte, *Martin Luther und Thomas Münzer, oder Die Einführung der Buchhaltung* (Frankfurt: Fischer, 1981), 94 and 95 (all German texts, including Luther's, are translated by P. J. B.).
2. Forte, *Martin Luther und Thomas Münzer*, 96.
3. See Forte's discourse, "Zur Methode," at the end of the text (*Martin Luther und Thomas Münzer*, 206–7). His claim to be using only Luther's words ("But they are after all his words" [206]), might also be taken as a parody of Luther's own claim of being entirely true to the biblical word, even as he is translating it, that is, interpreting it, and placing it in the service

inaccurate presentation of history, accurately *re*presents the potential for the common people's misunderstanding of Luther and, even if putting words in Luther's mouth, accurately captures the import of his rhetoric, which justified, even encouraged, such misunderstanding. My focus will be on the textual proof of this, on exploring the rhetoric of Luther's text—that is, tracing the construction of his argument and examining how his text says what it says and thus had the effect it had.

The text under consideration, aside from a brief excursus toward the end into *The Freedom of a Christian (Von der Freiheit eines Christenmenschen)*, is Luther's *To the Christian Nobility of the German Nation (An den christlichen Adel deutscher Nation von des christlichen Standes Besserung)*, the first of his three revolutionary polemics of 1520 (completed in June and published in August). Luther's *To the Christian Nobility* experienced an unprecedented dissemination and a disastrously split reception, being taken by the nobility as a justification of their power and by the peasants, as well as by Luther's Catholic critics, as an incitement to rebellion.[4] How could this happen? Because the text is not rhetorically unified and coherent. I argue that the text pursues two types of rhetoric that compete with one another—a rhetoric of authority and subjection and a rhetoric of equality, democracy, and revolution—even if it is clear in hindsight, indeed was clear by 1525 at the very latest, that Luther's intent lay with the first.

Authority and Subjection

One might justifiably wonder how a text addressed *To the Christian Nobility of the German Nation*, a text designed to convince the nobility that it is superior to the papacy and should wrest control of the church and of religious life and property from Rome, could be governed by anything but a rhetoric of authority and control. The celebration of the nobility is clear from the first page, not only in the title, but in Luther's false modesty and obsequiousness, when he says "that I won't remain uncastigated for, as a lowly, unworldly person, daring to address those of such high and great station in such formidable and great matters."[5] This tone continues, as he follows his preface with another

---

of his argument, sometimes tendentiously so. See my discussion of Luther's use of the Bible in the "Power to the People" section of this essay.

4. See Mark Edwards's informative and important work on the early reception of Luther: Mark U. Edwards Jr., *Printing, Propaganda, and Martin Luther* (Minneapolis: Fortress Press, 1994), esp. ch. 7.

5. "Daß mir's nicht wird unverwiesen bleiben, daß ich verachteter, weltabgewandter Mensch solche hohen und großen Stände wage anzureden in so gewaltigen, großen Sachen": Martin

bow "to the most supremely high and mighty Imperial Majesty and Christian Nobility of the German Nation," whereby he rhetorically, with the superlative adjectives doing double duty, raises this nobility to the level of the emperor (*Kaiser*).[6]

While we might expect such bows to authority and such pandering as a convention, this rhetorical elevation of the general nobility is not such a commonplace. It is the nobility in whom Luther repeatedly invests or wishes to invest unprecedented authority and control, uninhibited by the traditional authority and control of the church, over their domains and their subjects, as well as over the pope, bishops, and priests. For this he frequently employs a rhetoric of martial force, the office of the sword (*Schwertamt*): "thus temporal authority holds the sword and the fasces in its hand."[7] "Therefore temporal Christian power should exercise its office freely and unhindered, regardless whether it befalls the pope, a bishop, or a priest."[8] "On the basis of divine order the temporal sword has power over the guilty priests."[9] "Therefore, whoever can do it first should see to it that a proper free council takes place, which no one can achieve so well as the temporal sword."[10]

Luther, *An den christlichen Adel deutscher Nation*, in *"An den christlichen Adel deutscher Nation," "Von der Freiheit eines Christenmenschen," "Sendbrief vom Dolmetschen,"* ed. Ernst Kähler (Stuttgart: Reclam, 1977), 9, LW 44:121. (Subsequent quotations from this text are referred to as Luther Reclam. The German original, available in the notes, is quoted from this edition because of its easy accessibility. Where it differs significantly from the Weimarer Ausgabe on which it is based, the wording of the latter is restored and the change noted. Translations by P. J. B., with occasional assistance from published translations, notably C. A. Buchheim's translation, *Address to the Christian Nobility of the German Nation Respecting the Reformation of the Christian Estate*, Harvard Classics 36, part 5. Furthermore, all equivalents in the LW are noted in square brackets.)

6. "Der allerdurchlauchtigsten, großmächtigsten Kaiserlichen Majestät und Christlichem Adel deutscher Nation": Luther Reclam, 10, LW 44:123. Grammatically, the superlative adjectives do not do double duty, since they are part of the dative feminine construction beginning with "Der" and ending with "Kaiserlichen Majestät"; "Christlichem Adel" constitutes a separate dative (masculine) construction. However, the connection of majesty and nobility by the conjunction "und" encourages us to read those adjectives as attributes of both, as does their connection through the genitive attribute "deutscher Nation," for Luther is addressing not only the Christian nobility of the German nation, but also the emperor of the German nation (of the Holy Roman Empire of the German Nation).

7. "So hat die weltliche Obrigkeit das Schwert und die Ruten in der Hand": Luther Reclam, 17, LW 44:130.

8. "Drum soll weltliche christliche Gewalt ihr Amt üben frei ungehindert, unangesehen, ob es der Papst, ein Bischof oder Priester sei, den sie trifft": Luther Reclam, 18, LW 44:130.

9. "Aufgrund göttlicher Ordnung [hat] das weltliche Schwert über [die schuldigen Priester] Gewalt": Luther Reclam, 19, LW 44:131.

10. "Darum . . . soll dazu tun, wer am ersten kann, . . . daß ein rechtes freies Konzilium werde; welches niemand so wohl vermag wie das weltliche Schwert": Luther Reclam, 24, LW 44:136.

The German nobility might have objected, or not, to being addressed "Oh noble princes and lords"[11] by a celebrated but also notorious friar, but certainly not to being endowed with such expansive authority and control. Luther proceeds to make it even more attractive by linking the power invested in the princes through the office of the sword to the retention of wealth that otherwise went to the Vatican, for example: "Kaiser Karl has the right, because of his office of the sword, not to let any more fiefs and benefices in all of Germany go to Rome."[12] Moreover, as is commonly known, many of Luther's other suggestions for improvement in this later part of the text, which grow out of the gravamina he enumerates in the second part, not only declare that temporal nobility alone should hold sway over temporal matters and that spiritual power is not superior to temporal power, but also accrue to the direct fiscal benefit of the nobility.

Hand in hand with this rhetoric of authority and control goes, as one might expect, a rhetoric of subjection governing those who are not among this privileged class. For this, Luther enlists the Bible, both Paul—"Every soul (and I include the pope's) should be subjected to authority, for it is not for nothing that it carries the sword"[13]—and Peter: "Subject yourselves for God's sake to every authority instituted among men."[14] The fate of Luther's call for subjection will become apparent in what follows.

Rebellion

With such an explicit rhetoric of authority and subjection, how could it be that this text was understood as an incitement to rebellion by the common people? The twelve articles, especially the third, and the Peasants' War of 1524–1525 ultimately demonstrated this understanding emphatically, while Luther saw it as a fundamental misunderstanding of his polemics, as his unspeakable pamphlet of 1525, *Against the Robbing and Murdering Hordes of Peasants* (*Wider die räuberischen und mörderischen Rotten der Bauern*), would so mercilessly

---

11. "O edle Fürsten und Herren": Luther Reclam, 35, LW 44:148.
12. "Kaiser Karolus . . . [hat das Recht], von wegen seines Schwertamtes [in ganz Deutschland kein Lehen und Pfründe mehr gen Rom kommen zu lassen]": Luther Reclam, 34, LW 44:146.
13. "Ein jegliche Seele (ich halte dafür, des Papstes auch) soll untertan sein der Obrigkeit, denn sie trägt nicht umsonst das Schwert": Luther Reclam, 18, LW 44:130; Luther conflates Romans 13:1 and 4.
14. "Seid untertan allen menschlichen Ordnungen um Gottes willen": Luther Reclam, 18, LW 44:130. Luther conflates 1 Peter 2:13 and 15.

demonstrate.[15] Already in his first responses to Luther's polemics, starting in late 1520, the Catholic Thomas Murner revealed an understanding of those polemics as supposedly mistaken as that of the peasants, when, as Edwards has formulated it, he warned that Luther's theology "could easily mislead 'simple Christians' not only into religious error but also into rebellion against authority" and that "Luther was attempting to subvert the traditional order of society and promote rebellion" with his doctrine of the priesthood of all believers.[16]

Again, how could Luther be so (mis)understood? As I stated at the outset, the answer to this question lies in the fact that the text is not governed by one primary rhetoric, but by two that confront and compete with one another. A rhetoric of equality and democratic revolution runs through the text that serves Luther's purpose up to a point, insofar as it rallies the Christian nobility to Luther's anti-Vatican cause by undermining the hierarchical differentiation between spiritual and temporal power. This rhetoric cannot, however, ultimately be subsumed under the rhetoric of authority and subjection, but rather frees itself from the latter and escapes Luther's control. Which means that, in terms of the text itself, the rhetoric of authority and subjection fails. Which in turn would mean that the peasants, and Luther's Catholic critics, and anyone else who saw the text as a call to rebellion by more than just the nobility, did not misunderstand it.[17]

The text may be addressed to the Christian nobility, but it begins with a dramatic call to revolution: "The time for remaining silent has passed and the time for speaking has come."[18] The call is repeated in the plea to God to give "us" a trumpet like that used to blow down the walls of Jericho.[19] Of course, the new Jericho Luther is talking about is Rome, and the walls that give rise to oppression and exclusion here are the so-called "three walls" on which his polemic famously focuses and that oppress the Christian nobility, namely: wall

---

15. Text in LW 46:45–55. On Luther's feeling that he was misunderstood, see Richard Marius, *Martin Luther: The Christian between God and Death* (Cambridge: Harvard University Press, 1999), 221 and 231–34, as well as Edwards, who remarks on the "fateful misunderstanding of what he was all about" (*Printing, Propaganda, and Martin Luther*, 12).

16. Edwards, *Printing, Propaganda, and Martin Luther*, 61.

17. Edwards addresses the misunderstanding of Luther's intent by the peasants and the Catholics, but acknowledges (see *Printing, Propaganda, and Martin Luther*, esp. 157–61 and 168–71) that "his Catholic critics could also reasonably argue that whatever Luther said, his writings had the effect of encouraging rebellion" (171). While we agree on this conclusion, my focus is on showing precisely how Luther's text itself, how *To the German Nobility*, in its rhetoric and the construction of its argument, is responsible for the seeming misunderstanding that had that effect.

18. "Die Zeit des Schweigens ist vergangen und die Zeit zu reden ist kommen": Luther Reclam, 9, LW 44:121.

19. Luther Reclam, 13–14, LW 44:127.

(1) that temporal power is subordinate to spiritual; wall (2) that no one but the pope may interpret Scripture; and wall (3) that only the pope may convene a council. But once invoked, the revolutionary sentiment of blowing down the walls of oppression is not so easily restricted. Moreover, Luther begins and ends his polemic by saying he is "forced to scream and shout," "forced . . . to bay, to scream."[20] He repeats the revolutionary call at the beginning of the second part of the text when he says, "Therefore let us awake, dear Germans, and fear God more than we fear men."[21]

Luther himself, even as he invokes Jericho as an allegory for Rome and calls on his fellow Germans to awake, already attenuates the restriction of his revolutionary zeal to the affairs of the nobility in that he uses the first-person plural pronoun "us." This might seem a minor matter. It is anything but, for it is a constitutive part of his rhetoric of equality and democratic revolution. In the context of his rhetoric of authority and subjection, Luther uses definite articles—"*the* authority," "*the* sword," etc.[22]—but he otherwise uses the first-person plural pronoun repeatedly and makes it clear that he is talking about everyone, including himself. Luther can hardly be using "we" to refer only to himself and the Christian nobility he is ostensibly primarily addressing, for that would equate him, a friar, with the temporal Christian nobility. As we have seen, Luther is far too obsequious for that. Indeed, it is clear when he says "Since, then, the temporal power is baptized in the same way we are,"[23] that the "we" does not constitute an exclusive party of Luther and the nobility. We might at first think, here as well, that Luther is employing a royal "we" to refer only to himself, but the proof that this is a "we" that literally includes everyone, at least all Christians, from the highest to the lowest, comes in phrases such as "not me alone, but everyone," "we, all of us," "thus we, all of us," "we all in the same way," "we all," and so on.[24] That this can also mean those of lowest station is clear when Luther says that those in the "the crowd . . . all have the same power," when he explicitly includes "peasant" (*Bauer*) and "burgher" (*Bürger*) in the new priesthood, and when he says that the common people, listing "tailors, cobblers, masons, carpenters, cooks, cellarers, peasants, and all

---

20. "Gezwungen, zu schreien und zu rufen," "gezwungen . . . zu . . . bellen, schreien": Luther Reclam, 11, 108, LW 44:124, 217.
21. "Drum lasset uns aufwachen, lieben Deutschen, und Gott mehr denn die Menschen fürchten": Luther Reclam, 27, LW 44:139.
22. "*die* Obrigkeit," "*das* Schwert," etc.
23. "Dieweil denn nun die weltliche Gewalt ist gleicherweise wie wir getauft": Luther Reclam, 16, LW 44:127.
24. "Nicht allein mich, sondern jedermann": Luther Reclam, 11, LW 44:124; "wir allesamt": Luther Reclam, 14; "wir also allesamt": Luther Reclam, 14; "wir alle gleicherweise": Luther Reclam, 16; "wir alle": Luther Reclam, 22.

temporal tradespeople," should provide nothing to the pope, bishops, priests, and monks.[25] One need only imagine being a commoner of whatever station at the time and reading this or, more likely, hearing it read or reported, in order to understand why the common people would have ample reason to believe Luther meant them, too. Luther's rhetoric of "we" is a rhetoric of equality and democratic revolution that anticipates by two and a half centuries the familiar revolutionary rhetoric of "We the people."

Luther's text experienced a previously unheard-of dissemination through its multiple printings and reprintings and the still much broader circulation through quotation from those many thousands of copies by countless preachers, teachers, and officials, all of which would have led to an even more extensive word-of-mouth propagation.[26] Even more significant than this, however, is the proof either of an actual democratically revolutionary intention, which hardly seems likely, or of an epic miscalculation on Luther's part that is offered not only by the fact that he wrote the polemic in German, thus guaranteeing himself a vastly wider audience, but also by the simple fact that he used the press to disseminate his ideas. By the time he wrote *To the Christian Nobility*, he was already well familiar with the press and its possibilities. As Edwards has shown so convincingly, the pamphlet form is itself a democratic form.[27] It is hard to imagine that Luther, having already used it repeatedly, would be ignorant of this, so this was no innocent mistake. Still, it is of course possible that he truly did not imagine just how broad the circulation of this pamphlet and its ideas would be and thus did not anticipate or appreciate its democratically revolutionary potential. Especially if he was unaware of the degree to which he had lost control of the democratic rhetoric he employed in the service of his rhetoric of authority and subjection.

Power to the People

Luther wastes little time in getting to the heart of his novel argument for empowering the Christian nobility vis-à-vis Rome, but in doing so he lays the foundation for empowering Christians of all stations. Luther storms the first Roman wall, the position that spiritual power is superior to temporal, by declaring that "all Christians are in truth of the spiritual estate and there is no

25. "Haufen . . . alle gleiche Gewalt haben": Luther Reclam, 15, LW 44:129; Luther Reclam, 16, LW 44:129; "Schneider, Schuster, Steinmetzen, Zimmerleute, Köche, Kellermeister, Bauern und alle weltlichen Handwerker": Luther Reclam, 18, LW 44:130.
26. Edwards, *Printing, Propaganda, and Martin Luther*, 38.
27. Edwards, *Printing, Propaganda, and Martin Luther*, 58.

difference among them except office alone,"[28] and by concluding from this democratic assertion, which happens to disregard any accepted understanding of what constitutes the spiritual *estate*, that "according to this, we are all of us thus consecrated as priests through baptism."[29] He will repeat that "we are all priests"[30] several times, so that it is impossible to miss. Of course, it is such a radical claim that it would have caught the attention of every reader and the many more listeners.

Luther grounds his revolutionary declaration of the universal priesthood of the baptized, along with his equation of spiritual and temporal power, with a quotation from the Bible: "You are a kingly priesthood and a priestly kingdom [1 Peter 2:9]."[31] However, he manipulates the Bible for his purpose here, in that he turns the "holy people" or "nation" into a "priestly kingdom" in order to establish the chiastic relation to the "kingly priesthood" and thus give the equation rhetorical force.[32] This is neither the first nor last time he turns his translation and use of the Bible to his purpose. The first is his initial revolutionary declaration that "the time for remaining silent has passed and the time for speaking has come," which becomes revolutionary only through his transformation of the simple statement in Ecclesiastes (3:7) that "there is a time to be silent and a time to speak," but which he presents as a direct quotation from the Bible.[33] He will later quote Paul's letter to the Corinthians (2 Cor. 10:8): "God gave us power not to corrupt but to better Christianity."[34] In doing so, Luther shifts the power God gave Paul to himself and to those who take up his cause, the cause of bettering Christianity, which diverges from the Bible, where not all of Christianity is at issue, but rather the bettering to be done is

---

28. "Alle Christen sind in Wahrheit geistlichen Standes und ist unter ihnen kein Unterschied denn des Amtes halben allein": Luther Reclam, 14, LW 44:127.
29. "Demnach werden wir also allesamt durch die Taufe zu Priestern geweihet": Luther Reclam, 14, LW 44:127.
30. "Wir sind alle Priester": Luther Reclam, 22, LW 44:135.
31. "Ihr seid ein königlich Priestertum und ein priesterlich Königreich": Luther Reclam, 14, LW 44:127.
32. See Johannes Dickhut, "Rhetorik als konstituierendes Moment der Textkomposition in Luthers Schrift *An den christlichen Adel deutscher Nation von des christlichen Standes Besserung*," *Daphnis* 35 (2006): 486. Luther's sometimes dubious translations and manipulations of the Bible have been pointed out from time to time (see, e.g., Edwards, *Printing, Propaganda, and Martin Luther*, 167); Dickhut's study, however, is the most useful in its demonstration and analysis of what he calls Luther's "utilization of the Biblical text" in *To the Christian Nobility* (485–92).
33. Luther Reclam, 9, LW 44:123; Dickhut, "Rhetorik als konstituierendes Moment," 485–86.
34. "Gott hat uns Gewalt gegeben, nicht zu verderben, sondern zu bessern die Christenheit": Luther Reclam, 25, LW 44:138. The Reclam edition elides the word "Christenheit."

the building up of Corinth.[35] Such passages might make one wonder about the privilege Luther implicitly claims for himself in the interpretation of the Bible, since he uses translation here as interpretation—tendentious translation and tendentious interpretation. For our present purpose, however, it is enough to recognize Luther's subjection of Scripture to *his* purpose, namely, drawing as many as possible into a revolution against Rome.

Luther's rhetoric of "we all" grounds the democratic appeal of his message, but he uses an even more powerful rhetorical strategy to assert that appeal when he introduces the metaphor of the "one body." Immediately following the equation of spiritual and temporal power, and as an elaboration on the claim that we are all of the spiritual estate, we read "that we are, all of us together, one body," although what Luther really means, as he makes clear, is that we are all members of the one body: "each member"; "each of us a member of the other"; "the members of the body"; "all members of the whole body"; "each and every member."[36] What is so powerful about this is not only that it offers a striking image of unity and equality, but also that the one body of which we are all members—like the "community"[37] Luther repeatedly mentions and that in at least one instance is characterized by codetermination[38]—arouses communal, democratic sentiments in which all members participate. The "one body" could be taken as the very image of a democracy.

Moreover, Luther encourages his readers and listeners to understand it this way, for he takes many opportunities to explicate the duties of one body member to another. When the metaphor is first introduced, we read that every member "has its own work with which it serves the others."[39] Elsewhere we read that "everyone should be of use and service to the others through his work or office"; that "the members of the body all serve one another"; that it is unnatural and un-Christian "if one member does not help the other, does not prevent the other's ruin."[40] These last three exhortations to service and help all

<hr>

35. See also Dickhut, "Rhetorik als konstituierendes Moment," 487.
36. "Daß wir allesamt ein Körper sind": Luther Reclam, 14, then again 17, LW 44:127, 130; "ein jeglich Glied": Luther Reclam, 14, LW 44:127; "ein jeglicher des anderen Gliedmaß": Luther Reclam, 17, LW 44:129; "die Gliedmaße des Körpers": Luther Reclam, 17, LW 44:130; "alle Gliedmaßen des ganzen Körpers": Luther Reclam, 19, LW 44:131; "einem jeglichen Glied": Luther Reclam, 23, LW 44:136.
37. "Gemeinde": Luther Reclam, 16, 22, 24.
38. Luther Reclam, 16, LW 44:129.
39. "Sein eigen Werk hat, mit dem es den anderen dienet": Luther Reclam, 14, LW 44:127.
40. "Ein jeglicher soll mit seinem Amt oder Werk den anderen nützlich und dienstlich sein": Luther Reclam, 17, LW 44:129; "die Gliedmaße des Körpers alle eins dem andern

occur on one page. Luther also tells us that "each member is ordered [by Scripture] to care for the other," and that in cases of crisis "every burgher is bound to rouse and call in the others."[41] He thus not only employs the democratic metaphor of the one body. He expands on it in a way that encourages rebellion among the oppressed common people, for it gives them reason to expect that not only those of their own station, but *all* Germans—peasants, commoners, burghers, and nobility alike—should be and are being exhorted to serve one another, to help one another, to take care of one another, and thus reason to object openly to and rebel against any oppression.

Luther calls the pope a thief, a devil, and the Antichrist. He likens his Roman enemies to Turks, a particularly aggressive insult at the time, and calls them bloodsuckers and princes of hell. And the Vatican he calls a whorehouse to end all whorehouses.[42] The coarseness in the incendiary and almost frenzied excess of these condemnations might either be read as a sign of Luther having lost control of his rhetoric or of him employing a rather lowly rhetorical device to draw in the peasants: coarse and out-of-control language to draw in coarse people and incite them to rebellion, being *bäurisch* (peasantly or boorish) in order to appeal to peasants (*Bauern*), perhaps being the "peasants' apostle" ("Bauern-Apostel") that Nietzsche would one day call him.[43] But Luther also makes *explicit* the call to rebellion against oppression and the laws that ground it, as well as the peasants' justification in expecting help, care, protection, and service from everyone, when he says, "If a priest is killed, a land lies under an interdict; why not also if a peasant is killed? Where does such a great difference among equal Christians come from? Only from human laws and inventions."[44] To any peasant hearing this, the meaning would have been unmistakable.

---

dienen": Luther Reclam, 17, LW 44:129; "daß ein Glied dem anderen nicht helfen, seinem verderben nicht wehren soll": Luther Reclam, 17, LW 44:129.

41. "Einem jeglichen Glied [befohlen wird], für das andere zu sorgen": Luther Reclam, 23-24, LW 44:135; "ein jeglicher Bürger schuldig [ist], die anderen zu bewegen und zu rufen": Luther Reclam, 25, LW 44:136.

42. Luther Reclam, 30, 33; 12, 14, 15; 20, 26; 29, 43; 12; 41.

43. Nietzsche repeatedly refers to Luther as "bäurisch." See Friedrich Nietzsche, *Dawn* § 88, in *Sämtliche Werke: Kritische Studienausgabe in 15 Einzelbänden* [KSA], ed. Giorgio Colli and Mazzino Montinari, 15 vols. (Munich: dtv, 1988), here 3:82; and Nietzsche, *Beyond Good and Evil*, § 50 (KSA 5:70); he refers to him as a "Bauer" in Nietzsche, *On the Genealogy of Morals*, section 3, ch. 22 (KSA 5:394), and as the "Bauern-Apostel" in Nietzsche, *The Anti-Christ*, § 53 (KSA 6:234).

44. "Wird ein Priester erschlagen, so liegt ein Land im Interdikt; warum nicht auch, wenn ein Bauer erschlagen wird? Wo kommt her solch großer Unterschied unter den gleichen Christen? Allein aus menschlichen Gesetzen und Erdichtungen": Luther Reclam, 19, LW 44:131.

Retraction

However, those peasants would have been mistaken nonetheless, it seems, for, after having thus drawn them in, Luther *takes it all back*. The equality he preaches is only part of the story and only an appearance. When, in a rather loose paraphrase, he reminds us that Christ said "each one should consider himself the lowest and least important,"[45] "each one" ("jeglicher") resonates with all those iterations of "each member" and thus would encourage a peasant or commoner to think that they and the nobility are to be on the same level. This passage, however, while evoking the democracy of "each one" and thus giving an appearance of equality of station, simultaneously maintains the hierarchy of the highest and the "lowest," and this is how the nobility would certainly have understood it.

How does Luther take it all back? Most strikingly and insidiously, I would say—insidious because he holds out a hope that proves to be no hope at all—in his retraction of the "all members of the one body" metaphor or, more accurately, his qualification of it such that its democratic force is vitiated. To be fair, Luther retracts it or at least anticipates its retraction practically in the very act of offering it. Immediately following the initial statement "that we are, all of us together, one body,"[46] we read "*but* each member has its own work with which it serves the others."[47] No sooner is the democratic metaphor introduced than it is qualified and partially taken back by a "but." Still, the clause the "but" introduces expands the metaphor with the notion of us each being a member of the one body and emphasizes that each member serves the others. As we have seen, Luther then repeats this metaphor and the various calls on each equal member to serve, help, and care for the others, but that first "but," as easily overlooked as it was, returns with a vengeance two pages later when Luther qualifies dramatically his notion of the priesthood of all the baptized: "For whatever has crawled out of baptism can boast that it is already consecrated priest, bishop, and pope, *although* it does not beseem everyone to exercise such office."[48] Then, a page and a half later, immediately following the third of those three exhortations on a single page to mutual service and help

---

45. "Ein jeglicher soll sich für den Untersten und Geringsten halten": Luther Reclam, 20, LW 44:133.
46. "Daß wir allesamt ein Körper sind": Luther Reclam, 14, LW 44:127.
47. "*Doch* ein jeglich Glied sein eigen Werk hat, mit dem es den anderen dienet": Luther Reclam, 14 (emphasis P. J. B.), LW 44:127.
48. "Denn was aus der Taufe krochen ist, das kann sich rühmen, daß es schon zum Priester, Bischof und Papst geweihet sei, *obwohl* nicht einem jeglichen ziemt, solches Amt zu üben": Luther Reclam, 16 (emphasis P. J. B.), LW 44:128.

among all members of the one body, we read: "Indeed, the *nobler* the member, the more the others should help it"!⁴⁹ With this, for those who notice it and its implications, Luther has taken back his rhetoric of equality and democracy and reinstated his rhetoric of authority and subjection. But again, it is hard to notice in the midst of or after those far more numerous "one body" and "each and every member" declarations.

In the next pages, Luther follows his retraction with demands that "temporal Christian power should exercise its office freely and unhindered, regardless whether it befalls the pope, a bishop, or a priest,"⁵⁰ and, a paragraph later, that "temporal rule has become a member of the Christian body . . . and thus should do its work freely and unhindered upon all members of the whole body, should punish or convict, as guilt may deserve or need demand, regardless whether pope, bishop, or priest."⁵¹ This radical empowerment of the nobility vis-à-vis the papacy and clergy might not disturb the peasant or commoner who has justifiably come to see himself as a member of the one body. However, following as it does so closely on the retraction of the equality of the body parts, peasants should have reason to worry about such punishment and conviction, especially when they learn that the nobility is to exercise its power over "all members of the whole body." Then again, while using this catchphrase, which is so hard to overlook or not to hear, Luther has veiled, if not buried, the subjection of "all members of the whole body" to the nobility's power in a call to action against Rome and the clergy. Only careful reading of or listening to this passage enables one to recognize the double trajectory of the power Luther invests in the nobility, as opposed to the other members of the supposedly unified Christian body, and such careful reading and listening by the vast majority of recipients hardly seems likely.

Luther has thus moved from a rhetoric of authority and subjection to a rhetoric of equality and democratic revolution and then back again to the rhetoric of authority and subjection, the rhetoric of equality and democratic revolution having functioned as a tool to draw as many Germans as possible into his and the nobility's battle against Rome. The proof that this "inclusive" rhetoric has been put in the service of his "exclusive" rhetoric is the very fact

---

49. "Ja, je *edler* das Gliedmaß ist, je mehr die andern ihm helfen sollen": Luther Reclam, 17 (emphasis P. J. B.), LW 44:129.
50. "Weltliche christliche Gewalt ihr Amt frei ungehindert [üben soll], unangesehen, ob es der Papst, ein Bischof oder Priester sei, den sie trifft": Luther Reclam, 18, LW 44:130.
51. "Weltliche Herrschaft ist ein Glied geworden des christlichen Körpers . . . und soll darum ihr Werk frei ungehindert gehen über alle Gliedmaßen des ganzen Körpers, strafen und überführen, wo es die Schuld verdient oder Not erfordert, unangesehen Papst, Bischof, Priester": Luther Reclam, 18-19, LW 44:130.

that he takes it back, takes back especially the democratic aspect of the "one body" and "each member" metaphor, and takes it back in a way that is relatively easy to overlook.

Failed Rhetoric

Having traced the two competing rhetorics of *To the Christian Nobility*, I would like to return, at least briefly, to the structure and strategy of Luther's core argument: that all Christians are in truth of the spiritual estate, which grounds the doctrine of the priesthood of all believers. I have been speaking of Luther's "equation" of spiritual and temporal power, when it would be more accurate to say that what Luther undertakes is a deconstruction of the hierarchically organized binary opposition of spiritual power and temporal power, whereby the previously unprivileged term in the opposition, temporal power, is reinscribed in such a way that it can no longer be constitutive of the binary opposition: by positing that all Christians are of the spiritual estate, Luther reinscribes "weltlich" *as* "geistlich," "temporal" *as* "spiritual," and as a result the binary opposition collapses as such.

This collapse reverberates, for with the leveling, the egalitarianism of "estate" (*Stand*), the hierarchy of estate over "office and work" (*Amt und Werk*), is also undermined. Thus, very democratically, "we are all priests *in the same way*," and thus, continuing the deconstruction of spiritual and temporal, "a station of priest should not be different in Christendom from that of a civic official."[52] Since we are all priests, that would also make us all "civic officials" (*Amtsmänner*). This, however, is where the deconstruction stops, indeed where it is reversed, for Luther uses it in order to reinstate precisely the kind of hierarchy he had ostensibly been undermining. The deconstructed hierarchy of estate over office and work is replaced by another hierarchy, that of the different offices and works: "there is in truth fundamentally no other difference between spiritual and temporal persons than that of office or work, and not of estate; for they are all of spiritual estate, truly priests, bishops, and popes, but not of the same, unified work."[53] Here Luther makes it clear, by the way,

---

52. "Wir [sind] alle *gleicherweise* Priester": Luther Reclam, 16 (emphasis P. J. B.), LW 44:128; "ein Priesterstand [sollt'] nicht anders sein in der Christenheit denn wie ein Amtmann": Luther Reclam, 16, LW 44:128.
53. "Geistliche und Weltliche [haben] wahrhaftig im Grunde keinen anderen Unterschied denn des Amtes oder Werkes halben und nicht des Standes halben; denn sie sind alle geistlichen Standes, wirklich Priester, Bischöfe und Päpste, aber nicht gleichen, einheitlichen Werkes": Luther Reclam, 16–17, LW 44:128. The Reclam edition has "letztlich" in place of "im Grunde," which has been restored by P. J. B.

that equality of estate did indeed imply unity, and with the differentiation and hierarchization of works and offices, that unity dissolves. The differentiation of works and offices then grounds the differentiation of the nobler from the less noble members of the one body that I discussed earlier. By tracing the strategy of Luther's argument, we can see more clearly just how it is that an ostensible rhetoric of equality reveals itself as, or is transformed into, a rhetoric of subjection.

But Luther is either too clever by half here or does not have sufficient control over his own discourse, for there are too many nuances, turns, and reversals in this argument, in his ostensible logic, for there to have been any hope of its "subtlety" being appreciated by his vast audience. What is more, Luther, in pursuing something like a deconstruction of the hierarchical opposition of estate over office and work, falls into what we might consider a trap of his own making, the trap of his own German language. The name of the trap is *Stand*. The word is generally translated in Luther as "estate," and indeed this is what he usually means by it, in its historically specific sense. But "Stand" also means, generally, "standing" in the sense of "station" or "class." That it can also mean this in Luther's text is demonstrated by his use of the word "Priester-stand," which I translated above as "a station of priest" and which refers more to a class than to an "estate," especially when preceded, as here, by an indefinite rather than definite article.[54] When he repeatedly tells us we are all of the same "Stand," he is thus also telling us that we are all of the same class and is undermining, it seems inadvertently, precisely the social hierarchy that he is trying to reinstate with his differentiation among works and offices. Thus his argument continues to encourage democratic and democratically revolutionary thinking, whether he wants it to or not.

The Freedom of a Christian

To the Christian Nobility is not the only text where Luther fatefully lost control over his rhetoric. In his polemic of October 1520, *The Freedom of a Christian*, which, apparently mistakenly, grounded the peasants' claim to freedom, he begins with the famous paradox that "A Christian is a free master over all things and subject to no one. A Christian is a subservient slave of all things and subject to everyone."[55] He proceeds, just a few lines later, to resolve the paradox

54. See also the use of the word "Laienstand" ("laity") at the beginning of the text, which sooner means "standing" or "station" than "estate": Luther Reclam, 9, LW 44:121.
55. "Ein Christenmensch ist ein freier Herr über alle Ding und niemand untertan. Ein Christenmensch ist ein dienstbarer Knecht aller Ding und jedermann untertan": Luther

by restricting the freedom in the first claim to the spiritual realm (*geistlich*) and the servitude in the second to the bodily realm (*leiblich*), although such a resolution could already be implied in the formulations "free master *over* all *things*" and "subservient slave *of* all *things*." This differentiation might have forestalled the kind of confusion and unintentional consequences that *To the Christian Nobility* would provoke, except that in the very formulation of the paradox and in the failure of his own resolution of it, Luther once again encourages precisely the kind of thinking he expressly forbids, namely, thoughts of freedom in the bodily, thus temporal and social, realm.

With regard to the formulation of the paradox: each statement, not just the first, is in itself democratic, insofar as each includes *all* Christians, regardless of estate or station. Thus the immediate conclusion to be drawn from both, even before Luther sets about resolving the paradox, is that everyone is in the same position. That, however, would mean that everyone is equally free and everyone is equally subject, that no one is placed higher than, that no one is master over anyone else (except non-Christians, of course, but the text only addresses the freedom of Christians), thus, paradoxically, that everyone is free, whether free or subject, either by virtue of equally ruling over all things or by virtue of being equally, with all others, ruled by everyone (implying collective self-rule, otherwise known as democracy)—equality being the, or at least one, ground of freedom.[56] The second half of the paradox is particularly interesting, and itself paradoxical, since if everyone is subject to everyone, then no one is subject to anyone, because no one is *more* subject to anyone than anyone else is, as Luther formulates it, and thus there is no hierarchy, no rule of one over the other. The paradox Luther expresses, in other words, is far more fundamentally paradoxical than he thinks and cannot be resolved by his attribution of freedom to the spiritual and servitude to the bodily, temporal, social realm, but rather already resolves itself in the very paradoxicality of the second statement, which renders it equivalent to the first, so that, whether one understands why or not, it would not be mistaken to take this first and most prominent section of the text, the one most readers and listeners would remember best, as a justification for claiming social freedom.[57]

Reclam, 125, LW 31:344; the imprecise LW translation reads: "A Christian is a perfectly free lord of all, subject to none. A Christian is a perfectly dutiful servant of all, subject to all."

56. "Freedom cannot be adequately defined in terms of relationships of inequality," argues Peter C. Hodgson in his essay, "Luther and Freedom," in ch. 3 (p. 35) of the present volume, an essay that addresses *The Freedom of a Christian* at length.

57. Herbert Marcuse articulates a very different paradox that he traces back to Luther's *The Freedom of a Christian*, the paradox of freedom as the precondition of servitude: "The amalgamation of inner autonomy and outer heteronomy, the fracture of freedom to unfreedom,

With regard to Luther's resolution of the paradox: it depends, as I have said, on the attribution of freedom to the spiritual and servitude to the bodily realm. Luther further articulates these realms in order to maintain their strict separation and thus to preclude the contamination of one by the other. The realm of freedom he inscribes not only as the spiritual realm, but also as that of the new, of interiority, of faith, and of the word, as opposed to the realm of servitude, which is inscribed not only as the bodily realm, but also as that of the old, of exteriority, of works, and of commandments.[58] In the eighth section, where he directly expresses the doctrine of justification by faith alone,[59] he already runs into some trouble when it comes to the word versus works and commandments, since Scripture contains so many of the latter; he solves this problem, with some sleight of hand, by dividing the Bible into two kinds of word—the commandment or law of God, which he ascribes to the Old Testament, and "promise" or "assurance," which he attributes to the New Testament.[60] There is a clear hierarchical opposition here of free–spiritual–new–interior–faith–word over subject–bodily–old–exterior–work–commandment, and in order to maintain the hierarchy, Luther needs to maintain these strict dualities. But the opposition collapses: first, when we read that "Thus it should justly be the sole work and practice of all Christians properly to internalize the word and Christ, constantly to practice and strengthen such faith, for no other work can make a Christian"[61] and discover that both the word and faith have been inadvertently reinscribed *as works*; second, when we learn that, when "humiliated and undone"[62] by the burden of commandments and unable to find one's way to piety, "then the other word comes, divine promise and assurance, and speaks: if you want to fulfill all commandments, rid yourself of

---

is the decisive characteristic of that concept of freedom that has ruled bourgeois theory since the Reformation"; "[freedom] is—an astonishing formulation to be held fast in all its paradoxicality—the precondition of unfreedom": Herbert Marcuse, "Theoretische Entwürfe über Autorität und Familie: Ideengeschichtlicher Teil," in *Studien über Autorität und Familie: Forschungsberichte aus dem Institut für Sozialforschung*, ed. Max Horkheimer (Paris: Félix Alcan, 1936), 137 (translation P. J. B.).

58. Luther Reclam, 125; 128; 127; 125; 126; 127; 129.
59. "Der Glaube allein kann fromm machen": Luther Reclam, 129; "faith alone can make pious," translated in LW as "faith alone justifies" (LW 31:347).
60. Luther Reclam, 129, LW 31:348. I should emphasize that I am addressing the correlation between law/gospel and Old/New Testament only as it is articulated in *The Freedom of a Christian*.
61. "Drum sollte das billig aller Christen einziges Werk und Übung sein, daß sie das Wort und Christum wohl in sich bildeten, solchen Glauben stetig übten und stärkten, denn kein ander Werk kann einen Christen machen": Luther Reclam 128, LW 31:347. The Reclam edition has "mit Recht" in place of "billig," which has been restored by P. J. B. It also has "sich recht einprägten" for "wohl in sich bildeten"; P. J. B. has restored the latter.
62. "Gedemütigt und zunichte geworden": Luther Reclam, 130, LW 31:348.

evil covetousness and sin, as the commandments compel and demand, behold, believe in Christ, in whom I assure you all grace, justice, peace, and freedom."[63] Here, in the imperative "believe in Christ," faith has been inadvertently reinscribed *as a commandment*. If faith is a commandment and faith and the word are works, then the new is also the old, the interior is also the exterior, the spiritual is also the bodily. Freedom, then, is no longer contained within the sphere of the spiritual and the interior, but rather is released into that of the bodily and exterior, into the world, thus giving all Christians reason to claim freedom not only in spiritual life, but also in the world.[64]

Conclusion

In his address *To the Christian Nobility*, and in his treatise on *The Freedom of a Christian* as well, Luther played a dangerous game with his rhetoric and lost. The historical proof that he lost is the Peasants' War. Certainly it was by no means specifically Luther's doing, but would it have happened at all without the catalyzing democratic and revolutionary rhetoric of his 1520 polemics? It is hard to answer this question in anything but the negative, even if we know, at the very latest from his 1525 pamphlet *Against the Robbing and Murderous Hordes of Peasants*, that Luther condemned democratic revolution, condemned any attempt to undermine social hierarchy.[65] But it was too late. For he had already sowed the seeds of rebellion with his rhetoric of equality and democratic revolution. Even if, in *To the Christian Nobility*, he employed this rhetoric strategically, in order to draw as many to his side as possible, when he

---

63. "Dann kommt das andere Wort, die göttliche Verheißung und Zusage, und spricht: willst du alle Gebote erfüllen, deine böse Begierde und Sünde los werden, wie die Gebote zwingen und fordern, siehe da, glaube an Christum, in welchem ich dir zusage alle Gnade, Gerechtigkeit, Friede und Freiheit": Luther Reclam, 130, LW 31:348.

64. Servitude would then also be associated with faith and the word, thus rendering the latter less clearly the source of freedom (Luther Reclam, 131, LW 31:349)—another instance of Luther's loss of control over his text.

65. It is not as if the 1525 pamphlet is the first time Luther used violent rhetoric, this time in encouraging the nobility to slaughter the peasants. Consider his call in *To the Christian Nobility* to hang and behead the Roman enemies, "let us justly hang the thieves and behead the robbers, why should we let Roman greed, which is the greatest thief and robber, go unpunished?" ("hängen wir mit Recht die Diebe und köpfen die Räuber, warum sollen wir frei lassen den römischen Geiz, der der größte Dieb und Räuber ist?": Luther Reclam, 43, LW 44:156), when read alongside lines such as the following from *Against the Robbing and Murderous Hordes of Peasants*: "Therefore, dear masters, redeem here, save here, help here. Take pity on the poor people [the princes]. Whoever can, should stab, smite, and choke [the peasants]" ("Drumb, lieben herren, loset hie, rettet hie, helfft hie, Erbarmet euch der armen leute [a misleading reference to the princes], Steche, schlahe, würge hie, wer da kan": WA 18:361, LW 46:54).

returned to his initial rhetoric of authority and subjection, it was too little, too late. The problem is that the revolutionary democratic rhetoric of all Christians being equal members of the one body, once deployed, can no longer be contained—in the text, as I hope to have shown, and in the world, because Luther wrote it in German and published it, thus spreading it among the masses, and what would the masses have heard but the rhetoric of equality and freedom from oppression?

Luther lacked control over his rhetoric of control, lacked mastery over his rhetoric of mastery. To the nobility he says "rebel" and to the peasants and commoners he says, ultimately, "behave and serve," but only after he has included them in the call to rebellion. In other words, Luther's text itself is, despite itself, rebellious, and the misunderstanding of the peasants and of Catholic critics like Murner was a justified misunderstanding, and thus not a misunderstanding at all, as much as Luther may have thought otherwise. In the end, Luther's rhetoric is not a masterful rhetoric, for the text achieved the opposite of what it set out to do: it grounded violent democratic revolution against the masters instead of assuring the downfall of the papacy and the simultaneous subjection of the common people.[66] It may be that Luther stood there and could not do otherwise, but, as Nietzsche would say, "he knew not what he did."[67]

---

66. Nietzsche comments on another way in which Luther achieved the opposite of what he set out to achieve: "And Luther *rebuilt the Church*": Nietzsche, *The Anti-Christ*, § 61 (KSA 6:251); "Luther rebuilt the Church right at the moment *when it had gone under*. The Catholics would have reason to celebrate Luther festivals, to compose Luther plays": Nietzsche, "Why I Write Such Good Books: The Case of Wagner," in *Ecce Homo*, § 2 (KSA 6:359).
67. "Er wusste nicht was er that": Nietzsche, *The Gay Science* § 358 (KSA 3:604).

CHAPTER 17

Power and Politics
– Incursions in Luther's Theology –
Vítor Westhelle

J ust as it was once the monk, so it is now the philosopher in whose brain the revolution begins."[1] And so it did with this Augustinian monk's nailing of the Ninety-Five Theses, followed by a prolific career: writing incendiary pamphlets, Bible translations, catechisms, treatises, and commentaries. The revolution had metamorphosed into a religious reformation. But its impact, also in political and economic life, was and continues to be remarkable. Notable among Luther's varied contributions was the label used by twentieth-century Lutheranism to frame his thoughts on the relationship of God's grace and everyday life in the midst of its institutional realities: the two kingdoms doctrine. It soon became the litmus test to diagnose the Lutheran stance on social issues. And with it came its own promises and problems.

The so-called two kingdoms doctrine has dominated much of Luther research on power and politics since Franz Lau published an essay on the subject in 1933,[2] and it continued to be discussed through the middle of the 1970s. During this time, it was "one of the most debated issues in Luther's theology," as Heinrich Bornkamm aptly said.[3] In Gerhard Ebeling's opinion, the

---

1. Karl Marx and Frederick Engels, *Collected Works*, trans. Richard Dixon et al. (New York: International Publishers, 1975–), 3:182.
2. Franz Lau, *"Äusserlich Ordnung" und "weltlich Ding" in Luthers Theologie* (Göttingen: Vandenhoeck & Ruprecht, 1933).
3. Heinrich Borkamm, *Luther's Doctrine of the Two Kingdoms in the Context of His Theology*, trans. Karl H. Hertz (Philadelphia: Fortress Press, 1966), 5.

two kingdoms doctrine expressed nothing less than "the fundamental prob-lem of theology."[4] For the last three decades, however, there has been almost a complete silence regarding this "doctrine." The "two kingdoms," born as a "doctrine" merely in 1933, lived a short life indeed.[5]

Did the concern about politics and power in Luther's theology fade accordingly with the malaise that brought to naught a once famous and highly debated doctrine? Does the discussion of the topic in a collection on the global Luther indicate the contrary? The answer is a qualified yes! Qualified because the topic does not appear to be the same topic that was raised before. Of the two kingdoms doctrine, it can be said what was stated years ago in graffiti on the wall of the University of Bogotá, Colombia: "When we had almost all the answers, the questions changed." Indeed, the questions have changed. Europa 1989 stands as an indicator of the change; it has become a political marker, as it is also the name of a trendy café in downtown Copenhagen, once run by Brazilian immigrants.

Migration and the Economy

This is the symbol: the 1989 Europa Café in Copenhagen. It is not so much about changing regimes (*die Wende*)—the political transition that was precipi-tated by the fall of the Berlin Wall marking the end of the Cold War—as it is about the changing of places within a global hegemonic regime. More diver-sity is presently coming to the fore under this new regime: for example, the growing diversity in feminism, the gay movement that has an acronym that is ever expanding to accommodate different pleas (the last time I checked it was LGBTQ), bringing the relationship between gender, human sexuality, and reproductive rights to a new plateau.

In addition to these, one must add immigration, considered to be one of the social markers of the turn of the century, particularly as it affects the tra-ditional places where most Lutherans live—the United States, central Europe, and Scandinavia. Most immigrants to these places come to find a source of livelihood. Strictly political refugees are a minority among them, although the

---

4. Gerhard Ebeling, "The Necessity of the Doctrine of the Two Kingdoms," trans. James W. Leitsch, in *Word and Faith* (Philadelphia: Fortress Press, 1963), 389.
5. See Vítor Westhelle, "The Word and the Mask: Revisiting the Two-Kingdoms Doctrine," in *The Gift of Grace: The Future of Lutheran Theology*, ed. Niels Henrik Gregersen, Bo Holm, Ted Peters, and Peter Widman (Minneapolis: Fortress Press, 2005), 167–78; also Vítor West-helle, "The Dark Room, the Labyrinth, and the Mirror: On Interpreting Luther's Thought on Justification and Justice," in *By Faith Alone: Essays on Justification in Honor of Gerhard Forde*, ed. Joseph A. Burgess and Marc Kolden (Grand Rapids: Eerdmans, 2004), 316–31.

distinction between the two categories is imprecise, according to the United Nations High Commissioner for Refugees. The most common cause of migration is the search for a place to secure a livelihood and to establish a household, to have an "economy." Politics and economics are, indeed, bundled together, but they remain remarkably distinct. And it is only timely and salutary that we revisit Luther's theology with regard to this distinction. It presents intricacies that the two kingdoms doctrine has not effectively addressed. Indeed, theologians discussing the two kingdoms doctrine have tended to overlook this important yet nuanced distinction between politics and the economy.

The word "economy" in its original sense covers the search and the means to sustain livelihood together with the propagation of life. The modern West has striven arduously to keep the two senses apart: one belonging to the public realm and the other to the private sphere. However, migrant workers in search of sustenance for themselves or their families raise issues about sexual ethos and reproductive rights that are closely intertwined with labor and the economy. The issues are raised in this regard in such a way that they reconnect the split between the private and the public. This split is unheard of, where the means for survival are at their minimum. One does not need to search far for such examples. Consider the case of many places in the Third World, where survival and reproduction are so closely knit together so as to form an economic-political Gordian knot that defies unlacing.[6] The separation between production and reproduction can only be afforded in societies, as in modern Western societies, where the matters of the house or the bedroom have been privatized and the economy has moved out of the household's domain. But it is not so in other parts of the world—mainly, but not exclusively, in the planetary south. For many of the poor in the world, raising children is the parents' pension plan. The knot that intertwines sexual reproduction (and the moral problems it raises) with a sustainable livelihood can only be untangled when reasonable levels of international justice and economic equity are achieved.

Lutheranism is now moving south to places where survival is often negotiated on a daily basis. Half a century ago, 90% of Lutherans worldwide resided in the North Atlantic axis; that is, Europe and North America. This number is now less than 60% and falling. Lutheran churches in the south, particularly in Africa and Asia, are registering escalation in membership, while dwindling

---

6. It is not helpful to attribute positions of moralistic pietism or political opportunism to church leaders and politicians in these places when they articulate a stance pertaining to the AIDS epidemic or homosexuality. It is not helpful insofar as it does not address the intimate relationship between sexual reproduction and the production of the means of sustenance, meaning, this relationship is about the economy.

numbers in Europe and the United States predict a likely near future in which the majority of Lutherans will live in the southern hemisphere. This shift, though primarily not the result of physical migration, does, however, register a symbolic change, a symbolic "migration." It is expected that this shift will determine the future agenda of Lutheran theology and ecclesial practice. Also expected is that Luther will be read in new ways to address this changing agenda; the hegemony that Germany and Scandinavia have exercised and still exercise in Luther research will be upset.[7]

The questions will change as a result, as much as they changed in regard to politics at the end of the Cold War. Changing *agenda* affects the *credenda* (that which is believed). In short, these issues addressed to church and theology are not only, or primarily, of a political nature; they pertain, rather, to the household, to the "economy" in the broad and traditional sense of the term. The term *household* was used prior to the emergence of financial capitalism and the industrial revolution in the etymological sense of the Greek term *œconomia*, meaning the rules and workings of the house.

The Three Estates

The question of the economy brings us to address anew to Luther the question of power and politics, particularly in view of the fact that the two kingdoms has apparently faded to near oblivion. Around 1530, Luther's more general references to the worldly regime (*weltliche Regiment*) became more nuanced. He was already familiar with and had used the popular medieval division of society into three "estates" or "hierarchies"[8] that distinguished civil governance from household (*œconomia*).[9] But the distinction became most prominent with and after his *Confession* of 1528 and the Catechisms of 1529.

In the middle ages, these hierarchies were often used in the sense of distinct classes, social strata, castes, or rank, and regarded as part of natural law. The division of these estates took many forms, but they were all made in general reference to the clerics, the nobility, and the common people. The three

---

7. In 2007, the International Congress for Luther Research was held in Canoas, Brazil. This was the first time that the International Congress was held in the planetary south since its first meeting in 1956 that took place in Aarhus, Denmark. This fact is of symbolic significance.

8. Luther names them variously as *Orden, Stifte, Stände, Hierarchien, Ertzgewalten, fora, mandata*, etc. See Ulrich Duchrow, *Christenheit und Weltverantwortung: Traditionsgeschichte und systematische Struktur der Zweireichenlehre* (Stuttgart: Klett, 1970), 503.

9. Luther refers to the three estates for the first time in his 1519 pamphlet, *The Holy and Blessed Sacrament of Baptism*, in LW 35:39, WA 2:734, 24–28.

estates were united like the persons of the Trinity for the sake of the earthly good of the *corpus christianum* ("Christian body"). In the words of Ruth Mohl, in her study *The Three Estates in Medieval and Renaissance Literature* (1933): "God created this threefold society, and so it must be right. He instituted the prayers of the clergy, the defense of knighthood, and the labor of the commons . . . Moreover, Holy Church is dependent on all of them and without any of them could not stand. Just as the Trinity would be inconceivable without Father, Son, and Holy Ghost, so the Church would be inconceivable without its three estates."[10] The estates were discrete parts of Christendom that served as the natural infrastructure to its spiritual expression in the Holy Church, which was the head and the expression of the Christian body. With his adoption of the three orders, however, Luther distanced himself from the medieval notion of the *corpus christianum*.[11]

Luther made a few changes to this model of the three estates that are worth noticing. For example, he did not see the clergy as a distinct class (thus his criticism of monastic life), but included in this estate the entire human race insofar as it descended from Adam (the preachers, but the listeners as well). Luther saw the church as an institution; it was one of the orders instituted by God. It was the first estate given to humans with the mandate of the Sabbath. The same is the case with the household and the civil government. Luther writes in the *Lectures on Genesis* of 1535–1536: "Here we have the establishment of the church [*Ecclesiae*] before there was any government of the home [*Oeconomia*] and of the state [*Politia*]."[12]

For the Reformer, the church is an instrument for the Word of God to be announced to the whole of creation and for the human response to be expressed. The household or economy was instituted to provide sustenance and nourishment, while the civil government was instituted for the sake of social order, defense, and protection. Luther calls these institutions the masks (*larvae*) through and by which God works. In Luther's words: "God ordained the three institutions (*Stände*) in which we live in good conscience with God. The first is the household; the next the political and worldly regime; the third the church or priestly order—all according to the three persons of the Trinity."[13]

---

10. Ruth Mohl, *The Three Estates in Medieval and Renaissance Literature* (New York: Columbia University Press, 1933), 330.
11. Jürgen Küppers, "Luthers Dreihierarchienlehre als Kritik an der mittelalterlichen Gesellschaftsauffassung," *Evangelische Theologie* 8 (1959): 370.
12. LW 1:103 (to Gen 2:16-17), WA 42:79, 3.
13. WATr 6:266, 16-20 (no. 6913) (Translation V. W.); see Oswald Bayer, "Nature and Institution: Luther's Doctrine of the Three Orders," trans. Luís H. Dreher, *Lutheran Quarterly* 12/2 (Summer 1998): 152, n.24.

For Luther, the three orders do not form classes, strata, or castes separately from each other, but are functions of human society in which all humans participate in one form or another, both passively and actively. Luther does not regard the church to be composed exclusively of the priestly class, but of all who worship; the same is true of the household and the civil government. The distinction between the active life (*vita activa*) and the contemplative life (*vita contemplativa*) as attributes of classes collapses.[14] Luther, thereby, brings dynamism into the static character of the hierarchies, even as he is still captive to hierarchical language and the imagery it evokes.

The medieval estates' typology relied on the Aristotelian distinction between the spheres of the house (*oikos* in Greek, *domus* in Latin) and of the public order (*polis* in Greek, *civitas* in Latin). The church (*ecclesia*) or clergy completed the tripartite division.[15] In the tradition of Plato and Aristotle, these divisions correspond to the fundamental human vocations of nourishing life (Luther: *neeren*), protecting it (*wehren*), and teaching (*lehren*).[16] According to Mohl, Aristotle, influenced by Plato's *Republic*, developed this distinction between household and public order in view of his own position on the natural state of slavery. Aristotle, for Mohl, distinguished between those who held responsibilities to carry out the duties of the state—namely, the free citizens and the oligarchy—and those who did not—namely, the farmers, craftsmen, and laborers of all kinds that "will of necessity be slaves or barbarians."[17] The latter category might correspond to what we would now call "immigrants."

Luther's important contribution to the medieval typology is the functional or instrumental connotation that he attributes to the three estates, particularly as it concerns the distinction between the household or economy, and the political order. In this regard, Luther reestablishes the Aristotelian distinction, lost in the middle ages, between production or labor (*poiesis*) and practice or action (*praxis*).

---

14. See Küppers, "Luthers Dreihierarchienlehre," 361–74.
15. Duchrow, *Christenheit und Weltverantwortung*, 501. A lengthy discussion on the important question of the particular conception of the church's institution that includes all humanity (it was instituted for Adam and his descendents) is very tempting. Nevertheless, this task is beyond the scope of this chapter.
16. This last vocation does not coincide with the church, but belongs to all three orders. See Reinhard Schwarz, "*Ecclesia, oeconomia, politia*: sozialgeschichtliche und fundamentalethische Aspekte der protestantischen Drei-Stände-Theorie," in *Protestantismus und Neuzeit*, ed. Horst Renz and Friedrich W. Graf (Gütersloh: Gerd Mohn, 1984), 83.
17. Aristotle, *Politica*, trans. Benjamin Jowett, revised edn. W. D. Ross (Oxford: Clarendon, 1921), 1329a26. Cited in Mohl, *The Three Estates*, 11.

The Distinction between Household and Political Realm

Luther was certainly familiar with Aristotle's distinction between free citizens (those who act in the political realm) and slaves (those who labor or produce). Luther had read Aristotle and had lectured on Aristotle's works in his early years at the University of Wittenberg. What is not clear is whether Luther was aware of the anthropological reason Aristotle gives for this division as it is presented in the *Metaphysics*. At the beginning of Book VI, Aristotle distinguishes between three—and only three—fundamental and discrete human faculties (*dianoia*): namely, that by which motion causes production or labor (*poiesis*), that by which the will causes a deed or an action (*praxis*), and that by which observation or speculation causes theory (*theoria*).[18] I will concentrate the discussion of this section on the distinction between *poiesis* and *praxis*, which is directly pertinent to Luther's own use of the distinction between household (*œconomia*) and political realm (*politia*). I will leave the discussion of *theoria* aside, for which Aristotle gives the examples of physics and mathematics.

The distinctiveness of production (*poiesis*) in contrast to practice (*praxis*) is that it designates an activity that results in the making of something. Production entails an objective result. Practice or action (*praxis*) conveys an accomplished deed that has an inter-subjective effect, but does not result in a positive and material outcome. The analogy to the Greek theater is fitting. Production (*poiesis*) denotes the work of those who build the theater, set the stage, and write the play. Practice (*praxis*) denotes the activity of the actors performing the play. The verb, "to produce" (*poien*), is used in the Septuagint to translate the Hebrew terms for God's creative activity, including the Hebrew *barah*, of which God is the exclusive subject. In the New Testament, the verb is used to describe Jesus' healings: the miracle of water turned into wine, the lame walking, or the dead rising. The verb also occurs again in the Nicene Creed, which confesses belief in God, the "poet" of heaven and earth. In his *Hexameron* (circa 370), Basil of Caesarea explicitly appeals to the use of the term production (*poiesis*), as opposed to practice (*praxis*). While delivering his lessons to an audience of artisans, Basil employs "production" analogically to connect human labor to divine creation, even as he acknowledges the limits of the analogy.

The history of Aristotle's distinction between production and practice, particularly since its reception in the Latin world, is complicated. These two

---

18. Aristotle, *Metaphysics (Bilingual Edition)*, trans. Hugh Tredennick (Cambridge: Harvard University Press, 1933), 292–95 (1025b1-1026a33; VI.i.1.).

types of activity were conflated into the notions of either action (*actio*) or practice (*praxis*, since Duns Scotus) during the middle ages and well into modernity. The distinction between production or labor and practice or action would only return explicitly to the philosophical and theological vocabulary with Hegel's *Phenomenology*. In the section regarding the master and bondsman relation, Hegel represents "work as production" (*Arbeit qua poiesis*) as the human's self-actualization in transforming the material world in contrast to the inter-personal relation between master and bondsman.[19] The uniqueness of this concept of production as self-production is further developed by Marx's definition of "work" or "labor" (*Arbeit*) as a metabolism (*Stoffwechsel*) between worker and nature.[20] This metabolic relationship is distinguished from sociopolitical (inter-subjective) relations, to which the term practice (*praxis*) is normally applied. Practice (*praxis*), in its narrow sense, connotes inter-subjectivity; it is constituted discursively as explanatory narrative and public communication. It is the medium of human communicative action, moral deliberation, and juridical legislation: all that is required for procedural actions in the political realm. *Praxis* pertains to life in the political sphere and the actions necessary to administer it—in short, "politics." Production (*poiesis*) describes all activity that aims at providing the objective means for the sustenance of life. Of particular note is that production also includes intellectual nourishment. Hence, *poiesis* is the etymological root for the word "poetry." Production also includes preservation in the form of human biological reproduction. Both senses together, production and reproduction, are, in short, "economy."

Oeconomia (household) in medieval society—and Luther used the term in this specific sense—refers to the complex array of domestic relations, the relations of production and reproduction. The institutional reality of their distinction informs the opposition between the Aristotelian *poietic* (productive) faculty and the political faculty. The modern sense of the term differs from its medieval sense by conflating both sides—household and the economy— with each other.[21] I emphasize that Luther's distinction between household

---

19. Georg Wilhelm Friedrich Hegel, *Phenomenology of Spirit*, trans. A. V. Miller (London: Oxford University Press, 1977), 111–19. See my article "Theorie und Praxis III: Fundamentaltheologisch," in *RGG* 8:344–46.
20. Karl Marx, *Das Kapital: Kritik der politischen Ökonomie*, vol. 1 (Berlin: Dietz, 1962), 192.
21. Bonhoeffer recognized the difficulty with the modern separation of the household from the means of production, and as a result, he divided Luther's *oeconomia* into two mandates: marriage (including family) and labor. Dietrich Bonhoeffer, *Ethics*, ed. Eberhard Bethge, trans. Neville Horton Smith (New York: Macmillan, 1965), pp. 207–213, passim.

and economy should be interpreted against the medieval, not the modern, backdrop.

Luther employs the distinction between political realm (*politia*) and household (*oeconomia*) in order to stress two distinct institutional forms, that each offers particular ways in which humans cooperate with God.[22] God does not work without us; God works through human instruments or masks.[23] Luther's use of these two metaphors,[24] instruments (*Werkzeuge*) and masks (*Larven*)—even though he uses them interchangeably—is revealing. *Werkzeug* is an instrument or a tool for a work or labor to be accomplished; it is a metaphor imported from the economic, or *poietic* sphere, and thereby serves as a synecdoche by which a part (tool) is taken for the whole (labor). *Larve* is a mask taken either from Greek theater by an actor to represent a given role a person plays, or from the medieval carnival to represent an impersonation; it is the metaphor appropriate to describe the political person, the one who speaks on behalf of a cause, a person or a group representing and communicating interests for the common good, functioning thus as a metonymy.

For the Reformer, however, it is clear that the agent behind the tool or the mask is either God or the devil. Although both the household and the political realm are natural orders instituted by God, they are neither autonomous nor neutral. For Luther, natural law and divine law are one and the same, only *used* differently for distinct services to be accomplished through instruments or masks. The "supernatural" is not an additional realm, but lies buried in the depth of the "natural."[25] As Luther claims regarding the third mode of Christ's presence according to his humanity in the *Confession* of 1528 (a passage quoted at length in article VII of the *Solid Declaration*):

> He can be present in and with created things in such a way that they do not feel, touch, measure, or circumscribe him, how much more marvelously will he be present in all created things according to this exalted third mode, where they cannot measure or circumscribe him but where they are present to him, so that he measures and circumscribes them. You must place this existence of Christ, which constitutes him one person with God, far, far beyond created things, as far as God transcends them;

---

22. LW 33:243 (*Bondage of the Will*; 1525).
23. See the use of these two terms for politics in the *Lectures on Galatians* (1535) in LW 26:96, WA 40/I:176.
24. "Instrument" functions, in fact, as a synecdoche, while "mask" is a metonymy.
25. See the similar distinction between "natural" and "spiritual" on p. 288 of this chapter.

and on the other hand, place it as deep in and as near to all created things as God is in them.[26]

But the distinction between household and political realm is decisive because it comprises two fundamental aspects of Luther's anthropology: the human as producer and as political animal.

Material and Formal Causes

Further evidence of the distinct operational principles behind the distinction of household and political realm is found in Luther's *Disputatio de Homine* of 1536.[27] In the initial nineteen theses on philosophy, Luther offers a revealing interpretation of Aristotle's "four causes." Luther flatly denies philosophy's capability of defining the efficient and the final causes for human existence. He had made a similar point just a few months prior to these theses in his first *Lectures on Genesis*: "God is the efficient and the final cause."[28] Theology alone, according to Luther, is entitled to make this pronouncement because these two causes belong to God's own agency. But Luther grants reason or philosophy some voice as to the material and formal causes. Philosophy may have something to say regarding the material cause if limited to the level of the appearance of things, or, in the case of the formal cause, philosophers will dispute but never agree upon it.[29] Luther does not spend much time discussing these two causes. The distinction he offers can be said to parallel the distinction in the institutions that I am treating in this chapter: hence, I relate the material and formal causes as the operational principles at work in, respectively, production and action.

The material cause gives humans knowledge of who they are, even as sinners in the midst of sin, or in the terminology of this chapter, in the midst of one's own production and self-production. The material cause, as the result of labor, provides for a visible and enduring result (*satis videre*). The human becomes "visible" by what is produced as result of labor or *poiesis*.[30] The formal

---

26. LW 37:222, WA 26:335, 29–336, 27; see also art. VII of the *Solid Declaration* in BoC, 609, 11.
27. Cited in Gerhard Ebeling, *Lutherstudien*, vol. 2, *Disputatio de Homine*, part 1 (Tübingen: Mohr Siebeck, 1977), 15–24.
28. LW 1:127 (to Gen 2:21).
29. "Nunquam conveniet inter philosophos" (thesis 15 as cited in Ebeling, *Disputatio de Homine*, vol. 2/1, 18).
30. The use of the word "labor" for the delivery of a child is still a linguistic relic of the close association between human production and sexual reproduction.

cause has to do with speech (*verbum vocale*) and communication[31]; it is about human representation in the political sense of practice (*praxis*).

Luther's brief treatment of the two causes reveals how closely he follows the Aristotelian distinction between the human faculties of production or labor (*poiesis*) and practice or action (*praxis*). For him, these faculties are the basis in human nature for the institutions of household and political realm, and these institutions are the instruments and masks of God by which humans present and represent themselves.

Luther summarizes his understanding of these institutions and their causes in his *On the Councils and the Church* (1539): "Thus Psalm 127[:1] says that there are only two temporal governments on earth, that of the city and that of the home. . . . The first government is that of the home, from which the people come; the second is that of the city, meaning the country, the people, princes and lords, which we call the secular government. These embrace everything—children, property, money, animals, etc. *The home must produce, whereas the city must guard, protect and defend.*"[32] The sense Luther assigned to these institutions was undoubtedly dependent on the static character of the medieval institutions. Luther did not know that the industrial revolution would move production out of the home. Nor did he know that the American and the French revolutions would do away with the entitlements of nobility. Yet he realized that the two fundamental anthropological dimensions could not be collapsed. The distinction is what really matters.

Keeping the Distinction

In the *Lectures on Genesis*, Luther does not assign a consistent origin to the political estate. Commenting on Genesis 2:9, Luther writes that God established "in Paradise . . . the administration of government and of the home."[33] In a subsequent passage, Luther examines Genesis 2:16-17, and says that in paradise, unlike the church and the home, "there was no government of the state before sin, for there was no need for it. Civil government is a remedy required by our corrupted nature."[34] Despite this inconsistency, Luther tends to hold the opinion that civil government is required after the fall. Politics, as opposed to economics, is post-lapsarian. This means that the political realm,

---

31. Ebeling, *Disputatio de Homine*, vol. 2/2, 347.
32. LW 41:177 (emphasis added).
33. LW 1:94.
34. LW 1:104.

even if mandated by God, is not an order of creation, whereas the economy and the church are orders of creation.[35]

In the draft notations to the *Lectures on Genesis*, Luther says: "At this point [in the story about Paradise] politics does not exist; it begins in the chapter on Cain [Gen 4]. Where politics is not posited, neither is the need for medicine or such things. All would be healthy; all would be right under the dominion of humans. Politics is the guard of fallen nature, economy is what remains of [original] nature, and the church is the redemption and restoration of nature."[36]

In his comments on Cain building a city for his "lust for ruling," Luther explicitly contrasts it to the true church, marking the difference between the political and the ecclesial realm.[37] Even more interesting is that Cain, exiled to the land of Nod (which in Hebrew means homelessness or wandering), was sent from his father's house, his "economy." Luther explains the difference found in Genesis 2:14 between being driven from the face of the ground (*adamah*) where Cain had his dwelling and home, and being a wanderer on earth (*'aretz*).[38] The curse on Cain is threefold: "Thus one sin is punished by a threefold punishment. In the first place, Cain is deprived of spiritual or ecclesiastical glory. . . . In the second place, the earth is cursed, and this is a punishment that affects his domestic establishment. The third punishment—that he is to be a wanderer and is to find a permanent dwelling place nowhere— involves civil government."[39]

It is certainly not the case that the economy has not been affected by sin. To the contrary. The point is that *politics* comes into existence when economy is affected by sin. The latter requires the former for the defense of its own damaged integrity.[40] Cain constitutes a household. To the extent that this household has been affected by sin, it has already entered into the realm of politics. In fact, household requires politics in the state of sin. Luther makes this claim in the "Preface" to the *Small Catechism* when he advises the teaching of the Seventh Commandment "to artisans and shoppers and even to farmers and household workers, because rampant . . . are all kinds of dishonesty and thievery."[41] Luther distinguishes here between two types of activity: on the

35. Bayer, "Nature and Institution," 128.
36. See WA 42:XXII, 20–26 (*Luthers Entwurf*, 1535) (Translation V. W.); See also Ebeling, *Disputatio de Homine*, vol. 2/2, 303.
37. LW 1:314.
38. LW 1:298 (to Gen 2:14).
39. LW 1:294.
40. BoC, 349, 18 ("On the Seventh Commandment").
41. BoC, 349, 18.

one hand, human self-expression in labor that produces and reproduces the means for the sustenance of life, from offspring to harvest, from the factory to the writer's desk and pen, from the cook in the kitchen to the canvas of the painter; on the other hand, the power to curb the effects of sin insofar as the second table of the Ten Commandments is concerned. This restraining power can range from the discipline imposed on a child to the waging of war, from the work of legislation to police patrols, from regulating international trade to codes of social etiquette. All the structures for intersubjective and political deliberation are the necessary remedies for an economy that has been corrupted and for labor alienated from the results of production.

Luther's distinction between the two realms, the spiritual and the earthly, falls short in addressing the distinct character of economy, politics, and the relationship between the two. Luther often insists on this relationship while keeping the distinction: "The will of God is to discern the orders."[42] In view of the spiritual realm, Luther sees the church as an order of creation and not an institution that belongs exclusively to the spiritual regime. Yet these careful distinctions are often misunderstood by the two kingdoms doctrine. The two kingdoms doctrine tends to collapse economy and politics into the earthly realm; the economy's production and reproduction differ from practice or political action. Luther's careful distinction helps us discern his anthropology and, thereby, his view of power, which is grounded in the economy but regulated by politics. Hence Luther establishes the primacy of economy over politics. In the words of Oswald Bayer: "Luther was definitely aware that politics is grounded in economy."[43] Politics is instituted for the sake of the production and reproduction of life, and not the other way around.

Instruments and Masks

As noted above, Luther uses the metaphors of "instrument" and "mask" interchangeably to describe the earthly institutions or mandates. Yet these concepts can be taken to suggest distinct forms that human self-representation take. Furthermore, they can be taken to correspond to the description of the human faculties of production and practice, which respectively ground economy and politics. Under the condition of sin, both are intertwined, but the distinction

---

42. "Vult Deus esse discrimina ordinum": WA 44:440, 25; see also WA 49:613, 1; 31/I:399, 26. For further discussion of this relationship, also as contrasted with Melanchthon's viewpoint, see Werner Elert, *Morphologie des Luthertums*, vol. 2, *Soziallehren und Sozialwirkungen des Luthertums* (Munich: C. H. Beck, 1931), 49–65.
43. Bayer, "Nature and Institution," 128.

remains; the two concepts are not exactly interchangeable. In order to understand the human in her most clear profile as the image of God (*imago dei*), one must attend to her capability of reproducing and producing the means for the sustenance of life. Even more precisely, she can be taken to *be* this very means, which is conveyed by the word "instrument." The most basic form that power assumes is this capacity for production that cannot be fully transferred to the political realm. In Luther's terms, production remains a residue, a relic of uncorrupted nature (*reliquum naturae*).[44] One should not romanticize the Reformer's insistence in finding Christ among the poor, the laborers, the little ones. Such a romanticized interpretation uses Luther's view of the laborers as an epistemological gesture. According to this interpretation, these little ones are those whose labor has not produced the surplus necessary to control and alienate the labor of others. They do not have political power, and are therefore to be seen as the privileged expositors of Christ's presence.

The triune God is both the origin and goal of this economy; God is the economy's efficient and final cause. In the interstice between the two, Christ is present, as Luther writes, "as deep and as near to all created things as God is in them."[45] Luther adds that reason and nature do not recognize Christ's presence, but that faith makes use of both reason and nature to see Christ in the world. Faith is the means by which both God works and the human cooperates with God (the human is a *cooperator dei*). God operates in the world through human labor and only through humans.[46] Luther can joyfully exclaim that "labor is in itself pleasure,"[47] while politics is a function of labor's alienation; unhappiness indicates the distortion of labor's metabolism.

One can understand Luther's high estimation of labor only if one brackets it from the political context into which it is inevitably plunged after the fall. Luther's own insistence that politics enters into the picture as a divine mandate after the fall indicates that something happens to labor with human sin. Karl Marx evokes Luther in view of this relation. Marx called Luther "the oldest German political economist,"[48] and discussed Luther's "Admonition to Pastors to Preach against Usury" (1540) at length in both the first and the third volumes of *Das Kapital*. Alluding to Luther, Marx insightfully remarked that

---

44. WA 42:XXII, 24 (*Luthers Entwurf*).

45. LW 37:222 (*Confession concerning Christ's Supper*, 1528); see footnote 26.

46. LW 33:241–43 (*Bondage of the Will*), WA 18:754, 14. Luther's formulation in Latin is: "sed non operator sine nobis."

47. "Labor est demum ipsa voluptas": WA 6:120, 25–26; see also LW 42:145 (*Fourteen Consolations*; 1520), where the translation is a paraphrase of the original.

48. Marx and Engels, *Collected Works*, 29:448.

the "primitive accumulation [of capital] plays in political economy a role akin to the original sin [*Sündenfall*] in theology."[49]

As far as the economy is concerned, politics emerges as the register of sin and corruption. The expression "political economy" claims this association. In the *Lectures on Genesis*, Luther sees traces of economy and politics in the twofold mandates given to Adam to work and watch. After the fall, they are disoriented from their originally intended goal.[50] In the description of Adam tilling the fields and cultivating the garden, Luther notices that the human being labors the very ground from which Adam was formed and out of which nourishment is produced. To quote Marx again, labor consists in a metabolism (*Stoffwechsel*) between the human and the rest of nature.[51] This metabolism is the foundation of household and economy. The term metabolism is indeed very appropriate in its etymological sense. *Metabolein* in Greek means "to bring together." The opposite of *metabolein* is corruption or alienation, which is nothing other than the sheer *diabolical*. (*Dia-bolein* in Greek means "to throw apart," which is the work of the devil.)

Politics consists of administering the *polis* (the city) and protecting it from corruption. Hence politics can only be exercised for the reason of restoring labor to its true metabolic function. Though the sword is a common trope for the way Luther describes politics and civil government, the actual formal cause for anything that happens in civil government is reason. The material cause, the objective result that politics should produce, is equity (*aequitas* in Latin; *Billigkeit* in Luther's German).[52]

I have now arrived at the distinction between two realms that the human being occupies. The human being occupies both the economic or poetic realm (*homo œconomicus aut poeticus*, where *poeticus* is taken in the Greek sense of *poiesis*) and the political realm (*homo politicus*). The former, *homo œconomicus aut poeticus*, is an instrument of the work of the triune God and presents God's continuing creation in and through humanity. The latter, the *homo politicus*, also represents God's creative work through humanity, but does so as a mask revealing God's judgment of the world on the economy's perversion. This is why, for Luther, the political sphere does not have autonomy: not because it fails to recognize Christ's lordship,[53] but because its legal structure (*nomos*) is

---

49. Marx, *Das Kapital*, 1:741.
50. LW 1:102.
51. Marx, *Das Kapital*, 1:192.
52. Duchrow, *Christenheit und Weltverantwortung*, 498, 565.
53. In the Barmen declaration of 1934, Karl Barth and his followers defended the "lordship of Christ" over all aspects of life. They developed this idea as a critical principle against an understanding of the two kingdoms doctrine that they claimed informed the notion of the

grounded in the household (*oikos*). Politics exists only for the goal of achieving economic justice. It must be exercised solely with this goal in mind, however complex and challenging to reason this task might be. If politics administers power relations, labor and economy are the material foundation of power. If politics refuses to achieve justice according to the intrinsic right of the household, of labor and reproduction, politics is distorted and corrupted. The mask is fractured and its fissures expose only the unbearable sight of a hidden god that is at once the devil's own self.[54]

Looking Forward to Luther

Marx was right in his polemical acclamation of Luther as the first German political economist. How right was Luther in distinguishing clearly between economy and politics? As seen in his exposition of Genesis and study of Aristotle's *Metaphysics*, Luther carefully discerns the unique distinction between the household, or economy, and the political. Sadly, the traditional form of the two kingdoms doctrine has not sufficiently attended to this distinction. Furthermore, this insufficiency has not translated into an adequate account of the world or earthly regime, as Luther would call it. It is precisely the earthly realm—the rules and workings of the house, so to speak—that has been taken in a different direction since Luther.

Two interrelated phenomena—the immigration from the south to the old bastions of Lutheranism and the increasing presence of Lutherans in the southern hemisphere—have brought the question of economy, distinct from politics, to the Lutheran agenda in a quite different perspective. Yet Luther's theological anthropology and his understanding of society offer resources that have not yet been fully explored. I have offered in this chapter an incursion into Luther's theology in order to provide an itinerary for this task of distinguishing economy from politics according to two principles in Luther's thought on power and politics, which can best be expressed by the Aristotelian human faculties of production (*poiesis*) and practice (*praxis*). Careful study of Luther's distinction between economy and politics reveals a view of power the foundation of which is in the economy that politics should protect and defend. Such a theological incursion on the distinction of politics and

---

autonomy (*Eigengesetzlichkeit*) of the secular sphere. See in particular article 2 in Arthur C. Cochrane, *The Church's Confession under Hitler* (Philadelphia: Westminster, 1962), 237–42.
54. "To summarize, the devil does not become and is not a devil without first having been God. . . . For what the devil speaks and does must first have been said and done by God": LW 14:3 (*Commentary on Psalm 117*; 1530).

economy provides a conceptual frame to address pressing questions at the turn of the millennium. Prophetic were the words of Anders Nygren in his presidential address to the first assembly in 1947 of the Lutheran World Federation in Lund, Sweden: "Forward to Luther."

Acknowledgments

First, I thank my husband Robert A. Orsi for saying, "here we stand" with me, with all its consequences, particularly during these years when I was working on the "global Luther."

The chapters in this book are written by scholars who take the risk of thinking with Luther beyond Luther. The authors take Luther seriously as a thinker whose contributions in a number of different areas—religion, theology, literature, politics, psychology, musicology, and history—have taken on global significance. I thank the authors, who not only braved the famous Chicago winter to participate in the Global Luther conference but who risked the challenges of international, interdisciplinary, and interreligious dialogue—sometimes even misunderstanding—to come to greater appreciation for the relevance of Luther's ideas today. I am moved by the willingness of these scholars to press Luther beyond common lines of interpretation in order to catch exciting glimpses of what it means to be human in relation to God and neighbor in a contemporary global context.

The book documents a conference titled *The Global Luther: Rediscovering the Contributions of Martin Luther* held at Northwestern University from February 21–23, 2008. The conference was generously funded and joyfully supported by many individuals and institutions. I thank Northwestern University's Office of the President (Henry Bienen); Weinberg College of Arts and Sciences Dean's Office (former WCAS Dean and current Provost Daniel Linzer and especially Estelle Ure for her coordination of conference details and her thoughtful artistic design of conference poster and programs); the Alice Kaplan Institute for the Humanities; and Departments (and relevant Department Chairs) of Art History (Claudia Swan), Philosophy (Kenneth Seeskin), German (Peter Hayes), and Religion (Richard Kieckhefer). I am very grateful for the enthusiastic support of the conference by the Consulate General of the Federal Republic of Germany in Chicago (Wolfgang Drautz), the German Academic Exchange Service (DAAD) (Ulrich Grotius), Garrett-Evangelical

Theological Seminary, University Lutheran Church at Northwestern (Lloyd and Janet Kittlaus), Fortress Press, Thrivent Financial for Lutherans, and the Lutheran congregations in Evanston of Trinity Lutheran Church and Immanuel Lutheran Church. My special thanks goes to Immanuel Lutheran Church's Music Outreach Endowment Fund for graciously cosponsoring the concert (available as a recording in this volume) and to all my friends at Immanuel who organized the wonderful musical evening, especially to Pastor Frank Senn for envisioning a concert of historical chronology on the medieval Sequence, *Victimae paschali laudes*, and for welcoming this project and all the scholars and participants associated with it to Immanuel.

I thank my assistants, Jennifer Donndiego, Veronica Roth, and Matthew R. Robinson, who helped me to prepare the book's manuscript for publication with contagious enthusiasm and extraordinary patience every step of the project. I also thank Michael West, senior editor at Fortress Press, for making complete sense out of an extensive email, phone, and communication history, and to Josh Messner of Fortress Press, particularly for his creative suggestions, among them the "Luther and music" dimension of the book. I am especially grateful to my father, Paul Helmer, for creating the musical program and for writing the program notes. After so many years of canoeing together and pointing bricks, it was wonderful to join my father in another project, this one of shared musical and intellectual interest.

My sincere thanks go to Northwestern University for generously funding the recording, particularly the Religion Department, as well as the Graduate School (Andrew Wachtel) for a University Research Grants Committee (URGC) award. I thank Seabury-Western Theological Seminary in Evanston, particularly Ron Fox, for kindly making the Charles Palmerston Anderson Chapel of Saint John the Divine and the organ available for the recording. I am honored to have worked with Andrew Lewis, conductor, the Bella Voce choir and musicians, and Ed Hoke, sound engineer. I thank them for their enthusiasm and delight in producing the recording as a beautiful work of art.

Select Bibliography

Altmann, Walter. *Luther and Liberation: A Latin American Perspective*. Translated by Mary M. Solberg. Minneapolis: Fortress Press, 1992.

Arffman, Kaarlo. "The Lutheran Reform of Poor Relief: A Historical and Legal Viewpoint." In *Lutheran Reformation and the Law*, 205–30. Edited by Virpi Mäkinen. Leiden: Brill, 2006.

Bainton, Roland H. *Here I Stand: A Life of Martin Luther*. Nashville: Abingdon, 1990.

Bayer, Oswald. "Nature and Institution: Luther's Doctrine of the Three Orders." Translated by Luís H. Dreher. *Lutheran Quarterly* 12/ 2 (Summer 1998): 125–59.

Benedict XVI. *Glaube und Vernunft: Die Regensburger Vorlesung: Vollständige Ausgabe*. With commentaries by Gesine Schwan, Adel Theodor Khoury, and Karl Lehmann. Freiburg: Herder, 2006. English text online.

Blume, Friedrich. *Geschichte der evangelischen Kirchenmusik*. 2d edition. Kassel: Bärenreiter, 1965.

Bonhoeffer, Dietrich. *Ethics*. Translated by Neville Horton Smith. Edited by Eberhard Bethge. New York: Macmillan, 1965.

Bornkamm, Heinrich. *Luther im Spiegel der deutschen Geistesgeschichte: Mit ausgewählten Texten von Lessing bis zur Gegenwart*. 2d revised edition. Göttingen: Vandenhoeck & Ruprecht, 1970.

_____. *Luther's Doctrine of the Two Kingdoms in the Context of His Theology*. Translated by Karl H. Hertz. Philadelphia: Fortress Press, 1966.

_____. "Luther und sein Vater: Bemerkungen zu Erik H. Erikson, *Young Man Luther: A Study in Psychoanalysis and History*." *Zeitschrift für Theologie und Kirche* 66 (1969): 38–61.

Braaten, Carl E. and Robert W. Jenson. Eds. *Union with Christ: The New Finnish Interpretation of Luther*. Grand Rapids: Eerdmans, 1998.

Bräuer, Siegfried. *Thomas Müntzer: Deutsche Evangelische Messe 1524*. Berlin: Evangelische Verlagsanstalt, 1988.

Carlson, Åsa. Ed. *Philosophical Aspects on Emotions*. Stockholm: Thales, 2005.

D'Costa, Gavin. *The Meeting of Religions and the Trinity*. Maryknoll: Orbis, 2000.

de Unamono, Miguel. *Tragic Sense of Life*. New York: Dover, 1954.

Dickhut, Johannes. "Rhetorik als konstituierendes Moment der Textkomposition in Luthers Schrift: An den christlichen Adel deutscher Nation von des christlichen Standes Besserung." *Daphnis* 35 (2006): 449–93.

Dieter, Theodor. *Der junge Luther und Aristoteles: Eine historisch-systematische Untersuchung zum Verhältnis von Theologie und Philosophie*. Theologische Bibliothek Töpelmann 105. Berlin: de Gruyter, 2001.

Dörfler-Dierken, Angelika. "Luther und die heilige Anna: Zum Gelübde von Stotternheim." *Luther-Jahrbuch* 64 (1997): 19–46.

Donaldson, David. "On the Very Idea of a Conceptual Scheme." In *Inquiries into Truth and Interpretation*, 183–98. Oxford: Oxford University Press, 1984.

Duchrow, Ulrich. *Christenheit und Weltverantwortung: Traditionsgeschichte und systematische Struktur der Zweireichenlehre*. Stuttgart: Klett, 1970.

Dykema, Peter A. and Heiko A. Obermann. Eds. *Anticlericalism in Late Medieval and Early Modern Europe*. Leiden: Brill, 1993.

Ebeling, Gerhard. *Lutherstudien*. Vol. 2: *Disputatio de Homine*. 3 Vols. Tübingen: Mohr Siebeck, 1977, 1982, 1989.

Ehrlich, Ernst Ludwig. *Luther and the Jews*. Geneva: Lutheran World Federation, 1984.

Erikson, Erik H. *Young Man Luther: A Study in Psychoanalysis and History*. New York: Norton, 1958.

Estes, James. *Peace, Order, and the Glory of God*. Leiden: Brill, 2005.

Fabiny, Tibor. "The Strange Acts of God: The Hermeneutics of Concealment and Revelation in Luther and Shakespeare." *Dialog* 45/1 (Spring 2006): 44–54.

Forte, Dieter. *Martin Luther und Thomas Münzer, oder Die Einführung der Buchhaltung*. Frankfurt: Fischer, 1981.

Gerrish, Brian A. *Grace and Reason: A Study in the Theology of Luther*. Oxford: Clarendon, 1962.

Grosshans, Hans-Peter. "And the Truth Will Make You Free: On the Relationship between Religion, Truth, and Power." *Studies in Interreligious Dialogue* 17 (2007): 184–204.

Hadot, Pierre. *Philosophy as a Way of Life: Spiritual Exercises from Socrates to Foucault*. Translated by Michael Chase. Edited by Arnold Davidson. Oxford: Blackwell, 1995.

Halpérin, Jean and Arne Sovik. Eds. *Luther, Lutheranism, and the Jews: A Record of the Second Consultation between Representatives of the International Jewish Committee for Interreligious Consultations and the Lutheran World Foundation Held in Stockholm, Sweden, 11–13 July, 1983*. Geneva: Lutheran World Federation, 1984.

Hegel, Georg Wilhelm Friedrich. *Lectures on the History of Philosophy*. Vol. 3. Translated and edited by Robert F. Brown et al. Berkeley and Los Angeles: University of California Press, 1990.

_____. *Lectures on the Philosophy of World History. Introduction: Reason in History*. Translated by H. B. Nisbet. Cambridge: Cambridge University Press, 1975.

_____. *Phenomenology of Spirit*. Translated by A. V. Miller. London: Oxford University Press, 1977.

_____. *The Philosophy of History*. Translated by John Sibree with an introduction by C. J. Friedrich. New York: Dover, 1956.

Heim, S. Mark. *The Depth of the Riches: A Trinitarian Theology of Religious Ends*. Grand Rapids: Eerdmans, 2001.

Helmer, Christine. *The Trinity and Martin Luther: A Study of the Relationship between Genre, Language, and the Trinity in Luther's Works (1523–1546)*. Veröffentlichungen des Instituts für Europäische Geschichte/Abteilung Abendländische Religionsgeschichte 174. Mainz: Zabern, 1999.

Helmer, Paul. *Le premier et le secont livre de fauvel in the version preserved in B.N. fonds français 146*. Ottawa: The Institute of Mediaeval Music, 1997.

Hiley, David. *Western Plainchant: A Handbook*. Oxford: Clarendon, 1995.

Hodgson, Peter C. *Hegel and Christian Theology: A Reading of the Lectures on the Philosophy of Religion*. Oxford: Oxford University Press, 2005.

Hoffman, Bengt. *Luther and the Mystics: A Re-Examination of Luther's Spiritual Experience and His Relationship to the Mystics*. Minneapolis: Augsburg Fortress Press, 1976.

Helmer, Christine. "Introduction to Luther's Theology in Global Context." *Religion Compass Online Journal* (Blackwell) 3/3 (April 2009):1-13.

_____. *Theology of the Heart: The Role of Mysticism in the Theology of Martin Luther*. Edited by Pearl Hoffman. Minneapolis: Kirk House, 1998.

Holm, Bo Kristian. *Gabe und Geben bei Luther: Das Verhältnis zwischen Reziprozität und reformatorischer Rechtfertigungslehre*. Theologische Bibliothek Töpelmann 134. Berlin: de Gruyter, 2006.

Joest, Wilfried. *Ontologie der Person bei Luther*. Göttingen: Vandenhoeck & Ruprecht, 1967.

Joint Declaration on the Doctrine of Justification by the Lutheran World Federation and the Roman Catholic Church. Grand Rapids: Eerdmans, 2000.

Jones, James W. *Contemporary Psychoanalysis and Religion: Transference and Transcendence.* New Haven: Yale University Press, 1991.

_____. *Terror and Transformation: The Ambiguity of Religion in Psychoanalytic Perspective.* London: Brunner-Routledge, 2002.

Jungmann, Joseph, S. J. *The Mass of the Roman Rite: Its Origins and Development (Missarum Sollemnia).* 2 Vols. Translated by Francis A. Brunner, C.S.S.R. Westminster: Christian Classics. New York: Benziger, 1951–1955.

Kepler, Johannes. *The Harmony of the World.* Translated by E. J. Aiton, A. M. Duncan, and J. V. Field. Memoirs of the American Philosophical Society 209. Philadelphia: American Philosophical Society, 1997.

King, Martin Luther, Jr. *A Testament of Hope: The Essential Writings of Martin Luther King Jr.* Edited by James Melvin Washington. San Francisco: Harper, 1986.

_____. *The Papers of Martin Luther King Jr.* 3 Vols. Edited by Clayborne Carson et al. Berkeley and Los Angeles: University of California Press, 1992–1997.

_____. *Why We Can't Wait.* New York: Harper, 1964.

Kittelson, James M. *Luther the Reformer.* Minneapolis: Fortress Press, 1986.

Kohut, Heinz. *The Search for the Self: Selected Writings of Heinz Kohut (1978–1981).* Vol. 2. Edited by Paul H. Ornstein. New York International Universities Press, 1991.

Leaver, Robin A. *Luther's Liturgical Music: Principles and Implications.* Lutheran Quarterly Books. Grand Rapids: Eerdmans, 2007.

Leppin, Volker. *Martin Luther.* Gestalten des Mittelalters und der Renaissance. Darmstadt: Wissenschaftliche Buchgesellschaft, 2006.

_____. " '*omnem vitam fidelium penitentiam esse voluit*': Zur Aufnahme mystischer Traditionen in Luthers erster Ablassthese." *Archiv für Reformationsgeschichte* 93 (2002): 7–25.

Lindbeck, George A. "The Rabbinic Mind." In *Understanding the Rabbinic Mind: Essays on the Hermeneutics of Max Kadushin*, 141–64. Edited by Peter Ochs. South Florida Studies in the History of Judaism 14. Atlanta: Scholars, 1990.

Lindberg, Carter. *Beyond Charity: Reformation Initiatives for the Poor.* Minneapolis: Fortress Press, 1993.

Lindner, Andreas. "Was geschah in Stotternheim? Eine problematische Geschichte und ihre problematische Rezeption." In *Martin Luther und das monastische Erbe*, 93–100. Edited by Christoph Bultmann, Volker

Leppin, and Andreas Lindner. Spätmittelalter, Humanismus, Reformation 39. Tübingen: Mohr Siebeck, 2007.

Loimeier, Roman. "Is there something like 'Protestant Islam'?" *Die Welt des Islams* 45/2 (2005): 216–54.

Luther, Martin. *Address to the Christian Nobility of the German Nation Respecting the Reformation of the Christian Estate.* Translated by C. A. Buchheim. Harvard Classics 36, part 5.

_____. "An den christlichen Adel deutscher Nation," "Von der Freiheit eines Christenmenschen," "Sendbrief vom Dolmetschen." In *An den christlichen Adel deutscher Nation.* Edited by Ernst Kähler. Stuttgart: Reclam, 1977.

_____. "The Freedom of a Christian." In *Reformation Writings of Martin Luther.* Vol. 1. Translated by Bertram Lee Woolf. New York: Philosophical Library, 1953.

Mannermaa, Tuomo. *Christ Present in Faith: Luther's View of Justification.* Edited and introduced by Kirsi Stjerna. Minneapolis: Fortress Press, 2005.

Marius, Richard. *Martin Luther: The Christian between God and Death.* Cambridge: Harvard University Press, 1999.

Marshall, Bruce D. *Trinity and Truth.* Cambridge: Cambridge University Press, 2000.

Marty, Martin E. *Martin Luther.* New York: Viking, 2004.

Marx, Karl. *Das Kapital: Kritik der politischen Ökonomie.* Vol. 1. Berlin: Dietz, 1962.

Maurer, Wilhelm. *Kirche und Synagoge: Motive und Formen der Auseinandersetzung der Kirche mit dem Judentum in Laufe der Geschichte.* Stuttgart: Kohlhammer, 1953.

Miller, Gregory J. "Luther on the Turks and Islam." In *Harvesting Martin Luther's Reflections on Theology, Ethics and the Church*, 185-203. Edited by Timothy L. Wengert. Grand Rapids: Eerdmans, 2004.

Nussbaum, Martha. *Upheavals of Thought: The Intelligence of Emotions.* Cambridge: Cambridge University Press, 2001.

Oberman, Heiko A. *The Harvest of Medieval Theology: Gabriel Biel and Late Medieval Nominalism.* Cambridge: Harvard University Press, 1963.

Overbeck, Franz. *How Christian Is Our Present Day Theology?* Translated by Martin Henry. New York: Continuum, 2005.

Pabst, Adrian. "Partizipation durch Relationalität." *Ökumenische Rundschau* 57 (2008): 205–13.

Panichas, George. Ed. *The Simone Weil Reader.* Wakefield: Moyer Bell, 1977.

Press, Volker and Dieter Stievermann. Eds. *Martin Luther: Probleme seiner Zeit.* Spätmittelalter und Frühe Neuzeit 16. Stuttgart: Klett-Cotta, 1986.

Raunio, Antti. "Divine and Natural Law in Luther and Melanchthon." In *Lutheran Reformation and the Law*, 21–61. Edited by Virpi Mäkinen. Leiden: Brill, 2006.

Saarinen, Risto. *Gottes Wirken auf uns: Die transzendentale Deutung des Gegenwart-Christi-Motivs in der Lutherforschung*. Veröffentlichungen des Instituts für Europäische Geschichte/Abteilung Abendländische Religionsgeschichte 137. Stuttgart: Franz Steiner, 1989.

_____. Guest Ed. *The Future of Luther Studies*. Dialog 47/2 (Summer 2008): 91–175.

Senn, Frank C. *Christian Liturgy: Catholic and Evangelical*. Minneapolis: Fortress Press, 1997.

Simon, Wolfgang. "Worship and the Eucharist in Luther Studies." *Dialog* 47/2 (Summer 2008): 143–56.

Stolt, Birgit. "Luther on God as a Father." *Lutheran Quarterly* 8/4 (Winter 1994): 385–95.

_____. *Martin Luthers Rhetorik des Herzens*. Uni-Taschenbücher 2141. Tübingen: Mohr Siebeck, 2000.

_____. "On Translating Ave Maria as 'Hello there, Mary'." *Lutheran Quarterly* 12/1 (Spring 1998): 105–7.

Taubes, Susan A. "The Absent God." *The Journal of Religion* 35/1 (January 1955): 6–16.

Taylor, Charles. *A Secular Age*. Cambridge: Harvard University Press, 2007.

_____. *Sources of the Self: The Making of the Modern Identity*. Cambridge: Cambridge University Press, 1989.

Thompson, Deanna A. *Crossing the Divide: Luther, Feminism, and the Cross*. Minneapolis: Fortress Press, 2004.

Tierney, Brian. *Foundations of the Conciliar Theory: The Contribution of the Medieval Canonists from Gratian to the Great Schism*. London: Cambridge University Press, 1968.

Tietz, Christiane. *Freiheit zu sich selbst: Entfaltung eines christlichen Begriffs von Selbstannahme*. Forschungen zur systematischen und ökumenischen Theologie 111. Göttingen: Vandenhoeck & Ruprecht, 2005.

Torvend, Samuel. *Luther and the Hungry Poor: Gathered Fragments*. Minneapolis: Fortress Press, 2008.

Tracy, David. "The Hidden God: The Divine Other of Liberation." *Cross Currents* 46/1 (Spring 1996): 3–16.

von Loewenich, Walther. *Luther's Theology of the Cross*. Translated by Herbert J. A. Bouman. Minneapolis: Augsburg Fortress Press, 1976.

Weil, Simone. *Waiting for God*. Translated by Emma Craufurd. New York: Harper Perennial, 1992.

Westhelle, Vítor. "The Dark Room, the Labyrinth, and the Mirror: On Interpreting Luther's Thought on Justification and Justice." In *By Faith Alone: Essays on Justification in Honor of Gerhard Forde*, 316–31. Edited by Joseph A. Burgess and Marc Kolden. Grand Rapids: Eerdmans, 2004.

_____. "The Word and the Mask: Revisiting the Two-Kingdoms Doctrine." In *The Gift of Grace: The Future of Lutheran Theology*, 167–78. Edited by Niels Henrik Gregersen, Bo Holm, Ted Peters, and Peter Widman. Minneapolis: Fortress Press, 2005.

Witte, John. *Law and Protestantism: The Legal Teachings of the Lutheran Reformation*. Cambridge: Cambridge University Press, 2002.

Yeago, David. "'A Christian Holy People': Martin Luther on Salvation and the Church." *Modern Theology* 13/1 (Jan. 1997): 101–20.

Zachman, Randall C. *The Assurance of Faith: Conscience in the Theology of Martin Luther and John Calvin*. Minneapolis: Fortress Press, 1993.

Zovko, Jure. "Die Bibelinterpretation bei Flacius und ihre Bedeutung für die moderne Hermeneutik." *Theologische Literaturzeitung* 132 (2007): 1169–80.

List of Illustrations

Index of Biblical Passages

Index of Names

Index of Subjects

Diet of Worms, 20, 40
doctrine
  authority of, 254
  and freedom, 39, 43
  in interfaith relations, 60, 64
  in the Reformation, 30
  in relation to experience, 66

ecumenism, 50, 54, 184, 207-208,
  241
ego, 80, 102-103, 106, 109-110
emotion (*see also* reason and
  emotion)
  in cognition and thought, 135-
    137
  and the human, 5, 6, 8
  in Luther's thought, 65, 133
  and music, 153, 160
  and psychoanalysis, 68, 81, 83
  in text, 132, 141, 145
the Enlightenment, 25, 131, 174,
  180
equality, 13, 28, 36, 38 n. 23, 40, 64,
  117, 241
  rhetoric of, 267-283
eschatology, 58-59, 113-117, 120,
  123
ethics
  and freedom, 44-45
  and justice, 9
  and justification, 9, 188
  in Roman Catholic teaching,
    214
  sexual, 25-28
  social, 13, 31, 212
evangelical, 17, 27, 51, 124, 134,
  165, 229
evil, 1, 121, 148, 173, 179, 197,
  219, 231
  forces of, 40, 45
  and God, 89, 230
  Holocaust, 54
  in humans, 71
  power of, 89, 92
  radical, 116, 119

sin as, 26, 37-38
  suffering, 116
exclusivity, 234-236, 238-241
  in doctrine, 61, 191
existence, 12, 27, 65, 101, 191-192,
  198, 293
experience
  and conversion, 17, 31, 81
  and doctrine, 66
  faith and, 140, 203, 208, 245
  and freedom, 11, 65
  the human, 66, 69, 96, 119,
    128, 196
  individual or personal, 31, 71,
    97, 107, 110-111, 140, 237
  religious, 15, 65, 71-72, 88,
    144, 147
  as source of understanding, 76,
    98, 110-111, 119, 140-141,
    150, 195, 203, 345
  and suffering, 60, 96-112, 113
the Fall, 36, 183, 219, 222, 294,
  295, 297-298
feminism, 285
feminist theology, 102-103
forgiveness, 50, 63, 64, 98 n. 5, 140-
  141
  of God, 72, 79, 81, 119
  of sin, 140, 147-148, 197,
    255
freedom, 4, 5, 65, 111, 163-164,
  178
  and Christ, 11, 61, 79, 93
  concept of, 24, 33, 280 ns.
    56-57, 280-282
  and faith, 6
  God's, 34, 36, 242-243
  history of, 8, 11-12, 32, 42, 47
  and human being, 12, 25, 33,
    39, 107, 195
  individual, 13, 23, 215, 224
  and reason, 36, 44, 183
  salvation, 43, 48
  and the will, 37-38, 40 n. 24

Luther's Easter Hymn

Christ lag in Todesbanden, derived from
Victimae paschali laudes and *Christ ist erstanden*

Facsimile of *Christ ist erstanden gebessert*, from *Das Babstsche Gesangbuch von 1545*. Courtesy of Luther Seminary, Saint Paul, Minnesota.

Program

Bella Voce and the Evanston *Stadtpfeifer*
Andrew Lewis, conductor
Program created by Paul Helmer

1 Chorale Prelude for organ, John Eggert (1996)
2 *Victimae paschali laudes*, Sequence for Easter Sunday, attr. Wipo of Burgundy (c. 1050)
3 Sepulcher Ceremony, *Quem queritis . . . Victimae paschali laudes . . . Christ ist erstanden*, Aquileia, Italy (c. 1100)
4 *Victimae paschali laudes*, Sequence for Easter Sunday, polyphonic setting in two parts from the Cistercian Nunnery of Las Huelgas, Burgos (c. 1300)
5 *Victimae paschali laudes*, Sequence for Easter Sunday, Johannes Galliculus, Wittenberg (1539)
6-13 *Christ lag in Todesbanden*, contrafact of *Christ ist erstanden*, Martin Luther, Wittenberg (Easter 1524)
    6 Chorale Prelude for organ, Johann Heinrich Buttstedt (c. 1700)
    7 Verse 1—Martin Luther, unison with congregation
    8 Verse 2—Balthasar Resinarius a 4 (1544)
    9 Verse 3—Arnold Bruck a 4 (1544)
    10 Verse 4—Lupus Hellingk a 4 (1544)
    11 Verse 5—Martin Luther, unison with congregation
    12 Verse 6—Johann Walter a 5 (1544)
    13 Verse 7—Michael Praetorius a 8 (1607)
14 Chorale Prelude for organ, Johann Sebastian Bach, *Orgelbüchlein*, BWV 627 (c. 1714)

Program Notes

The "global Luther" must include the music that Luther introduced into the history of the West and world. The musical selections in this performance are based on one of the great hymns that Luther composed in 1524, *Christ lag in Todesbanden*. The hymn is perhaps best known for its intonation as an organ prelude and chorale in the work of the Lutheran composer Johann Sebastian Bach. Perhaps less known is that Luther built on a tradition of medieval composition that goes back to the eleventh century. The famous Latin Sequence from this century, *Victimae paschali laudes* (*Praise to the Paschal Victim*), was a text sung at the Catholic Easter Mass. As a Sequence, it would have been sung right before the reading (and in the case of the middle ages, the singing) of the Gospel. The Latin Sequence is one of only four medieval sequences to have been retained by the Council of Trent's liturgical reforms. It was published in the *Missale Romanum* of 1570.

Both tune and text fascinated generations of church composers, who used and reused the material in ever changing reflections on the Easter deed—the foundation of Christian faith. The Latin Sequence was rewritten as a German *Leise*, meaning a liturgical song reworked into the vernacular, called *Christ ist erstanden* (*Christ is Arisen*). Luther continued this tradition of rewriting German versions in his hymn composition *Christ lag in Todesbanden*. The program here offers a chronological working of a few compositions modeled on the Sequence from the eleventh through the seventeenth centuries.

Chorale Prelude for organ, John Eggert (1996)

This first organ prelude is a contemporary American setting of the hymn. John Eggert is Professor of Music at Concordia University, Saint Paul, Minnesota, where he teaches organ, music theory, and composition. Eggert's prelude is a dance setting littered with open fifths and constantly toying with fugal ideas taken from the cantus firmus. It would be fair to say every melodic and rhythmic motive is close cousin to the hymn tune. The entire prelude is unmeasured and takes full advantage of the mixtures and reeds of the organ.

Victimae paschali laudes, Sequence for Easter Sunday, attributed to Wipo of Burgundy (c. 1050)

The Sequence was sung after the Gradual at the Easter Mass services. It arose in the later eleventh century in the western German states or eastern French states. Its attribution to Wipo, the court chaplain of the Emperors Conrad II and Henry III, may be merely an acknowledgment of his status as an ecclesiastical personage of note rather than a proof of authorship.

The Sequence is in double-versicle structure (a bb cc dd) with internal rhymes set syllabically (one note per syllable) but with neumes on the final "Amen, Alleluia." It is written in the Dorian mode.

The text is a narrative of the resurrection story played out as a dialogue in lines 3a and 3b between an observer and Mary (Magdalene). The words of Mary are set off from the question by a lower tessitura. The opening melodic phrase from line 2a with its fourth leap upward in the higher tessitura is repeated in 4a, giving the work a dramatic focal point. The chant closes with an Alleluia circling around the low D final.

The Sequence was widely disseminated throughout Europe and soon became the cantus firmus in polyphonic settings. The first of these compositions was set in Saint Martial, Limoges c. 1100 (ms. 3549) and, in this particular case, to an organal voice that crosses it in melismatic flourishes.

Sepulcher Ceremony, *Quem queritis . . . Victimae paschali laudes . . . Christ ist erstanden*, Aquileia, Italy (c. 1200)

The town of Aquileia is in the province of Udine in northeast Italy. It has a magnificent basilica in which the present piece undoubtedly was performed. The piece was sung by the choir at the end of the Night Office on Easter morning in Latin, with the congregation joining in the German *Leise, Christ ist erstanden*. The question as to the appropriation of the German version of the drama and the use of the *Leise* in this Italian city is of scholarly interest. The music historian David Hiley claims in his book *Western Plainchant* (Oxford, 261–63) that Aquileia received the ceremony from the Augsburg canon Heinrich, who was patriarch of Aquileia from 1077 to 1084.

This setting of the *Victimae* Sequence involves a dramatic dialogue. In the medieval period, a number of scriptural texts were subjected to dramatic treatment and performed as part of regular Mass or Office services. *Victimae paschali laudes* readily lent itself to its performance as a "staged" presentation in church. The original Sequence already included a dialogue between an observer and Mary Magdalene spoken at Christ's tomb on early Easter morning. The present version sung here expands the incipient dialogue to include sung roles for the women, as well as for Peter and John, who were also early at the tomb on Easter. Hence this version might be considered an incipient opera.

The redactor begins with a conflation of the biblical narrative taken from Matthew 28:6-7, Mark 16:6-7, and John 20:3-4, but apportions the roles to the individual actually speaking. The work then goes on to quote the third and fourth stanzas of *Victimae paschali laudes* in their entirety. Then follows the rubric, *deinde populus*, which refers to congregational participation. The assembled faithful are to sing the German *Leise, Christ ist erstanden* together, an early form of Reformation hymnody! The drama concludes with the congregation singing the Te Deum.

The melodic relation between the hymn, *Victimae paschali laudes* and the *Leise, Christ ist erstanden*, is extremely close. The redactor quotes the three melodic phrases of the second verse of the Sequence and by repeating the second phrase creates a four-phrase entity, an ABCB structure. This is followed by a formulaic Kyrieleis. The striking Dorian figure A-C′-D′-A used at the beginning of the *Leise* ("Agnus redemit oves") immediately catches our attention. The A lifts off to the higher third, C′, and on to the upper fourth, D, followed by a descending fourth leap, D′-A. The answering phrase, A-G-A-F-E-F-D

("Christus innocens Patri") returns the gravitational pull back to the low D, the final of the mode. The third phrase again plays on the descending leap of a fourth now G-D ("reconciliavit peccatores") heard in the opening phrase and cadences on the dominant A. The final phrase repeats the second phrase. The melody concludes with neighboring tones of the mode final, E and C. The third verse of the *Leise* begins with a threefold Alleluia, the first two phrases of which are melodically new. The first uses B flat, the flattened sixth degree of the mode, the only time in the entire hymn that this note is used. The second phrase centers on the triad F-A-C, a nice diversion from the dominant modality. The remainder of the verse repeats the previous pattern, BCB, Kyreleis. Thus the entire German hymn is derived from the melodic components of the second verse of the Sequence.

Victimae paschali laudes, Sequence for Easter Sunday, polyphonic setting in two parts from the Cistercian Nunnery of Las Huelgas, Burgos (c. 1300)

Victimae paschali laudes also found its way to the Iberian peninsula. It was sung by the fourteenth century in the nunnery of Las Huelgas, in the vicinity of Burgos. The Cistercians were, in general, interested in a stricter and more austere form of the Benedictine rule. In spite of this commitment, they did not hesitate to cultivate the most advanced forms of polyphony available in their day. A male priest would perform the obligatory intonations and canonic portions at liturgical services. All other parts of the liturgy were performed by female voices. The present setting in two voices is an elaborate fantasy on the chant with florid contrapuntal writing.

The melody and text were often used in polyphonic elaborations by fifteenth- and sixteenth-century composers, among them Antoine Busnois, Orlando di Lasso, and Josquin des Prez. Josquin's six-voiced setting uses the text of the Sequence but sets it as a motet in point-by-point imitation.

Victimae paschali laudes, Sequence for Easter Sunday, Johannes Galliculus, Wittenberg (1539)

This setting has seven verses, each of which is sung in alternation between unison choir and four-part polyphony in motet style.

Christ ist erstanden is cited in verse 4. This setting was printed by Georg Rhau, an enterprising publisher well acquainted with Luther. Polyphonic settings of the Latin texts for Masses and Offices flowed from Rhau's presses in a steady stream.

Luther in no way wanted to discontinue the Latin musical heritage of the Catholic Church. In fact, he but cultivated it with vigor. He admired the polyphonic settings of the Franco-Flemish masters of the fifteenth and sixteenth centuries, particularly Ludwig Senfl and Josquin des Prez. German composers took up the challenge and learned the complex techniques of the Northern masters. The verse selections here offer different examples of the new techniques.

Christ lag in Todesbanden, contrafact of *Christ ist erstanden,* Martin Luther, Wittenberg (Easter 1524)

Chorale Prelude for organ, Johann Heinrich Buttstedt (c. 1700)
Verse 1. Martin Luther, unison with congregation
Verse 2. Balthasar Resinarius a 4 (1544)
Verse 3. Arnold Bruck a 4 (1544)
Verse 4. Lupus Hellingk a 4 (1544)
Verse 5. Martin Luther, unison with congregation
Verse 6. Johann Walter a 5 (1544)
Verse 7. Michael Praetorius a 8 (1607)

Chorale Prelude for organ, Johann Sebastian Bach, *Orgelbüchlein,* BWV 627 (c. 1714)

Luther wrote many of his hymns between 1523 and 1524. It is very likely that he composed *Christ lag in Todesbanden* in 1524, particularly because phrases from the hymn have textual parallels to the sermons Luther held at the Easter service in 1524.

Martin Luther composed his mighty contrafact of *Victimae paschali laudes* but entitled it surprisingly "Christ ist erstanden verbessert," in English, "Christ is Arisen, Improved." The medieval custom of "improving" on an earlier composition actually means a substantial expansion of its model. The Reformer knew the German *Leise* well and praised it in his writings. Luther quotes the text in his own hymn.

Luther's composition has seven majestic stanzas in the well-loved Bar form, aab (2 *Stollen* and an *Abgesang.)* Rhymes abound. The rhyming plays on homespun images—baking bread, roasting meat, and Christ the Son as our metaphorical sun (the German homonym, "Sohn," is "Sonne"), giving the work a solid, earthy flavor. Luther's text emphasizes the Sequence's reference to the struggle between death and life. In Luther's version, the struggle becomes an epochal battle in which Christ emerges as victor only after a protracted life-and-death struggle.

The melody uses and slightly alters the first three phrases from the *Leisen*. The fourth phrase of the model is, however, subjected to an elaborate two-phrase expansion. Instead of the somewhat anticlimactic "Kyrieleis," Luther appends a jubilant "Alleluia" refrain.

The version of the sung hymn chosen here calls upon settings for each verse composed by various musicians from the Wittenberg circle. The final sung verse (verse 7) is the magnificent eight-part setting by Michael Praetorius from 1607. Our composers have set the text in motet style, often using imitation between the voices. The Praetorius setting is more homophonic, setting the text in block-like chords, reminiscent of the polychoral Venetian style of Giovanni Gabrieli. Two verses are sung by the congregation (verses 1 and 5). This practice recalls Luther's recommendation that the boys from the Latin choir school be placed amongst the congregation to support the congregational singing.

The series of compositions on Luther's contrafact begins with an organ prelude by Johann Heinrich Buttstedt (1666–1727), an organist in Erfurt. The final organ prelude is by J. S. Bach (1685–1750), who composed the forty-six chorale organ preludes that make up the set around 1714 when he was working in Weimar.

—Paul Helmer

I. *Victimae paschali laudes*

1. Victimae paschali laudes immolent Christiani.

1. Let Christians offer praises to the Paschal Victim.

2a. Agnus redemit oves: Christus innocens Patri reconciliavit peccatores.

2a. The Lamb has redeemed the sheep and the guiltless Christ has reconciled sinners to the Father.

2b. Mors et vita duello conflixere mirando: dux vitae mortuus, regnat vivus.

2b. Death and life contended in a wondrous battle, our master was overcome by death but he reigns victorious.

3a. Dic nobis Maria, quid vidisti in via? Sepulcrum Christi viventis, et gloriam vidi resurgentis:

3a. "Tell us, Mary what saw you on the way?" "I saw the sepulcher of the living Christ and the glory of his resurrection,

3b. Angelicos testes, sudarium, et vestes. Surrexit Christus spes mea: praecedet suos in Galilaeam.

3b. the angelic witnesses, his shroud and garments. My hope, Christ, has risen, he will lead his own into Galilee."

4a. Credendum est magis soli Mariae veraci quam Judaeorum turbae fallaci.

4a. We should believe Mary rather than the Jews who deny Christ's resurrection.

4b. Scimus Christum surrexisse a mortuis vere: tu nobis, victor Rex, miserere. Amen.

4b. We know that Christ is truly risen from the dead: thou art our conqueror and king, have mercy on us. Amen. Alleluia.

II. Text for Easter Ceremony

Angelus: Quem queritis O tremule mulieres: in hoc tumulo gementes.

Mulieres: Iesus Nazarenum crucifixum querimus.

Angelus: Non est hic quem queritis sed cito euntes nunciate discipulis eius et Petro: quia surrexit Iesus.

Mulieres: Ad monumentem venimus gementes: angelum domini sedentem vidimus et dicentem: quia surrexit Iesus.

Petrus et Ioannes: Currebant duo simili: et ille alius discipulus precurrit citius Petro et venit prior ad monumentum alleluia.

Petrus et Ioannes cum sudario: Cernitis O socii: ecce lintheamina et sudarium: et corpus non est in sepulchro inventum.

Chorus: Dic nobis Maria quid vidisti in via.

Maria: Sepulchrum Christi viventis: et gloria vidi resurgentis.

Chorus: Dic nobis . . .

Maria: Angelicos testes: sudarium et vestes.

Chorus: Dic nobis . . .

Maria: Surrexit Christus spes mea: precedet suos in Galileam.

Chorus: Credendum est . . . Scimus Christum . . .

Deinde Populus: Christ ist erstanden

Postea Te Deum laudamus.

Translation

Angel: Whom do you seek O fearful women, weeping in this place of burial?

Women: We are seeking Jesus of Nazareth who has been crucified.

Angel: He is not here whom you seek but run quickly and tell the disciples and Peter that Jesus had risen.

Women: We came to the sepulcher weeping. We have seen an angel of the Lord who told us that Jesus had risen from the dead.

Peter and John: Both ran together and that other disciple ran more quickly than Peter and went in before him to the sepulcher, Alleluia.

Peter and John with the grave clothes: Here are the linen wrappings and the
    grave clothes but the body is no longer here in the sepulcher.
Chorus: Tell us Mary, what did you see on the way?
Mary: I have seen Christ's sepulcher and the glory of his resurrection.
Chorus: Tell us . . .
Mary: [I have seen] the angelic witnesses, his shroud and garments
Chorus: Tell us . . .
Mary: My hope Christ has risen: he will lead his own into Galilee.
Chorus: We believe . . .
We should believe . . .
Then the congregation: Christ is arisen
Afterwards, We praise Thee O Lord.

III. *Christ ist erstanden*

1. Christ ist erstanden von der Mar-
   ter alle;
   des solln wir alle froh sein, Christ
   will unser Trost sein. Kyrieleis.
2. Wär er nicht erstanden, so wär die
   Welt vergangen;
   seit daß er erstanden ist, so
   lobn wir den Vater Jesu Christ.
   Kyrieleis.
3. Halleluja, Halleluja, Halleluja!
   Des solln wir alle froh sein, Christ
   will unser Trost sein. Kyrieleis.

1. Christ is arisen from the deepest
   agony.
   Glad should we be that Christ is
   our true comfort, Kyrieleis.
2. Were he not arisen, the world
   would have perished,
   But since he is arisen, we praise
   the Father of our Lord, Kyrieleis.

3. Alleluia, Alleluia, Alleluia,
   Glad should we be that Christ is
   our true comfort, Kyrieleis.

IV. *Christ lag in Todesbanden*

1. Christ lag in Todesbanden, für
   unsre Sünd gegeben,
   der ist wieder erstanden und hat
   uns bracht das Leben.
   Des wir sollen fröhlich sein, Gott
   loben und dankbar sein
   und singen Halleluja. Halleluja.

2. Den Tod niemand zwingen konnt
   bei allen Menschenkindern;
   das macht alles unsre Sünd, kein
   Unschuld war zu finden.
   Davon kam der Tod so bald und
   nahm über uns Gewalt,
   hielt uns in seim Reich gefangen.
   Halleluja.

3. Jesus Christus, Gottes Sohn, an
   unser Statt ist kommen
   und hat die Sünd abgetan, damit
   dem Tod genommen
   all sein Recht und sein Gewalt; da
   bleibt nichts denn Tods Gestalt,
   den Stachel hat er verloren.
   Halleluja.

4. Es war ein wunderlich Krieg, da
   Tod und Leben 'rungen;
   Das Leben behielt den Sieg, es
   hat den Tod verschlungen.

1. Christ lay in death's dark prison
   sacrificed for our sins
   He is arisen and has brought us
   life,
   Glad should we be, let us praise
   God and be thankful and sing
   Alleluia.

2. No one of all creation could master death
   This we know that all had sinned
   Thus death came down and held
   dominion over us, kept us under
   his sway, Alleluia.

3. Jesus Christ the Son of God came
   for us
   He cast away sin and thus death's
   power
   All its power and might is
   removed, nothing is left, the prick
   has been taken away, Alleluia.

4. It was a wondrous war when
   death and life contended
   Life retained the victory and has
   swallowed up death.

Die Schrift hat verkündet das, wie
ein Tod den andern fraß,
ein Spott aus dem Tod ist worden.
Halleluja.

Scripture tells us how one death
ate the other and made a mockery
of death, Alleluia.

5. Hier ist das recht Osterlamm,
davon wir sollen leben,
das ist an des Kreuzes Stamm
in heißer Lieb gegeben (Luther:
gebroten)
Des Blut zeichnet unsre Tür, das
hält der Glaub dem Tod für,
der Würger kann uns nicht rühren.
Halleluja.

5. Here is the proper Easter lamb
through which we should live.
This one was given on the cross in
wondrous love.
His blood shows us the way
which faith wields against death,
the destroyer cannot touch us,
Alleluia.

6. So feiern wir das hoh Fest mit
Herzensfreud und Wonne,
das uns der Herr scheinen läßt. Er
ist selber die Sonne,
der durch seiner Gnaden Glanz
erleucht' unsre Herzen ganz;
der Sünden Nacht ist vergangen.
Halleluja.

6. And thus we celebrate this high
feast with joyful hearts and
pleasure,
The one the Lord shows us, he is
the true sun,
Who through the light of his grace
brightens our heart, the night of
sin is removed, Alleluia.

7. Wir essen und leben wohl, zum
süßen Brot geladen;
der alte Sau'rteig nicht soll sein
bei dem Wort der Gnaden.
Christus will die Kost uns sein
und speisen die Seel allein;
der Glaub will keins andern leben.
Halleluja.

7. So let us eat the proper Easter loaf,
The old unleavened bread should
not be found beside the word of
grace.
Christ shall be our proper meal
and feed our souls, faith would
have no other, Alleluia.

—Translations by Paul Helmer

About the artists

Founded in 1982 as His Majestie's Clerkes, Bella Voce performs classic a cappella repertoire, early music of the Americas, and contemporary music from all over the world. In 2004, Bella Voce received the prestigious Alice Parker ASCAP Chorus America Award for programming that was "an adventurous stretch" for both singers and audience. Distinguished guest conductors including Sir David Willcocks, Paul Hillier, Simon Preston, and Alice Parker have led the ensemble over the years. The ensemble has recorded for Centaur, Harmonia Mundi, Narada, and Cedille Records, and has three self-produced recordings in release. A noteworthy contribution of Bella Voce to the arts has been its commissions of choral works by Midwestern composers, including Frank Ferko, Gustavo Leone, and Rami Levin. The latest of these commissions, *Mar*, a setting of a Garcia Lorca poem by Janika Vandervelde, was premiered in the spring of 2005. In 2005, the organization's longtime artistic director, Anne Heider, retired after more than sixteen years leading the group. In 2006, after a year-long search, Andrew Lewis was named Bella Voce's new artistic director. Since his appointment as artistic director, Lewis and the ensemble have garnered unanimous critical praise and have debuted at the Harris Theater for Music and Dance in Millennium Park.

Andrew Lewis is artistic director of Bella Voce, music director of the Elgin Choral Union, founder and artistic director of The Janus Ensemble, a professional chamber orchestra specializing in Baroque and new music, director of the Chancel Choir at Glenview Community Church, and is on the conducting faculty at the University of Illinois at Chicago. He is also artistic director emeritus of the Lutheran Choir of Chicago and formerly taught conducting at DePaul University. Mr. Lewis has been a guest lecturer at Concordia University Chicago, the nationally recognized *Lectures in Church Music* series, Garrett-Evangelical Theological Seminary in Evanston, and has appeared as a guest conductor with the Elgin Symphony Orchestra. Mr. Lewis's performances have been heard live on WFMT 98.7.